FOR THE LOVE OF
North Dakota

AND OTHER ESSAYS

FOR THE LOVE OF
North Dakota

AND OTHER ESSAYS
SUNDAYS WITH CLAY
IN THE BISMARCK TRIBUNE

Clay S. Jenkinson

Foreword by Sheila Schafer

Illustrations by Leon Basler

The Dakota Institute Press
of the Lewis & Clark Fort Mandan Foundation

Library of Congress Control Number 2012943445
ISBN 978-0-9834059-1-7 (Hardcover)
ISBN 978-0-9834059-2-4 (Paperback)

Distributed by The University of Oklahoma Press

Created, produced and designed in the United States of America
Printed in Canada

Book layout and design by:
Margaret McCullough corvusdesignstudio.com

*The paper in this book meets the guidelines for permanence and
durability of the Committee of Production Guidelines for Book
Longevity of the Council on Library Resources.*
10 9 8 7 6 5 4 3 2 1

The Dakota Institute Press
of the Lewis & Clark Fort Mandan Foundation
2576 8th Street South West . Post Office Box 607
Washburn, North Dakota 58577
www.fortmandan.com
1.877.462.8535

MIX
Paper from
responsible sources
FSC® C016245

DEDICATION

for Catherine Missouri

These words are my invitation
that you cast your lot with Dakota,
when the time comes.

and for Patti Perry of Marmarth

Hail and Farewell
Great Spirit

Past the Missouri

for Clay Jenkinson

Frederick Jackson Turner—in my youth
I studied immigrants, competing strands
of settlers groping westward for the truth.
The land was ours before we were the land's.

"Step in a Lutheran church, you'll go to hell."
So I was brainwashed fifty years ago.
But I swiftly escaped that priestly spell,
playing with Lutheran children in the snow.

Frost had it wrong. The land cannot be ours,
we are custodians at best. When we are cursed
the sheriff shivers, the accountant cowers.
The Seven: is avaritia the worst?

Sixty years old—I hope before my end
I will grope west and sunset down some days
where you, stranger, have become my friend
and horseman is the highest term of praise.

—Timothy Murphy, 2011

TABLE OF CONTENTS

PREFACE i

FOREWORD ii

INTRODUCTION vi

INTRODUCTORY LETTER by Ken Rogers viii

SEASONS 1

CULTURE 55

PEOPLE 111

WERE I LIVED AND WHAT I LIVED FOR 163

FAMILY 221

CONSERVING OUR HOMELAND 263

THE MISSOURI RIVER 281

THE FUTURE OF NORTH DAKOTA 301

ENERGY and THE SPIRIT OF NORTH DAKOTA 315

WHEN THE LANDSCAPE IS QUIET AGAIN
by Governor Arthur A. Link........................... 342

ACKNOWLEDGEMENTS 344

BOOKS CITED 349

INDEX 356

"Perhaps the rarest courage of all—for the skill to pursue it is given to very few men—is the courage to wage a silent battle to illuminate the nature of man and the world in which he lives."

—John F. Kennedy, *February 26, 1961*

PREFACE

God has Billy Graham and North Dakota has Clay Jenkinson.

Anyone who has read his weekly column in the Sunday edition of the *Bismarck Tribune* (and they are legion, thanks to the World Wide Web) knows of what I speak here. He is truly evangelical in the passionate manner in which he presents the virtues of his beloved North Dakota.

Since returning to his native land several years ago, after sojourning in such non-Dakota places as Reno, Nevada, Clay has found great joy in expressing his feelings in this weekly forum. Indeed, my preference was to title this book "Sundays with Clay," but the author insisted that North Dakota get top billing. Such is his humility and such is his love for perhaps the least understood state in the Union.

At times, Clay will gingerly touch upon the "third rail" of topical issues, social and political. However, this book is filled with what he unabashedly calls his "love songs to Dakota." Only the love he often expresses for his daughter supercedes his feelings for North Dakota. And these feelings only grow in intensity as he now glides through his fifties.

Complemented by new essays, this collection will delight those of us who also call North Dakota home, while enlightening those unfamiliar with our prairies, rivers, and badlands of our mystical beauty. More than anything else, it would be Clay's wish that you read this book and then engage in a conversation of our sense of place, whether you are a citizen of Dakota or the world at large.

Read. Enjoy. And perhaps find yourself joining the choir, led by Clay, singing love songs to North Dakota.

—David Borlaug

FOREWORD

There was a time when I would pick up my Sunday *Bismarck Tribune* to check the headlines, the obituaries, and the sports, then head to church. Since meeting Clay S. Jenkinson about six years ago, I have a different pattern. I now grab the paper, turn to the Dakota section, and immediately read his column. Arriving at church, I will inevitably be asked: Did you read Clay's column? Did you like it? Do you agree?

When I first met Clay he was delivering a lecture on Theodore Roosevelt—in character and in costume—for the Theodore Roosevelt Medora Foundation. He was and is a marvelous performer. At a reception after the performance, we were having our picture taken together. He loves to tell people that I said, "I don't like your politics, but I like you." Never!!! While I don't always agree with his point of view, I admire his writing and respect his opinions. I am always amazed, and I enjoy that this provocative and sometimes sentimental, informative, and humorous column is a part of our weekly newspaper. We have come to be very close friends, and we share many splendid things—a love of North Dakota, the Badlands, the rolling plains, the people of our state, our mutual friends, and a great gift of laughter.

WHO HE IS.

Clay S. Jenkinson is a complete genius. In Douglas Brinkley's book, *The Wilderness Warrior*, he writes that Theodore Roosevelt "had multi-dimensional sides and that some people felt he had thousands of sides." There is no doubt that those close to Clay would agree that he also has multi-dimensional sides to his personality. Every aspect of his life's accomplishments has been honed to perfection.

People aren't always aware of his vast array of talents. He has many plates spinning at all times. Clay is the author of eight books, with three more to be published before year's end. He is a humanities scholar, a social commentator, a Jefferson scholar, a Lewis and Clark scholar, a producer, director, and creator of renowned documentaries, a presenter of historical figures, and a weekly participant on radio program covering whatever subject he has chosen. Clay has a one-hour radio program, *The Jefferson Hour*. In this popular presentation, he appears for the first half as Thomas Jefferson and the second as himself, answering questions about Jefferson. The program airs on fifty-plus public radio stations and has tens of thousands of followers. Among the many characters he portrays in addition to

Roosevelt are: J. Robert Oppenheimer, John Wesley Powell, Meriwether Lewis, John Steinbeck, and Thomas Jefferson (who is Clay's hero). He has presented before two US presidents, Supreme Court justices, and state legislatures in twenty-three states.

AND (this is going to be a much-used word) this extraordinary man lives in Bismarck, North Dakota, where he is surrounded by at least sixteen thousand books. He has read more than one thousand of those books several times. Clay admits to being a "carnal lover of books," as opposed to "courtly lovers" who never make notes in the margin or dog-ear pages. Not only has he read them, but he knows the names, the dates, and the subjects. He can lecture on any one of them at a moment's notice. Certainly one of his greatest gifts is his memory.

And he has created, directed, and helped produce three documentaries—winning a national award for *When the Landscape is Quiet Again* about former ND Governor Art Link. He has conceived, hosted, and moderated eight symposiums since he returned to North Dakota. These events invariably draw people from all over the United States. He is currently working on three more. I want to tell readers about two incredible symposiums. The first was in the fall of 2010 and focused on the life of ND native Eric Sevareid. Clay conceived, organized, and moderated this three-day event. He brought to Bismarck, ND, a number of nationally famous radio and television personalities including Dan Rather, Bob Schieffer, Nick Clooney, Bob Edwards and others. In the fall of 2011, he composed, directed, and moderated a commemorative three-day symposium dedicated to the ten-year anniversary of 9/11. In planning for this special presentation, Clay invited insightful authors and personalities such as HLN's Chuck Roberts, Peter Bergen, Thomas Frank, and Geoffrey Wawro.

Now, hanging in the new Rough Riders Hotel in historic Medora, ND, are seventy 24 x 36" panels, doubled matted and beautifully framed, each representing a different episode of Theodore Roosevelt's life. Those panels, written by Clay, were recently published in his beautiful book called *A Free and Hardy Life: Theodore Roosevelt's Sojourn in The American West*. For fans of TR, you will find it hard to discover a more thoughtful and beautiful coffee-table book.

In 2008, Clay and the president of Bismarck State College, Larry Skogen, began a series of "conversations" on a variety of topics, which are streamed live on the internet and later broadcast on local television. At Dickinson State College, he serves as the principal consultant of the Theodore Roosevelt Center, which was his idea, born in the Little Missouri Badlands. Clay has spearheaded the digitization of more than four hundred thousand national documents related to Theodore Roosevelt. A portion of these documents are catalogued and ready for use by authors, scholars, historians, biographers, and libraries. This is an incredible project.

And yet—more. Clay has hosted cultural tours all over the world to places like London, the Panama Canal, the classical world of Italy and Greece, the Middle East, Alaska, Jefferson's Virginia, and up and down the Lewis & Clark trail.

This is just a small sampling of his talents. I saved Clay's incredible hike until the end of "who he is," for his legacy will always include this adventure. Clay is a champion of the Little Missouri River. Alone, during a hot August in 2005, he hiked the 173 miles from Marmarth, ND, to the North Unit of Theodore Roosevelt National Park (one of his favorite places in the world). He finished this trek in seventeen days.

All these accomplishments of Clay's have been in the last five-and-a-half years. To everyone he raises his arms and shouts, "This is the best time of my life."

What These Columns Are About

So . . . I can finally turn to "what these columns are about." It's about time! *For the Love of North Dakota: Sundays with Clay in the Bismarck Tribune* is a collection of one hundred fifty-plus columns selected from more than 350 that he has so far written. I have chosen that the first chapter begin with his very earliest column called "Coming Home." Clay has written, "Other than deciding to have a child, coming home to North Dakota was the greatest decision I ever made in my life." You will read many columns devoted to his love and passion for this state.

Clay is the most prominent voice for North Dakota, not only for sharing the beauty and uniqueness of the state, but also for addressing issues important to North Dakota people. He is very humorous and clever. But he does more than entertain. Clay is brave enough to tackle some controversial topics on the minds of North Dakotans—the state's infrastructure, the oil boom and its impact, the future of our state. Every column shows evidence of his poetic use of words, his enormous power of observation. He can be serious, argumentative, sentimental, caring, and funny. One woman wrote to Clay, "I love your columns, but they are too damn long." However, Clay can also use only a few carefully chosen words to get right to the point. For instance, in describing the conversation during a ride to Kansas with his beloved young daughter Catherine (the center of his universe), he wrote:

Clay: "Well, Catherine, what do you know about sex?"
Catherine: "Not much."
Clay: "Me either."
End of conversation.

I believe that in the columns selected, you will discover Clay's deep concerns about our state and our country; his devotion to books and learning and teaching; his love for family—many columns about Catherine, and so much love shown for his grandmother, his father, and a very special person in his life, his very attractive and "forever young" mother.

So reader, come. Enjoy learning about and being with Clay S. Jenkinson. Come walk beside him on a Badlands butte or along the Little Missouri River. Climb with him to the top of a pyramid in Egypt. Sail with him through the Panama Canal or to Alaska, or tour London or the Holy Land or the Lewis and Clark Trail. Know the joy of silence as you sit with him in some sacred place, and feel his spirituality as he is at peace and understands his sense "of being alive and in the place." Here you can sit and think and imagine.

Imagine yourself on an early walk with Clay, just a short walk, maybe only two hundred feet. In these few steps, Clay would embrace the breeze, listen to a bird, identify the song, be aware of a wildflower, caress the ground, feel the grass, examine the view from every direction. Perhaps you will also feel the joy and the sense of just being there. And always, you will feel his ever-present love for North Dakota and for the weather. You will read repeatedly, "How great is this" or "This is the best day ever," and "I love my life." I believe that when Clay achieves the level he strives for, it is pure magic and joy for him. He makes every column come alive because his heart and soul are in each one. Because of his genius and expert use of words, you are there. That's the magic of Clay.

Finally, why did I, an eighty-six-year-old woman with no writing experience, agree to write an introduction for this book? Just because he asked me to.

—Sheila Schafer

INTRODUCTION

Let's see if I can make this briefer than any column I have written. My close friend David Nicandri quoted Lord Reading recently when he gave his farewell address as director of the Washington State Historical Society: "Always be shorter than anyone dared hope."

This book consists of one hundred twelve newspaper columns and a handful of other essays that celebrate or explore the idea of North Dakota. I have not made any changes to the columns, though I was tempted.

In the six years I have been publishing a weekly column for the *Bismarck Tribune*, I have written about a wide variety of subjects. My interests are catholic. My goal in life is to remain widely curious deep into my 80s, and then one day to die while hiking in the Badlands. Ideally I would be struck by lightning and then eaten by a mountain lion, somewhere north of Marmarth, but that may be dreaming too high and requiring too much specificity of the fates. The most inspiring thing I ever read comes from Francis Bacon (1561-1626): "I have taken all knowledge to be my province." While I would love to be able to call myself "a man for all seasons," I certainly aspire to be a man for at least a season and a half.

The bulk of the essays in this book are about North Dakota. I have chosen not to print here columns on national politics, my travels abroad, or about things that are intensely time-specific. My goal has been to create a body of work celebrating this place in all of its moods, to sing a love song to North Dakota, and to help put North Dakota on the map without removing it from the margins. Given Thomas Friedman's flat world and the kind of work I do, I could live just about anywhere. I choose to live in North Dakota because I think it is one of the most beautiful places on earth, in its improbable contours and endless space at the heart of the North American continent. I know that I am happiest when I am out driving or hiking the Great Plains, as far from the nearest paved road as possible, and preferably along the sinuous path of the Little Missouri River. In fact, I have a wall calendar on which I keep track of the number of days between visits to the Badlands. That chart tracks my mental health.

I have organized these essays by subject, not by chronology. In selecting less than half, I have left open the possibility of a sequel (!), and tried to concentrate on North Dakota. My goal is to put you into the places I go and the stories I tell, to let you smell the dust of the gravel roads west of Grassy Butte, to invite you to listen to the heartbreaking clarity of the meadowlark's song, to feel the heavens crack when the lightning bursts from the earth to the top of the sky, and to listen with me to my favorite sound, the dance of the cottonwoods in a moderate breeze.

There's one really important thing I want to say before we get started.

When I returned to North Dakota six years ago, the dominant story was outmigration and rural decline. I remember a dinner party in which one of my wisest friends said the population of the state would probably wind down to about five hundred thousand and hold there, and that we'd have a series of regional service centers in places like Bowman and Harvey. He said the state would come to resemble the Australian outback. We debated over dinner as to whether North Dakota would eventually revert to territorial status.

Oh my.

Now the story is the wholesale industrialization of the landscape of western North Dakota. In 2011 the population of the state surged to 683,932, the highest in our history. Western North Dakota is in the first phase of a massive oil boom—a carbon rush—that will transform the landscape and the social structure of this place beyond recognition. Tens of thousands of workers are converging on Williston, Watford City, Dickinson, Killdeer, Stanley, and a range of smaller places. Their presence, and the work that they do, are putting unprecedented pressures on the agrarian values of North Dakota. While I welcome the oil boom, generally speaking, I fear that it will destroy what I love most about this place—the silence of vast empty spaces, our ability to commune with the godhead in nature, and the pristine heritage of the North Dakota Badlands (broadly defined). In the months and years ahead, I fear that I will be compelled to write a good deal about the industrial tsunami that is crashing over our quiet landscape. This gives me no pleasure whatsoever.

Stay tuned.

Sometimes, but not always, I have written a little after-note to say something about how my readers (or some of them) responded to the column, or to add a little thought or correction in retrospect. The dates of the columns are printed in tiny type after the last sentence.

I hope you enjoy reading these essays as much as I have enjoyed writing them.

—Clay Jenkinson

DEAR READERS,

Please welcome Clay Jenkinson to the pages of the Tribune.

Beginning here and now, Clay will be taking my place as a columnist for the Tribune. He will be offering his ideas and insights in regular columns, often touching on things North Dakota because that's where his love lies. He's a personal friend, and I step aside with pleasure.

Clay is also a friend to public discourse, about issues large and small. He has a first-rate mind and, as those who have heard him take on the persona of Meriwether Lewis, Teddy Roosevelt or Thomas Jefferson can attest, he has the gift of language. Clay can be witty and wise, thoughtful and probing, certainly knowledgeable, and, always, interesting.

A genuine love for North Dakota drives Clay. That love is for the state's history. For its landscape and people, back roads and small towns. For its peculiarities, as well as common comforts of family and heritage.

Although he's grounded in the state's past, he has rich dreams for North Dakota's future.

For the record, Clay is a humanities scholar, born and raised in North Dakota. He is now returning home at the age of 50, the author of six books, including two about North Dakota: *A Vast and Open Plain: The Writing of the Lewis and Clark Expedition in North Dakota* and *Message on the Wind; A Spiritual Odyssey on the Northern Plains.*

Readers will find him here most Sundays, and occasionally on the Tribune's editorial page.

Meanwhile, I will be developing a new column for the Tribune.

It's all yours, Clay.

—Ken Rogers

When Ken Rogers wrote this welcome on October 1, 2005, he was the managing editor for the Bismarck Tribune. *Ken still works with the Tribune as Opinion Page editor.*

SEASONS

COMING HOME

Clay Jenkinson:

A native son's letter from the Plains

And so I am finally moving home. I was born in Minot and I grew up in Dickinson. I left to go away to college in 1973, and though I have come home on average six times a year ever since and lived in North Dakota for a full year, twice, in early adulthood, the truth is that I have been away for twenty-five years now. For about ten years I have been trying to figure out a way to move home. Now that I'm fifty and at least at the meridian of my life, I have finally just done it. Over the summer I drove four stout U-Hauls from Reno to Bismarck at the high water mark (so far) of American fuel prices. It was mostly books in the back, ruinously heavy and (when you count the moving costs) ruinously expensive.

Twenty-five years is a long time, longer than what my hero, Thomas Jefferson, regarded as a full generation. It is possible that I am no longer really a North Dakotan. I worry about that almost incessantly now that I burned my bridges behind me. The environmental essayist Barry Lopez has asked, "How far can you venture out and still come back?" Perhaps I have been gone too long. I know that I am extremely proud to be from North Dakota and, whenever anyone has asked where I'm from during this long sojourn, I have always said, "I live in X, but I'm really a North Dakotan." That gets some quizzical looks.

Everyone knows that North Dakota suffers from serious outmigration, especially of our children. The 2000 census showed a net growth of just 3,400 people since 1990, the smallest of any state. Without the vibrant birth rates among North Dakota's minorities, particularly American Indians, the state would have suffered a considerable population decline. I'm bucking the trend. I'm one of the returnees. It turns out that there are a surprisingly large number of us—OK, a few. We return for a variety of reasons: aging parents, nostalgia for the golden prairies of our youth, cultural exhaustion from life in more hectic places. I think a significant number of return-ees are worried that some hard-to-define cataclysm or cultural collapse is looming. When the crisis comes and there is no food in the grocery stores and no work to be had, I want to be in North Dakota, not L.A. or New Orleans or even Denver. My faith is that North Dakota is still a community in some meaningful sense of the term, some remnant of *Little House on the Prairie*, where neighbor reluctantly but without real hesitation helps neighbor in times of peril and communities pull together without gunfire.

I may be wrong. I've changed in twenty-five years. So, no doubt, has North Dakota. There are dramatically fewer farms. That fraction of the rural population that has stayed in North Dakota has migrated to the cities. Bismarck and Fargo are booming. They look like other prosperous suburban places. North Dakota is less isolated culturally, less provincial in character, less distinctive in personality. This is good and bad as far as I'm concerned. It is not the clunky wheat state of my youth. A good friend of mine, a few years after her divorce, married a myth from her youth. It was a big mistake. She should have known better. Beware of making decisions on the basis of mythology. Be especially wary of nostalgia for one's youth.

Ironically, the future of the United States is, for once, more uncertain than that of North Dakota, and my intuition visits me in the night to predict turbulence ahead for the western democracies. That is good reason to get home to the Northern Plains. But it is not a very positive reason, and it certainly is not my main reason.

I am returning for the meadowlarks—the purest sound there is, the signature sound of the Great Plains.

I am returning for the thunderstorms and the northern lights and, yes, the blizzards and the wind. I want to live where nature still demands our attention. In that sense we still are Jefferson's people.

I am returning for the buttes; for the prairie potholes; for the pine ridges; for the antelope; for the coyotes.

I am returning to spend more time with my mother and with the friends I have kept yet sorely missed through this long period away.

Almost more than anything else, I am returning for the Little Missouri River and the crazy, fragile, and deeply imperiled valley it has carved in southwestern North Dakota. North of Marmarth is the heart of all that I love best about the Great Plains.

Above all, I am returning to learn to live again in the hope that someday my daughter, who is just eleven, will choose to cast her lot with Dakota.

I am so glad to be home.   *10/1/05*

Sheila Schafer insisted that I publish this column and put it at the beginning of the book. This is the column that inspired Leonard Baenan of Mandan to denounce me in a letter to the editor. Great start!

Moving Home to a Kinder,

Gentler—and Chattier—State

Moving to North Dakota is a revelation. It's also a gift from the gods. I've been away so long that I got used to the rest of the country and forgot how different North Dakota is.

First of all, everyone is shockingly friendly here. In the grocery store the other day, the bag girl (approximately sixteen years old) chatted amiably with me throughout my time in line, and then thanked me for our conversation. The cable guys apologized when something went slightly wrong with my installation. Then someone from the cable company called me to thank me for my patience. My neighbor volunteered to mow my lawn when I am gone even before I had a lawn to mow.

In Reno, Nevada, where I most recently lived, service is rude and deplorable. As often as not, the low-paid employee at Office Max or Sears is on the phone with friends, annoyed to see me appear at her or his cash register, and utterly indifferent, if not hostile, to any request I might make. Trying to purchase a replacement ink cartridge was like obtaining a passport in Kenya. After ten minutes of attempting to pierce through the ennui and self-absorption of the employee, I always wanted to say, "Sorry to interrupt your meth haze."

That was Nevada or Oregon or Minneapolis, for that matter. At Menards in Bismarck a couple of weeks ago, I was looking for coaster pads to put under my couch. Given my experience in box stores elsewhere, I had resigned myself to pushing my mega-cart up one aisle and down the next until I stumbled into the right section sometime around closing time.

Then the most amazing thing happened. A young man in his late teens asked me if I needed help. I stammered out my question with the same confidence that one asks to change seats at the airline counter. The young man not only told me what aisle I needed, but insisted on escorting me there, and then gave me thoughtful advice about which widget would protect my hardwood floors best. Then he offered to guide me to other obscure hardware zones across the acre of merchandise.

Altogether we spent about twenty minutes together, during which he told me about his academic plans while solving one new-homeowner puzzle after the next. And when I asked for five copies of my house key, he did not give me the universal "don't bore me by making me grind you house keys" look. As I left the store I wanted to tip him, or contribute to his college fund or invite him to dinner.

The stout young men who helped unload my U-Hauls behaved as if they were my nephews. They reckoned that I own too many books, and they exchanged glances when the fleet of file cabinets appeared, but they thanked me (twice) for supplying them Gatorade, and in the course of three hours each one told me his story. One of them actually apologized for chipping the molding.

In North Dakota everything is clean, crisp, efficient, honest, and straight forward. I won't say you can eat off of the floor of a Hardees or the bathroom at Pizza Hut, but if I had to undertake that unlikely act, I would choose to do it in North Dakota rather than anywhere else. Travel elsewhere in the United States and check out the general hygiene level, particularly below the Mason-Dixon Line. North Dakota is the kind of place that Howard Hughes would have admired.

The only thing I dreaded about moving was … well moving. Selling a house, buying a house, boxing stuff up, hiring moving vans, canceling phone, newspaper, gas, electric, water service and engaging all these services all over again in a faraway place. The North Dakotans made it easy, almost fun. I have not heard a rude word since I arrived, and nobody has given me the runaround.

My real estate agent Kristi can only be called a saint. I picked her out of a real estate guide while eating a fleishkuechle one evening last spring when I was passing through Bismarck, and we met the next morning at Starbucks. She asked me what kind of house I was looking for. I told her precisely what I wanted. After that she never veered from my criteria. Because she was so honest and forthright and agreeable, I eventually bought my new house on the strength of her recommendation—sight unseen (my mother was not so sure this was a good idea). I would never have done this anywhere but North Dakota. The house turned out to be perfect. Then, in my absence, Kristi both initiated and supervised work I had done in the basement, contacted drape, security, cabinet, sprinkler, landscaping, and lawn companies, and ordered corrections when things were not what she thought I would want. Her son installed my mailbox, and she stored my telescope until I moved to town. Even after all the money had exchanged hands and all of her duties were completed with outstanding professionalism, she continued to volunteer to do favors for me—things I wouldn't do for my sister or mother and they certainly wouldn't do for me. In all the time we spent together (lots), she never spoke like a used car salesman, never tried to talk me into anything, and never made a commitment she did not immediately keep.

All I can say is, try this anywhere else. Kristi behaved as if we were friends. Now we are.

The real estate agent I employed in buying a house in Reno, Nevada, a decade ago treated me like I was a seven-year-old child learning cursive, carted me around to a series of houses that conformed to her, not my, agenda, and then abandoned me entirely when the sellers cheated on four or five commitments they had made to get out from under their property. Friends told me this was standard procedure in the real estate industry.

And then I went to the North Dakota Department of Motor Vehicles. This is, of course, the most dreaded of all bureaucratic errands, the equivalent of Dante's seventh circle of the Inferno. I took a book, a notebook, cell phone, a voice recorder, bottles of water, and a snack just to be sure. By sheer coincidence my business partner Janie (a Nevadan) and I (a North Dakotan!) went to our DMVs on the same day in September 2005. She was in Reno and I was in Bismarck. She spent four hours in line, behind a group of twenty-seven hookers from the Mustang Ranch east of Reno. They caused quite a stir, I'm told, as they drank their lattes and worked their PDAs, but they did not hold up the progress of the line. When Janie got to the front of the line in Nevada, though she is as prepared a person as I have ever met, she was turned away rudely for not having some document in her possession (something like her second college semester's tuition payment stub), and so she had to do it all over again the next day, without the benefit of legal prostitutes for diversion. In Bismarck, meanwhile, I stood in line for a sum total of seven minutes before encountering a wonderful woman who engaged me in a genuine human conversation before taking my check for $10 (ten dollars!!!!). I walked out of the DMV glad to be alive. Once in southern California I waited six and a half hours to pay $753 to put a license plate on a Honda Civic.

It's so gratifying to be in North Dakota again. The only thing I don't understand is that everyone I have encountered in these late-summer homecoming errands has asked me if I like winter.

Citizens of North Dakota. NEVER take North Dakota for granted. You (we) live in paradise. All we need are a few more people, better-paying jobs, and better cheese. *10/8/05*

Kristi the realtor is still my friend. Turns out the house wasn't quite perfect. The suburban sprawl of Bismarck has eaten my view of the open plains to the south and west of Bismarck. The coyotes don't howl most nights any more, and I am worried about the meadowlarks. I should have thought this through. I loved living on the edge of civilization.

FINALLY, THE EXHILARATION OF GENUINE WINTER

Finally, some real winter. The cold snap of mid-January was the first severe weather I have experienced in the sixteen months that I have been home. It was exhilarating and delightful. It was, at times, awe-inspiring. And there were a few moments when it was actually appalling. You never feel more present, more completely alive, than when it is so cold that it bites, so cold that you have to take precautions if you wish to remain alive.

All this is easy for me to say, of course, since I don't have creatures huddling in a pasture, don't earn my living outdoors, don't have to gather my own fuel. Still, in such weather you truly feel like a North Dakotan. In fact, you feel a little smug. You can get summer anywhere. But you can only experience cold this dramatic in a few places in America. In one of his greatest paragraphs, Theodore Roosevelt wrote of the Dakota Badlands in moments of "iron desolation." "In the coldest midwinter weather, not a breath of wind may stir; and then the still, merciless, terrible cold that broods over the earth like the shadow of silent death seems even more dreadful in its gloomy rigor than is the lawless madness of the storms. All the land is like granite; the great rivers stand still in their beds, as if turned to frosted steel."

> **I know that it is neither polite, nor, for that matter, any of my business, but I regard the snowbird phenomenon with chagrin. And remote car starters—are we reduced to this?**

The winter gear is so good now that it is possible to be out in extreme cold weather for extended periods of time. With snow on the ground and clear, crystalline, bitterly cold skies, the visual payoff is stunning. All the contours of the rolling bluffs of Dakota stand out in brilliant relief. The stars on cloudless nights are piercingly beautiful and close at hand. Every shrub in every ravine is a revelation against the blinding white.

The recent pattern of bitter cold spells, with temperatures in excess of 20° below, followed by days at or slightly above freezing, is actually normal for the northern Great Plains. It's the one season when you never really know what the dawn will bring.

Lewis and Clark kept a detailed weather log during their time in what is now North Dakota. Like his mentor Thomas Jefferson, Lewis recorded weather data at sunrise and 4 p.m. In January 1805, the highest temperature recorded at Fort Mandan was 36°F on Jan. 16. The lowest temperature was 40° below on Jan. 10. On Jan. 21, 1805, 202 years ago today, it was 2° below at sunrise, cloudy, wind from the northeast, and 8° above at 4 p.m., fair skies, wind from the southeast.

Quiz: What is, without question, the coldest walk in North Dakota? Answer: Yes, you guessed it, the campus of the University of North Dakota in Grand Forks on a winter day when the wind is blowing. I was there late last week to do some research on Theodore Roosevelt. By sheer good fortune, I found a parking space three blocks from the Chester Fritz Library. Because it was such a short stroll from car to microfilm reading room, I made the walk with an open jacket and no gloves. How cold, really, could it be? I was carrying a small computer bag in one hand and a satchel of books in the other. After I slammed shut the door of my car against the wind, the wall of cold hit me like a blast furnace—in reverse. "Oh my God!" I said, involuntarily, out loud. It was dangerously cold. Within a block, my hands were screaming in pain. I shifted my bags to try to get at least one hand into a pocket. Halfway to the library, I remember thinking, "I can walk three blocks this way in this cold, but I probably could not walk a mile without frostbite at this temperature."

By the time I got to the library, I had actually stopped two or three times to beat my hands against my thighs to get some blood into them, like a character out of a Jack London story. That's cold. That's also a real nitwit.

It was so cold that people from elsewhere checking into the Holiday Inn were fretting at the front desk about whether their cars would ever start again. The politely smiling desk crew explained that there were plenty of parking spaces with access to an electrical box, but some of these folks had never used a head bolt heater before. Some had not heard of such a thing. A few guests left their cars running all or most of the night. In the morning, when I ventured out dressed in everything I owned, I found twenty stiff electrical cords hooked up to cars and a handful of plastic Heet bottles strewn around the icy parking lot. As I drove around Grand Forks at sunrise (at 8:14 a.m.), every thousandth car had its hood open and a couple of grumpy, worried-looking people fumbling with jumper cables. At stoplights, the exhaust accumulated above every car like a cloud of doom. At major intersections, visibility was seriously impaired. It was like a dreamscape. The already slow traffic inched almost to a halt to avoid fender benders on such a morning.

When it is breathtakingly cold, starting a car requires a strategy. You will always know when it is that cold because when you get onto the driver's seat, it does not yield a millimeter no matter what your body mass. No give. Even a bucket seat is literally frozen into place. It feels exactly like sitting on an aluminum bleacher on a very cold day. When I feel that granite seat below me, I always pause (and occasionally pray) before turning the ignition key.

There are basically two approaches to extreme cold weather starts. You can just hold your breath and turn the key as if it were July and hope that the car fires up. Logic: We trust technology, and we certainly don't want to flood the engine. Disadvantage: No matter how good your battery, if it is extremely cold, you have got no more than a couple of minutes of grinding—and then chaos. Every turn of the key is critical. Or you can pump (once, no more than twice) or feather the gas pedal before attempting a pathetic little trial start. It is hard to think of a sound more absolutely disheartening than when the engine whine begins to slow down and ebb on a bitter day and the car almost—just about—nearly fires, but in the end does not, and your battery reserves are spent or dying. And if the car does start, you treat the engine like a newborn baby in the intensive care unit, praying that somehow it does not stall out before it has a chance to warm up.

It was so cold that one Alpha Male at the Grand Forks hotel bar—fifty men and three women at the bar all storm-giddy, the three women in a protective phalanx together at a table—claimed that earlier that day his spit had frozen before it hit the ground. I was sitting alone reading a book in my geeky way, definitely minding my own business, but when he said that I raised an eyebrow (inwardly). "That cannot be true," thought I. And indeed, since I got home, I have looked it up on the Internet and, indeed, the frozen spit story turns out to be an urban myth or, rather, rural myth.

According to meteorological experts, spit can in fact freeze before it hits the ground, but it requires temperatures at 50° below or worse, and North Dakota almost never gets that cold. The coldest temperature ever recorded in North Dakota was 60° below at Parshall on February 15, 1936. Last week in Grand Forks didn't even come near frozen spit weather. Liar.

Most of my mother's friends who can afford it have winter homes in Arizona, California, or Florida. I know that it is neither polite, nor, for that matter, any of my business, but I regard the snowbird phenomenon with chagrin. And remote car starters—are we reduced to this?

We're North Dakotans. We endure, not flee. Bring it on. *1/20/07*

Spring has Sprung, a Sea of Snirt, but Will We Ever See the Dirt?

The light has returned. Now we need the heat. It's hasn't been a particularly harsh winter this time. I don't recall many days in which it was 40 or 30 or even 20° below this winter. My unscientific impression is that the temperature range has been from 20° above to 10° or so below. For North Dakota that has to be regarded as a mild winter. I live up on a ridgey part of Bismarck, and yet I don't have the impression that it was a particularly windy winter, either. Lots of calm, gray days with the temperature hovering in the teens. It feels as if the sun didn't shine much between Halloween and, well, today. A melancholy winter.

But in spite of its relative mildness, it has turned out to be a very long and an unusually lingering winter. Several times in the past couple of weeks, I have looked out in the morning and thought, "Ah, spring at last," but then an hour later watched as winter, like a grumpy old patriarch, effortlessly scattered the merest hint of spring.

I made the mistake of thinking that last big snowstorm would be ephemeral. The wind-whipped snow was so full of moisture that I stupidly reckoned it would melt away by itself as soon as the storm blew itself out. Every institution in western North Dakota was canceling everything in every direction. But the storm seemed pretty slushy to me. I was the only person on my block who didn't drag out the big snowblower one last time. The morning after the storm, simultaneously, at first light, all my neighbors were out walking behind identical looking snow rigs, clearing their driveways. It was like a snowblower ballet, or like watching identical groundskeepers at work at a major league baseball park. It felt like a scene from "North Dakota: The Musical." As I sipped my tea and read from Boswell's *Life of Johnson,* I pitied them for being slaves to the internal combustion engine.

Alas.

Their driveways have been clear and dry ever since, and mine is like a vast and lethal iron meringue, with sharp ridges jutting up every couple

> "The morning after the storm, simultaneously, at first light, all my neighbors were out walking behind identical looking snow rigs, clearing their driveways. It was like a snowblower ballet, or watching identical groundskeepers at work at a major league baseball park."

of yards, and my tire tracks from the first day of the storm etched paleon-tologically into the snowscape. The few places where the snow has actu-ally melted a little are now glassy seas of black ice. On the two occasions when I have returned home from the grocery store, with heavy plastic bags in either hand, I have slipped virtually head over heels on that ice and then scrambled and lurched to keep my balance like a cartoon char-acter whose legs are churning at 7,000 rpms. It's a very wrenching sort of Dakota yoga.

My neighbors now all look at me with pity.

Now that we are into April, time finally appears to be on our side—though stay tuned! We've reached the interlude of snirt that marks the transition from winter to spring in North Dakota. This is the moment of the year when North Dakota is least beautiful. Nothing is blooming yet. Everything has a winter-scoured look about it, and the landscape appears sterile and dead now that the mantle of white snow has ceased to shroud it. This will soon change. I intend to genuflect before pasque flowers in the Badlands sometime in the next two weeks. The various pavements are finally starting to emerge. My contract postman is significantly less apoplectic than he was even a week ago. As the snow recedes from my yard, I'm starting to glimpse forgotten newspapers, that Tupperware con-tainer of turkey I put out on the deck Christmas evening because my refrigerator was too full, and the ends of hoses that didn't get attended to last fall.

So, to review. Winter comes to North Dakota sometime in mid- to late October, and it lingers until sometime in April. That's a full six months of winter, and we all know all too well that the first winter storm can come in early October, and it is not uncommon for there to be a half-hearted snow-storm in late May or early June. Lewis and Clark saw their first mosquito on April 9, 1805, near Stanton. The prairie grass greened up and the cotton-woods budded, and the silly Virginians reckoned that spring had come to stay. Then, on May 2, a late winter snowstorm blew through. Meriwether Lewis, who was a gentle man and a great lover of plants, fretted that the storm would stunt the prairie flowers and kill the cottonwood leaves, which were already as large as dollar coins, he said. "The (water) friezed on the oars as they rowed," Lewis reported.

I've been making long lists of things I want to do if winter ever releases its grip on us. I'm not talking about yard improvement projects, though there is no avoiding some of that. I mean picnics on butte tops, Badlands hikes, a pilgrimage to Inyan Kara in the Black Hills, the musical with Sheila Schafer, kayaking on the Little Missouri and the Big, a leisurely re-con trip through the oil patch, long overland walks, a venture up to the Big Muddy Badlands in Saskatchewan, a long afternoon on a scalding sandbar in late July. The list is long.

We North Dakotans know how to squeeze the most out of the compacted window of shirtsleeve and shirtless time that comes to us every year, later than we remembered, on or about June 25.   *4/3/11*

I'm sorry to say I didn't do everything on this list. In spite of my friend Valerie's best efforts, we did not find a time to hike up Inyan Kara. I did not use my kayak on any river or lake. Nor did I venture up to the Big Muddy Badlands in Saskatchewan. All those things are high on my list, plus more. I did see the Medora Musical three times with Sheila Schafer, which is the best way to see it. She whoops.

You Call That Winter?

And Hail to the Crocus

> "If there is a heaven, the day begins with the sound of the meadowlark. "

You call that winter?! After twenty years away, I was looking forward to a big, spirit-crushing whopper of a winter, a riff-raff disincentive winter, a scan of the parking lot for head bolt heater plug-ins winter. In my diary I wrote that very sentence—"You call that winter?"—on January 26, with the idea that it would be pleasant when I had to eat crow sometime much later in the year. And perhaps it is not quite over yet. Beware of hubris. It can snow in any of the twelve months in North Dakota.

I wanted my first winter home to be so appalling and even dangerous that it would make us meditate on the fragility of life on the northern Plains. I wanted a Laura Ingalls Wilder winter in which I'd have to store wheat kernels between the walls of my tarpaper shack so that my neighbors wouldn't force me to share it, so that even Almanzo Wilder, courting my daughter, wouldn't know we had a teeny hidden reserve. I wanted a winter that we could later be smug over.

Instead, we got the only January in recorded history in which the temperature did not drop below zero. As far as I can remember, we had one pitiful little cold snap in November and another in February, and that's it.

The journals of Lewis and Clark are filled with appalling accounts of the cold November-February 1804-05. Coldest day, December 17—45° below. It was so cold the whiskey froze. It was so cold, as Sgt. John Ordway put it, that frost accumulated on the inside back of a Fort Mandan chimney even though the Corps of Discovery kept logs burning twenty-four hours a day.

But our winter was merely balmy. Citizens, this cannot be good.

I've been puzzling over this phenomenon for months, and I have developed a little theory, which I would like to try out on you. My editor, Ken Rogers, has said that this weekly column is a place where I can float some original ideas and see what our readers think. So here's my theory.

It's like the Earth is heating up or something.

OK, it's a lame and improbable explanation, but it's all I've got.

My neighbor is a retired farmer from Napoleon. He has a lovely new house with a driveway the size of Rhode Island, and he bought himself the largest snow blower that does not require a power takeoff to make it turn. It had to be delivered. It's the size of a Suburban. It's the size of the Zamboni at a hockey rink. Employees of the state highway department drive by the neighborhood just to drool over it. It's so large that he could save a lot of fuel if he just parked it in the driveway as soon as the snow started to fall, and moved it a few days later.

It appears to have a small V-8 engine and a Plexiglas protective hood (which, depending on one's domestic situation, could serve as a kind of cone of silence). I cannot tell, but I think there is a DVD player in there somewhere. On the two occasions when he actually got to use the thing this winter, he looked like a cleanup engineer from a toxic spill or the first farmer on Jupiter. It took him about ninety unheroic seconds to sweep his vast driveway. Sparks flew. I couldn't tell whether he was clearing snow or rototilling his driveway. I was afraid I'd see chunks of concrete blowing into the empty lot next door. I begged him just to sweep the entire neighborhood, maybe even the street itself, if only to give the rig time to warm up. I'm going to buy him the GPS attachment for Christmas.

I saw him out there the other day, rotating the tires a little sadly and putting it away until November.

Spring has sprung.

I heard my first meadowlark on March 31. Is there any more beautiful sound on the Great Plains? It stopped me in my tracks.

Here is a Sunday morning exercise more satisfying than Sudoku.

Make a list of the loveliest or most evocative sounds you know (and e-mail me your list if you like). Here are a few personal nominees. The sound of a cow's milk hitting the bottom of a pail. Garrison Keillor taking a long pause and then saying, "Well, it's been a quiet week in Lake Woebegon." As long as we are on public broadcasting, Carl Castle of NPR at dawn saying, "Good morning, this is Carl Castle," before intoning the news.

Anyone pronouncing, "Monongahela."

My daughter is eleven. For ten years, I have been monitoring the way she says "daddy" when she talks to me. If she says it in a certain way, it just buckles my knees. I have a recording of her, in a fiftieth birthday teddy bear, saying, "I love you, daddy," and about two days out of five when I squeeze that bear, the way she says "daddy" makes me burst into tears. She is about to embark on the Black Sea of puberty, and lately when she calls me daddy I am hearing a little "Daddy, will you please buy me a Ford Mustang?" tone in her voice. But I told her she had to learn German first, so that's that.

The grass has riz.

More sounds: The breeze in the cottonwoods at the campgrounds of Theodore Roosevelt National Park as the fire burns low and the tug of sleep begins to dull your senses. The sound of a distant coyote. The train in the middle of the night on the prairie. Jazz saxophone after a glass of wine.

And yet, if I could only keep one sound except "daddy," it would be the sound of the meadowlark. It's the signature sound of the Great Plains. If there is a heaven, the day begins there with the sound of the lark. Theodore Roosevelt, who knew what there was to know about birds, wrote, "One of our sweetest, loudest songsters is the meadow-lark; this I could hardly get used to at first, for it looks exactly like the eastern meadow-lark, which utters nothing but a harsh, disagreeable chatter. But the plains air seems to give it a voice, and it will perch on the top of a bush or tree and sing for hours in rich, bubbling tones." That was in *Hunting Trips of a Ranchman,* 1885.

The wind has been blowing lately in that wonderful brassy spring way. I was in flatter-than-a-pancake Kansas last weekend, and I experienced the most punishing wind of my life. It nearly blew my eighty-seven-pound daughter off her feet. And in the wind I can smell the good earth coming back to life.

Spring has sprung. The grass has riz. I wonder....

Actually, it's Palm Sunday and I don't wonder where the flowers are. The crocuses (pasque flowers) are blooming today in the Badlands. The early Christian church wisely understood that tying Easter to pagan fertility celebrations marking the renewal of spring only deepens the profundity.

Oh, and I bought a bicycle the other day. *4/8/07*

My neighbors have been good sports about my work. I write about them with some frequency and never ask their permission. Nobody has ever complained, and the widow of the snow blower farmer from Napoleon has said that she enjoys my wry references to the neighborhood.

THE RITES OF SPRING:

WHITE CARP LOOSE AMONG OUR STREETS

The moveable feast of Easter was perfectly set for North Dakota this year. It was the precise line of demarcation between winter and spring 2009. I went to Kansas to visit my daughter for the holy day. When I left Friday morning, the snow, though diminished, still covered my big backyard. It was snirty and heading toward the consistency of a soiled snow cone, but it looked as if it might linger until June. When I returned Monday afternoon, it was entirely gone. Just like that. And none of it in my basement.

The snowpack in my backyard was so vast this winter that, at one point, I nearly bought a Bobcat—to conduct "preventative trenching" and become "a snow emergency hero in my neighborhood." The fact is that, like nearly all men, I yearn for a Bobcat. It's all that's left of my dream of life. The fact that I have absolutely no reason to own one does not diminish the craving. For one brief shining moment in February, it seemed to me that I could justify owning one—a spanking new one with lots of attachments and the inevitable trailer—to save my house from flooding. (And my neighbors' houses, I quipped sanctimoniously). Somehow good sense returned. Thanks to a generous friend, I obtained a snowblower on the black market instead, at a time when they were as rare as a unicorn. It is now, except for cars, my most serious industrial object. I know the upshot: the snow blower's gleaming hopeful existence in my garage virtually assures a decade of dry and open winters in North Dakota.

I have good news and bad news about my garden, which is visible for the first time since November. The good news is that I did not, in fact, leave my rototiller out all winter, at the spot where it ran out of gas on that Saturday afternoon when it seemed as if Indian summer would last forever. The bad news is that the retreat of the snow has revealed a real mess of rusted-out coffee can tomato shields, strewn about in a most un-Jeffersonian manner, hoses and sprinklers, a perpendicular pitchfork with a snow-line clearly visible about four inches from the top, and other detritus of a grasshopper's lifestyle. Ah, but there are already green shoots of voluntary (or leftover) onions and garlic.

If the BTUs come soon and hard enough, I predict that this will be a bumper crop year for tomatoes. Last year, for me, was just so-so. Against my garden partner's strenuous protests, I'm intending seventy-three tomato plants this year, and I'm going to lay in a box of Mason jars every time I go to the grocery store between now and September.

Every evening now in my neighborhood, folks are inventing reasons to be outside doing stuff: picking up trash that had been mummified by the snowpack, raking and, in some cases, combing the sand from their boulevards into the street, trying to jack their supine mailboxes back to vertical, bouncing balls and practicing golf swings, hosing the grit from the porch and driveway, and even washing their SUVs by hand. People are wearing shorts when we all know it is not really shorts weather yet. If anyone doubts that this is a Nordic enclave at the top of the nation, just walk through any subdivision after supper and observe the flashes of blinding white flesh that has not seen the sun for six months. We all look like the underside of humanoid carp. And it is sadly clear that we have let ourselves go during the long winter.

It's delightful that these rites of spring so far do not involve the internal combustion engine. We are in that glorious interlude between the muffled and huddled winter and the obsessive drone of summer lawn care. People are actually leaning on rakes and talking to their neighbors, so glad are we to be able to spend as much time as we want outside after work.

I want to ride the gazillion dollar bike my friend Melanie made me buy. The salesman, her friend, realizing that the famous triathlete was talking Mr. Schlump into buying a bicycle worthy of Lance Armstrong, actually asked me if I wanted streamers for it. There are two problems, however. I don't dare open my garage door for fear that the mountain of stuff I literally threw into the maw—in the dark, wind howling, at 20° or more below zero—throughout the winter will cascade down on me like a closet in a sitcom. And, as far as I can remember, I wrecked the tire pump when I used it to prop open the hood of my Jeep on several of the occasions when I had to jumpstart the engine.

I've been trying to run after a winter of appalling torpor. At fifty-four, the old snap and resilience of my body is a bittersweet memory. As I lug my carcass down the street, I feel like a freight train powered by a Ford Pinto engine or a tugboat powered by an old D-cell battery you find at the back of a drawer in the laundry room. I no longer prance along scoria roads and ridgelines, but merely jog around the block—it is a big block—so that if I collapse I won't have very far to crawl home.

Normally I disdain running to music because it interferes with my reverie with nature, but this spring I have been listening at high decibel to the Beatles on an iPod merely to drown out my wheezing. It feels as if I am running in medieval chain mail and armor, on lead legs. There are moments, startlingly frequent, when I literally think, "Oh the hell with it, I'll just sit in a Barcalounger and give up altogether. The terminally sedentary life is much under-rated."

I drove to Dickinson and back on Tuesday. The snow was entirely gone except in heavily shaded places, and the countryside was as drab and gray and lifeless as it can ever be. Ah, but there was bright blue water running in every coulee, creek, stream and culvert. The geese honked lustily high overhead as they chevroned towards the North Pole.

In the next few weeks, the land of North Dakota is going to burst back to life as if the world were just emerging from the Great Flood—which is precisely what has happened. *4/18/09*

Melanie Carvell is the best garden partner in the world. She rebukes me for the extravagance of my tomato patch, but her reward is to harvest all that she can carry away, and she makes outstanding salsa.

Lilac Time on the Northern Great Plains

My theme is anticipation.

After so long and unyielding a winter, we all feel that summer owes us a long series of windless eighty-degree days and slightly breezy sixty-degree nights.

We've had a couple of teaser rumbles of thunder, but I won't feel right until we get pounded and punished with a thrashing, smashing, clashing, flashing thunderstorm that makes you almost wet your pants. One that splits the heavens down the middle with that sickening sound like a watermelon ripped open at cosmic decibel. I want a wild evening thunderstorm that moves in slowly from far off in the West, and you just sit out on the deck and watch it gather its energy as it advances over the Great Plains right at you. When it finally arrives in full force, I want to stand out in it as long as it is arguably safe—and then for a while longer—and watch the cottonwood trees bend over to what would seem like the snapping point, all their leaves trilling in orgiastic ecstasy, and the whole world magnificently alive. But I want the dawn thunderstorm too, the one that sneaks up on you and wakes you up on the second crack of thunder. You really want to go back to sleep, but the dawn storm is so strange and wonderful that you drag yourself out of bed and to the best window. And start the teakettle.

It was light until 9:15 p.m. last night, but because the weather has been so wet and chilly, I have not yet experienced that first May night when you sit out in a light jacket well after sunset and realize that the longest night of the year is not far off. That moment when you feel the need to exclaim, "Can you believe that it is still light at 10:15 p.m.? This is why we live here. I have waited nine months for this moment."

Two nights ago, after a long stressful day, I literally forced myself out into my garden to till. It took about an hour to get the tiller started and running properly. That was frustrating but exhilarating, too, because whenever a completely moronic and sedentary man can get any reluctant machine to work for him, he feels a strange sense of triumph. If I can bloody my knuckles and do something that a real man is supposed to be able to do, I light up and feel—for a few seconds at least—that I am equal to the challenge of life. And if getting something to work requires a trip to a hardware store for "stuff" (tools, blades, plugs, replacement caps, or a caulking gun!), well that's just hog heaven.

My mechanical ability includes changing the oil in this or that and replacing spark plugs, and I can deploy WD-40 (or PAM cooking spray) as well as the next man, but if there is anything more serious than that wrong with any of the four or five internal combustion engines in my world, I throw up my hands and begin making calls. My expertise breaks down well this side of the torque wrench.

> "For me the herculean gumption of the bean is as potent a parable as Jesus and the mustard seed (Matthew 13:31-32). One reason to plant a garden is to learn all over again that life is a miracle."

I tilled the ground for a couple of hours and got dirty and gazed around at the greening plains and felt the evening chill on my face and neck and felt like a human being again. I actually went over and caressed the soft green needles of my Ponderosa Pines.

So now I am anticipating three garden events. First, the moment when the leaf heads of the beans push through the black soil, sometimes moving whole lumps of earth in their effort to rise up into the air to breathe. When that happens, I lie face down on the good earth to study the magical iridescent green of the bean sprout. It fills me with wonder that the life force can be that strong, that this little bean can overcome such odds (including the law of gravitation) to perform its appointed role. For me the herculean gumption of the bean is as potent a parable as Jesus and the mustard seed (Matthew 13:31-32). One reason to plant a garden is to learn all over again that life is a miracle.

Second, I love the moment when you walk out into the garden late on some July afternoon and suddenly smell the unique odor of the tomato plants for the first time. It's just a little localized waft, but it makes me take my first deep breath of the season, and for that instant all is right with the universe. There's aromatherapy! The smell of a tomato plant places me instantaneously at the side of my grandmother back of the old farmhouse in Fergus Falls, MN, though she has been dead for twenty years. She is wearing a thin, bleached-out calico apron. The apron pockets are full of her small tools: a carefully rolled length of bailer twine, a brown pocket-knife, four or five safety pins, a needle threaded with an eight-inch piece of white carpet thread, one of grandpa's discarded pairs of pliers. Her hair is silver gray. One of her front teeth has a gold rim. She is clucking and fussing among the plants like Andy Griffith's Aunt Bea, pinching off a sucker shoot with supreme confidence or crushing a potato bug like an ogre between her fingers. She was the Tomato Queen.

Third, the moment in late August when I walk out into the garden after work and snap off a cob of sweet corn, a cucumber, and a tomato, and pull an onion gently up out of the ground, and go into the house to eat a meal I produced (with a little help from God) with my own two hands. *5/5/11*

LEARNING TO LIVE AGAIN IN THE GARDEN:

WHICH GREEN DO YOU TRUST?

The freak freeze just before Memorial Day damaged my potatoes and to-matoes. Because I live abstracted from nature and to a certain extent from life, I was unaware that there had been a freeze. For decades, until last year, my whole experience with living plants has consisted of maintaining a grass lawn. And my standard, until now, has been very low: It shall not actually die on my watch.

A lawn in the age of sprinkler systems demands very little attention, though some of the folks in my neighborhood lavish the same loving care on their quarter-acre lawns that they would on bonsai trees or an expensive stamp collection. Several have mowed six or seven times already this year, and a few have taken to mowing the borrow ditch between their homes and the formerly county road. There is almost no time during the weekends when the drone of a small internal combustion engine is not breaking the silence of the neighborhood. The lawn mowers don't much bother me, but the ning-zing-wing of the weed whackers and the leaf blowers is enough to detract from the pleasure of a cup of coffee or a glass of wine.

My neighborhood is like a small paramilitary unit of lawn tractors. If we could coordinate our aggressions, we could invade Lincoln or Wilton and declare the republic of John Deere. My pathetic little push mower (which cost a fortune) is looked down upon as a "starter mower," and I'm sure more than one neighbor has speculated that I will soon see the light and get myself a rig. But, for me, there is no middle ground between a mower and something heroic. I'm holding out for a Bobcat, which I believe is every man's dream. With a Bobcat, I could mow my lawn in twelve minutes (and use my regular mower as an edger) and dig some post holes too.

Grass will survive almost anything, including a late spring freeze, but a garden is a much more delicate organism, I'm discovering. The little insights of gardening are obvious to almost everyone, I know, but they are new (or renewed) to me. At this time in American life, at the pace we live, with the myriad of distractions and over-stimulations that we daily absorb, it is possible to lose touch with life and to live a kind of mediated, digitized existence, and simply to move from one laminated surface to the next. Even our lawns now, thanks to the superb (if toxic) chemical treatments of our time, are preternaturally lush, even and weed-free, and as I drive around I often have the impression that the lawns look a little—well, colorized. When we reconnect with life in some simple Thoreauvian way— planting a garden, say—it feels to me that we have to learn very basic understandings again, as if we just returned from a long sojourn on Mars. Things my grandmother did daily with effortless mastery I have to learn as if they were a foreign language.

The great Jefferson believed that gardening was the sanest thing humans can do, that when we have our hands in the soil our souls cannot be meditating mayhem or investment strategies. He wrote a famous letter to his old friend Charles Willson Peale in 1812, in which he called himself "an old man, but a young gardener." "No occupation is so delightful to me as the culture of the earth, and no culture comparable to that of the garden," wrote Jefferson with his characteristic grace and serenity. "Such a variety of subjects, some one always coming to perfection, the failure of one thing repaired by the success of another, and instead of one harvest a continued one through the year." In other words, a field of wheat or corn is monoculture. If the hail or blight comes, the crop is a write-off.

> " My neighborhood is like a small paramilitary unit of lawn tractors. If we could coordinate our aggressions, we could invade Lincoln or Wilton and declare the republic of John Deer. "

But in a garden, the peas may miscarry but the tomatoes bury you in salsa.

For Jefferson, the variety of a garden was one of its principal delights. When I visit Monticello and see the huge gardens terraced on the red soil of the mountain, I think, "Well, of course, that's why Jefferson was Jefferson. There is no other American historical figure for whom a garden is so central to his life and achievement."

The day after the freeze, I walked out in purple Crocs (purchased by my whimsical daughter) to survey my domain, and discovered to my horror that about half of the potato leaves were black and the majority of my tomato plants were prone on the black earth. I was horrified. It was the first time in a life of five decades when it actually mattered to me that the temperature had dropped below 32°F. I actually felt like crying as I wandered among the stricken plants, and I actually thought, "I killed them. I have failed in my stewardship responsibility. Why wasn't I out at midnight with old blankets and towels?"

I got down on my hands and knees—as one must in a garden. In the little tilled patches behind our houses, we kneel and crawl and thereby humble ourselves. We embrace the earth from which we came and to which we will return like a spent cornstalk. It's liberating because it is so overwhelmingly real and basic and undeniable.

At ground zero, it soon became clear that the freeze had been a partial one and that the potatoes would surely survive, and many, perhaps most of the tomatoes will recover, if the sun ever chooses to shine again. The onions were undaunted, and the garlic (planted in the fall, like winter wheat or tulips) looked magnificent with their eight-inch spires reaching toward the heavens. Nearby, the beans were breaking through the crust of the earth with their shields folded before them. Jefferson was right.

Of the forty trees I planted not long ago, some are probably dead, though I won't know that for a few more weeks; others are waiting for more BTUs before they leaf out. The lilacs are flourishing. When I walk out to the garden, I cannot really believe that anything could thrive so quickly after being transplanted. They have been in the ground for two weeks and somehow their root structures have stabilized and begun to spread, and the leaves are proliferating like bubble bath. Lilacs are European colonists.

The cottonwoods, though native, may or may not survive. What I don't understand is how cottonwoods can flourish in the Darwinian jungle of the prairie, but have such a hard time of it in the ICU atmosphere of my backyard. I've tried to transplant them to every home I've lived in since my father died in 1995, never with any success. If one of the six survives, I'll regard it as victory.

Possibly there have been greener springs in Dakota, but I cannot remember any. I had occasion to go to Medora recently. On the drive out, when I wasn't marveling at how much serious maintenance an interstate highway seems to need, this year one long section, next year another, I just relaxed and looked around, not without some reckless careening across the broad concrete surface of the highway. We all know we live in the North American grasslands, but in a spring like this you experience that moment when you realize all over again, it's GRASSland.

Square Butte south and west of Medora was a vast green giant, never more beautiful than that afternoon.

On the drive home, I stopped at the twin buttes between Glen Ullin and Almont to stretch. The two conical hills were as green as organic green can ever be, and in the soft evening light the scoria road rolling over hill and valley and hill again to the south was as brilliantly pink-orange as scoria can ever be. The temperature was sixty-five degrees. A very light breeze caressed the evening. It was a magic kingdom called North Dakota.

And there was not a single plastic surface in the world. *6/2/07*

OF WIND AND TRAVEL IN THE UNSETTLED SEASON

It wasn't the isolation and the hard work that made Great Plains pioneers go mad. It was the wind.

When the annual Santa Ana winds come to Southern California, the crime rate soars. The novelist Raymond Chandler might just as well have been writing about North Dakota when he said, "It was one of those hot dry Santa Anas that . . . curl your hair and make your nerves jump and your skin itch. On nights like that every booze party ends in a fight. Meek little wives feel the edge of the carving knife and study their husbands' necks. Anything can happen."

The storms that passed through North Dakota last week were impressive even by Great Plains standards. Everywhere I have gone, people have been buzzing about it in a way that is normally reserved for the aftermath of the severest of blizzards. I walked into the same coffeehouse two days in a row only to find the same man telling the same story to the same people about the miasma of fog, wind, and blinding rain on the highway west of Mandan Tuesday.

Stuff has blown off of my house and deck and driveway that I didn't know could blow off. On the highway Tuesday, I was mesmerized by the way the fierce gusts created wave and dervish patterns in the lush, tall, green spring grass. My little Honda was buffeted like a piñata from shoulder to shoulder and everywhere in between. The rubber door and window seals just gave up the fight and played an Aeolian trumpet riff all the way across the state.

A friend of mine who was walking in downtown Fargo was almost beaned by a flying pizza box.

Some folks flew in from faraway to attend an important meeting in Dickinson this week. They had never been here before. When they walked into the room, they had a wide-eyed wind-blasted look, as if they had spent the afternoon with King Lear on the heath. "So this is North Dakota!" They were so impressed by our climate that one of them—who was here to pitch his company's services—actually told us, unapologetically, "You are really the middle of nowhere here."

People who have lived here all of their life have told me they are not sure they have ever seen anything quite like the winds of the last few weeks. Which is probably an exaggeration.

When Meriwether Lewis was trying to move his flotilla of six canoes and two pirogues past today's Williston into Montana, the Corps of Discovery was delayed for so many days by such appalling winds that he actually wondered—for a day or two—if they would ever get to the Great Falls. Two weeks later, all was calm. Temporarily.

As a very frequent flyer, I have more flight delays and missed connections in May and June than in the worst months of the winter. Once, seven years ago, in June, I was delayed in Tulsa by a lightning storm, which made me miss my connection to Durango at Denver International. My lecture was scheduled for 8 a.m. the next morning, and I make a point of never failing to show up, no matter what. I was completely exhausted by the time (10:15 p.m.) the airline agent finally informed me that my luggage had been lost. So I rented a car and drove literally all night to get to the conference. That meant I-70 from Denver to Grand Junction (243 miles), then US 550 from Grand Junction to Durango (169 miles).

It was, of course, a dark and stormy night.

I got to the point on that all-nighter drive—we have all been there—where I was so bleary that I had to sing at the top of my lungs to stay awake. I had to open all the windows on the rental car to let the rush of air blast me into some semblance of consciousness. It was the kind of fatigue wherein you try a range of unprecedented eye stretches and blinks, including rough eyeball massages with your thumb and fingers. The kind of fatigue in which eventually you actually slap your face hard to stay awake and shake your head like a rag doll, and engage in yogic breathing to try to super-charge your lungs and bloodstream. The kind of fatigue in which several times per hour you are jolted back to consciousness by the rumble strips on the shoulder of the road.

> " My little Honda was buffeted like a piñata from shoulder to shoulder and everywhere in between. The rubber door and window seals just gave up the fight and played an Aeolian trumpet riff all the way across the state. "

And that was the easy part of drive! The last stretch, the road between Ouray and Durango, is one of the most beautiful in America—during daylight hours for a confident and well-rested driver. Just at the time I had reached maximum exhaustion and despair, I drove up three of the most spectacular and breathtaking passes in Colorado: Red Mountain Pass (11,275 feet) between Ouray and Silverton and Molas (10,899) and Coal Bank Passes (10,640) between Silverton and Durango. These are the kinds of mountain passes on a narrow road without more than perfunctory guard rails that used to send my acrophobic father onto the floor of the back seat with a blanket over his head. I got out once, to stretch, and looked over the lip of the road into the abyss in dawn's early light. I was literally gaping down thousands of feet into the valley below, without a guardrail of any sort between me and eternity. I recoiled like someone who has come snout to snout with an angry bat.

When I finally got Durango at 6:49 a.m., I was as bleary and sweat-gluey and rumpled as it is possible to be. My one remaining dream in life was to take a shower (no time to buy a toothbrush) at the hotel before going to the lecture hall, even if it meant putting on the same foul and fetid clothes. I walked up to the desk like a survivor of the Bataan Death March. The young clerk crisply informed me that there was no room available, because, of course, my reservation had been voided at midnight. *5/30/10*

The "middle of nowhere" folks did not get the contract.

BITTERSWEETNESS AND THE SUMMER SOLSTICE

Here we are closing in on the summer solstice, and as usual I'm bracing myself for a wave of melancholia, a week or so from now, when I realize that the longest day of 2007 has come and gone. In the days before June 21, I always start to feel a little unsettled. A rivulet of sadness stains my summer high, because I know we are about to drink in the moment of maximum light, after which, slowly but inexorably, the sunset will come a minute or two earlier every day.

There's the glass half empty! At the moment when I should be dancing in a Druidic bed sheet at Carhenge in Nebraska or Cross Ranch State Park southwest of Washburn, worshipping the life force and the sun, I feel bittersweetness at the inevitability of the retreat of the light.

On the other hand, at the other end of the calendar, just after the hangover of Christmas madness, I feel an annual elation because I know that each day, no matter how cold, windy or raw, the number of minutes of light will inexorably increase, and the end is in sight. I believe for most Dakotans the issue is not winter, but the way night gobbles up the world in December and January. That's the source of what Theodore Roosevelt called the "iron desolation" of the northern plains.

So far as I know, I don't suffer from Seasonal Affective Disorder (SAD—did they choose these words merely to get to SAD?), an affliction said to bring depression to between 6 percent and 14 percent of the

American people during the months surrounding the winter solstice. Some people sneer at the idea of Seasonal Affective Disorder, and I admit being skeptical, but I have known people who have been diagnosed with the syndrome, and they have suffered acutely in the dark winter months.

Why should we sneer? If, from a quarter of a million miles away, the moon can lift the oceans by six to ten feet, it must surely lift the liquids in my body (65 percent to 70 percent water) too. Only my lack of sensitivity prevents me from feeling the tug of tides within me. If it is true that plants respond as much to the quanta of light as to BTUs, then surely the human plant perks to the light, just as a sunflower twists its fibrous neck to keep its flower pointed at the sun.

It is only because we humans are so determined to distance ourselves from the organic, so anxious to deny our place in the symphony of nature, that we pretend to be immune to forces that indubitably influence my potatoes and corn.

Run any software you want—from Presbyterianism to "shop till you drop" consumerism—but your hardware, your slushy body, marches to the drum of cosmogonal forces that are as strong as dogma and infinitely more healthy. We are creatures of the Earth and subject to all sorts of lunary and sublunary forces. The problem for most of us is that the universe is FM and we are running AM only in our souls.

> "We are creatures of the earth and subject to all sorts of lunary and sublunary forces. The problem for most of us is that the universe is FM and we are running AM only in our souls."

My tomatoes are showing signs of reluctant recovery.

This is that time of the year when we are still shocked when we come in at dusk—from the garden, from a walk through the neighborhood—and find that it is already 10 p.m., although it feels no later than 7:45 or 8 p.m. Whoa, we say, it really stays light late. The fact that we have to relearn this truth every year is one of the great joys of life in a northern latitude.

Is there anything in North Dakota life better than that first endless early summer evening, when the day lingers forever? The sun finally slips down over the horizon, as if reluctantly, but leaves behind a broad gash of light the color of bloody mary mix in the western sky and a pink roseate crown above the horizon all the way around the compass. Time to find a jacket. As the dusk deepens, the color drains out of the sky. Gray and charcoal-black streaks appear, impossibly elongated and parallel with the horizon, bearing just the faintest hint of lightning.

So far this year, perhaps because of my travels, I haven't experienced a sockdolager of a thunderstorm. That moment, when fear and awe run a dead heat across the heart, is yet to come. But even better than a massive thunderstorm, when the great cottonwoods bend like reeds against the frontal blasts, is the slow motion spectacle of heat lightning all around. For some reason I associate that phenomenon with being in the back seat of my parents' car, and my father saying, with edgy reassurance, "It's only heat lightning. Besides, the tires will protect us."

So far this summer everything is growth and green and promise. The stress of our characteristic aridity has not yet touched Dakota.

I love North Dakota in all of its guises. I love the moment in August, when it is still hot summer, and yet somehow, for an instant, out walking, gazing about, you think, "There's a hint of fall in the air today." Something physical happens in the body just then. I love the moment in late September when the cottonwoods explode into the yellowest golden light nature ever produces and you just want to cry, it is so beautiful. I love the moment in November when you are driving somewhere on back roads and the weather suddenly turns threatening, and you are made aware all over again of how fragile life is on the northern Great Plains.

I love the warm January afternoon (ten degrees) when North Dakota is covered in a low-hanging canopy of dark gray clouds and yet there is a band of wan yellowish light on the western horizon, and the wind comes in short hard gusts, which—if you relax—are actually quite pleasant to experience. I love dusk in the Badlands, camping along the river, when you quiet down and begin to listen to the stirring to crescendo of the cottonwoods.

Yesterday, I sat on the banks of the Missouri River near Washburn and gazed out on the shimmering current of America's second most myth-silted river. The temperature was somewhere in the low eighties. There were wisps of sandbars a couple of hundred yards out. How I wanted to get to one of them in a kayak and spend the day lying on my back as close to moving water as was safe and dry, and just turn vegetable. What could be better than dozing and musing and rising on one's elbows to look at the river and the huge dense cottonwoods far off on the other side? There is a reason why *Huck Finn* is the great American novel. The light from the cloudless sky and the wide expanse of the river was so bright that, at times, it overwhelmed my retinas and created that wonderful gray-scale effect wherein it feels as if you are wearing sunglasses. Eventually, I shut off my addled busy brain, and all that is trivial flowed downstream to the Gulf. For a cluster of minutes, I just WAS for a change, and just existing turned out to be the peace that passeth understanding.

The light is not forever. We must drink it while we can.

My thirty-seven little corn stalks are so very beautiful against the wet dark earth.

It's summer in North Dakota! *6/16/07*

As I reread my seasonal columns yesterday to prepare this book, I realized that this is my Walden, *this set of essays constitutes my attempt to listen to the hidden voices of this place. I don't expect everyone who reads the Bismarck Tribune to hearken to these same voices. I can imagine some readers throwing down the Sunday paper and saying, "That guy's just weird." But my overall purpose is to celebrate North Dakota in ways that is not usually described, to try to explain my own sense of spirit of place because I believe that others feel it too, to lesser and greater degrees, and that we must all awaken ourselves to a deeper sense of place if we are going to make the right choices in the difficult years ahead.*

CELEBRATING THE AMERICAN PROMISE

ON THE FOURTH OF JULY

My Fourth of July was as unabashedly American as it can get.

It started at the Medora Musical, to which I took my twelve-year-old daughter and her cousin on Monday night. There is something magical about sitting in that perfectly embedded Badlands amphitheater as the evening temperature begins to drop, wondering if you are going to need a jacket, watching the broken country south of Medora turn roseate. And then the show!

When the Burning Hills Singers slowed the hectic stage business to sing "Home to North Dakota," every North Dakotan, and particularly those home for the holidays from somewhere far away, felt a little pulse of emotion, of longing and nostalgia and loss. A woman a few seats down from me sat in solemn pride with a tear making its way slowly down her cheek.

Then we drove to Montana to America's first national park, Yellowstone (1872).

If there were only one state, it would have to be Montana. California, Texas, and Colorado each have some claim to being singly representative of what America means to itself and the world, but Montana trumps them all as the heart and essence of America. The Yellowstone River Valley is a breathtaking reminder of what the Missouri River corridor might have been.

My mother has a tiny cabin, about the size of the Unabomber's hideout, near Cooke City, not far from the northeast portal of Yellowstone National Park. It's possible in that one-room cabin to whap a close relative with a spatula and honestly proclaim one's innocence.

Unlike the palatial designer log homes all around it, Mother's wee hut is precisely what a wilderness cabin should be. Thoreau could not have found it lavish, except for the Direct TV satellite dish, which scars the whole experience and which I would like to unabomb.

We fried eggs and bacon for breakfast. Naturally, they tasted better among the mountain pines than they would have in some marble-countered kitchen. Black bears lumber through the property with some regularity. Mother and her terrified lapdog cowered in the house one evening while a grizzly bear peered through the window and tested the screen door.

> " We have Indians. We are so fortunate to have indigenous people still living in America. "Though they have made accommodations to survive…" amongst the dominant white culture and to accept some of the benefits of industrial culture, American Indians continue to an astonishing degree to retain their aboriginal ways. "

S'mores and German potato salad. Sparklers and a hammock. I taught my nine-year-old nephew to catch with a baseball mitt. We made bars for the picnic in Cooke City, a fundraiser for the volunteer fire department.

What's the most American place in America? Old Faithful is certainly near the top of everyone's list. Even so, I had to drag my kin kicking and screaming to the world's most famous geyser on the Fourth of July.

It was, they rightly argued, a long drive on the most congested day of the year to a place that will be overwhelmed by the press of humanity.

They pointed out that the very faithfulness of the geyser (every ninety-seven minutes) was such that we could visit it any other time of the year.

But I reminded them that it was the nation's birthday, that I intended to be as corny and patriotic as Clark Griswold in *National Lampoon's Vacation,* and that we were going to Old Faithful whether they liked it or not. An over-zealous patriarch and reluctant auto hostages—hard to get any closer to the heart of an American vacation than that.

And there she blew at 4:25 p.m. There were five thousand people watching, many of them foreigners. I gasp out loud every time and take dozens of useless photos of one of the most photographed places on Earth.

Meanwhile, we saw elk, antelope, bison by the hundreds, a black bear, a coyote, deer, a pelican, and—far down in a magnificent valley—a microscopic grizzly bear. How did we know? Because of thirty cars perched precariously on the steep shoulder of the road and a dozen spotting scopes triangulating precisely the same distant speck.

Later, as we lay on my Grandma Rhoda's quilt waiting for the Silver Gate fireworks show, I gave over gastronomic self-indulgence to ponder the Fourth of July.

So what's really admirable about the United States on our 231st birthday?

We are profoundly blessed in our national Constitution. Even though Thomas Jefferson hoped that we would tear up the Constitution of the United States every nineteen years, it is now the oldest and most venerated social compact in the world.

More admirable still, after a period of doubtful adherence to the Constitution and serious erosion of the Bill of Rights, we the people have begun to reassert ourselves. The Constitution is a self-righting ship, as long—said Jefferson—as the people remain vigilant.

The fruited plains and the purple mountains' majesty will take your breath away if you let them. My favorite patriotic song is "America the Beautiful," composed by Katherine Lee Bates in the shadow of Pike's Peak in 1893. America: "God shed his grace on thee."

Our population is now more than 300 million and that seems like a lot of people, but the thing that strikes you the minute you fly over the American West or drive anywhere west of the Mississippi River is how vast and empty the rugged arid lands of America still are. Every pessimist, everyone disillusioned with America, should be encouraged to spend a week driving the American West. It is impossible not to cheer up at Ekalaka or Moab.

We have the national park system, which may be the greatest thing America ever invented. The names alone fill you with transcendental reverence: Arches, Crater Lake, Yosemite, Glacier, Death Valley, Grand Teton, Big Bend, the Grand Canyon.

We have Indians. We are so fortunate to have indigenous people still living in America. Though they have made accommodations to survive amongst the dominant white culture and to accept some of the benefits of industrial culture, American Indians continue to an astonishing degree to retain their traditional ways.

Just for a minute, try to imagine North Dakota life without Indians in it: Mandan, Hidatsa, Lakota, Dakota, Ojibwe, Assiniboine, Arikara, Cree. Think of what powwows, drum groups, prayers at public gatherings, flute music, oral traditions, Sacagawea, the legendary resistance of Red Cloud, Sitting Bull and, above all, Crazy Horse, and the automatic Indian skepticism about "development" have brought to our national consciousness. Even a single tepee on a plains vista deepens our cultural experience and reminds us of what is unique about America.

Fields of wheat, flax, sunflowers, corn, soybeans and alfalfa. There is something about growing more than our share of the world's food that entitles us to the deepest pride. God forbid that North Dakota ever veer from its primal status as breadbasket of the world.

And, finally, there is the document that lit what Jefferson called the "little flame" of liberty on the Fourth of July 1776. Outstanding wordsmith that he was, Jefferson said his intention was "to place before mankind the common sense of the subject, in terms so plain and firm as to command their assent." Mission accomplished, Mr. Jefferson.

Jefferson wrote what I call the thirty-six most important words in the English language. Has there ever been a sentence better than this: "We hold these truths to be self-evident, that all men are created equal, that they are endowed by their Creator with certain unalienable Rights, that among these are Life, Liberty, and the pursuit of Happiness"?

The unfinished purpose of these words is for us to find a way to live up to the promise of America.

The western writer Wallace Stegner envisioned a "society to match the scenery." Theodore Roosevelt said, in Dickinson, on the Fourth of July 1886, that the magnificence of the American landscape challenged us to develop an equal magnificence in the American character, and that if we failed to do this, we would have squandered the greatest advantage any people ever had.

We've got a lot of work to do.

Where to start? Visit the national parks, preferably in off-season. *7/7/07*

Northern Lights Drop the Curtain

on the Moon Anniversary

Did you see the northern lights on Tuesday night? It was well after 11 p.m., and I was winding down for the night. I was weary in body and soul. For no good reason, I ventured for a moment out onto my deck—just to feel the night air and internalize the midnight breeze.

I looked up. There in the northwestern quadrant of the night sky hovered an aurora borealis, a luminous miasma of soft white diffused light, with a little tincture of gray-green, looming like a vague celestial amoeba over Saskatchewan and Alberta all the way up to the pole. It was making a little tentative visit to North Dakota, and I was lucky enough to have stepped out of my interiorized life in time to see it.

So much of life is accidental.

Immediately I thought of getting out into the country to see it right.

It was late and I had a full schedule on Wednesday—including writing this column. I'm sleep starved virtually all of the time. The smart thing to do would be to watch it for a few minutes from my deck and then turn in. But at the end of our protracted winter (was that early June or early July?), I pledged that I would not fail come summer to "live deep and suck out all the marrow of life," as Thoreau put it in *Walden*.

Even now, in the midst of some achingly beautiful extended dusks, I look out from my house at the hills to the southwest and I can almost see the winterscape and almost feel the biting wind in my bones six months from now either direction. "Soon enough, sooner than you think," I find myself saying, sometimes out loud. Carpe diem, you silly Dakotan.

Here were my first serious northern lights since I returned to North Dakota almost four years ago—and I was contemplating just going to bed? How pathetic is that? So, with that literal internal dialogue we sometimes find ourselves hosting on our shoulder—"this is stupid, just go back into the house and go to bed," versus, "seriously, you prefer sleep to wonder?!"—I drove out to Double Ditch Indian Village State Historic Site on N.D. 1804 north of Bismarck. Needless to say, I was the only car in the parking lot.

> "When you turn off your car lights in the middle of a nightscape away from the grid, there is always a little inrush of anxiety."

When you turn off your car lights in the middle of a nightscape away from the grid, there is always a little inrush of anxiety.

It was a dark and still and brooding night. It was at the low end of shirtsleeve weather, fifty-six degrees, no perceptible breeze. The grass was never less than six inches deep, thick, dense and trippy. The air was gelid. I was a little afraid, the way we get when we first face the night away from the umbilicals. For the first time I noticed that Double Ditch has some serious contours and ridgelines. They were silhouetted—slightly menacing and yet powerfully inviting—against the glow of the aurora.

Even in daylight, Double Ditch is a place of palpable mystery. At night you can feel the sacred inching up your legs.

I lay down out there on top of the remains—ruins is the wrong word—of that once-bustling Mandan Indian village, bustling at the time of the Declaration of Independence, quiet now for more than two hundred years. For as long as my work-conscience permitted, I lay on my side looking up at the aurora, watching it dance in the northern sky.

At times it faded as if it might just blink out and leave me there in the darkness. In its periodic retreats, the left edge of the constellation Cassiopeia (shaped like a splayed W) emerged. The most important person in my adolescence taught me to identify Cassiopeia. That in itself brought on a rush of memory and wonder.

At times the aurora seemed to form itself into columns, into vague shafts of greenish white light not so different from Albert Speer's light symphony at the Nuremberg rallies in the 1930s. My head told me that the aurora is a mere soulless phenomenon of physics, the atoms of solar wind interacting with charged particles in the magnetosphere. Blah blah blah. But if you haven't utterly banished your sense of wonder, you know that the Cree were closer to the "truth" when they called the northern lights the Dance of the Spirit Beings.

As I lay there gazing in wonder at the aurora and peering through to the stars, I found myself in the midst of one of those periodic attempts we make to fathom the universe and our place in it. The aurora is a neighborhood phenomenon, a fluorescent glow against the razor-thin veneer of atmosphere that envelopes the Earth and makes it habitable. But the stars are—at least to the mind of humanity—infinitely far away. The moon (a mere quarter of a million miles away) we can visit a couple of times if we throw the whole weight of our will and technological concentration at it. For a staggering cost, we can plant our flag on the lunar soil and then come back and crow about the majesty of man.

But the stars stagger all our pretentions. They put us back in our place— a very insignificant place in a puny corner of a modest-sized solar system in a back bend of a fair-sized galaxy, which is merely one of an estimated 125 billion-500 billion galaxies in an expanding universe.

It wasn't always so. The contemporaries of Thomas Aquinas (1225-74) believed that the Earth was the center of a young and finite (almost miniature) universe made of up concentric circles with God himself hovering over the crystalline outer firmament like the aurora of auroras. Theologians and philosophers like Aquinas made much of man, because back then, for all of his faults, man was still the center of the universe.

That was before Copernicus, before Galileo's telescope. That was before Freud, who taught us that most of what goes on in our souls takes place below the radar of consciousness, and before Darwin, who taught us that if we are the most extraordinary of created beings, we also are disappointingly temporary and certainly not the final product to which all things tend.

Just how alone we are in the cosmos depends on which lens you wear, but I know I looked around a little helplessly out on the ridge Tuesday night in the midst of my prayers of gratitude to have the good fortune to live in North Dakota.

A minor meteorite, a little shooting star, streaked down to the black earth somewhere very far away. Suddenly, the aurora felt like a security blanket. *7/22/09*

When I was young I belonged to a "northern lights club." If any of us saw the aurora, we had to call five other people, and they in turn called five other people, until everyone in the club had the opportunity to drop what they were doing and venture outside. UND philosopher Ben Ring was one of the founders. The northern lights are comparatively rare nowadays, I'm not quite sure why.

Summertime and the Living is (Un)Easy

Summer finally rolled in this last week—go cool off in the river summer, micromanage the windows and window shades summer. Corn and tomatoes summer. Drive to King Cone on the edge of town summer. Too hot to eat summer.

I was beginning to wonder, actually. But the Great Spirit finally cranked up the BTUs on the northern Great Plains. Now is the time to go see the Medora Musical, to sit in that fabulous amphitheater just at that moment when the heat relents and the temperature starts to drop a degree per minute, gazing out before the show at the massif of Bullion Butte and forgetting for a moment that North Dakota is not always so hospitable. Now is the time to wade through the Little Missouri River looking for a gravel shelf to lie down on and take in the sun for a couple of hours, a hedge against the "iron desolation" of January.

I have been gone for two full weeks, a fortnight chock full of labor, adventure, and sensory overload in a place far away. Even so, I found myself thinking about North Dakota throughout my travels, and fussing over my garden the way absent parents worry about their teenage children left alone in the house for the first weekend ever. I don't know quite what I expected to unfold in my absence, but I reckoned I'd get back to find the garden ripe enough for a continuous daily mini-harvest between now and first frost. I got periodic reports from my friend The Triathlete—cool and rain, mostly, said she—but in my gardener's optimism I reckoned that time and the endless light were on my side.

As soon as I got home, I walked out to check the garden, even before walking through the house. Good news. The weeds are under control this year. Last year, they got ahead of me and then went on to get the best of me. This year, thanks to firmer supervision by The Triathlete, I spaced the tomatoes better and once even engaged in what I regard as horticultural heresy: namely, using the rototiller between rows as a weed control device.

More good news. The corn is in full profligate exuberance. I have four rows of corn this year, perhaps forty plants in all. The corn grew at least a foot in my absence, and it is tasseling and heading out.

In my Wobegonian world, corn is the parable of the mustard seed (Mark 4:30-32). The Kingdom of Heaven, Jesus said, "is like a grain of mustard seed, which, when it is sown in the earth, is less than all the seeds that be in the earth? But when it is sown, it groweth up, and becometh greater than all herbs, and shooteth out great branches." Just yesterday, it seems, on a cold morning in May, I poured a packet of dry corn seeds into the cup of my left hand and crawled through my garden planting a dull yellow, wrinkled, seemingly inert seed every six inches or so. Now, two months later, those improbable parched kernels have metamorphosed into lofty towers of steroid green, higher in proportion to their surroundings and girth than the Empire State Building, and a far greater miracle of engineering. All that stalk and leafage to produce a cob of corn. I eat them as languidly as possible to savor the miracle. The earth is awash in the Life Force.

"Just yesterday, it seems, on a cold morning in May, I poured a packet of dry corn seeds into the cup of my left hand and crawled through my garden planting a dull yellow, wrinkled, seemingly inert seed every six inches or so. Now, two months later, those improbable parched kernels have metamorphosed into lofty towers of steroid green, higher in proportion to their surroundings and girth than the Empire State Building, and a far greater miracle of engineering."

Meanwhile, frankly, I am worried about my tomatoes. I hope I am not being a nervous Nellie (or Nigel), but my eighty-seven plants are bushy, still blossoming, and the tomatoes that have already developed are solid green and no larger than plums. Some have a black rot below their tropics of Capricorn. By this time in August, one in ten tomatoes should be red or reddening. My two Topsy Turvys continue to turn my life upside down.

I decided to make a wee little cherry tomato salad for supper, to celebrate the best of all experiences: homecoming. So I plucked a dozen of the ripest grape-sized tomatoes and, with my hands cupped together, carried them like rare quail eggs into the kitchen, washed them in cool water and spread them out on a sunny plate. With the most delicate knife in my drawer I carved them up into teeny little slices and salted each one liberally. Then I ate them, Charlie Chaplin-like, in little delicate miniature bites the size of your thumbnail, and sighed with animal content between each bite.

Summertime, and the living is easy.

At the Denver airport, I discovered that I was returning home at the moment of the annual Perseid meteor shower. So as soon as I had washed up my little plate and fork, I gathered a blanket and pillow and drove out north of Bismarck to an undisclosed meteor-viewing location and lay flat on my back on the prairie I love more than Paris, Alaska, Santorini, London, or Montana. It turned out to be a mediocre meteor shower (a modest burst every ten minutes or so and a few spectacular strikes in two hours of doze-and-wake observation), but an unbelievable night.

As I lay on my back gathering what strength I could from our collective grassland, like Antaeus of Greek myth, lamenting how few constellations I can identify, I was startled to observe the gibbous moon rise like an overripe orange over the eastern horizon. It was as parched and mottled as those seeds of corn, infinitely far away, remote and unapproachable. Lifeless—and a little menacing out there in the middle of nowhere. Do you believe there are spirits abroad in the night?

As the moon rose over that open plain, it grew brighter and brighter until it cast a mystical wan yellow light over all the Missouri bluffs. It's hard to explain how something that dim could be a little overpowering, a garish low-watt moonshine that cast long foreboding shadows over the plains. Fool that I am, I first concluded that the moon's intensity would ruin the meteor shower. I stood up and stretched every muscle I can still access like a New Age Great Plains yoga dork, and breathed deeply, and tried to get present—to live in this single moment completely and with no withholding. It dawned on me there on the vast plain, as I teased out muscles I had neglected for years, that the mooncast was, in fact, most of the magic of the night. You are never present if you wish what is were otherwise.

I made a slow, awkward pirouette to drink it all in—the lights of Bismarck to the south, Mandan's lesser cast to the southwest, the dipper and Cassiopeia circling the pole above me to the north, the bold borrowed light of the moon, my own shadow fifty feet long, apparently trying to jump off into the Missouri River, and the glorious Jupiter bursting out of the southeastern sky like the king of solar system.

Tomato growing weather.   *8/16/09*

I'm including this one, even though I have certain misgivings about it. It feels a little "literary" for a newspaper column, but it wrestles with some things that are really important to my love of North Dakota. The Triathlete is Melanie Carvell. It's the same moon I experienced on my seventeen-day hike along the Little Missouri River—overpowering somehow.

THE FIRST BITTERSWEET MOMENT

OF AUTUMN IN ND

I can pinpoint the precise moment when fall came this year. It was last Monday at about 4:30 a.m. All summer I have been sleeping with nothing but a thin sheet, and that only for the security of it.

Ever since the Fall, humans have felt the need to cover up. I'm one of the most emphatic coverees. My house is air conditioned, but I refuse to use it, because this is North Dakota. I woke up at 4:30 Monday morning because

I was cold—really cold. The windows were open throughout the house. There was a quilt, made for me by my grandmother fifty or more years ago, on a chair nearby. Rather than fetch that blanket the other night, I tried to huddle up in the fetal-est of fetal positions, and wound up wrapping myself in that sheet as in swaddling clothes or a medieval funeral shroud. When I finally did get up, I had to begin by escaping, Houdini-like, from the sheet.

Fall.

I turned my sprinkler system off this week. I reckon if I time it right, I'll need to mow the lawn just one more time this year.

The irony of this is that just as the signs of autumn begin to accumulate, we had the hottest days of 2010. For a couple of days, the heat was almost oppressive. The air felt oven-heavy and unsettled, and I found myself looking to the West for signs of a gargantuan thunderstorm. None came. For a couple of days, I couldn't get enough water onto my tomato plants.

This has been quite a summer. North Dakota summers are more complex and subtle than we tend to remember come January. June is typically volatile, wet and often quite cold. This is the time when the Medora Musical rains out a number of times. Sometime around July 1, reliably hot weather arrives, pretty suddenly, and then a period of "timelessness" ensues for four or five or six weeks. It's summertime and the living is easy. During this period, thunderclouds build on the western horizon almost every day, sometimes becoming storms and just as often fizzling out in a few squibs of heat lightning. The high temperatures tend to be in the eighties or lower nineties, and at night we get temperate open-window sleeping weather.

Then, sometime after the first week in August, dog days come to the Northern Plains. This is when you most want to get to the river in the heat of the afternoon. There is nothing quite so satisfying as being on a sandbar, with nowhere to go and nothing to do, when it is blistering hot, when the light is blinding and all the countryside a mirage, and you just surrender into a vegetative state and for once just be.

In any given year, you get only a few such experiences. In North Dakota, you have to store them up against the protracted season of iron desolation, like squirrels or ground mice.

My tomatoes are many, but tardy and only the size of baseballs. Furtive night critters are taking bites out of the ripest of them. My corn looks fabulous in three haughty rows. Each stalk towers like a corn god. The corn has tasseled but not yet filled out. I can't wait for the moment when I boil my first ear from my own crop and slather it with butter. I've been eating tomatoes and onions for about two weeks. For a few weeks per year, I graze in the evenings. The cost of that experience, in water and seed and nurturing, is irrationally high, especially if you bring farmers' markets into the equation, but the soul pay is just enormous. When I gather up a few things from my garden and eat them with the earth still hovering about their husks, I feel more present, integrated, in tune, and authentic than at any other time. Alive. To grow a cucumber and then eat it too is to reconnect with something so fundamental as to be too good for language. (But you see it has not stopped me, alas).

Now, every evening that I can, I take a long walk in the evening breeze. As I walk off the strains of the day—the strains are heavy these days—I try to look around and open my eyes fully, not just to see the plains but to *see* them, if possible, to drink it all in to the fullest. I try to remind myself that two months from now it will be dark by that time of evening, and if I go walking, I'll have to suit up first. I'm going to can tomatoes, of course, but how do you can a North Dakota summer? I take deep breaths and talk out loud—as often as not, to myself—about what I see around me, so that the experience gets deeper in. Every night that I can, I read out on my deck until dusk, knowing that all too soon in the evening, I will be inside shutting the cold out, not urging the cool in.

> "There is nothing quite so satisfying as being on a sandbar, with nowhere to go and nothing to do, when it is blistering hot, when the light is blinding and all the countryside a mirage, and you just surrender into a vegetative state and for once just be."

I went out with friends to Chuck Suchy's Bohemian Hall music festival last Saturday night. There were several hundred of us, splayed out in lawn chairs, listening to North Dakota's troubadour, his marvelous wife, Linda, their son, Ben, and their friends. The nearly full moon rose between the hall and the droll little church on the hill across the road to the southeast. It was as magical a night as I can ever remember, with Chuck singing and storying the agrarian experience, giving the Dakota experience its best and most authentic voice in his usual self-depreciating and gentle way. It was just this side of blanket weather after the sun went down. It would have been a perfect night at any time of the summer, given the von Suchy family talent, but, of course, its annual arrival marks the moment when summer begins to surrender and we coil up the hoses. That made the evening more enchanting and more poignant.

Because in the back of our minds, we all knew. *8/29/10*

OK, in reading through all of my columns to determine which to include and which to omit, I see that I go back to Roosevelt's phrase "iron desolation" too often. I will hereafter try to find other ways to express that period of the year when winter locks up the plains and forces all rational people to stay indoors.

Relishing the Autumn

with a Wary Eye on the Skies

When I finish writing these words, about ninety minutes from now, I am going to go hiking in Theodore Roosevelt National Park with one of its principal admirers. I'm sitting out on the deck of the Rough Riders Hotel in Medora in shirtsleeves trying not to shiver. I'd be more comfortable inside, in the big TR-sized chairs next to the fireplace, but I'm trying to squeeze every moment, every squib, out of the "summer of 2011," and I refuse to move inside. Yesterday I drove from Bismarck to Dickinson without using the heater in my car, even though my fingers were numb on the steering wheel. Nor have I turned on the heat in my house yet, in spite of the fact that I could actually see my breath the other morning when I inserted sourdough bread into my toaster. I warmed my hands over the toaster chutes, like a character in a Jack London story.

My scientific friends tell me that these gestures of defiance are unlikely to change the weather in my favor, but what do they know? They're the ones who subscribe to the theory of evolution. They're the ones who have been warning us about global climate change.

As I repeat here two or three times a year, I love North Dakota in all of its moods. I love it when it is a scene straight out of a *ND Horizons* calendar (all crocus and round bale), and I love it when the winds are blasting us into oblivion and making it literally difficult to stand up straight. I love North Dakota on those nurturing, picture postcard mornings amid prairie flowers and azure skies, but equally when it is so appallingly cold on the northern plains that you have to beat your hands on your pants to keep them from freezing and falling off. I love North Dakota on the days when it is hospitable, of course, but I have a much greater love of this stark improbable place when it feels a little heroic to stake out a claim here at all. I prefer O.E. Rolvaag's Per Hansa to Michael Landon as Pa Wilder. Whether the long, punishing winters really keep the riff raff out, as the icky cliché has it, is a proposition that will be tested in the decade ahead, I believe.

We have four seasons here, though of radically unequal measure. Like everyone else, we observe the standard demarcations at the solstices and the equinoxes, but no North Dakotan would actually shape his or her life according to such weak abstractions (in 2011, March 20, June 21, Sept. 23, and Dec. 22). I may be a little pessimistic, but I would place the North Dakota markers a little differently. I'd put the goal posts of winter at Oct. 31 and April 15. That's 167 days or 46 percent of the year. My spring runs from April 15 until June 25. That's 71 days, or 19 percent of the calendar year. Summer in North Dakota runs from June 25 until Sept. 5: 72 days, 20 percent. Thus autumn runs from Sept. 5 to Oct. 31: 56 days, 15 percent.

You may have a different sense of where the goal posts belong. If so, I would like to see your figures. My logic is pretty simple. You cannot really count on genuine summer weather in North Dakota until almost the Fourth of July. A June wedding is almost certainly going to be moved indoors. A family reunion in June is likely to feature a gale force picnic with the tablecloths weighted down with bricks. June is usually a blowsy, chilly, cloudy, and drizzly month in North Dakota, with lush green grass along the highways that is whipped into waves by the strong late spring winds. Memorial Day and Labor Day are typically "ruined plans" weekends in North Dakota. Winter can start at the end of September and it can continue well into May, but typically the first snow falls half-heartedly around October 15. That moment sends dread and melancholy through the North Dakota population, but it is almost always followed by a magnificent period of Indian summer, in which it nearly freezes at night and gets up to sixty or even seventy by day. Summer, fall, and winter follow the pattern I have laid out pretty reliably in North Dakota, but spring is the wild card season. Spring in North Dakota is like the curriculum of a US History class. The professor says you are going to survey American history from Plymouth Rock to Vietnam, but, as things turn out, you seldom ever get past World War II. Very few North Dakota springs behave as they should. Winter and summer are always nipping away at the margins. There are many years in which we get about a twenty-day spring, when the transformation is so sudden that it feels like winter one day and summer the next.

I love North Dakota in good times and bad times, in sickness and in health, in rain, snow, sleet, and dark of night, in blizzard and thunderstorm, sultry, muggy, bone-dry or heart-sickeningly cold, in dust storm, bathed in northern lights, when the wind is whispering in the cottonwoods or bending their ancient trunks to the ground.

But I love autumn best of all in North Dakota, days just like today. My fingers are thawing out. The sun has dispersed the morning clouds. The grasses of the badlands have finally turned rust-and-tawny, though there is still more green grass than I have ever seen this late in the year. I'm off now to find a slice of toast and a perfect rasher of bacon, and then to go out to see how the cottonwood leaves are shaping up. My friend, the lover of the badlands, says they are going to be magnificent. I cannot wait for that moment when we come around the bend and catch sight of the Little Missouri River for the first time, threading out its loopy sine curves in perfect blue against the bluffs on its long sluggish journey towards the Gulf.

My heart always leaps at that. *9/25/11*

I've proposed a couple of alternative calendars over the years I have been writing these columns, but this one is the most accurate, I think.

CLAY JENKINSON'S NORTH DAKOTA SEASONS

SPRING April 30 – June 25

SUMMER June 25 – September 5

AUTUMN September 5 – October 31

WINTER October 31 – April 30

November	December	January
	WINTER October 31–April 30	
Februay	March	April
May	June	July
SPRING April 30 – June 25		**SUMMER** June 25 – September 5
August	September	October
		AUTUMN September 5 – October 31

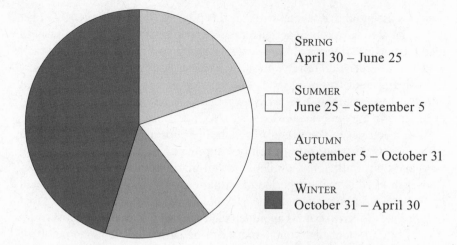

SPRING
April 30 – June 25

SUMMER
June 25 – September 5

AUTUMN
September 5 – October 31

WINTER
October 31 – April 30

ONE LAST STOLEN PERFECT DAY
IN THE DAKOTA BADLANDS

For no really compelling reason, I drove out to the Elkhorn Ranch mid-week, the day before I wrote these words. My intention was to write about something completely different—about the legacy of Steve Jobs—but my experience there, on an absolutely stunning Indian summer afternoon, was so purely satisfying that I want to write about it now, before the exquisite-ness fades into the blandness of memory. A week from now I will still know what I meant to say about Steve Jobs, but I won't any longer be able

> "The awareness
> that you may get
> lost is essential to
> experiencing the
> American West."

to find words to express an October interlude at the Elkhorn in the heart of the heart of the North Dakota Badlands.

No matter how many times you have been to the Elkhorn Ranch, thirty-five miles north of Medora, it's possible to get a little lost. I wound up making two wrong turns (briefly) even with the detailed Little Missouri Grasslands Map spread out on the seat next to me. That's part of the joy of the experience. The Elkhorn Ranch is remote. It was remote in 1884, when Theodore Roosevelt chose it and named it and made it his Dakota Territory ranch headquarters. I hope it will always be remote, that it will never be possible to reach the Elkhorn by paved road. It's essential that whoever makes this pilgrimage will think, "OK, I get it. You have to earn this experience, you cannot just pop off the highway to read the two hundred-word historical sign and snap a photograph of yourself with teeth bared like Teddy." In 2011 you can only get to the Elkhorn by threading around on gravel roads that never quite match the rational layout on the grasslands map. The awareness that you may get lost is essential to experiencing the American West.

When you get to the Elkhorn Ranch Site parking lot, you have to pass through a pedestrian gate (recently "improved" in a silly and upsetting way) and then walk about a mile on a well-marked trail to TR's homestead. Roosevelt lived in the last period of human history that was not dominated by the internal combustion engine. He could only get to the Elkhorn on foot or horseback (or rowboat for about ten days per year, if he timed it just right). It's really important that you cannot visit the shrine of the human embodiment of the strenuous life and wise conservation without using your legs.

Once I got to the cabin site, I quickly took the still photographs and the video that had justified the mid-week journey, so that I could spend a couple of hours just drinking in one of the handful of best places in North Dakota without any industrial clutter. I ate a little lunch: baguette, two types of cheese, a glass of Merlot, and a square of superb chocolate.

Then, for about half an hour, I just sat in complete stillness under the ancient cottonwoods that stand directly west of TR's cabin site. The cabin is long gone. Only a handful of foundation stones remain to show visitors the outline of what was once a 30 x 60-foot ranch house. The old cottonwoods rise above what was back then the bank of the Little Missouri River. A few of them may be as old as Roosevelt's sojourn in Dakota.

This year's cottonwood leaves are not as profuse, as brilliantly yellow-golden, or as "radioactive" as they sometimes are. There's a certain half-heartedness to them this time around, though they are still magnificent. When fall cottonwoods are at their best, their leaves are like wafer-thin amulets of the sun itself, storing solar intensity and the life force in an organic memory device the size of an irregular drink coaster, thousands to every tree, hundreds of thousands of cottonwood trees lacing and gracing the banks of the Little Missouri River all the way from Devils Tower to Twin Buttes, ND, and back again. If you stand up on the overlook of Wind Canyon in one of those 23-carat autumns, it makes your knees buckle, the beauty is so profound and heartbreaking.

I listened to the leaves dance in the intermittent breeze as long as I could. It was as perfect a moment as there will ever be in my life: the sky, the muted colors, the temperature, the breeze, the ancient shattered trees, the heritage of the place, the fierce life and endless legacy of TR, and of course the Little Missouri River running through it with its usual unhurried serenity.

Part of the joy was a kind of sweet melancholy in knowing that two months from now the northern plains will be locked in what Roosevelt called "iron desolation," and it will be much more difficult, and possibly impossible, to get to the Elkhorn Ranch. We've had a magical fall in North Dakota. Almost every day starts blowsy and chilly and gray and then somehow, by early afternoon, is metamorphosed into perfection—a wan, but brassy sun illuminating the stubble fields and the grasslands with gentle yellowish light, just enough breeze to stir the soul, just enough to rasp and crackle the dry grasses, and waft a few dead leaves from one pinpoint in the vastness of the Great Plains to another pinpoint ten yards away. Above, that blue blue blue blue sky with high wispy autumn clouds, some of them thickening into a gray and charcoal half-front moving in from the west. The feeling of being out in the most beautiful place on earth in shirtsleeves this deep into October, but living on borrowed time, a bonus day, a tender unearned Great Plains day to store up in one's memory for the long string of severe ones lining up somewhere over the horizon, like the line of impatient taxis at a New York airport. One morning soon, we will wake up, stretch, look out the window, and say, "It's here now."

Oh, one more thing. All the way up and all the way back, more than a dozen giant oil trucks hogged the gravel trail and thundered a very different ode in TR's beloved Badlands: the unquestioned industrial anthem of the twenty-first century in North Dakota. *10/16/11*

First Portrait of Winter in a Parking Lot

And so, winter. I woke up Wednesday morning in the Honeymoon Suite of a motel in north Minot. Just why I was staying there, alone, resolutely unmarried, is an interesting story, but it has nothing to do with the sudden and dramatic onslaught of winter. We've enjoyed one of the best autumns I can ever remember. It lingered beautifully through most of October. Lulled by its russet loveliness and the wan October sun, by the chill mornings and the just-short-of-hot afternoons, we had all begun to take it for granted, and we had foolishly let ourselves almost believe, in direct violation of a lifetime of experience, that fall might extend deep into November. This week North Dakota reasserted itself, reminded us that this is a place that punishes its admirers.

So I wake up alone in a huge bed, set on a kind of nuptial platform or stage, surrounded by mirrors, in the largest hotel room I've ever been in, and the windows are rattling off their frames.

It took me a few minutes to make sense of where I was and why, and to "place" the rattling of the windows in my consciousness. Finally it dawned on me that the wind must be blowing like a son of a gun (as they say). I climbed out of the vast honeymoon bed to investigate, but I had forgotten that the bed sat on a foot-high carpeted dais. In my rattled bleariness, I stepped off the platform like Wily Coyote in the Road Runner cartoons, and literally plummeted forward about ten feet before I could regain my balance. If the windows had been closer, I would have plunged right through them out into the parking lot. Perhaps that is a metaphor of some sort.

You have all seen this same parking lot at some point in your winter lives. Forty or fifty vehicles were parked in quasi disorder in several haphazard rows in a four-inch gray soup of ice, slush, snow, and mud. The steps up into the motel lobby had been shoveled once, at dawn, but in a lazy single lane about two feet wide. Since then enough snow had drifted in to make it uncertain just where the steps might be. On the glass door at the front of the lobby, someone has scotch-taped a "use other door" sign made with a magic marker. Those who obediently used the other door had to throw their whole weight against it to wedge it open against the gale force wind. In front of the hotel, the brave early morning pickups had formed a two-track trail that sashayed its way towards the side street. All the parked vehicles were blanketed with pure white snow on their north and west sides, but left clean on the south and east. Men who had not expected this sudden appearance of winter were using their forearms as windshield scrapers and issuing sharp curses against the howling wind. When they had completed the excavation, they rubbed their hands together violently or beat them on their pant legs. Most of the diesel vehicles in the lot were running, with nobody in the cab, making that characteristic ball bearing snorting sound that diesel engines make. When people opened their car doors, whatever was loose was blasted out into the storm and then the driver chased the errant envelope or circular through the parking lot like Charlie Chaplin. In the corner of the parking lot, a man in a Bobcat was doing his best to clear away the snow, but mostly waiting for everyone to clear out so that he could do his work efficiently.

I wanted to be in that Bobcat.

As I hiked down the long corridor of the Honeymoon Suite to the bathroom, I had time to process two lines of thought. First, I love North Dakota. In fact, I love North Dakota especially when it is an acquired taste. I love the sub-arctic hostility of the climate, the winds, like Tuesday's, that whistle the windows, rattle all the commercial signs, and strip siding right off unfinished houses. I love winds that make the TV weathermen—snug against their green screens using the latest acu-this or 3-D-that software—shudder, and explain to us, in gluey sympathetic tones, as if we were children or cancer patients, that "I'm afraid things might be a little gusty out there today." I love North Dakota when you have to want to live here, when you realize why most people born elsewhere regard this as a state where no rational being would live. You never see last Tuesday and Wednesday's North Dakota on glossy calendars or in the state tourism brochures. But that is at least as much North Dakota as a photo of a serene family picnic by the big lake on one of the few calm days of the year.

> "Most of the diesel vehicles in the parking lot were running, with nobody in the cab, making that characteristic ball bearing snorting sound that diesel engines make. When people opened their car doors, whatever was loose was blasted out into the storm and then the driver chased the errant envelope or circular through the parking lot like Charlie Chaplin."

Second, grasshopper that I am, I have neglected once again to gather up my hoses before the first winter blast. That means that sometime in the next few days, when the wind calms—if it calms—I will be out there issuing sharp curses, pulling them out of the snow stiff as frozen licorice, and trying to coil them without snapping them into shards of hoses.

Next year I will be ready. I promise. *10/31/10*

Suddenly, While We Slept, Winter Grazed the Plains

When I ventured outside the other day, there was more than a dusting of snow on my roof and my windshield. The wind was blowing at about 35 mph straight out of the north. The sky was low, dark, and menacing. In an instant, I wanted to cancel everything, make some popcorn, curl up in my late father's favorite reading chair, and start in on a big fat classical novel.

Here comes the winter of our discontent.

One day we are lollygagging along, enjoying one of the finest autumns I can ever remember, thinking the crisp mornings and serenely warm afternoons will never cease. The next day we awaken to a short fierce blast of what is to come, like the brief first burst of the train whistle at the far edge of town.

It's like daylight-saving time. Silently and without warning, in the middle of the night, a magic invisible line is crossed, and we wake up to the inaugural gust of another North Dakota winter. When we venture out, the weather bites for the first time. We involuntarily look up to the sky with a mixture of wonder and apprehension. It is one of those moments when we are most present, most alive. And sad, too, for the death of summer and the loss of light.

It's the first day you leave the lights on in the kitchen all day. Folks turn on their headlights as they drive to work. Some forget to turn them off and pay the price.

On days like this, I want to be somewhere out in the Badlands, hiking alone, a little uncertain of just where I am, and watching the sky for signs.

I love this season of northern Plains life almost more than any other. It's cold, but not yet unbearable, somewhere between crisp and bitter. A jacket is usually sufficient, and many folks still scurry about in shirtsleeves, a little faster than usual, like characters in a Keystone Kops movie.

Windy, cold, grim days are intermixed with afternoons of Indian summer so beautiful that they make you ache. The walking trails are virtually empty.

From far above a faint whirring. You look up, and there are two hundred geese high overhead, beating their wings madly as they hasten south. Then a couple of harsh faraway honks—the alpha goose firming up the chevron and browbeating the laggards.

A North Dakota summer is not that much different from summer in Colorado or New Mexico or Arkansas, but early winter here is unique. Because the cloud cover is so low and dense, the focus of our eyes gravitates from the sky back to the land, our home, which seems to stretch out like tawny uneven taffy endlessly in every direction.

Late fall, before the snow cover comes, is when I feel most swallowed up by the sheer brown vastness of the Great Plains. Often enough, at sunset, there's a narrow band of pale blue sky along the southwestern horizon, and the egg yolk sun makes its only appearance of the day as it slips quickly below the horizon.

I'm always the grasshopper, never the ant. When the first ground blizzard sweeps through North Dakota, I'm the guy out wrestling with the stiff and brittle hoses, engaged in a little home experiment in physics. How far can you bend a frozen plastic hose in a gale force wind without snapping it into shards like stale licorice? I'm the guy on his knees scraping the dead grass off the bottom of his lawnmower with a screwdriver. When I try to stand up, the knees of my jeans are half frozen to the ground. They stay wet for hours after I peel them off the grass.

I'm the guy parked on the side of the road who thought he could defrost the windshield with his wipers and washer fluid, now reduced to using an old audio cassette or CD case as a makeshift scraper. Those are my bloody knuckles at the morning meeting. I'm the guy who never bothers to check the radiator fluid until the first below-zero day and then expresses annoyance when the dealership explains, admittedly in a sellers' market tone, that they cannot possibly fit me in until two weeks from Thursday.

I'm the guy who put the snow shovel in an obscure corner of the garage in June, and now crawls and tumbles over boxes wondering if it would just be smarter to go buy a new one. I'm always the last guy in town to get his sprinkler system blown out. The young man informs me of my dubious honor and shakes his head.

My father was the ant.

He had checklists that he kept in a little wooden file box next to his favorite chair in the den. Every week or so, he'd take out his seasonal "to do" list and study it like the Kabala. Sometime around the last week of September, he'd begin to winterize his world, working his way through his list of chores as methodically as an Apollo astronaut strapped on top of a Saturn V rocket before launch.

When he had come in from some routine yard task, he'd pull out the checklist and ostentatiously draw a line through item 15c. By the time the first snow flurries appeared, he would have drained fluids out of the lawnmower, positioned his shovels and scrapers as if they were dental tools, and fired up the snow blower for at least two test runs. He tested every string of Christmas lights in October, not wanting a crisis at tree time. He paid his bills—always—on the day they came in the mail, never at the end of the month. Around March 1, he would begin to ask me how my tax preparations were coming.

I've read my Freud. I know that the son is engaged in a deadly struggle with his father, no matter how benign it might appear to the casual observer. He's required by a deep law of human nature to rebel against the modus operandi of the old man and to chart his own course through life, no matter how illogical. I get it. But the fact is that the struggle lasted for a full forty years, and each of us had innumerable opportunities to make his point, and now there is nothing left to prove.

My father has been dead for a dozen years. He would have been seventy-nine on Nov. 1. I miss him every day, always a little and sometimes in open pain.

I don't want to be a grasshopper any more.

My life would be so much better if I just surrendered and bought a snow blower and kept it in fighting trim. But that would require me to go shopping for a snow blower, which would require me to admit that I am middle-aged, and I'd be reminded that my father would have comparison shopped and studied the consumer reports for half a year before making his purchase.

Besides, there is no room for it in the garage, and if I cleaned the garage sufficiently to accommodate a snow blower, I'd find four or five shovels in the process.

Early dusk. A coyote calls west of my house. It is a winter call. The stubble in my garden rustles against the biting wind, and it says, you promised to till me.

Soon. *11/10/07*

Eventually, I received a big snow blower as a Christmas gift. I try to use it as seldom as possible because I don't really like the idea of being the owner of a snow blower.

A Nocturnal Upon St. Lucy's Day,

Being The Shortest Day.

by John Donne

'TIS the year's midnight, and it is the day's,
Lucy's, who scarce seven hours herself unmasks;
   The sun is spent, and now his flasks
   Send forth light squibs, no constant rays;
      The world's whole sap is sunk;

The general balm th' hydroptic earth hath drunk,
Whither, as to the bed's-feet, life is shrunk,
Dead and interr'd; yet all these seem to laugh,
Compared with me, who am their epitaph.
Study me then, you who shall lovers be
At the next world, that is, at the next spring;
   For I am every dead thing,
   In whom Love wrought new alchemy.
      For his art did express

A quintessence even from nothingness,
From dull privations, and lean emptiness;
He ruin'd me, and I am re-begot
Of absence, darkness, death—things which are not.
All others, from all things, draw all that's good,
Life, soul, form, spirit, whence they being have;
   I, by Love's limbec, am the grave
   Of all, that's nothing. Oft a flood
      Have we two wept, and so

Drown'd the whole world, us two; oft did we grow,
To be two chaoses, when we did show
Care to aught else; and often absences
Withdrew our souls, and made us carcasses.
But I am by her death—which word wrongs her—
Of the first nothing the elixir grown;
   Were I a man, that I were one
   I needs must know; I should prefer,
      If I were any beast,

Some ends, some means; yea plants, yea stones detest,
And love; all, all some properties invest.
If I an ordinary nothing were,
As shadow, a light, and body must be here.
But I am none; nor will my sun renew.
You lovers, for whose sake the lesser sun
   At this time to the Goat is run
   To fetch new lust, and give it you,
      Enjoy your summer all,

Since she enjoys her long night's festival.
Let me prepare towards her, and let me call
This hour her vigil, and her eve, since this
Both the year's and the day's deep midnight is.

THE WHOLE WORLD'S SAP IS SUNK:

AH, BUT SUCH LIGHT

Read fast. Today is the shortest day of the year. As I wrote this a few days ago, the sun came up at 8:23 a.m., a huge bloody egg yolk disk in the southeast.

Thanks to the appalling blanket of cold that currently envelops the Great Plains, the rising sun was as gigantic as it was impotent. Just as there is a wavering effect in the light near the horizon on extremely hot days, so too, in the bitterest days of winter, the air between you and the rising sun is so dense with trillions of microscopic ice crystals that it has a magnifying effect, a kind of ice pixelation of the sky.

Here's a paradox. At Rugby (or Rio), the sun is 93 million miles away, a distance so great that any Earth distances are negligible. It's the same toaster at both latitudes, the same distance away, and yet merely by virtue of the tilted axis of the earth (23.5 degrees) and the consequent daily quantum of direct sunlight, Rugby's temperature this week was 5° below zero and Rio's 71° above.

From every chimney between my kitchen window and the horizon, sluggish house-hovering smoke, as if every building housed a College of Cardinals that had just elected a new pope. Brutally cold mornings like these are strangely quiet and lovely, as if God turned the sound down a few decibels to pay respect to hibernation.

When I walked out to my car, in a thick stocking cap, I listened to my feet breaking the surface of the snow. The muffled crunching as the surface crust gives way is one of my favorite sounds of the Great Plains. On a winter hike of any distance, it has a beautiful hypnotic effect. You can hear it in your tires, too, on snowy streets, if you drive slowly and keep the radio off. Unless the wind is blowing, life on severe winter days here is like living in a glycerin aquarium.

My favorite poet, John Donne (1572-1631), captured the essence of this time of year in his solstice poem, "A Nocturnal upon St. Lucy's Day," which was in fact written about the longest night and shortest day of the year.

The sun is spent, and now his flasks
Send forth light squibs, no constant rays;
The world's whole sap is sunk.

Donne's great poem—worth reading in its entirety—suggests that all life at the winter solstice feels as if it has shrunk down to the foot of the bedcovers. I've spent a few winters in England where houses, then and now, have no central heating, and I've done my share of hunkering at the foot of the bed in the fetal position under a mountain of blankets.

"From every chimney between my kitchen window and the horizon, sluggish house-hovering smoke, as if every building housed a College of Cardinals that had just elected a new Pope. Brutally cold mornings like these are strangely quiet and lovely, as if God turned the sound down a few decibels to pay respect to hibernation."

Today is the first official day of winter—as if any North Dakotan needed that coy Bureau of Standards announcement. The conventional international designation of seasons has little meaning in North Dakota. If Greenwich were located at Rugby, not east of London, the seasons might run a little differently. Winter: Nov. 15-April 15 (five months). Spring: April 16-June 25 (ten weeks). Summer: June 26-Sept. 20 (fourteen weeks). Autumn: Sept. 21-Nov. 14 (ten weeks).

Good news. At 7:04 a.m. today Eastern Standard Time (6:04 a.m. here), the sun reached the far other end of its annual pendulum swing, lingering for an instant over the Tropic of Capricorn. The word "solstice" commemorates that almost imperceptible pause at the end of the pendulum swing. It literally means "the sun stands still."

Today is the longest day of the year in Alice Springs, Australia, Easter Island, Kruger National Park in South Africa, and Rio de Janeiro in Brazil. At high noon in those places, the sun today will be directly overhead. Up here in Dakota, the sun will make a lazy little horizon-hugging arc from southeast to southwest, lighting our frigid world for just 8 hours, 31 minutes, and 55 seconds. At the summer solstice, on June 21, we get a full 15 hours, 52 minutes, and the afterlight lingers, as you all know, forever.

Why is the solstice good news? We all know winter is just getting rolling in North Dakota, (and with any luck it will be a doozy), but every day hereafter, between 6:04 this morning and your first wind-shattered picnic of 2009, will provide a few more precious minutes of light. For those, like Donne, who suffer from seasonal affective disorder, the worst is now behind us. We stoic North Dakotans, wedded to a fault to common sense, tend to sneer at upstart diagnoses like SAD, which, like gout in the eighteenth century, have the feel of being disorders of people with too much leisure on their hands. But who among us does not feel a rush of regeneration sometime in February, no matter how cold the weather, when we become aware that the days are noticeably longer?

Theodore Roosevelt was no John Donne, but he lived in North Dakota, not in temperate England, and he wrote about our landscape and climate as well as anyone ever has. More than a hundred years ago, he wrote a perfect description of last week's furious blizzard: "When the days have dwindled to their shortest, and the nights seem never ending, then all the great northern plains are changed into an abode of iron desolation. Sometimes furious gales blow out of the north, driving before them the clouds of blinding snow-dust, wrapping the mantle of death round every unsheltered being that faces their unshackled anger."

I got a full dose of iron desolation when I returned early last week from a business trip to Memphis, where I had walked around carelessly in my shirtsleeves. Unfortunately, I missed the brunt of the storm, but when I lurched out into the airport parking lot, I found drifts of snow inside my car. That's a brisk wind! Truly, there was an inch-high crust of snow on my steering wheel and a fairly large bank of snow on the back seat.

I had never experienced that before. I turned the key with the confidence of a featherweight in a bout against Mohammed Ali. As I paused on the iron leather seat, strategizing what I knew would be my one and only one attempt at starting the car, I indulged myself with hope, but in my heart I knew the truth. I was welcomed home by the official North Dakota blizzard sound: "click nick click nick … phut."

When the taxi got me home, ninety minutes later, for the first time in my life I actually had to shovel my way into my house—in the grasshopper jacket, no gloves, no hat, I had worn to Memphis. My house appeared to have been blown about four feet off of its foundation.

Ah, but there is good news. The house was toasty. There were no drifts of snow inside the house. And when the next day broke, I discovered that my garden is covered with about five feet of drifted snow.

I'm going to have great tomatoes in 2009.

Merry Christmas to you all. *12/20/08*

I write about light as often as I can. My North Dakota is about the quality of the light, about the silence of the open plains, about the different varieties and sounds of wind. Those are things hard to depict in photographs. The Grand Teton Mountains are about magnificence and sublimity. It is hard to take a bad photograph of them. But most of the good photographs of North Dakota are about a very selective North Dakota, not about the general feel of the plains as you look out at them. Because a photograph wants to be about something, it is always tempting to break up the endless plains with a grain elevator or a copse of trees. The plains really lend themselves more to painting than to photography. Unfortunately that is one of the many, many talents I don't have.

CULTURE

It's a Small World, After All ...

Not Including Lines

For a number of years, my mother has been trying to take my daughter to Walt Disney World. Mother subscribes to the iron-cross code of grandparental fairness. She took my nieces to Disney World a decade ago, so she was determined to get my daughter to Florida, too, to even things up.

The journey finally came together—after several years of talk—last week. They took me along as baggage boy. I went kicking and screaming, and now, of course, I find myself humming, off and on all day, "It's a small world after all, a small, small world."

Once the paperwork on my second mortgage came through, we were ready to take on America's premier amusement park.

One of mother's motives for getting this done now is that she is seventy-four years old, and she was afraid that she won't be able to hobble around the large acreage of Disney World and Epcot Center much longer. She need not have worried.

Every ride at the park is so popular that you wind up half-sprinting from line to line from the moment the morning starting gun goes off until the ushers toss you out of the park sometime after 11 p.m., just in time to stand in line (forever) for the last bus back to your hotel. You don't even really want to stop to buy the nine-dollar hot dog because that might jeopardize your chance of getting in to see the Haunted Mansion.

It's the Disney mania, which is hard to explain until you are standing there envying and resenting everyone who is closer to the front of the line than you are. I wouldn't stand in line for an hour to see a great movie or hear the Rolling Stones or watch the New York Yankees play the Mets. So why do I stand in line for sixty-seven minutes to spend six minutes on a relatively tame, themed roller coaster ride?

It's true that the park has a system called Fast Pass, which allows you to "reserve" your ride in advance and thus cut the line time from an hour to about twenty minutes. The problem with Fast Pass is that you have to obtain the pass at the ride site well in advance, for a "reserved" return several hours later, so it effectively doubles your hiking mileage within the park.

And it means that, at breakfast, my family poured over the park map like Churchill over maps of Berlin, debating our "ride distribution strategy" for the day. We power-walked six to eight miles each day, because who does not want to see a quarter-sized replica of the Eiffel Tower and eat lefsa at the Norwegian pavilion at Epcot's World Showcase?

Mother need not have worried about declining vigor. She was indefatigable. By the end of two days, I was exhausted, but I had to pretend to be strong as a bull moose. My daughter looked as if she had run consecutive marathons, and she actually requested that we take a four-hour swimming break on the second day. My Germanic mother was just hitting her stride. We worked Disney World like a panzer division. I half expected Mother to suggest we invade Czechoslovakia.

The upside of Disney World is that it is clean, safe, and amazingly well run. The downside is that it's a zoo. It's the most densely packed cluster of random humanity you will ever see, except in Tokyo or New York City, and they all want to ride on Space Mountain and Big Thunder Mountain Railroad at the same time.

We happened upon the Magic Kingdom during the National All-Star Cheerleading Championship, which meant that approximately 50,000 girls, between the ages of 12 and 18, all dressed in provocative and inappropriate costumes, egged on by their mothers and chaperones, who were former cheerleaders or cheerleader wannabes, swarmed the park, and chattered and cried and broke into spontaneous cheers and hugged one another and did each other's makeup and worked their cell phones and argued with their mothers and flirted with boys and bickered. It was as if the gymnast Mary Lou Retton were cloned into a phalanx of fifty thousand identical little bundles of uninhibited estrogen, but without much compensatory talent.

As I studied their obsessive urge to be Dallas Cowboy Cheerleaders in thirteen-year-old bodies, I mumbled, over and over, "Daddies, don't let your daughters grow up to be cheerleaders. Let them be doctors and lawyers and and such." I have now seen enough midriffs for a full lifetime.

I prefer the really traditional Disney rides, like the Tea Cups and Snow White's Scary Adventures and Dumbo the Flying Elephant. These rides, transported from the original Disneyland, now exactly fifty years old, are low-tech and clunky and even cheesy, but they appeal to me because they remind us of how much America has changed—especially technological-ly—since 1956. At one time, It's a Small World was a thrill ride featuring cutting-edge solenoid technology and "robotics."

My daughter, who is eleven, prefers rides that involve G-force warning signs and interactive high-tech wizardry, rides designed for children who have grown up with Xboxes and Game Boys. I prefer Epcot Center, be-cause it is at least possible there to argue that your outing is "educational," thus justifying pulling your daughter out of sixth grade for two days to fly to an amusement park halfway across the continent.

My daughter saw through Epcot Center in an instant and realized that what passed for techno-futurism in the 1980s is pretty ho-hum in 2006. She preferred a Mars Mission ride before which you get a serious seminar on how to use the "in-flight sickness" bag and how to avoid passing out during liftoff.

In short, my daughter and I were at slight odds about our Disney World priorities. Mother provided the diplomatic breakthrough: "Let's do it all!" she said. And so we did.

The pleasure of going to Disney World with the two most important women in my life, one 11, one 74, was seeing them both as wide-eyed and joyous as seven-year-olds, suspending their disbelief, laughing out loud, exchanging nervous glances before a wild ride and then debriefing afterward, barking out drinks and snack orders to their baggage boy. It was pricey, but it was, as the commercial says, priceless, too.

Is the Disney experience really worth the cost and the chaos? Personally I say no. I prefer that other hectic American theme park, Yellowstone. But visiting one of the Disneys is an important American rite of passage, and it really is impossible not to have fun there, if you can avoid being crushed by a collapsing cheerleader pyramid, spontaneously assembled in front of your monorail car.

The only bad moment came at the end, when we took advantage of the Disney resorts' offer to check your bags in their lobbies rather than at the Orlando airport, which has the feel and press of humanity of Cairo in an Indiana Jones movie. For technical reasons, this proved to be impossible for my mother's ticket.

My frustration level steadily mounted because I have been through this before elsewhere, and I knew that the two friendly, but essentially indifferent, men at the concierge desk could solve the problem if they looked deep enough into our flight record. Finally, in his perplexity, one of the men said, "Bismarck. Is that a domestic flight, sir?" And the other young man, who had been attending to something else, walked over and said, "Is North Dakota in the United States?" They were both serious.

So it's not such a small world, after all. *3/18/06*

This one has a very special place in my heart. A perfect stranger, the famous triathlete Melanie Carvell, wrote to chide me (gently) for my assault on high school cheerleading. This led to one of the great friendships of my life.

NEKOMA FORTY YEARS ON

Last Sunday marked the fortieth anniversary of the protest march at the ABM missile site at Nekoma. On May 16, 1970, approximately 1,500 people gathered one mile north of the village of Nekoma to protest what the anti-ballistic missile system represented—nuclear proliferation, the idea that nuclear war was survivable, the widening of the War in Vietnam, and the killing of four students at Kent State University just two weeks previously.

More or less on a whim, I drove up to Nekoma last Saturday. I was only fifteen at the time of the protest in 1970, queasily negotiating my adolescence in a cow town almost five hundred miles away from the action.

> "Unless you lived through that decade, it's hard to comprehend how the combined dynamics of Vietnam, rock music, the counterculture, recreational drugs, the martyrdom of the Kennedys and Martin Luther King, unprecedented freedom and mobility, the civil rights movement, the birth control pill, and Bob Dylan shaped a whole generation of American young people"

I wished I were driving my old brown Ford Falcon with its tube type radio and roll down windows (and gas at 35 cents per gallon), but it was a Honda with satellite radio and gas at $2.95, instead. I drove the back way, in no hurry whatsoever, listening to Janis Joplin just to get into the spirit of the thing. My plan was to be at the ABM site at dawn on May 16, 2010, forty years on, and to plant a tree "in remembrance of things past."

A number of prominent North Dakotans participated in that march. Now they are in their sixties. A great deal of water has flowed under the bridge since that weekend forty years ago—a different time in a different America. Unless you lived through that decade, it's hard to comprehend how the combined dynamics of Vietnam, rock music, the counterculture, recreational drugs, the martyrdom of the Kennedys and Martin Luther King, unprecedented freedom and mobility, the civil rights movement, the birth control pill, and Bob Dylan shaped a whole generation of American young people. Even for those who lived through that period, it is—on any given day in the twenty-first century—a kind of hazy pixelated Oz. It makes you understand the meaning of British writer Leslie Hartley's great sentence: "The past is a foreign country."

In that tumultuous decade, we went from *Where the Boys Are* and "I Want To Hold Your Hand" to *Apocalypse Now* and "Hey Jude."

1970 was the year of Kent State, the release of Robert Altman's film *M*A*S*H* and the Beatles' last album, *Let It Be*, the completion of the World Trade Center, Apollo 13, the first Earth Day (April 22), the creation of the Environmental Protection Agency, and the first broadcast of *Monday Night Football* on ABC, starring Keith Jackson and Howard Cosell.

The ABM protest march in May 1970 was called a "Festival of Love and Life." It was a very serious protest against the further nuclearization of North Dakota by people, mostly young, who believed that if they ever got their hands on the levers of power, they would launch the Age of Aquarius. It's impossible to meditate on that concept without smiling a little wanly. I can hear Sarah Palin saying: "How's that hopey-changey thing workin' out for ya?"

The ABM site was activated and deactivated in the same year: 1976. It was operational for just a few weeks. Total cost: approximately $6 billion.

I finally arrived at the Nekoma site about 8 p.m. on Saturday after infinite digressions—the McClusky Canal, Lonetree Wildlife Management Area, Minnewauken (now being eaten by Devils Lake), Sullys Hill National Game Preserve, etc. By the time I set up my cameras to catch the sunset, I was "empty and aching and I don't know why." The vast sky was full of late-spring, early-summer bilious clouds piling up in a dome so blue it made you ache to look at it. A hint of localized rain. I gazed from a half-mile away at the centerpiece (the photo-op) of the ABM site, a huge abandoned concrete pyramid with the top cut off. On each of the four faces of the truncated pyramid, there is a giant oculus, the unblinking eye of the military-industrial complex, like something out of Orwell's *1984*.

It's eerie and in its own way incredibly impressive and imposing.

As I stood there trying to make sense of what it signifies—in the history of North Dakota, in the history of the Cold War, in the history of human folly, in the history of my friendships—a rainbow suddenly appeared with one foot right over the great pyramid. In that perfect, serene, late-evening moment, at the end of a wonderful day of driving Dakota on obscure roads, I so wanted to believe that I lived in the world of Genesis 9:13, in which God could balance a rainbow above the Nekomas of the earth to say, "Never again will you practice the arts of annihilation."

But we are fallen creatures, all.

I drove slowly into Langdon and got myself a room at the local motel. The woman who checked me in lived in the apartment suite behind the desk—that kind of motel. She gave me an actual key attached to a plastic diamond etched with my room number. That kind of motel. I walked over to the Sportsmans Bar for a beer and a bar pizza. Perfection.

At first light I was back out at the site, closer now, cameras ready.

With considerable furtiveness, I planted my lilac tree. I did not wish to become the only casualty of the ABM Protest March! I said a little prayer. I was utterly alone. So far as I know, I was the only human being who commemorated the fortieth anniversary of the Nekoma peace march.

Heartache. There were three very different individuals that I so intensely wanted to see drive up the dirt road where I was parked Sunday morning, in search of the same thing. Had any one of them ambled up, out of the blue, on that anniversary, at that place, I would have regarded it as nothing less than the redemption of the project of our lives. But I could not invite them, because that would make it a mere rendezvous rather than a miracle or a sign of grace. *5/23/10*

Former North Dakota Governor William L. Guy handled the ABM protest so masterfully that it could be cited in a textbook case study of how to exhibit true leadership in such a crisis. That episode is part of a documentary film the Dakota Institute made on Bill Guy called The Charisma of Competence.

DROOLING WITH ELVIS AND MERIWETHER LEWIS

IN A CONVENIENCE STORE

NEVER WRITE A BOOK!

As I type these words, on the oak desk before me are several unopened copies of my just-off-the-press book, *The Character of Meriwether Lewis: Explorer in the Wilderness*. There it is in its gleaming blue dust jacket, a product rather than a project now, officially birthed into the world, and—for good or ill—out of my hands forever. Is it *War and Peace*? Or just *Bing: The Cocaine Years*? I have no idea—but I have purchased a truss.

Some people think the life of a writer is glamorous. There are, I admit, little flashes of glamour, at a book signing when someone sidles up with a big shy smile and blurts out some lovely unstudied compliment. When people write a letter to say that something you wrote touched their heart or changed their mind.

On one of those few—very, very few—occasions when you "get into the zone" while writing and the words flow magically through your fingers onto the screen and you are able to say precisely what you wanted to say in language that has its own syntactical beauty or sound. When the phone rings and it is someone saying she cannot imagine doing the big event next September without you in it, since what you wrote about X was so insightful.

You have to live for those rare moments, because they are really all the reward you are ever going to get for months and years of lonely research and countless hours of staring at the blank screen, hacking out flabby sentences. So you want to be a writer? Hemingway (or Red Smith or someone else) said, "All you have to do is sit in front of a typewriter eight hours a day and sweat a pint of blood through your temples."

Like most writers, I don't like writing nearly as much as I like having written. Since yesterday I have been holding my Lewis book in my hands, turning it over, feeling its heft, goofily gazing at it with a kind of wonder, as if someone else who shares my name had written a big book about one of my favorite subjects. I have not really cracked the book open yet, for fear that there is a whopper on the opening page or that after the first paragraph it just reads "peas and carrots, peas and carrots" for the following 496 pages.

I wrote this book on Meriwether Lewis in about fifteen months, though it had been percolating in my head for many years. When I finally sat down to "write the damn thing," if I may use the technical term of the industry, my goal was to produce approximately two thousand words a day.

For the first two months of serious writing, I worked about six hours a day, partly at home and partly at my favorite coffee house. During that period I was able to maintain something like a regular life. I was preoccupied but still recognizably human.

People were beginning to avoid me in public places, however, because if they asked about the Bakken oil field, I flashed from Bakken to bacon and from oil to kidney suet and responded with a passage about the average daily caloric intake on the Lewis and Clark Expedition; if they said, "How about those Twins!" I held forth about the only brothers of the expedition, Reuben and Joseph Field, not twins, but twin-ish in their capacity as hunters and runners .... People's eyes glazed over if I said the words, "Now Lewis ... " and even my mother, a Lewis and Clark buff, stopped returning my calls.

Then things began to heat up.

For the next five weeks, I worked about eleven hours a day. By the end of such days, when you finally stand up and stretch and blink yourself back into the world, you are essentially a human zucchini: brain-dead, numb, stammery, confused, and unfit for human contact, like the folks emerging from the cave in Plato's *Republic*.

This is the phase in which at the end of the day your back is fused into the osteoporosis position, your breath is some fetid combination of stale coffee and a pole barn, and your body has that gluey, clammy sheen that you feel after flying from Sydney, Australia, to Bismarck, in one forty-hour sequence of human degradation and germ-pooling. After such days you are really only capable of sitting in front of the TV screen watching a *Three's Company* marathon. (By the way, Jack Tripper is apparently not really gay).

During the final month, I literally sat in the same chair at my kitchen table (where all the light is), working seventeen-hour days, and occasionally twenty, on autopilot. By then there were approximately 250 books strewn about the kitchen, in crazy "National Geographic collector" stacks, dozens at a time held open by staplers, pliers, and other books—dog-eared, coffee-stained, Post-it marked, some backs split.

The great Dr. Johnson (1709-1784) said, "A man will turn over half a library to make one book." By now I was working every waking minute, literally sleeping just enough to allow myself to go on, eating only to banish hunger and employing the rare "all Cheetos and Diet Coke" diet.

At that phase, if I woke up at 2:38 a.m., I was up for the duration. I would sometimes wake up in the middle of the night with a verb in my mouth, or wake up in a cold sweat realizing that I had somehow wintered Lewis and Clark in Fort Sumter rather than Fort Mandan or made Meriwether Lewis President Reagan's aide de camp. Or wondering whether you spell it grizzly bear or bare or bier.

Or bore.

By now I didn't even like Lewis and Clark any more, and I no longer cared whether Lewis was killed on Oct. 11, 1809, or committed suicide, or was spotted with Elvis in a convenience store in San Antonio in 1983.

When I wasn't sitting in a corner in the yoga position facing the wall drooling or playing solitaire on three computers at once for seven hours straight, I found myself cursing Thomas Jefferson for ever consummating the Louisiana Purchase and wondering what sort of mother would name her son Meriwether.

And then, suddenly, it was over. I typed the last sentence, the only short sentence in the whole book: "I like mystery."

I took a very long hot bath. And started on my next book, which, I believe, is Einstein's definition of insanity. *11/20/11*

My book turned out to be a big success. I'm immensely proud of it. I was not exaggerating the process of writing, though it was not really a burden. Now that I look back upon it, I can hardly believe that I actually wrote the book.

Of Cottonwoods in the Breeze & Rhubarb Flan

Summer finally came to me last Sunday. I was asked by my colleagues at Fort Mandan to be on hand as a judge for the annual Rhubarb Festival. Naturally, I jumped at the chance. This is as close to the judges' table at "American Idol," "Dancing with the Stars," or Miss Universe as I am ever likely to get. Besides, I love rhubarb.

Come January, I can actually make my mouth pucker just by conjuring up my grandmother, Rhoda Straus's, rhubarb sauce. She cut rhubarb stalks into inch-sized pieces and then boiled them in well water perfectly saturated with sugar. When you bit into the sauce, months later, it disintegrated, almost dissolved, in your mouth like beef cooked for several days at a low temperature.

Meanwhile, you puckered up as if you had been stung by a squad of rhubarb bees. It was heavenly. I'd give anything for a few quarts of that sauce.

When my grandmother died in 1993, there were more than five hundred quarts of farm produce in her basement, on crude 2-by-12 shelves my grandfather had thrown up for her back when she was a mere canning machine. She's my inspiration for all the genuine things I do in life.

When I moved back to North Dakota four years ago, one of my first excursions was to Fergus Falls, MN, to dig up some rhubarb from just south of the lilac bushes behind her farmhouse. She has been dead these many years, but I got permission from the present owners to take enough stock to get my own Rhoda Straus crop started. It gives me enormous pleasure to make my first rhubarb dessert of the spring. I use my grandmother's recipe. Next year, I'm going to enter the Fort Mandan contest surreptitiously, under the nom de plume Mr. Rheum Rhabarbarum (of New Leipzig). Hint: Graham crackers.

Last Sunday was as beautiful a summer day as you could ever imagine: seventy-two degrees, a sweet breeze, the Missouri River sliding by just to the west with lazy sandbars and a few half-sunken tree trunks, and a perfect, pure blue sky. The great Merrill Piepkorn and the Radio Stars from faraway Fargo were to perform more than two hours of music in the picnic pavilion.

As soon as I arrived at Fort Mandan, I started the rumor among the assembled multitude that I was a rhubarb judge who could be bought. I made it clear that the price would be comparatively low (a new Bobcat skid-steer loader) and that the deal could be done by way of a secret handshake. My hope was to "throw" the contest and possibly touch off the Great Washburn Rhubarb Scandal of 2010. Several matronly women approached me waving giant rhubarb fronds—which I took to be a sign—but there was a deputy sheriff on the grounds and nothing came of it.

These women are serious about their rhubarb concoctions—if that is the right word. Rhubarb cake, rhubarb muffins, rhubarb swirl, rhubarb bars (called "rhubars"), rhubarb Bundt cake, rhubarb upside-down cake (I regard that as a decadent form), a rhubarb conserve, rhubarb reduction and, of course, rhubarb pie. It's easy for me to make light of the contest, but some of these women approach the scoring table with the menacing determination of a duelist. They all say North Dakota things like, "Oh, shucks, the only reason I brought my celebrated sour cream rhubarb syllabub is to make sure you have enough entries this year," or "My pie is OK, but not as good as the one I won the Western Hemisphere Pan-American Grand Championship with last summer."

I didn't dare make eye contact with several of them, lest they force me to my knees employing nothing but a glare worthy of a Jedi knight in a *Star Wars* episode. These prize homemakers saw through me immediately as someone who may know a bit about raspberries or possibly even about Lewis and Clark, but who had no business whatsoever judging the viscosity of a rhubarb glaze. I was so nervous I could not add up the scores for creativity, taste, and presentation. We had to bring in a professional accountant.

By the time I had tasted my twenty-fourth rhubarb flan, I was a nervous wreck. Just to be safe, I slipped out the back door gripping a black powder musket and a pipe tomahawk like someone fresh from the White Perogue. I made my way as unobtrusively as possible to a grassy spot behind the picnic area just under the magnificent cottonwood trees of Fort Mandan, some of which are well more than one hundred feet high. There, I lay down in a rhubarb- and sugar-induced diabetic coma, and half-dozed in the warm, but not hot, sunlight of that Sunday afternoon.

The genial Piepkorn (North Dakota's answer to Garrison Keillor) was at his absolute best. The music was just what you'd want to hear on a lazy summer afternoon on the banks of the mighty Missouri, at just the right volume. The only downside of the Radio Stars concert was that the results of the rhubarb contest were to be announced at 3 o'clock from the very same microphone at which the Radio Stars crooned, and before long the most confident of the rhubarb babes sat down together in the front row, grim and surly, arms crossed, like the four horsemen of the apocalypse.

I love North Dakota. I am in love with North Dakota.

Fortunately, I dozed off just at that point. For the first time this summer, I slowed down long enough to listen to the breeze make the cottonwood leaves dance. The tree directly in front of me was one hundred twenty feet high—at forty-five feet, the trunk exfoliated into five graceful branches perfectly in balance. I don't know if there is any Great Plains sound finer than the dance of the cottonwood leaves—especially when the breeze ebbs and flows. It's astonishingly beautiful.

With what was left of my consciousness, I could hear Piepkorn singing "Get Along Little Dogies." When he came to, "It's your misfortune and none of my own," I thought the rhubarb queens were going to rush the stage. *7/4/10*

THE SOUNDS OF TRAINS AND AMERICAN MEMORY

Spring has sprung. I've been out walking the trail from my house to the end of the line and back, a distance of about five miles. The meadowlarks are singing with such joy and lucidity that it's impossible not to smile when I walk outside. It's as if they have been waiting all winter to have the chance to sing their liquid magic song again. I'm pretty sure that's not good science, but that's how it feels. The representative sounds of Dakota-the meadowlark, the croon and whoop of the coyote, the train whistle off on the horizon, the breeze moving through the cottonwoods until it rises in growing waves to a jangle, and then very slowly subsides until it almost, but not quite, goes still. We live in paradise.

When I go home to see my mother, I lie in bed at night listening to the trains. She lives in Dickinson two blocks from the railroad tracks. Somehow that sound in that place arcs straight into the heart of my nostalgia. "Nostalgia" derives from two Greek words: *nostos*, which means homecoming and *algos*, which means pain. I'm not sure why we feel an agreeable pain over that which is past, but we do. Trains meant much more when I was a child than they do now. They still routinely carried passengers back then. Airplanes were exotic. The roads were all two lane-fragile ribbons that rode the contours of the plains like an organic roller coaster.

> "The countryside would be punctuated at long intervals by lonely little farmsteads, set well back from the tracks, half a mile or a mile away, with a single orange yard light half illuminating a ghostly barn and chicken shed, and the two-story Dakota farmhouse."

When I was a student at the University of Minnesota, I used to ride the train home for the Christmas break. Once, as a luxury, I got a couchette with a black porter who came in to make up the bed after supper. I'd be dog tired after final exams. I used to sit up in the observation car, in sweet end-of-term melancholy as we chugged along past the fields and lakes and forests and villages of Minnesota, dozing off to the sway and "clackedy clack clackedy clack" of the train. The trains that I rode then were never more than half full—maybe that's why they are gone.

As often as not, a young bearded man with a guitar would appear in the observation car around dusk. He'd strum in a lazy Woody Guthrie kind of way, and maybe sing a few bars of this or that. Sometimes this would draw a couple of young women—which, no doubt, was the point. I gazed out at the countryside, wishing I had musical talent, wishing he did, for that matter. At some point I'd drift off to my berth and use the droll little bathroom, and climb up into the snug little bed. The sheets were invariably tight as a drum. There is something heavenly about slipping between cool sheets on a moving train. I'd read myself to sleep, which never took very long.

Sometime later—minutes? hours? —I'd wake up as the train huffed and jerked to a stop at some small Dakota town like Medina or Tappen. We'd be motionless for a few minutes and I'd look out, if I could keep myself awake, at the depot and the platform, and see perhaps an older woman with a modest valise standing near the depot on a light carpet of snow, patiently waiting to board the train. Finally, after what seemed like an interminable delay (and often was), the train would inch forward, pulled taut by the engine, and then slowly press further out onto the short-grass plains. As we began to pick up a little speed on the outskirts of town, I'd watch the village infrastructure play out, and the vast prairie open up and swallow the train again. And then the pendular rhythm of the train would rock me back to sleep, with an occasional shriek at the curves as the iron wheels glanced against the rails.

As we thrummed slowly towards home through the night, the Willa Cather, O.E. Rolvaag countryside would be punctuated at long intervals by lonely little farmsteads, set well back from the tracks, half a mile or a mile away, with a single orange yard light half illuminating a ghostly barn and chicken shed, and the two-story Dakota farmhouse. There were people living in those houses, all bedded down for the night, in the heart of the heart of America, so far from the centers of power, money, entertainment—and other people.

The prairie light would wake me up at dawn-bleary, blinking, disoriented. I don't sleep soundly on a train, any more than on the first night of a camping trip. The porter would appear with coffee and a menu, and I'd eat a full breakfast as I gazed out on the stubble fields and the gathering buttes, my mind now bent on home. It was often bitterly cold outside. Some of that cold would press through the big window. Once the bed was murphy'd back up into the wall, I'd wrap myself in a blanket and read and doze and daydream and gaze about.

When we crossed the bridge at Bismarck, I'd sigh in satisfaction that I was home, in the part of North Dakota I loved (and love) best, with its laughingly low population density and its stark landscape and big big sky. When we reached that astonishing bluff and breaks country between New Salem and Glen Ullin, I'd start to pack up my books and notebooks, and anticipate the first sight of my father standing alone in the Dickinson depot glancing at headlines in the *Minneapolis Tribune*.

Somehow all the romance of America is riding on that train, crossing North Dakota almost forty years ago. When I hear the sound of the train from my house in north Bismarck, I experience a little rush of satisfaction, especially late at night. But when I hear the trains moving through Dickinson, from my bedroom in the house I grew up in, I am transported to an America that is gone, by a spiritual locomotion that I wonder at but do not fully understand. *4/11/10*

North Dakota is an Acquired Taste

You've probably seen the story about the Florida family that moved to Hazelton four years ago, lured by the promise of free lots and home purchase subsidies, and now has given up on North Dakota and plans to move back to Florida. Michael and Jeanette Tristani and their twelve-year-old twins have had enough of us. Michael's conclusion: "No one really wants new people here." Jeanette: "People prejudge you without getting to know you."

Let's face it. North Dakota is an acquired taste. I know people who have moved from somewhere far away to Dickinson, Bismarck, and Fargo, who find our Dakota cultural landscape frozen and forbidding. They quite literally talk about "culture shock," not in the "wow, they actually serve borscht in that restaurant" sense, but "it's not very comfortable to live here and frankly I don't feel very welcome" sense. They literally wonder if they are going to be able to tough it out here.

And those newcomers are living in our metropolises! Imagine moving from somewhere like San Diego to Osnabrock or Bowman or Hazelton. Before they began their 1,800-mile odyssey to the Great Plains, did the Tristanis read Sinclair Lewis's *Main Street*?—America's classical account of the smug saccharine suffocation of small town life? For that matter, did they listen to Garrison Keillor's more genial monologues about the white-bread clunkiness of Lake Wobegon?

If you suffer from agoraphobia (fear of wide open spaces), you might not want to move to North Dakota. Or ancraophobia (fear of wind), or psychrophobia (fear of cold) . . . not to mention treelessnessophobia, velveeta-phobia, coupedupophobia.

I know a highly educated man who teaches at the University of North Dakota, who told me that after ten years of living and working in North Dakota, he now believes he has finally learned how to survive this place. Ten years. "You still cannot get a good bagel here," he concludes with a world-weary sigh.

Look folks: North Dakota is a low population, windswept, splayed out and seemingly featureless place, stuck up in the middle of nowhere, about as far away from the cultural hot spots of America as it is possible to get. Average annual temperature: 42°F. One of the five windiest places in America. If Los Angeles is the film capital of the United States and Nashville the music capital, and New York the financial capital, and San Jose-Palo Alto the high tech capital, then North Dakota is the _____ (fill in the blank).

Oh, yeah, it's Eric Sevareid's "large rectangular blank spot in the nation's mind." Note to newcomers: You're going to want satellite TV.

When I travel, I sometimes tell people elsewhere that there are times when Applebee's is the best restaurant in my hometown. They howl with snobby derision at this, and they often say, solemnly, "I could never live in a place like that." Fair enough—that's good natural selection. What they don't understand, when they speak condescendingly about our amenities and our isolation, is that there are a hundred towns in North Dakota that would give anything to have an Applebee's.

What we need is a mandatory North Dakota Orientation Course (NDOC) for folks who are transferred here, stationed here, marooned here, incarcerated by marriage vows here, and for that anecdotal handful who actually choose to move here to "get away from the rat race."

Upon entering North Dakota airspace, every newcomer would get two handsomely laminated conversion charts. One chart redefines automobiles. If you want to fit in here, you need to know that in North Dakota the Chevrolet Impala and Ford Taurus are regarded as sub-compacts and the Suburban three-quarter ton a mid-size. The Ford F-150 is officially defined here as a "starter pickup." On the back of the card, we'd print the following bit of homespun wisdom: "If you don't like to buy gasoline, don't move here."

The other card (personalized for Hazelton or Mott) would indicate distances. Nearest movie theater. Nearest Wal-Mart. Nearest bookstore. Nearest Thai food. Nearest "chain restaurant of any sort." And the 800 number for Allegiant Airlines.

Forget Larry Woiwode and Louise Erdrich. I'd make Mylo Hatzenbuhler the poet laureate and cultural czar of the NDOC project. Just so they know they're not in Florida or California anymore, for a solid week newcomers would be strapped into bar-caloungers to listen to such Hatzenbuhler classics as "To All the Cows I've Milked Before," "Hens in Low Places," "I Feel Yucky," "Born to Be Wide," and "Oh, Little Town of Amidon."

> "If you suffer from agoraphobia (fear of wide open spaces), you might not want to move to North Dakota. Or ancraophobia (fear of wind), or psychrophobia (fear of cold)… not to mention treelessnessophobia, velveetaphobia, coupedupophobia."

The NDOC orientation program would consist of several broad subject categories:

Cuisine. Courses would include "666 Uses for Velveeta (Including Velveeta Fudge)," "The Tao of Hot Dish," and "Serving Bars at Weddings, Funerals, Baby Showers, Bridge Club, Graduations, Anniversaries, Family Reunions, Holidays, the Ballet, and a Few Other Occasions." Plus the graduate seminar on "The Twelve Month Grill on the Northern Plains."

Gadgets. Newcomers would first be taught to identify and later to use head-bolt heaters and remote car starters; and issued two sets of solid steel picnic tablecloth clips, cleverly shaped like giant paleo-mosquitoes, welded during the winter by the Welcome Wagon Farmers Auxiliary of Wishek. Each immigrant would memorize the recreation mottos of North

Dakota: "Why sweat? It's a lot more fun with an internal combustion engine," and "Pinochle-The Game that God Plays."

Architecture. I haven't really worked out the details, but I know the course begins with units on "The Four Car Garage: Best Practices" and "The Four Car Garage with the Extendo RV-Boat Port."

I think you begin to see the kind of the orientation I have in mind for new immigrants—to avoid another Hazelton-Tristani debacle. Optional non-credit courses would include, "Hey, That Gray Treeless Gale Force Lake is our Weekend Hideaway," "Why a Butte Is Called a Mountain," and "Yes, as a Matter of Fact, it IS Always This Windy." What do you think? *2/21/10*

I got some negative feedback on my proposed orientation course. The urge among North Dakotans to be like the folks of Maple Grove, Minnesota, or Aurora, Colorado, is powerful. I prefer to celebrate what North Dakota is—including those things that seem backward to the cosmopolitan among us—rather than what we wish it could be.

SHOVEL MANIA IN THE HOOD

This has been a winter to remember and, as they say, it ain't over yet. We appear to have moved into a wet cycle on the northern Great Plains. That's good news on the whole—for agriculture, especially ranching, for the great reservoirs on the Missouri River, which are refilling after a long period of drought. It's not such good news for the folks who live along Apple Creek, at Devils Lake, or along the Red River in Fargo and Grand Forks.

My mailbox is more or less buried now, like the cache of vintage Scotch whiskey from the 1909 Shackleton expedition that was recently found under the Antarctic ice. From time to time I go out and hack away at the snow and ice embankment—especially after I get one of those "Last Warning" or "LAST WARNING, and this time I really mean it" or "Don't make me go postal" notices from my contract mailman. Recently he has taken to cutting out letters from magazines and newspapers and pasting his warnings on the Violation of Mail Protocol forms. I think he's getting a little testy.

I feel genuinely sorry for the postal carriers in a hard winter like this one. Even during the summer, trying to get slippery sheaves of junk mail into the boxes through the window of a mini-van while lurching forward, twenty yards at a time all day long, sounds like yoga to me. In the heart of winter, when the snow removal embankments pile up, it must be extremely frustrating and contortionistic. If you add up the number of times per run that an inaccessible mailbox gums up the process, you will understand why the carriers get a little peevish.

This winter I know only two things: that I now have nine, count them, nine, different snow removal devices—some purchased at enormous expense; and that in spite of that array of snow weapons, I have the worst snow removal record in my subdivision.

May I rant for a moment here? I love my neighbors, but from an "estate grooming" perspective they are really annoying. One April when the grass was still in hibernation, my neighbor was out mowing his lawn in a heavy coat. In the course of an hour of precise quincunx swathery, he didn't fill the mower bag even once.

Eventually I went out to ask him why he was doing so unproductive (meaning insane) a thing. He said, and I quote, "I just like to mow."

Now that's just wrong.

This winter, my neighbors have been so disciplined—and may I say so obsessive—about snow removal that it would seem as if we had all met in the fall and agreed to compete in the international Clean As a Whistle snow removal festival. They don't just remove a utilitarian amount of snow from their sidewalks and driveways. They do plumb-line edge work, on the principle, apparently, that concrete, like fine red wine, must be allowed to breathe. If there were a miniature snowblower edger, like a 6HP minivac with teeth, they'd have it.

When the snow starts to fall, I sit at my kitchen table with a good book looking out at their houses waiting to see who will break first. I imagine them suited up in polar wear just inside their front doors on catapults, going over their snow removal checklists, studying the weather channel like the Kabbalah, straining for the first possible moment when they can push the eject button and get out there to shovel. The moment the snowfall shows signs of slackening, they burst out of their houses and start to blow snow to kingdom come.

When the work is nearly done, they meet at their property boundaries to high five through inch-thick mittens, pluck ice stalactites from each other's beards, and talk rig specs (over the drone of those rigs). From where I sit across the street, they appear to be introducing their snowblowers to each other like two large dogs in a park. This year they are engaged in a friendly competition to see who gets the joy of clearing the driveway and sidewalks of the widow on our block. She has the back of an Olympic athlete—frankly, I think she's working them like a couple of internal combustion saps. They stand over there like Roman border guards at the barbarian frontier—reckoning that any snow that remains on concrete for more than a couple of hours will bring on the collapse of civilization as we know it.

And then they look over at my house and frown.

I'm regarded as the subdivision curmudgeon and killjoy—no seasonal flags, no Griswoldian Christmas light shows, no faux abominable snowman, no array of laser carved Halloween pumpkins. I mow my lawn at the longest intervals by far—just this side of hay or code violations—and I regard my driveway as "clean" if I can still get in and out of it.

The other day, just to show my neighbors that I, too, have the right stuff, I got out my snowblower and careened around my driveway for a while. I think (or at least hoped) they were on the verge of welcoming me to the Club. But then I hit a full Sunday newspaper buried under the snowpack and watched helplessly as my Death-to-Snow 4000 shredded it into 100,000 bits of confetti, and threw that confetti 200 feet in every direction, like a parade to my ineptitude.

I spent the rest of the afternoon until dusk (where are early sunsets when you want them?) on my hands and knees in the middle of the street gathering up bits of newsprint—and kissing suburban male bonding goodbye. *2/14/10*

LET US NOW PRAISE KING WHEAT

Last Sunday, I just drove around central North Dakota gazing at wheat. It's not very hard to find. There are, in fact, 8.17 million acres of wheat in North Dakota. That means that almost a fifth of the state is carpeted with wheat. Isn't that just about the loveliest of all statistics? It gives me limitless pride to know that we grow a fair amount of the world's wheat. Dakotans produce 1.6 percent of the world's wheat supply.

Only Kansas produces more wheat than we do, and that's not every year.

Of North Dakota's 30,000 or so farms, an estimated 19,200 produce wheat. We grow 44 percent of the nation's hard red spring wheat and 68 percent of the nation's durum.

It would be impossible to exaggerate the importance of wheat in the history of North Dakota. The state was built on a foundation of wheat kernels. No wheat, no North Dakota. Probably the state should have been named Wheat. It is wonderfully appropriate that the current Bank of North Dakota building has grains of wheat incised on its outer walls. It will be interesting to see if the new bank building finds a way to honor the simple grain that grew North Dakota.

Bonanza farms: wheat. Nonpartisan League and populist movements: wheat. The nation's only state-owned mill: wheat. Main purpose of the railroads that thread the state: wheat.

Is there anything more beautiful than a vista of heavy, ripe, tawny wheat in the days before the combines appear at the edge of the field? I love to stop the car next to a big wheat field on a hot, dry, July day and watch the wind work wave patterns across the grain. I love the dry, dust smell of ripe wheat and the sound of its brittle, unmistakably height-of-summer rustling. Hamlin Garland, whose autobiography *Son of the Middle Border* (1917) is one of the greatest books ever written about the Great Plains, used to lie out in the wheat fields in midsummer just to experience the grand fecundity of the Earth.

It's the only time we are ever overwhelmed by the color amber.

Wheat is the world's third-most important grain. Only rice and corn are more prolific. These three grains, in fact, were the foundation of world civilization, if by civilization we mean all that follows from surplus and storage of food: rice in Asia, corn (maize) in Mezo-America and wheat in the Middle East. The United States is the world's third largest wheat producer, after China and India. France, surprisingly, is fourth. Fully 20 percent of the protein consumption of the world's seven billion people comes from wheat. We Dakotans specialize in the production of one of the three essential plants of the world. Jefferson was right when he declared, "Those who labor in the earth are the chosen people of God, if ever he had a chosen people."

Wheat is one of the miracles of creation. It was one of the first wild plants ever domesticated, at least ten thousand years ago in the Fertile Crescent, which extends from today's Israel to the Black Sea. According to Jared Diamond (*Guns, Germs, and Steel*), wheat was relatively easy to domesticate, and even now it is not very different from the wild wheat grasses that still grow in the Fertile Crescent. Abundance created the world we know, from opera to air conditioning. A wheat kernel is inherently abundant— that's why it is the basis of civilization—and humans, well before they knew scientifically what they were doing, were genetically engineering wheat for ever greater abundance.

I'm looking at a full stalk of wheat as I write this. It's an unbelievably beautiful work of nature. Just go pluck one and contemplate it for half an hour. You will be filled with wonder. I have a couple of vases full of wheat stalks in my living room. Try that with corn or potatoes.

My grandparents had a modest little dairy and small grains farm just south of Fergus Falls, Minnesota. A third of the farm was pasture. The rest was planted in wheat, oats, flax, barley and silage corn. Probably there were never more than fifty acres of wheat. My grandfather was an International Harvester, not a John Deere man. He used a pull-type combine, and Grandma Rhoda and I would catch up in the 1957 red IH pickup when the hopper was full. It was, as one of my friends used to say when I went into my agrarian reverie, a "farmy farm."

Wheat harvest was always both the highlight and the critical moment of the entire year. Grandpa could not really sleep from the moment he swathed his wheat until the moment it was in the grain elevator in town. He was grumpier than usual and much less talkative during wheat harvest.

Grandma cooked special mid-day meals and the most amazing meringue pies. She packed them in an old wicker picnic basket, and filled up a plaid Thermos with coffee, and we'd drive out to meet the tractor in the field. Grandpa would sit on the running board of the pickup, in the shade, eating silently. His face would be blackened from the dawn-to-noon work. He never owned a tractor with an enclosed cab. They'd say grace out there on the good earth and he'd eat his dinner in silence. You could see the deep pride of the wheat producer in his eyes, though he would not have talked that way for all the world. And he'd sip the strong hot coffee from the plastic cup-lid of the Thermos and pucker from the sharpness of the brew.

Wheat harvest was like a sacrament. There was a palpable, though unspoken, excitement in the air. At the grain elevator, the farmers would remove their cloth caps (they were not all baseball caps then) and wipe their sweaty foreheads, lean on something and gossip about agriculture, and smile in a way that you didn't see other times in the year.

I have a black-and-white photograph of my grandfather gesturing for the pickup from his tractor seat the last year he farmed. It's framed on the wall of my entryway, right below one of my grandmother standing behind a picnic table, every inch of which is covered with tomatoes from her garden. I take enormous pride just knowing that such people existed in my family line. They remind me of what is really important in life, and what we are in such danger of losing as we sashay into the twenty-first century.

The other day, I saw two men standing together in a vast wheat field north of Bismarck. There were two combines side by side, and two 18-wheel trucks nearby, and far off at the edge of the field two pickups, one new and splendid and the other old and battered, and even more splendid. The red of the combines was almost shocking against the organic blonde monoculture of the wheat, which swallowed the men and their equipment almost as far as the eye could see.

As I drove away, I wondered what they were talking about. This, I said to myself, is the very essence of North Dakota. *8/4/07*

The old State Bank of North Dakota building is no more. The new one pays no tribute to wheat or agriculture.

The Fall Migration:

Birds Head South, Hunters North

I've been thinking a lot about hunting lately. Because I spend a good deal of my time at the Bismarck airport, coming and going, in the waiting lounge or at baggage claim (where there is always plenty of time to observe humanity), or inbound from Denver or Minneapolis, I have the opportunity to observe the great autumn migration of out-of-state hunters. Some of them are Dakotans who now live elsewhere; others are individuals who come to North Dakota for one reason once a year.

These days, the baggage carousel is frequently crowded with long rectangular cases, often aluminum, locked. It's not unusual to see (and hear) a couple of large dog kennels come out the special handling baggage shoot.

The hunters, some of whom I engage in conversation, are a mixed breed.

Some out-of-state hunters enter our boundaries with swagger. You can tell, just by observing their body language and the way in which they talk to each other and to us, that they regard North Dakota as a quaint backward place where they go to slum it for a few days every year, dining with the local yokels, whom they patronize in order to remind themselves that they have done very well in life, thank you very much, and made good choices. They throw their money around a little recklessly in Harvey and New Leipzig and Mott, and they regard our best rural steakhouses as rudimentary grub joints. They wink at each other as they order wine they would disdain back home and smirk knowingly at the bare-bones prices.

Such men often wear spotless designer hunting togs, purchased from Isaac Walton gear shops and Eddie Bauer. They carry leather satchels. They rent the largest vehicles in the local rental car fleet. They bring bottles of expensive whiskey in their luggage and cigars. When they board the plane, they thrust their gear into the overhead bins like men who have done it a thousand times before. They read the newest business books.

They are the minority, but they make my blood boil.

The great majority of the hunters who come here are folks just like us. They wear old-enough-to-be-comfortable casual outdoor clothing. They carry themselves with modesty and respect. They seem to appreciate the people of North Dakota as much as they do the hunting experience they have waited a full year to enjoy. They spend their money generously. They often form genuine friendships with the local citizens who are their hosts and servers. They fit in. They are curious, and they ask good questions. They express their gratitude freely. The sense of spiritual renewal we provide exhibits itself unmasked on their faces. They cannot believe how friendly, efficient, clean, and polite North Dakotans are.

Truth told, some of them seem to appreciate this place more than many of us do. In my experience, eight out of ten out-of-state hunters fall into this second category.

Still, something about this annual hegira fills me with disquiet. I don't begrudge these folks their hunting experiences in North Dakota. On the whole, it's very good for North Dakota that they come. In aggregate, they now represent a major source of cash flow for the villages of North Dakota. Most towns would suffer without the hunters' transfusion, and a few would wither up and die.

Any farmer who finds it possible to stay on the land by supplementing his ag income with some hunting or guiding fees has my respect. Nor is it any of my business how farmers manage the property they own.

The gas stations, quick shops, coffee houses, bars, motels, restaurants, and even the taxidermists benefit from hunting season. Hunters bring fresh energy, good cheer, and new perspectives and ideas to places where the rhythms of life seem to many to be pretty repetitive.

Those who venture here become ambassadors for the glories of the northern prairies. They help to raise North Dakota's stature in the world. Some of them fall in love with North Dakota. A few move here to take up the simple (albeit frigid) life.

But here's the source of my disquiet. First, many of these outsiders have so much net worth that it is in their interest to buy, not rent, their hunting grounds. Farmsteads in the most isolated places in North Dakota have "For Sale" signs posted where the gravel meets the pavement. Absenteeism is never good for rural America.

Second, the history of North Dakota is the story of extraction by outsiders: game (first furs, then robes, then meat, then bones), wheat, coal, oil and one might almost say, our young people.

On the whole, this pattern of extraction has enriched others at our expense, and at the expense of the land. Hunting is many things, many of them good, but it is, in essence, a practice of extraction. Third, moneyed out-of-state hunting locks up parts of the countryside and brings the specter of class and exclusivity to what has been traditionally the most equalitarian state in America.

Theodore Roosevelt prized the American West especially because it was open to hunters of all backgrounds and economic circumstances. He was well aware that in the East and in European countries, hunting preserves were usually privately owned, available only to wealthy landowners, their select circle of friends, and a number of paying clients whom they pretended to call "friends" to avoid admitting that they were selling hunting privileges. For Roosevelt, the West represented "democratic" access to outdoor recreation. He wanted to keep it that way.

I don't want the outback of North Dakota to become a playground for the rich.

Meanwhile, as we all spend less and less time outdoors—hiking, camping, picnicking, observing, loafing—it is essential that we don't send signals, including subtle ones, to our own young people that they are not altogether welcome in our own countryside.

This morning as I flew away toward Denver, the little United jet was mostly filled with hunters. They swapped stories as we waited for clearance. As we arced up toward the empyrean, the man across from me strained to look out the window at the tawny plains below. We flew over the state capitol and then trailed along the Missouri River for five or so minutes. The serpentine river was astonishingly blue against the drab fall grass. A wave of pure romance passed through me—oh, to be out along the river today with cheese and bread and a good book—and when I looked over at the departing hunter, who was from the Ozarks, I could tell exactly what he was thinking. He wore a wistful smile. "It's over now. I won't be back for a full year. I'm tired, but renewed. And now I have to go back to my real life."

For many years, I lived in Reno, Nevada. On the plane from Reno to Denver, I usually saw something quite different: guilt, exhaustion, remorse, spiritual depletion.

What happens in Vegas and Reno is said to stay there (though we know that is never really true). What happens on a hunting excursion in rural North Dakota becomes the stuff of much broad-smiled talk, in Little Rock and Newark, Seattle, and L.A. *10/27/07*

I got some serious negative feedback on this one. Some readers thought it a mistake to criticize out of state hunters, even those who look down upon us as prairie rubes. One man from a small rural community said we should simply be grateful for their presence, because they leave money behind them.

CULTURAL APPROPRIATION

It's a concept known as appropriation. What it means, in a nutshell, is taking something from another culture without permission or true understanding, without having earned it, and using it out of context in order to identify with some aspect of that culture. In other words, having invaded American Indian homelands in North America, conquered Indians in a series of border wars, killed off (accidentally) the majority of them with our diseases, forced them onto reservations and then permitted whites to buy large portions of reservation land, outlawed their religious practices, flooded their reservation homelands, done everything in our power to shatter their traditional culture and languages, and pressured them to assimilate, NOW the dominant white culture drags some portions of what it takes to be Indian culture out of context and uses (appropriates) it for its own purposes. A dominant culture that feared or detested Indians when they were still an active threat to settlement now cherishes "Indianness" and uses Indian iconography, terminology, and ritual to give itself a feeling of power or mystique or nativism.

Go into any large bookstore and you will find books and other materials designed to let non-Indians have access to those part of Indianness that non-Indians admire: bear medicine cards, new age Lakota meditation and sweat rituals, Indian-like prayers to the Great Spirit. The subtext of many of them is "How to Become a White Indian." I know. I've purchased them all.

Some American Indians are quite tolerant of this activity and perhaps even somewhat flattered by it. Better late (and out of context) than never. But many are offended by cultural appropriation. Their argument goes something like this: "You non-Indians don't really want to know us or concern yourself with our needs or our communities. You don't really like Indians or know Indians, but you think you have the right to take from us those parts of our heritage that make you feel exotic or authentic, and, by the way, you don't actually understand what you are appropriating. When white people come to Indian country, it is always to take something." I've heard this argument many times over the past thirty years, most eloquently in lectures by Vine Deloria, Jr., the Lakota educator and lawyer, and the author of *God is Red* and *Custer Died for Your Sins*.

The principle of the thing is very simple:

As a white Anglo-Saxon protestant male, I do not have the right to appropriate bits and pieces of black urban culture, African tribal dress or ritual, Islamic manners or iconography, or Japanese Samurai behavior. In most cases such posing would only make one ridiculous, even if it is intended as an act of respect, but in some instances it is positively offensive to the culture that has been appropriated without permission. The culture being appropriated gets to decide what is and what is not offensive, not the culture doing the appropriation. It's not so far different from identity theft or plagiarism. In the case of American Indians, taking icons, artifacts, rituals, and names without permission is yet another type of exploitation, even conquest, which signifies to many Indians that non-Indians think they have the right to take from Indians whatever they wish at any time without asking permission. For Indians, this is an old and very disheartening pattern. At earlier stages of our cultural encounters it meant taking lands, water, and other natural resources. Later it was burial objects, cultural artifacts, even human remains. More recently, it has meant taking the most attractive fragments of "Indianness" to provide some sort of cultural cache or sense of connection to nature for people who have spent little or no time among actual Indian peoples.

The University of North Dakota is a mostly non-Indian institution. Of the total student body of 13,187, approximately 400 are Native Americans. The percentage of Indians on UND's sports teams is miniscule. We all know that North Dakota is one of the least diverse places in America. Leaving aside tradition, and viewing the matter in purely rational terms, why would a community overwhelmingly white, with origins in Norway and Germany and the steppes of Russia, want to identify itself with native peoples they unapologetically moved out of the way in order to establish their own communities in North Dakota?

Do UND athletes call themselves the Fighting Sioux because they feel that the white conquest of the northern plains was unjust? No. Do they do it because they want to bring about race healing in North Dakota? No, for its effect is just the opposite. Do they do it because they would like to learn more about the history and culture of the Lakota, Nakota, Dakota, Ojibwe, Assiniboine, Cree, Mandan, Hidatsa, and Arikara? No. Do they even do it because they are dedicated to a better future for Indians in North Dakota? Unfortunately not. They do it because they wish to identify themselves as warriors. They do it because the name invokes an earlier period of American history in which the Lakota fought heroically—to keep white Americans from destroying their culture, sovereignty, economic life, and homelands. They do it because white people have decided that they Lakota were a warrior culture, as opposed to the more pacific Mandan and Hidatsa. They do it because the name is exotic, and team names are expected to stir up deep irrational energies in the hearts of athletes and fans. They do it because it is tradition, and we are exceedingly reluctant to tamper with tradition. These are not all bad reasons

> "Why would a community overwhelmingly white, with origins in Norway and Germany and the steppes of Russia, want to identify itself with native peoples they unapologetically moved out of the way in order to establish their own communities in North Dakota?"

to employ an Indian name for a University sports program, providing that the Indians in question have no problem with it.

But they do.

If UND were a new institution looking for a name for its athletic teams, it would certainly not and could not choose "Fighting Sioux" today. The only justification for keeping the name is that it has been around for a long time (since the 1930s), and that it is now on the whole used with good will rather than for what might be called racially insensitive reasons. But if UND would not create the name "Fighting Sioux" today in part because the Sioux actually call themselves the Lakota and fighting is not the core of what they are or do or how they see themselves or wish to be seen by others, and the historic fighting they engaged in was a response to invasion, it seems imperative that UND now yield to the will of the Indian community in North Dakota (and beyond), and acquiesce in the ruling by the collegiate athletic association of the United States, to whose collective judgment it has for decades agreed to adhere.

We need to start the twenty-first century with a new and basic respect for the Indian peoples of North Dakota. We have to break the long degrading cycle of appropriation. From now on we have to ask permission to take or borrow Indian traditions and nomenclature. We have to learn to call the Sioux Lakota—or Oglalla or Hunkpapa or Yanktonai. It wouldn't hurt to change all pace names using the term Sioux to something else, just as we have erased "squaw" and "savage" from the landscape. Peoples have a right to be called by the names they prefer, and they have the right to withhold their identity from any uses that trouble them.

The elimination of 'Fighting Sioux" is not the end of the process of curtailing white appropriation of Indian tradition. It is just the beginning. The University of North Dakota, the premier learning center of our state, should take the lead, set the tone, teach the rest of us, in this case and always do the right thing. *11/2/05*

> *I don't think the white people of North Dakota, overwhelmingly decent and generous, really yet understand the problem of cultural appropriation. I have tried to explain it here as well as I can. Needless to say, I got a lot of hate mail for this one.*

The Lure of the Open Road

Several of my friends and I had dinner the other night on the outdoor deck of a popular restaurant by the railroad tracks. We chose to sit outside, not because it was warm, but because it was possible. We knew from the start that we were going to freeze—and we did. We opted for outdoor seating as a vote of no confidence in the winter that now seems finally over.

Spring has sprung, the grass has riz, and all I can think about is gettin' out on the blacktop roads of America. I want to grab someone with a sense of spontaneity and a flexible work schedule, throw some clothes and a toothbrush into a duffel, jump in the car and drive off at random into the American West. With no destination in mind except the freedom of the open road. No hotel reservations, no mission statement except adventure and endless conversation, with nothing but a sad little return date tucked as far back as possible into our pockets. We wouldn't even gas up before leaving the city limits because any gesture of good sense might break the spell and scold us back to our desks. Gas and red licorice and sodas in … Beach or Sidney or Miles City. Thereafter? Let the road write the narrative.

We'll just drive all day, windows open if possible, eating up the miles at an unhurried pace, stopping for cheeseburgers at a home-owned roadside cafe, getting out to stretch or hike or change drivers. Gab endlessly about everything that comes to mind, laughing for the sheer joy of rekindled animal life, talking the issues, gazing silently for long periods at the endless western Badlands, buttes, pine ridges, clouds and sky, river valleys, rolling and sand hills and just plain open flowing plains in every direction, until you shudder at the sheer size of America and the audacity of torpedoing into the heart of it in a contraption you couldn't really fix if it broke down in the middle of all that nowhere.

Paradise.

And sometime around dusk, a shag carpet motel in a faraway marginal plains town, the local "nightclub" out on the curve at the city limits, a perfect ribeye medium rare, and a slightly wilted house salad with French dressing. And the coldest beer you ever drank.

After decades of loopy pointless auto trips through the American West, I know that thus far I have seen only a tiny, even pitiful, fraction of what is there to see. I've wandered along fragile filaments of roads on the back of the infinity of the continent and a handful of historic sites, parks and monuments scattered across a vast and largely empty landscape. In a place as obscure as the hills of Ekalaka, Montana, at the heart of Marlboro Man's America, there is more scenic beauty and romance than in most of Europe, and yet if you made a list of the one hunded best places in the American West, it wouldn't even register—except perhaps among Ekalakans. If you could put the land around Ekalaka on a flatbed and truck it to Germany, they'd instantly make it a national park, possibly their premiere national park.

In Oregon last week, out by McMinville, in a rental car, I passed a man on the side of the road with a foot-long black beard shouldering a twenty-foot wooden cross toward the Pacific Ocean. Traffic whizzing by, people shaking their heads in derision and disgust, turning to their road companion and saying, "Did you just see that?"

It's not clear what the proper thing to do is when you see someone carrying a large cross across the outback of America. Do you give him licorice or a crown of thorns?

> "If you could put the land around Ekalaka on a flatbed and truck it to Germany, they'd instantly make it a national park, possibly their premier national park."

I'm not sure what kind of crazy or divine (or crazy and divine) motivation put that long-haired beatific man under that cross on a Friday afternoon in the heart of Oregon, but in a country where 50 million people watch "American Idol" at the same time, I felt nothing but admiration for the blue highways pilgrim and his grail quest.

The other day I had the impulse to buy a big touring motorcycle. Does Bobcat Co. make a road bike?

You can hear the sense of joy and expectation in the journal entry of Meriwether Lewis on the day when the Corps of Northwestern Discovery finally threw off its winter sedentariness and got back on the road, April 7, 1805.

"We were now about to penetrate a country at least two thousand miles in width," Lewis wrote, "on which the foot of civilized man had never trodden ... entertaining as I do the most confident hope of succeeding in a voyage which had formed a darling project of mine for the last ten years, I could but esteem this moment of our departure as among the most happy of my life."

I know that feeling—toward the end of the first day of driving, when you've gotten into a smooth road rhythm and the car is running perfectly, and you are awake in a way you haven't been awake in a long time, drinking in the majesty of America, not quite sure just where, and you realize that you could drive evermore in that perfect zone.

Out in the Thunder Basin of Wyoming, between Gillette and Casper, the tribal homeland of the pronghorn antelope, it is still possible to wonder just how much the "foot of civilized man" has trodden the grass and sage. Which is why we go there. Somewhere between Havre and Browning, the West will swallow up all your cares and give you a momentary sense that anything is still possible.

Unfortunately for my sense of contentment, just at this time, for accidental (?) reasons, I'm reading the greatest of all American road novels, Jack Kerouac's *On The Road* (1957). If you haven't read it, give yourself that pleasure. It's one of the foundation texts of the Beat Generation and there is no other book that gets so close to the heart of the American trinity of car, freedom and the open road.

On The Road contains possibly the single best road sentence ever, a sad Tocquevillian utterance that gets to the heart of the essential restlessness of the American spirit.

"Whither goest thou, America, in thy shiny car in the night?"   *5/13/09*

The loopy, pointless auto trip through the American West is virtually my favorite thing to do. I know of no other country on earth where this is possible. Gas prices are no longer negligible, but I never let more than a few months pass between road odysseys, preferably to obscure places in the West that I have never visited before.

JUMP AND SHOW US WHO YOU REALLY ARE

This is a column you may wish to read while using the Internet to look at the photographs in question.

It's amazing what we discover when we are looking for something else. I've been reading biographies of J. Robert Oppenheimer (1904-67), the father of the atomic bomb. I'm fascinated by Oppenheimer, who was one of the most extraordinary and paradoxical men of the twentieth century.

What interests me most is that the great physicist did not seem to wrestle with the ethical implications of the atomic bomb (he called it the "gadget") until the first test occurred at Alamogordo, N.M., on July 16, 1945. Then—and only then, apparently—Oppenheimer had an inrush of moral consciousness about the grave thing he had done. Like the Greek mythic figure Prometheus, who stole fire from the gods and suffered profoundly for his crime, Oppenheimer became a haunted, even tragic figure in the two decades after Hiroshima and Nagasaki.

At Alamogordo, when the world's first atomic explosion occurred at 5:29:45 a.m., Monday, July 16, 1945, Oppenheimer suddenly found himself flashing to a passage from Hindu sacred literature. He had learned Sanskrit just for fun while teaching physics at Berkeley. As the nuclear age began, with a mushroom cloud that reached thirty-eight thousand feet, Oppenheimer blurted out a line from the Bhagavad Gita, "I am become death, the destroyer of worlds."

The minute I first read that, a dozen or so years ago, I knew I wanted to know more, much more, about the scientist who spoke those words on that occasion. If I had to list the ten most interesting people I have ever encountered in history, Oppenheimer would be high on the list. If you are interested, read Kai Bird and Martin Sherwin's *American Prometheus*. It won the Pulitzer Prize in 2006. I can assure you it requires no technical understanding.

In reading another biography, Jeremy Bernstein's *Oppenheimer: Portrait of an Enigma,* I learned that Oppenheimer had been photographed jumping, in an expensive three-piece suit, in his Spartan office at the Institute for Advanced Study at Princeton. It's an amazing portrait of an amazing man. Oppenheimer was thin to the point of gauntness. He is a picture of perfect elegance, one arm stretching up towards the ceiling and heaven, the other pointing, a little less emphatically, towards the floor... behind him is a blackboard partly inscribed with mathematical notations. Somehow the greatness of the man is clearly visible in the remarkable black and white photograph, and the vaulting ambition, and the sense that the usual boundaries of life are unable to contain him.

> "The usually-awkward Nixon looks balanced, calm, almost serene in the famous photograph. He should have jumped more and burgled less."

The photographer was a Latvian man named Philippe Halsman (1906–79), who came to the United States in 1940, and happened upon the notion of getting his subjects to jump in 1952.

The whole thing started when Halsman was photographing the Ford family for *Life Magazine* to commemorate the fiftieth anniversary of the Ford Motor Co. "I went to Grosse Pointe and found that the family consisted of nine bubbling adults and 11 laughing and crying children and babies." It was, said Halsman, a "cataclysmic sitting," by which he meant that it was an ordeal to create a more than blah photograph of a group so large and so stiff.

Mrs. Edsel Ford, the hostess, eventually offered Halsman a highball. Suddenly inspired, Halsman asked, "May I take a picture of you jumping?" "I have never seen an expression of greater astonishment," he later recalled. Mrs. Ford asked if he expected her to jump in her high heels. He did not. So she took of her shoes and jumped.

Thereafter, Halsman routinely ended his photo sessions by asking his subjects to jump. Odd though these requests must have seemed, coming from a famous photographer taking pictures of prominent individuals for important publications, a surprising number of people agreed to take the leap of faith. The photographs are collected in Philippe Halsman's *Jump Book*, first printed in 1959, reprinted in 1986. The Oppenheimer photograph is, in my opinion, the finest in the entire series.

Halsman argued that it is impossible to maintain an artificial pose while jumping. Jump photos, therefore, are a kind of Rorschach Test in which the core of a person's soul is revealed.

Some people refused to jump. Lord Mountbatten refused, period, and the great British philosopher Bertrand Russell, who understood what Halsman was trying to accomplish, explained that "he did not want to divulge his character." The great American journalist Edward R. Murrow refused, as did the secretary general of the United Nations, Dag Hammarskjold.

There are, of course, people you would expect to jump. Dean Martin and Jerry Lewis jumped together, with the usual hilarity. Dick Clark jumped—no surprise there. Carol Channing jumped—and a mighty jump it was. Red Skelton, Jackie Gleason, Phil Silvers, Milton Berle, and Steve Allen all jumped, as did Lucille Ball (splendidly), Dinah Shore (elegantly), Sophia Loren (not so sexy here).

Probably the most famous of all the jump photos is of the painter Salvador Dali. Not only is the surrealist Dali frozen in mid-jump, but everything else in the photograph is suspended in mid-air too: three flying cats, a menacing chair, an easel holding one of Dali's paintings, and a wide swath of water that looks like the Gulf Stream. It took twenty-six exposures to get the photograph right. Two things come to mind. First, I'd like to see the other twenty-five frames of what must have been an extremely frustrating photo session. Second, although I do not see a "no cats were harmed during the filming of this photo classic," I assume that they fared better than the famous painter, who must have been completely exhausted before the successful photograph was snapped.

It's an anti-gravitation tour de force, though Dali, who is holding paintbrushes, looks as if he might possibly just have sat down on a pitchfork.

It is little short of amazing that Halsman was able to talk such staid folks as Margaret Truman, Adlai Stevenson, Richard Nixon, and above all the Duke and Duchess of Windsor into jumping for the camera. The usually-awkward Nixon looks balanced, calm, almost serene in the famous photograph. He should have jumped more and burgled less.

I've gazed at the Oppenheimer photograph for hours at a time lately, trying to make sense of the strange man who loosed the atomic bomb into the world, then spent the rest of his life agonizing about whether even the "big toe of the Genie" could be put back into the bottle. In 1947 Oppenheimer famously said, "In some sort of crude sense which no vulgarity, no humor, no overstatement can quite extinguish, the physicists have known sin; and this is a knowledge which they cannot lose."

When my weak and pedestrian brain wearies of trying to make sense of the troubled genius, I turn in Halsman's book to his photograph of Audrey Hepburn jumping out of her sandals, in a blousy skirt and a tight cotton blouse. It is, in its modest way, one of the most beautiful and alluring photographs ever taken. *7/15/08*

How It Was in America on the Fourth of July

Do you remember those old *Life Magazine* stories that attempted to create a slice of life profile of the United States? They were usually titled "A Day in the Life of America." They featured sentences like, "At 7:04 a.m. in Cleveland, Ohio, a convoy of 23 garbage trucks at the Cuyahoga County Sanitation Facility begin to fan out into the city's 48 boroughs, to collect what will before day's end be a mountain of 497 tons of trash."

These *Life* magazine stories were stirring. They made the commonplace heroic. They simultaneously made you appreciate the vastness of our continental republic and the commonness, even intimacy, of our national experience. Garrison Keillor wrote a parody of the formula in the *New Yorker* in 1975. It was titled, "How It Was in America a Week Ago Tuesday." It was so well done that my friend Steve and I wondered if it was really a parody. A couple of years later, I had the chance to ask Keillor about the many "statistics" of the article: 4.6 million cans of soup, 160 million cigarettes, 40 million quarts of orange juice and 2 million plates of leftovers. "Made 'em up," he intoned in his best Wobegon voice. The plates of leftovers should have tipped me off.

Wouldn't it be wonderful if there were a way to create a precise and comprehensive profile of America for the Fourth of July weekend now ending, an exhaustive one-day cultural census of the United States on its 233rd birthday? If Thomas Jefferson could witness America this weekend from a lofty hot air balloon, what would he see? More to the point, what would he say? Would he weep for the American republic or shake his dreamy head in tolerant bemusement at the myriad of ways we have come to define the phrase, "the pursuit of happiness"?

How many bratwursts bit the dust this weekend? How many people experienced their first watercraft ride, ran their first marathon, assembled their first s'mores or attended their first Major League Baseball game? How many teenagers experienced their first furtive kiss this weekend? How many Americans hoisted or waved a flag? How many slept in a tent? How many people will be nursing a beety, painful sunburn tonight, shaking their heads at the folly of it all? How many Americans shot a bottle rocket? How many shot a gun?

Amber waves of grain. Purple mountains' majesty. America means wide open boundless space and rivers to make your heart ache with national pride.

It would be fascinating to have the weekend stats for the number of hot dogs eaten, and pounds of hamburger, and slices of cheese; for buns, brats, chicken wings, marshmallows, bottles and cans of beer, units of guacamole; for the national square footage of steaks, or (better yet) the length of all the steaks eaten this weekend laid end to end across America with a starting block at Mount Rushmore. How many of those steaks began their journey from creature to consumable on a ranch in western North Dakota?

Inquiring minds want to know.

If you added together the money value of all the food and fuel and stuff that has been consumed this weekend by America's 306,798,000 people, of which of the world's 192 countries would it equal the annual gross national product?

American means abundance.

How many bags of charcoal have been opened across America over the last three days? How many bags of ice? How many bags of potato chips? For that matter, how many bags of marijuana?

America means freedom not unmixed with a streak of misrule and anarchy.

If all the gunpowder in all the fireworks detonated over America this Fourth of July were put into a single barrel, how large would that barrel be and what could it blow up? (Would it finish the Crazy Horse Monument or merely smooth his war-weary forehead?) How many Americans are saying that this was the best fireworks display they ever saw? And how many have preferred to remember a Fourth of July long ago when the world was a magical place and red Radio Flyer wagons and homemade ice cream were the marker of the holiday and the measure of happiness?

> "How many bags of charcoal have been opened across America over the last three days? How many bags of ice? How many bags of potato chips? For that matter, how many bags of marijuana?"

How many Band-Aids have been applied across American in the last seventy-two hours with a kiss and words of comfort? How many casts have been set by doctors called away from picnics and pontoons, ball games, and the Boston Pops?

How many Independence Day babies were born this year? How many of the newborns were named Thomas Jefferson Schamansky or Thomas Jefferson Xiong? Or Liberty or Freedom Malloy?

America means diversity.

How many prayers have been spoken this weekend for our troops in Iraq (141,000), in Afghanistan (32,000), in South Korea (26,339); for the men and women serving their country at the 820 military installations in more than 40 countries worldwide? How many Americans have died in uniform this weekend? Imagine those calls.

America, in the twenty-first century, means empire. Mr. Jefferson would not have liked that at all.

How many times, in how many places, did citizens hear Lee Greenwood's patriotic anthem "God Bless the USA" and how does that compare to the frequency of the song's performance on the fourth of January or the fourth of October?

How many weddings were performed across America on Saturday? How many of those occurred in the six states that have legalized same-sex marriage?

America means tolerance.

How many men in bolo ties or top hats or funny wigs stood before a crowd of patriots Saturday and read aloud the preamble of the Declaration of Independence? How many featured speakers tried to articulate what it is about America that is so amazing, so inspiring, so breathtaking, so free, so important to the world, and got choked up and left the podium feeling a little embarrassed?

How many people, born in how many countries, became naturalized U.S. citizens Saturday? I know that 66 people, from 35 countries, took the oath at Jefferson's Monticello in its 47th annual naturalization ceremony. Seeing that ritual in that place is high on my bucket list.

How many people at some point during the weekend looked up from whatever they were doing, in the midst of the celebratory hoopla or the sheer relaxation of a sandbar, and said, "My God, I love this country. I'm so glad to be an American"?

I know I did.

America is still the last best hope of the world.   *7/5/09*

ROOSEVELT AND THE

CONSERVATION OF COWBOY CULTURE

Theodore Roosevelt is well known for his conservation efforts. During the course of his Presidency, Roosevelt set aside 230 million acres of the public domain for permanent federal protection against unrestrained economic development. He doubled the size of the National Park System, designated the first eighteen National Monuments, invented the National Wildlife Refuge System, and added 150 million acres to the National Forest. It was an extraordinary achievement—greater than that of any other president of the United States. At the end of his presidency, Roosevelt called the first national governor's conference. The subject was conservation.

Roosevelt's interest in conservation was not limited to land.

Like his friend Frederick Jackson Turner, Roosevelt understood that the long frontier phase of American history was ending. He came to the West in 1883 to experience frontier life before it disappeared forever. Ostensibly he came to kill a buffalo, but what he really sought was to immerse himself in the borderlands in order to incorporate into his own character something of what he saw in the heroes Davy Crockett, Daniel Boone, and George Rogers Clark.

Roosevelt believed that the frontier experience—courage, violence, raw simplicity, the test of the human will against the wild energies of nature and its creatures—was the fundamental shaping influence in American history. As he looked around him in New York or Boston, he saw increasing urbanization, industrialization, dependence, and alienation. He deplored the "taming" of the American soul. He determined never to be fully domesticated himself, and he became the nation's foremost advocate of the strenuous life.

Roosevelt would have liked to conserve those qualities of the American character, to find a way to keep alive a little of the Daniel Boone in each of us. That's one reason why he favored war—so long as it was righteous. Roosevelt saw the national parks and other federally protected recreational areas as landscapes in which Americans (particularly American males) could regenerate themselves when they became enervated by too much civilized life.

The best thing Roosevelt ever wrote about his time in the Dakota Badlands was his 1913 *An Autobiography*, which is regarded as one of the best in presidential history. In one of the most tantalizing passages of the book, Roosevelt wrote, "The punchers on night guard usually rode round the cattle in reverse directions; calling and singing to them if the beasts seemed restless, to keep them quiet."

Roosevelt participated unhesitatingly in "riding night guard around the cattle," though it is doubtful that he sang, "Oh, Bury Me Not on the Lone Prairie," or "The Old Chisholm Trail."

Roosevelt listened with fascination to those songs out on the edge of the herds. He was too busy to record them, but he had the intelligence to recognize that they were not mere ephemera. He realized that they were, in effect, the poetry of the cattle frontier and that they deserved to be preserved as an important manifestation of folk culture. What was needed was a patient and well-trained ethnomusicologist who would travel the frontier in search of that unique contribution to American culture.

Roosevelt found his man in John Avery Lomas (1867-1948). Born in Mississippi, raised in the Bosque district of Texas, Lomas became fascinated by cowboy songs and other working class songs, jokes, poems, and tales. Although he was cruelly discouraged by literature professors at the University of Texas, Logan persisted in his collecting, studied at Harvard under Barrett Wendell and George Lyman Kittredge, and went on to become the great American pioneer in the preservation and interpretation of cowboy song and poetry.

With his characteristic breadth, curiosity, and enthusiasm, Roosevelt encouraged Lomas to record the songs of the cattle frontier before the cowboy moment in American history disappeared and before the authentic folk material was eclipsed by commercial schlock. Lomax's *Cowboy Songs and Other Frontier Ballads* was one of the fruits of that presidential encouragement (1910). The collection is dedicated to "Theodore Roosevelt, who while president was not too busy to turn aside—cheerfully and effectively—and aid workers in the field of American balladry."

In a letter to Lomax written from Cheyenne, Wyoming, on August 28, 1910, Roosevelt exhibited his insight into the nature and importance of cowboy culture. "Your subject," he wrote, "is not only exceedingly interesting to the student of literature, but also to the student of the general history of the west. There is something very curious in the reproduction here on this new continent of essentially the conditions of ballad-growth which obtained in mediaeval England; including, by the way, sympathy for the outlaw, Jesse James taking the place of Robin Hood."

> "Roosevelt deplored the "taming" of the American soul. He determined never to be fully domesticated himself, and he became the nation's foremost advocate of the strenuous life."

All of his life, Roosevelt was fond of telling stories about ruffians and ne'er-do-wells, but he never celebrated them. He was too much a law and order man, a figure of righteousness, for that.

Of Lomax's collection, Roosevelt wrote, "It is...a work of real importance to preserve permanently this unwritten ballad literature of the back country and the frontier." In an era before the National Endowment for the Humanities, Roosevelt served effectively as a patron of authentic American culture. He championed the cultural significance of cowboy song and poetry at a time when most American scholars, like Lomax's professors in Texas, considered such Americana beneath contempt.

Roosevelt also encouraged North Dakota's poet laureate James Foley (1874-1939), whom he had known in the poet's childhood. Although Foley spent much of his life in Pasadena, California, where he died on May 17, 1939, he grew up in North Dakota, including Medora, where he served as a ranch hand. Foley published more than twenty books of poetry.

Roosevelt wrote the introduction to Foley's *The Voices of Song*. After explaining how much he appreciated his conversations with Foley's father, who was one of the few active readers in the Little Missouri River Valley in those years, Roosevelt wrote, "At that time the present poet was one of the small Foley boys, and seemed far more likely to develop into a cow-puncher than a literary man." Roosevelt told a couple of anecdotes, then concluded, "I can testify from personal knowledge that Mr. Foley writes his western sketches not out of books, but out of his own ample experience."

When Roosevelt visited North Dakota on his 1903 "conservation" tour of the American West, a trip which included prolonged stops at

Yellowstone and Yosemite National Parks, and Roosevelt's first glimpse of the Grand Canyon, California, and the giant redwoods near San Francisco, Foley wrote a welcoming poem for the former cowboy, now president of the United States.

Roosevelt's own western writings represent an extremely important contribution to the preservation of cowboy culture. His many articles, his trilogy about life on the Dakota frontier—*Hunting Trips of a Ranchman*, *The Wilderness Hunter*, and *Ranch Life and the Hunting Trail*—and above all the outstanding chapter in *An Autobiography*, "In Cowboy Land."

All these are backed by Roosevelt's magnum opus, *The Winning of the West*, in which he narrated and justified the conquest of the near-West (the trans-Appalachian West that included the Ohio Valley), and celebrated the "primordial violence and heroism" that characterized the frontiersmen who infiltrated the western wilderness between 1776 and 1890.

Historians have shown that Theodore Roosevelt, together with his friends Owen Wister (*The Virginian*), and Frederic Remington, played a critical role in actually creating the mythology of the American cowboy. These privileged easterners who came west to find themselves, reinvent themselves, and immerse themselves in what they regarded as the last great gasp of the first phase of American history, romanticized the rough culture of the frontier in ways that are now central to our understanding.

It would be impossible to improve on Roosevelt's summary statement about his adventures in the Dakota Badlands:

"It was still the Wild West in those days, the Far West, the West of Owen Wister's stories and Frederic Remington's drawings, the West of the Indian and the buffalo-hunter, the soldier and the cow-puncher. That land of the West has gone now, 'gone, gone with lost Atlantis,' gone to the isle of ghosts and of strange dead memories. It was a land of vast silent spaces, of lonely rivers, and of plains where the wild game stared at the passing horseman. It was a land of scattered ranches, of herds of long-horned cattle, and of reckless riders who unmoved looked into the eyes of life or of death."

The cultural intellectual Theodore Roosevelt conserved that life—himself and the men and women he encouraged. The adventurous Theodore Roosevelt lived that life in what is now North Dakota. *12/29/07*

WHAT IS READING GOOD FOR ANYWAY?

For many months, I have been reading the works of John Steinbeck (1902-68). So far, I've read *The Grapes of Wrath, East of Eden, Cannery Row, The Red Pony, Tortilla Flats, Of Mice and Men, The Log from the Sea of Cortez, Journal of a Novel, Travels with Charley,* and the *Acts of King Arthur.* That's about two-thirds of Steinbeck's immense literary output. Plus a couple of biographies and critical studies, particularly of *The Grapes of Wrath.*

At this point, I may as well keep at it until I read everything he wrote. That will be sometime around 2015.

I'm a slow reader, alas, painfully slow. From time to time, I determine to read through the works of X—Steinbeck, Dickens, Chaucer, Tolstoy, Dostoevsky, Twain, Cather, etc. But I never succeed. I cannot think of a single author whose every word I have read, except Jane Austen (six relatively short novels) and the Elizabethan poet and preacher John Donne. And time is running out.

It is sometimes said that no person could, in a lifetime, read the complete works of the Church Father St. Augustine, author of *Confessions* and *City of God,* among literally hundreds of other books. This cannot be true. After all, Augustine managed to write them in a lifetime (354-430). It is taking the editors of the Thomas Jefferson papers longer to edit and publish his collected correspondence (22,000 letters) than it took him write them during his eighty-three-year life. Something's wrong with that.

Once, I read a biography of the English poet and polymath John Milton. In addition to writing the epic poem *Paradise Lost,* Milton was one of the greatest intellectuals in British history. The biographer (whose name I have forgotten) said something like, "It cannot be said with any confidence that Milton had not read any book published up until the time of his death in 1674." This probably wasn't strictly speaking true, but what a compliment. I've always wanted to count myself among the great readers, but it is not to be. I haven't read a thousandth of what I want to read, or even a hundredth of what I ought to have read. This has been a source of disappointment and even self-loathing in my life.

In David Lodge's comic novel *Changing Places,* the English faculty at a California university play a game called Humiliation at their dinner parties. A professor thinks of a book she or he should have read, but never has, and the others try to guess the name of the book. The chairman of the English department, an eminent Shakespeare scholar, becomes the all-time world champion of Humiliation by confessing, in a moment of inebriation, that he has never actually read *Hamlet.* He becomes an instant legend in his profession, but he also is summarily fired by the university president the day after he blurts out this remarkable truth.

What is your dream of heaven? Mine is pretty nerdy, even geeky, not to mention slothful. The second slice of pizza, a gentle, but almost chilly breeze at the end of the day, the visitation of thunderstorms just infrequently enough to be a welcome surprise, and the capacity to read serenely at least half the day.

Are there days in heaven?

It's one thing to read. But it's heavenly to read when you are in the zone—when, as Thoreau insists, you read a book in the spirit in which it deserves to be read, when your attention does not wander, when now the sense, now the sentence structure, now the phraseology, now the euphony, now the bedrock theme, caresses your soul, and you know you could read on forever without feeling cloyed or restless. I get into that zone about one day in a hundred. And that's the day the plumber comes or the car payment is due or there is an essential (and pointless) meeting about that project.

> "The problem with the humanities is that they are immensely important and enriching."

Am I better off for having read most of Steinbeck? That's the paradox of the humanities. I want to say yes, that my soul, my perspective and my outlook have been deepened by the experience, that in some important way I am more fully a human being for my immersion in the works of one of America's greatest writers. A more skeptical or at least more realistic view is that, by the time you have lived fifty years, your character is pretty much a done deal.

What's the last book that really got under your skin, that knocked your socks off, that caused you to step back and rethink some pretty basic things you thought you understood?

My heaven would be for this to happen to me from time to time—often enough to indicate that my soul is open to possibility—but not so often that it made me flaky (or flakier than I already am). If I could snap my fingers and make anything purely selfish happen, I'd ask for my sense of wonder to be topped off like the freon in my car's air conditioner.

The only measurable effect of reading so much Steinbeck is that I have more gray hair, my eyes are a little weaker, and my checking account is diminished by a couple of hundred dollars. The problem with the humanities is that they are immensely important and enriching. At the same time, they are frustratingly unmeasurable as we go about the daily rhythms of our lives.

Don't we all want to be more than we are?

North Dakota has at least two Steinbeck connections. First, even though we don't think of them as Okies, the thousands of North Dakotans who left the state in the wake of the Depression and the Dust Bowl (more than at any other time in our history) were part of the mass movement that Steinbeck describes with such profound skill and compassion in

The Grapes of Wrath (1939). In writing about the "Joads," Steinbeck also was writing about us.

Second, Steinbeck came through North Dakota in 1960 on the fourteen-thousand-mile pickup camper trip that became *Travels With Charley* (1962). Steinbeck passed through North Dakota on old U.S. Highway 10. In *Travels with Charley*, he commented on Fargo, the Maple River, the significance of the Missouri River, and the Dakota Badlands. There ought to be interpretive signs at each of those locations.

Bismarck-Mandan evoked one of Steinbeck's most famous passages. "Here is where the map should fold," he wrote. "Here is the boundary between east and west. On the Bismarck side it is eastern landscape, eastern grass, with the look and smell of eastern America. Across the Missouri on the Mandan side, it is pure west, with brown grass and water scorings and small outcrops. The two sides of the river might well be a thousand miles apart."

If you haven't read Steinbeck, or read him recently, I heartily recommend three books (for a start!): *The Red Pony* (about the first darkness of adolescence), *Cannery Row* (light-hearted, amusing, life-affirming) and, of course, his masterpiece, *The Grapes of Wrath*, which is one of the world's great books, and which might, just possibly, knock your socks off. *7/21/07*

One of my plans is to write a book of the interpretive highway signs we should create to grace our landscape. Here's a good place to start.

It's Spring

and the Earth-Moving

Equipment is Waking Up

Ah, spring. How glorious these days in which the snow is still scattered across the Plains, but the great melt is on and the water runs down along the gutters of the streets. On the news last night, there were some stern warnings about getting fish houses off the lakes before mid-March. The smell of the earth is subtle but pungent in those places where the snow is entirely gone. And though in early spring the look of the land is as gray and dingy as it ever gets in North Dakota, here and there something green is already asserting itself. Time to go find crocuses (pasque flowers) in the Badlands. The quality of the air is enveloping, embracing, even at times enchanting. I've been doing a lot of walking, and I find myself saying, out loud, "It is a great day to be alive in Dakota," and then looking around, a little embarrassed.

Fall is my favorite season on the Great Plains, but for some reason I've been really thrilled by this spring. It was not a bear of a Dakota winter, but at least this time it was a true winter with some snow and cold snaps and the possibility of strandedness from time to time. If the head bolt heater does not come into play, it's not a true North Dakota winter. I have a couple of unused cans of Heet in the back seat of my car. That's my badge of honor. To anyone who sees them, the message is clear: "Oh, you went to Grand Forks this January." After such a winter, the kind that reminds us that this is not such an easy place to live, a spring like this one tells us that the compensations make it all worthwhile.

> "After my grandfather's health began to falter, they sold the cows at auction on the farm, together with a bunch of equipment. It's horrible to see your life's work spread across the yard, picked through by bargain hunters and the curious. When the bidding finally began on the cows, my grandfather was overcome with emotion, and he had to go into the house to be alone as the auction proceeded. After that, he was never quite the same."

It's wonderful to go out now to fetch something from the car, or walk to the mailbox in shirtsleeves, as I have done all winter, anticipating a bracing but endurable dash, and then finding the outside air warm and inviting, and not needing to hasten back inside as quickly as possible. My garden is still buried under three feet of snow, but it won't last long against this unseasonable heat, and I have begun to think about my rototiller. At the grocery store and at the hardware store, I have begun to toss a couple of packets of seeds into my cart every time. I have dreams of an unprecedented tomato crop.

I went out on my deck last night in the dark to look at Venus. I was surprised to discover shirtsleeve temperatures at 8:30 p.m. Well, not exactly, but the kind of warm spring night when you can stay out for ten or fifteen minutes before you begin to feel chilled. The laving of the warmish spring air is so welcome, so invigorating, after months of implementing a layer strategy each time you ventured outside.

The coyotes howled and yipped, back and forth in their contrapuntal way, on the prairie to the west of my house. It had been a spectacular sunset and one of the first lingering dusks of the year, and now, sure enough, the evening star dominated the western sky. There was a modest little breeze. Paradise.

I looked around at the vast bowl of the Great Plains, rolling plains stretching out forever, Bismarck and Mandan in some respects swallowed up by the valley of the Missouri.

I will be so sorry when the city eats my prairie and the coyotes drift away.

Driving somewhere yesterday, I heard a Bismarck city engineer on the "What's On Your Mind" show on KFYR radio. He was talking about the mighty road projects that will begin the minute the frost is out of the ground, connecting U.S. 83 and Washington Street in new ways, linking the new subdivisions as quickly as possible to everything else.

It sounded so gleeful on the radio. The city is growing. We're going to connect everything to everything. New neighborhoods are sprouting up all over, particularly the north end. New stores are coming. Coffee houses have sprung up like mushrooms all over the city. The infrastructure needs to be "upgraded to keep up with the phenomenal growth." I found myself thinking, "What's wrong with me? Why don't I share that sense of excitement?" I regard the growth dynamism of Bismarck with misgiving.

It would be silly to be against the change. It's coming, like it or not, and for many, many people it is a wholly welcome development: more of all the things we love to consume.

Meanwhile, we hear of the possibility of a single nine thousand-head mega-dairy operation in North Dakota, and we learn that Ramsey County has given up its attempt to prevent a five thousand-sow hog confinement facility from being thrown up near Edmore.

My grandparents, Dick and Rhoda Straus, had a dairy farm in Fergus Falls, Minnesota. They had sixteen head. Twice a day for decades, they milked those cows, first by hand and eventually with the help of Surge milkers. The milkers were a great innovation, but in those days, the milk canisters still had to be hauled into the milk room and poured into the bulk tank. I loved that role when I was a boy.

Each of the cows had a name—Daisy, Blossom, Gert, Brownie, Petunia—and each one, of course, lumbered to the same stanchion every time. On those few occasions when one tried to enter the wrong space, my grandfather flew into a rage and sorted things out with firmness. Grandma would voice a carefully restrained protest, and Grandpa would either say something snappish to her or just glare her way, but he always calmed down and made up to the cow, for he was a very tender man beneath all that Germanic bluster.

We arrived for a visit one year when an unusual Holstein calf had just been born: white over its entire body except for a black patch on either side of its face. It was a really beautiful calf, the daughter of Whitey, a huge cow with nearly identical markings. My grandmother "gave" me the calf, not in the economic sense, but as my "special milk cow." I named her Pal. Eventually, she became the best producing cow in the herd. For the next ten years, whenever we arrived at the farm, I went as soon as decently possible to the barn to see Pal. (Note: They don't seem to remember you quite the way a dog does).

After my grandfather's health began to falter, they sold the cows at auction on the farm, together with a bunch of equipment. It's horrible to see your life's work spread across the yard, picked through by bargain hunters and the curious. When the bidding finally began on the cows, my grandfather was overcome with emotion, and he had to go into the house to be alone as the auction proceeded. After that, he was never quite the same.

I wasn't there, but even recounting the story is heartbreaking to me.

I wish the mega-dairy's investors well. But—and I mean no disrespect—I do not call this farming. No Gert, no Daisy: barcodes and scanners. A hog operation that will produce 2,400 new pigs per week is not a farm. It is a production facility.

As March surges on, all over North Dakota, people are flowing to the trails for their first outdoor walks of the spring. It's great to see all those pale limbs and over-optimistic jogging outfits. People greet each other walking—as if to say I'm glad to be alive today, and I cannot help spreading my sense of joy.

It's spring, the time of renewal. The question is: what shall we renew?
3/17/07

The coyotes don't come around much anymore, now that Bismarck has grown to eat my little prairie cul-de-sac.

WAKING UP TO GREAT BOOKS IN ADOLESCENCE

My daughter called me about ten days ago to announce that she had read F. Scott Fitzgerald's *The Great Gatsby*. She is still young enough to belong to the "guess what?" school of conversation, so it took some time for me to prove that I was never going to guess right and that she may as well just report the news.

At the suggestion of her language arts teacher (what used to be called English), she had been trying to read Jane Austen's *Emma*. But she "couldn't get into *Emma*," so she picked up *The Great Gatsby* instead. She had read it in a single night—I hope under the covers, with a flashlight—and it had immediately catapulted into the best book she had ever read. If her experience is anything like mine, it will not be able to hold that position very long.

The Great Gatsby is a great novel, but it also is primarily an adolescent's book, which shines brightest for those who are just leaving the chrysalis. It gets at two extraordinarily important themes at the heart of adolescence.

Some of the people we will meet in life are not just "what they are." We all construct our personalities to a certain degree, and create a mask that we present to the world, but some people do this with special gusto. Such individuals fascinate us. We gravitate towards them like a moth to the flame. The persona they create has a sort of defiant brittleness about it, and they cling to that persona, that character armor, with such fierceness that it often winds up hurting others and hurting themselves. A great humanities text like *Gatsby*, by brilliant focused simplification of a very complex issue, allows us to process this phenomenon in a highly agreeable way. That's what the humanities do. That's why we need literature.

Jay Gatsby, it turns out, began his life as James Gatz from North Dakota, who at the age of seventeen shed his identity as the son of a marginal farmer, and, with the help of a temporary mentor, re-constructed himself as the great Gatsby.

Any adolescent trying to figure out how to navigate the fractured dissimulations of the adult world needs to process the problem of fashioning a "face to meet the faces that you meet," as T.S. Eliot (that other adolescent favorite) put it. I can imagine my daughter reading the novel alone in her room (we always read alone) and experiencing wanderings of the soul she has never known before. I can imagine her feeling exhilarated but also somehow a little guilty as she looks up from the text and tries to come to terms with Fitzgerald. And herself. And life.

The Great Gatsby also belongs to the "burning the candle at both ends as we dance recklessly against the fact of death and mediocrity" school of literature. For an adolescent, life is at the same time breathtakingly exciting and—as we look around at the odd way adults behave—routine, unpoetic, habit-bound, boring. When we face the first great disillusionments of our lives—and there are many—we have to decide whether we are going to shrug our shoulders and get on with life in a dogged and accepting way, or find some mad, heroic way to thwart the malaise. Here is a characteristic sentence from Fitzgerald, who coined the phrase "The Jazz Age": "So we drove on toward death through the cooling twilight."

Adolescents love the idea of Higher Law. Adults eventually come to realize it is hard enough to comply with the regular laws of life, much less higher laws. Our vital, questing, questioning children despise that in us. As they should.

It moves me to tears to think that my daughter is beginning to hack her way through the great texts with a mingled sense of mystery and perplexity.

I can imagine life without pizza—though I would be really sorry—but I cannot imagine life without great works of literature to divert us, delight us, disturb us, de-center us, and demand of us that we do the hard work of being authentic.

About the time of her fourteenth birthday in August, I wrote my daughter a letter straight out of First Corinthians 13:11, "When I was a child, I spoke as a child, I understood as a child, I thought as a child: but when I became a man, I put away childish things."

For a variety of reasons, I try to write her a couple of old-fashioned, hand-written letters per week. In this letter, I strongly urged her to begin reading the great books, made the best case for serious literature that a fourteen-year-old was likely to listen through, and offered several incentives for her to read such books with passionate commitment. I made a short list of the sorts of texts I had in mind: *Huck Finn*, *Robinson Crusoe*, *Their Eyes Were Watching God*, *Gulliver's Travels*, *My Antonia*. I did not think to put F. Scott Fitzgerald on the list. I had not read *The Great Gatsby* in thirty years.

I love our children's capacity to surprise us.

What does *The Great Gatsby* mean to a fourteen-year-old who is just beginning to understand that in the adult world there is a set of dynamics that she didn't even know existed two years ago?

As she makes the slow chemical metamorphosis from girl to young woman, from child to adult, from innocence to experience, she must have so much on her mind that nobody else—perhaps especially not her parents—can help her understand.

I reread *The Great Gatsby* last week, because the greatest gift we can give to a fellow reader is to read the same book on parallel runways. I found it a little thin in middle age, but I recognized its greatness and on every page I could almost, just about see my daughter tiptoeing like Alice in Wonderland or Dorothy in Oz. In those alone but not lonely hours, she was over the rainbow, and she was looking at the world through a lens she has never worn before.

She tells me that her class will be reading Dickens' *Great Expectations* later in the semester and Homer's *Odyssey* in about a month. Can there be anything more wonderful than that? That alone justifies public education. *Great Expectations* is one of my top five novels in the world, and Dickens is my number one author.

Better that her language arts teacher get her started on that than that her papa ruin the possibility of Dickens by over-selling him at the outset. I very much hope she reads the *Odyssey* in a prose translation, because you have to come to terms with it as a story before you are even half-ready to spend the rest of your life dancing with it as one of the world's four or five greatest poems and works of art.

Thomas Jefferson famously wrote to John Adams: "I cannot live without books." Right as always. *10/4/08*

This one is strangely moving to me as I reread it several years after I wrote it. Awakening into adulthood is the first great mystery.

So How Would You Change

the US Constitution?

In a few weeks, I am going to attend a Great Conversations program in Helena, Montana, wherein people sign up for dozens of conversation tables according to their interests and tastes. One table might be about the "Buffalo Commons" idea and another about "The Best Movie of All Time." The assignment I received today is to lead a discussion about "The Next American Constitution." I need your help.

Thomas Jefferson believed that we ought to tear up the US Constitution once every nineteen or so years, on the principle that "the earth belongs to the living not the dead." This splendid radical idea always gets a negative reaction when I try to make the case for it. Most Americans shudder as they try to imagine what a Constitutional Convention would look like in an age of tabloid 24-7 media, lobbying groups with virtually infinite funds and sophistication, and a public that is more interested in NASCAR than natural rights, more informed about Britney Spears than Great Britain.

Fair enough. But for the next few minutes, please ask yourself what you would change in the American Constitution if you had the power and wisdom of Solon, or for that matter Alexander Hamilton.

Here are a few possibilities.

The Electoral College. The Electoral College was created to serve as a filtering mechanism. By the time of the Constitutional Convention of 1787, many of the founders believed we needed to step back from the democratic principles of 1776 and create a more conservative social compact. Most of the founders had little, if any, respect for the common people of the country, Alexander Hamilton's "rabble, the beast." They were uncomfortable letting the people elect their own president, so they created the Electoral College to serve as a kind of College of Cardinals. The people would be permitted to elect electors, but the electors would have the authority to elect any president they chose. The system has broken down several times, and it makes thoughtful people wonder if they really live in a democratic republic. Perhaps we could clarify its purposes or just eliminate it altogether.

Impeachment. In my opinion, the 1787 impeachment (removal) mechanism is one of the principal flaws of the Constitution. There is a reason why there never has been a successful impeachment of a president or a Supreme Court justice. The bar was set too high. Either the number of votes needed for conviction needs to be lowered to something below a two-thirds majority in the Senate or (more sensibly) the criteria for removal should be widened beyond "high crimes and misdemeanors." Perhaps it should be possible to impeach a president for "gross ineptitude" or "unconscionable stubbornness" or "fundamentally losing the confidence of the American people." If we haven't successfully impeached a single president in a run of forty-three—a list that includes James Buchanan, Millard Fillmore, Richard Nixon and, er … Warren Harding—clearly the bar has been set too high.

The Second Amendment. I know we live in gun country (at the start of hunting season) and I am not, I repeat, not a gun critic. But given the almost incredible development in weapons technology since 1787, it might be useful to debate and clarify our national attitude toward gun access. After all, in Madison's time a high-tech weapon was a single-shot musket that took a minimum of twenty-five seconds to reload. Using such weapons (the weapons of the Second Amendment), the killers at Columbine High School (April 20, 1999) and Virginia Tech (April 16, 2007) would have been able to squeeze off one or at most two rounds before they were overpowered by their peers. At some point, technological developments represent a difference no longer of degree but of kind. It might be interesting to decide how the country really feels about guns as the twenty-first century begins. And where are our militias?

War powers. The founders, who lived in a three mph world, determined to muzzle the dogs of war and prevent presidential mania by insisting that the power to declare war lay exclusively with Congress, in fact, in the House of Representatives. Even Jefferson, the pacifist third president, found it impossible to respond to the rapidly changing world situation while wearing such a constitutional strait jacket. After World War II, the executive branch has effectively swallowed up the Constitution's war powers, irrespective of the occasional charade of the president seeking congressional authorization for war. Given that we now live in a world that travels at 186,000 miles per second, or at least at the speed of a ballistic missile, we ought to craft a new war powers doctrine that gives the president the constitutional flexibility he or she needs, at the same time that it provides Congress enough authority to prevent executive recklessness. It won't be easy, but the present arrangement is disingenuous and dangerous.

Judicial term limits. As you know, judicial officers, once appointed by the president and confirmed by the Senate, serve for life on "good behavior." Though the principle of judicial independence makes sense, life tenure was a bad idea even in the early national period. Of life-tenured judges, Jefferson famously said, "few die and none resign." In Jefferson's time, in an age before antibiotics, life expectancy was a little more than half of what it is today. Today, a man or woman appointed in their forties can expect to live (and therefore serve on the bench) for forty, maybe even fifty years. That's too much power too long in the hands of one individual. It might be worth setting a twenty- or thirty-year cap on judicial terms, or having a vote of confidence or no confidence every fifteen years or so.

It might be useful, too, to take advantage of a constitutional revision to remove some things that now are regarded as embarrassments. Although slavery is never mentioned by name in the Constitution, it is addressed (and perpetuated) eight times in the course of the document. The most notorious of these is the three-fifths clause, which counted every five Negro slaves as three for the purposes of apportionment and representation. At the moment of its crafting, this was a necessary compromise. That was two hundred twenty years ago. Now it's a blot on our national honor.

If we assembled a new Constitutional Convention, we might wish it to take up such vexing and intractable issues as abortion, the future of the public lands of the American West, access to health care in an advanced industrial society, America's participation in international bodies like the U.N. and the International Courts of Justice, women's rights, and the sovereignties of Indian tribes, which Jefferson's cousin, the great Chief Justice John Marshall, called "domestic dependent nations."

There are some constitutional theorists who believe the "Great Compromise" of July 16, 1787, apportioning House seats by population, but guaranteeing every state, no matter how small or lightly populated, an equal number of senators, is a violation of the principle of one person one vote, and that it permits determined minorities in the Senate to hold up the progress of a nation (a world power) of 300 million people. The famous compromise gives little North Dakota, with only 642,000 people, as much power in the Senate as California, with its whopping 38 million people. In other words, from a Senatorial point of view, each North Dakotan has as much power as fifty-nine Californians.

As a proud resident of the fourth least populated state, I would prefer now to change the subject. And please understand, I am not advocating gun control. *10/3/07*

Given the sheer insanity of corporate and individual Citizens United v. Federal Election Commission *(January 21, 2010), it would seem to virtually everyone who loves America that we should amend the constitution to prevent such anti-democratic distortion of the political process.*

At the time this book went to press, North Dakota had a population of about 685,000 people, the largest in our brief history.

For the Love of Books

I was sitting in my favorite reading spot the other night sipping tea and im-
bibing sentences from Theodore Roosevelt's *Rough Riders,* his 1899 account
of his heroics in Cuba. It's a wonderful book, written by a man for whom the
glass was always, even in the hard times, not only half but 98 percent full. It
is a surprisingly modest book, and generous to all the others who contributed
to the success of the expedition, though one of TR's friendliest critics, Finley
Peter Dunne, quipped that it should have been titled "Alone in Cuba."

It was one of those lovely occasions when we read purely for pleasure,
in a meditative frame of mind, at leisure, pausing to reflect or muse or
merely gaze off into space as often as the spirit moves us. The passage
I was reading indicated that, in the fetid jungle near Santiago, between
battles, in one of the headiest and riskiest moments of his sixty-year march,
Roosevelt was carefully listening to the life stories of the men he had re-
cruited for the First US Volunteer Cavalry. I looked up in silence for a few
minutes, then said to myself, this is one measure of Roosevelt's greatness.
He listened to the rough chaps with whom he shared a campfire in a war
zone. He remembered their stories. And he wrote about them in his book.

I happened to be reading Roosevelt at that moment, but later that night
I read a chapter from Edward Abbey's *Desert Solitaire,* a slender paperback that has been glowering at me from my nightstand for the past couple
of months. *Desert Solitaire* is an account of Abbey's time as a ranger in
Arches National Park in Utah in the late 1950s. I pulled it off the shelf in
September with the intention of reading it immediately, for some urgent
reason that I can no longer remember. Life intervened, but now, I'm not
sure why, I picked it up when I was winding down for the night, and it spoke
to me, all the way from Moab, 1,061.23 miles and half a century away. For
half an hour, the book and my imagination took me right into Abbey's
wind-rattled trailer in a remote part of Arches National Park, where, from
the corner, I watched him pour whiskey into his coffee and rave poetically
about the misuse of our public lands.

Think of the magic of books.

A white boy and grown black slave float down the Mississippi River to tease
out the possibilities of American freedom. A troubled Catholic priest tacks
ninety-five doctrinal propositions on the door of Castle Church in Wittenberg,
Germany, on Oct. 31, 1517, and changes the world. A mentally-ill sea captain
scours the high seas in search of a white whale he regards as evil.

Think of the infinite variety of worlds that lie behind the covers of books,
waiting patiently to be explored.

One million books are published worldwide every year now, a quarter of
them in the United States and Great Britain alone. Saudi Arabia publishes

fewer than 4,000 books per year, Egypt—once the most civilized nation on Earth—merely 2,215. Somewhere in the world, a new book is published every 30 seconds. As Mark Twain might put it, reports of the death of the book (in favor of the Age of Media) have been very much exaggerated.

> **"I have never thought about it until this moment, but I have more books than I have anything else, and aside from some photos and intensely personal objects, I cannot imagine anything I would less rather lose in a fire."**

Most books look more or less alike. The person sitting across the coffee shop holds a book. What is it? What world is she exploring this morning? It could be the Bible, but it might be the Quran or the *Bhagavad Gita* or the *Analects of Confucius*. Think of how different those four portals are, and yet they are all sacred books, and they are all about how we ought to align our souls with the divine energies of the universe. She might be reading Dickens' *Bleak House*, threading her way through the dank labyrinth of the London legal system in the mid-nineteenth century. But she might just as well be reading a book about breast cancer survivors or a how-to book about quilting. She might be reading *Charlotte's Web,* musing sweetly about her childhood and wondering if she will ever have a child of her own. But she might also be reading *Mein Kampf.* It could be a Danielle Steele romance, but it also could be Homer's *Iliad* or the autobiography of Lee Iacocca.

There is a scene in Bruce Beresford's film *Black Robe* that reminds us of the magic of the written word. *Black Robe* (1991) explores the coming of Jesuit missionaries to the Huron Indians of New France in the seventeenth century. In an effort to convince the skeptical Indians of the truth of Christianity, Father Laforgue tells the Huron chief that he can transmit any sentence the chief chooses to utter across the village without sound. The chief speaks a sentence. Laforgue writes it out on a sheet of paper. They walk to the other end of the camp, where Laforgue silently hands the white paper, with its curious black squigglings, to a colleague. The second priest reads out the sentence precisely as it was first uttered. The Huron chief jumps back in wonder and trepidation. These really are medicine men, these black robes.

We take all of this for granted, but, if you think about it, it is the most amazing thing in the world.

There are 26 letters and a handful of punctuation marks in the English alphabet. They can be combined to form more than 500,000 words (most of them technical). The greatest of English writers, Shakespeare, had a vocabulary of 29,066 different words. Francis Bacon used more than 20,000 words in his published works. Milton, the best educated of all English writers, used fewer than 8,000 different words in his immense output of poetry and prose.

The average American has a working vocabulary of about 2,500 words.

It's all about how writers combine those 26 letters and the words they are able to muster.

I have thousands of books in my library, most of which I have not read, of course. I have never thought about it until this moment, but I have more books than I have anything else, and aside from some photos and intensely personal objects, I cannot imagine anything I would less rather lose in a fire.

And all I have to do to leave my sorry life behind and enter into hundreds, even thousands, of alternative universes, most of which I have never seen and some of which I could never myself imagine, is to pluck one of those books off the shelf, open the door that is its cover and hurtle across the portal as magically as Harry Potter boards Hogswarts Express 5972 at the prosaic King's Cross Station in London.

Tonight, it's James Boswell's *Life of Dr. Johnson*, if my mood holds.
12/15/07

AT LEAST WE KNOW WE'RE FREE

So how was your Fourth of July?

Because my daughter was otherwise occupied this year, I allowed myself, in a moment of weakness, to be talked into a very long auto journey into the heart of Idaho. My friend David convinced me that we could attend four meetings he had set up along the Lewis and Clark trail, one on the Fourth of July in Missoula, but also attend the fiftieth birthday party of one of my best friends, and get into proximity with a Weber grill somewhere in the American West. All on modestly priced $4.18 per gallon gasoline.

So we packed up the truck and we drove to Lewiston.

Although I love North Dakota unreservedly, I nevertheless believe that, if there were only one state, it would have to be Montana. Generally speaking, the closer you can get to Yellowstone National Park on the Fourth of July, the better. Something about the big sky, the purple mountain majesty, the many free-flowing rivers and that never-far-from-the-surface anti-government edge makes Montana the heart of the heart of the country.

When you get deep into Montana, all the usual irritants—Osama bin Laden, the presidential race, Washington, DC, the IRS, Wall Street—seem far, far away. Montana is America's savannah, its Serengeti, its wide and empty outback, so far from the centers of power and commerce that it has a kind of primordial purity. The mountains and the plains intermingle in Montana better than in any other place in the American West. And two of the world's great rivers flow through it: the Yellowstone, which flows out of Yellowstone National Park, and the Missouri, which has feeder creeks there, too. The rivers arc in such different ways through Montana, and then meet rather solemnly just inside North Dakota west of Williston.

The unbelievably beautiful Yellowstone River was running bank full as we made the long drive from Bismarck to Bozeman. I have never seen the Yellowstone run so full into July. No wonder Lake Sakakawea is up twelve feet. Somehow, it filled me with pride to see the river run so abundantly.

We thought of William Clark, Sakakawea, York and Charbonneau (plus others) floating down the Yellowstone in the summer of 1806, essentially on a lark, killing a buffalo per day for supper, the canoes lashed together like America's first pontoon boat. It was probably the most relaxed period of the entire 7,689-mile expedition—for Clark. Long-suffering Meriwether Lewis, meanwhile, was up on the Marias northwest of Great Falls doing work of almost unbearable stressfulness.

Clark lived forever. Lewis committed suicide in 1809.

It takes a long time to drive across Montana, even with an essentially unenforced speed limit. In any Montana transit, it is quite possible to talk about the meaning of life until you are sick of the meaning of life and begin to recall and analyze episodes of *The Andy Griffith Show.*

By the time the sun set, after an insanely long day in the car, all we wanted in this world was a beer and a cheeseburger. That and nothing more. We had not eaten all day. We took the exit into a place called Big Timber, Montana. As an admirer of the twenty-sixth president, Theodore Roosevelt, one of the "Rushmore four," I regarded this as a very good sign. Big timber, big stick, big cheeseburger. We were in Big Timber to meet the daughter of a famous American historian for a beer and talk about a project, in a famous old hotel widely beloved for its fine food.

It was one of those places with a real or an imitation tin ceiling high above, a long beautiful wooden bar backed with a gigantic mirror, hunting trophies above each booth, and wisenheimer sayings on placards scattered across the walls. Everyone in the bar looked like they had just run a marathon or canoed to the source of the Missouri River. They all wore high-end recreational sports wear of the kind you see in Telluride or Aspen. The place was hopping. We were two hungry guys from North Dakota. It was still light outside.

We chose a booth. There was a moose hanging over our heads like the sword of Damocles. On the basis of this, we decided it would only be appropriate to sample Moose Drool beer. Our spirits were high. Perhaps we were road-giddy.

The waitress came. She was smiling. Our wallets were filled with rapidly devaluating American dollars. We were thirsty. And, my goodness, how hungry we suddenly were. "What can I get you?" she asked. "Burgers and beer!" said I. "It's America's birthday!"

She frowned in a nervous way. "Oh," she said, "you see, the kitchen closes at 9 p.m. and you can plainly see it's 9:10 p.m."

We pleaded. We begged. We nearly wept. She made a show, like a used car salesman, of going back to the kitchen to see if there were any possibility of a pair of all-American cheeseburgers on the eve of the Fourth of July. She returned with a set jaw. She could, if we ordered it immediately, stir up a couple of dinner salads and perhaps a bread stick.

"What sort of nation have we become?" asked Dave in a bewildered and crestfallen way. "If Jefferson had known this," said I, "he might have toned down the preamble of the Declaration of Independence to lower American expectations. For when you cannot get a burger on the third of July, at 9:10 p.m., in Montana, then in what sense can we still speak of the pursuit of happiness?" Somewhat bitterly, Dave said, "So the terrorists have won, after all."

In time, a couple of limp-looking salads came. We ate them slowly and without pleasure like a couple of valetudinarians on their last earthly journey. The carnivores all around us looked down on us with pity and contempt. I wanted to write out a cardboard sign: "I'll gladly pay you $2,000 Tuesday for a hamburger today."

"When you get deep into Montana, all the usual irritants—Osama bin Laden, the Presidential race, Washington, DC, the IRS, Wall Street—seem far, far away. Montana is America's savannah, its Serengeti, its wide and empty outback, so far from the centers of power and commerce that it has a kind of primordial purity."

As we sat there glumly, mumbling that perhaps George III was not such a bad despot after all, because at least under tyranny you can get a sandwich, the four waitresses of the joint kept emerging from the kitchen ostentatiously hefting large platters heaping with hamburgers. Almost every other table in the restaurant took delivery of pyramids of tall and steaming Fourth of July cheeseburgers (and Liberty Fries!), like a scene out of a Popeye cartoon, while we nibbled our carrots and tried to convince ourselves that a crouton, rightly understood, is really just a very small stale hamburger bun. We asked our waitress why we were the only people in the establishment who were not permitted to get burgers. The other patrons had placed their orders, we were told, well before 9 p.m. We asked if it were necessary for the staff to carry those platters within five or six inches of our famished and flaring nostrils as they delivered them to other hungry guests. We received a lecture about "standard food traffic lanes."

At ten o'clock, as we stared down at the table and drooled into our Moose Drool and talked about the sorts of frustrations the Unabomber must have endured before he cracked, Big Timber, Montana, administered the un-kindest cut of all. Almost everyone had gone home. Things were winding down. Then one of the waitresses came out of the kitchen with a plate, on which was poised the most beautiful cheeseburger in human history. She carried it to the bar, sat down, gave us a kind of "Montana attitude" look, and ate it in front of us.

After that, the Yellowstone was just a ditch, the Rocky Mountains mere protuberances, and the Fourth of July just another Friday in mid-summer. We left our sparklers, unopened, in the parking lot.

Next year, we'll have a strategy.   *7/13/08*

This one caused a little stir. Although this was clearly written tongue-in-cheek, we received a painfully defensive note from the hotel, and a rebuke from someone in Bismarck who wanted us to know that rules are rules. If you write, about a hamburger, "So the terrorists have won, after all," you would seem to be in the realm of humor, not complaint.

PEOPLE

The Importance of Friendship

in an Age of Incivility

At a time when the residual civility of American life appears to be collapsing, I want to write today in praise of friendship. I don't know how many people we get to know over the course of a lifetime. Probably it numbers somewhere in the hundreds. I'd divide that pool into the following categories: acquaintances; associates; "friends"; and true friends.

We routinely misuse the term "friend," spreading it like thin frosting over a range of relationships that are clearly something less. I regard friendship as a sacramental relationship—at the center of it there is some deep pool of affinity and good will and affirmation and joy. In my hierarchy, the best thing in life is being a parent, but nobody can deny that there are many, many sleepless nights. The second best thing is friendship, where there are no sleepless nights, except when you are too young to know when to quit partying.

Third best thing: Ginsu knives.

Friends are the ones we take the time to seek out. If you are not seeking them out, but just happily running into them from time to time, they are probably not friends. Friendship, like all important relationships, is hard work. In recent years I have become such a pathetic workaholic that I have neglected some of my friendships. That has lessened the joy of my life, and it often leaves me self-disappointed.

Friends are the ones who make our souls sing, the ones who affirm us even when we don't deserve it, who stand by us when "you have really done it this time," and who authentically cheer our successes and commiserate our failures and losses.

I'm with the Christian writer and lay theologian C.S. Lewis that, on the whole, friendship is a higher form of human relationship than romantic love. Love, at its best, provides ecstasies and intimacies that are uniquely satisfying, but they are hard to sustain. I know a fair number of good marriages, but not many great ones, and I have found—I hope this doesn't sound too dark—that marriage at times seems to be an institution that licenses people to treat each other with deliberate hostility and emotional indifference. The contractual permanence of marriage seems to encourage some of us to bring our least best selves to the equation. Knowing how hard it is to get out of a marriage—not to mention economically devastating—and fearing that the grass on the other side of the fence is mostly leafy spurge, keeps a lot of people in bad marriages.

It's the voluntariness of friendship that makes it so rich and delightful. You don't have to be together. You have to want to be together, and that makes all the difference.

It was C.S. Lewis, I think, who articulated the distinction between friends and lovers with the greatest insight. "Though we can have erotic love and friendship for the same person," he wrote, "nothing is less like a friendship than a love affair.... Lovers are normally face to face absorbed in each other; friends side by side absorbed in some common interest." Almost all the best adventures of my life have been side by side rather than face to face.

I had dinner the other night with one of my oldest friends. We've now known each other for a full forty years. We haven't yet reached the point in our friendship where we compare our current medication regimens—that's my definition of when old age begins. It was pure relaxed joy on a perfect summer night. We've long since ceased having anything to prove to each another. The pool of good will and shared experiences is so large that everything felt right with the world for a couple of hours. We know the contours of each other's minds and characters all too well, and yet we still find each other interesting, and want each other's "take" on current events, mutual acquaintances, cultural occurrences, the present state and future course of North Dakota, and the Badlands. Other true friends were present, and—as they say—a good time was had by all, but there was something deeply rewarding (though hard to articulate) in being with someone with whom there has been such a long and winding journey over so much common ground, with serious losses along the way, and no end yet in sight.

> "Friends are the ones who make our souls sing, the ones who affirm us even when we don't deserve it, who stand by us when "you have really done it this time," and who authentically cheer our successes and commiserate our failures and losses."

The best friendships are ones that have involved unforgettable adventures. My friend Douglas and I were arrested as possible spies in the old Yugoslavia—in 1977—and for about forty-eight hours, we did not know if our adventure would wind up being called "Much Ado about Nothing" or "Midnight Express," in which a young American winds up in a nightmarish Turkish prison. Though our lives have taken us in different directions, neither of us will quite let the friendship go, and no matter what else happens "we will always have Dubrovnik." We don't even have to talk about it anymore—though we do—because it marked our lives more than almost anything either of us has done. It doesn't hurt, of course, that we did not wind up in the Turkish prison.

Some friendships, like some campfires, require continuous stoking. Others have some kind of magic invisible fuel, and seem effortlessly able to pick up where they left off. Some friendships affirm us as we are, warts and all, and others call upon us to rise to our better selves. Most friendships find their level early on and never change—we often lock them into a certain set of interests and practices, and call them back to the old comfort level when they threaten to change. Others evolve, and like the on-again, off-again friendship between John Adams and Thomas Jefferson, find their fullest expression later in life, after the toxic cocktail of testosterone (or estrogen), ego competitiveness, and ambition loosen their grip.

That is my dream of the future. *8/8/11*

This is one of my friend's favorite columns.

TRYING TO SEE ROOSEVELT WITH FRESH EYES

I've been trying to figure out Theodore Roosevelt. You think you know something, but really how much do we finally know about the soul of any other human being, historical or contemporary? Or for that matter, how much do we really know about ourselves? It's so important to step back now and then from what we think we know (including those closest to us) and try to look at life with fresh eyes. We never really know anything in a final sense. We only know what we know at this moment.

Who was Theodore Roosevelt? What sort of man was he? What made him tick? What's the key to understanding him? Why is he important to us? What was his achievement? What is his legacy? How can we benefit from studying his life and outlook and achievement?

These questions could take up the rest of someone's life.

It's very easy to caricature Roosevelt as a kind of shrill whirlwind in spurs barking out heroic platitudes and doing reckless things on the slightest impulse. He's like the Tasmanian Devil in the cartoons or Jim Carrey in *The Mask*. It would be easier to combat this caricature if Roosevelt had not succumbed to it with such regularity. It is hard sometimes to take him fully seriously. This has made him a figure of myth, a legend, but it has in many ways prevented us from coming to terms with his intellectual and political greatness, and his personal integrity, which may be the most pronounced of any American president. In the end, we see Roosevelt as a comic figure, when he was so much more than that.

Last night, I began reading a book called the *Era of Theodore Roosevelt* by George E. Mowry. It's an old book (1958). I doubt that it now gets read five times a year anywhere in the world. Maybe less. I thought it would be useful, but dull. It has turned out to be marvelous. Mowry reminds us of just how unusual Roosevelt was. Mowry provides a five-page character sketch of Roosevelt that I now regard as the best short analysis of him ever written.

I believe it is fair to say that Theodore Roosevelt was one of the most extraordinary men who ever lived in America and that he, and he alone, is big enough for the magnitude of Mount Rushmore. Jefferson was a quiet, self-effacing man who would be embarrassed to be carved on a mountain. Washington and Lincoln were statesmen who played down their greatness. But the bigger TR became in the world's eyes, the more he liked it.

We know the facts. Roosevelt was born in 1858. He died in 1919. He was the twenty-sixth president of the United States. He lived in western Dakota Territory for a couple of years off and on, and thought of making the Dakota Badlands a more permanent home. He was flattered when folks speculated that he might be the first US senator from North Dakota. Then, he remarried and his political prospects in the New York-Washington corridor brightened. Sometime in 1886 or 1887, Roosevelt took life in Dakota out of the realm of possibility and put it instead into the scrapbook of nostalgia. Passing through Medora in 1900, he said, "It was here that the romance of my life began." I love that.

"A privileged and frail eastern intellectual with some off-putting personal traits and a love of opera, birds, and foreign literature comes to the lawless and raw frontier, and in the course of several years of uninhibited—even gleeful—immersion into frontier life is fundamentally transformed into the nation's first and most genuine cowboy president."

We take Roosevelt's western sojourn for granted. It is part of the core mythology of North Dakota. But think about it. A privileged and frail eastern intellectual with some off-putting personal traits and a love of opera, birds and foreign literature comes to the lawless and raw frontier, and in the course of several years of uninhibited—even gleeful—immersion into frontier life is fundamentally transformed into the nation's first and most genuine cowboy president.

Think Bill Clinton could do it? Remember John Kerry shouldering a shotgun in his camouflage fatigues? Lyndon Johnson faked (or at least fudged) his World War II record.

When the Spanish-American War broke out in 1898, Roosevelt, who was serving as the assistant secretary of the Navy, resigned his post, gathered up a scruffy company of volunteers from around the nation, and then worked with all of his might to get himself to the front in Cuba in time to be in a serious battle. His biggest fear in the late spring of 1898 was that the war would end before he could get his Rough Riders into some bloody action.

Think about that.

By the sheer force of his will, Roosevelt managed to get his "crowded hour" in Cuba on July 1, 1898. He later called it "the great day of my life." All eyewitnesses agreed that he led the assault up Kettle Hill with courage and even recklessness, and that it would be possible for a reasonable observer to conclude that he was trying to get himself killed or seriously wounded. He was carrying a pistol that had been salvaged from the wreckage of the battleship Maine. Roosevelt killed at least one Spanish soldier that day.

To understand this, imagine if, when the war in Iraq broke out, Vice President Cheney had resigned his post to go to the front to lead actual troops in an actual battle, or Sen. Barack Obama or Rep. Tom Tancredo. Imagine if Donald Rumsfeld had resigned as secretary of defense to personally lead an assault on Baghdad.

Roosevelt thrust himself into the war. He exhibited extraordinary bravery. He killed his enemy. And yet he was a rich and well-born man who was, when the war began, doing important work in the Navy office. If he had stayed there, advancing the American cause from his desk, sending telegrams to field commanders, dispatching coal to ships and supplies to the heat-bedraggled troops in Cuba, reporting naval affairs to Congress, nobody would have dreamed of questioning his patriotism or his integrity. In fact, his chief, John D. Long, the secretary of the Navy, insisted that Roosevelt stay at his desk where he could do the most good for the war effort. President William McKinley, not once but twice, appealed to Roosevelt to stay in Washington, DC, where his extraordinary energies were vitally needed, and not rush off to war, where he might get himself killed and where his contribution to the war effort could not possibly equal his administrative contribution. Roosevelt's wife, Edith, was recovering from a dangerous operation. She pleaded with TR to stay home to help, and not hurtle off and maybe render her a widow and their six children fatherless.

Here are some questions to ask yourself. If three armed and violent ruffians stole your car, would you hunt them down in really foul weather, sneak up on them in a camp or at a motel, disarm them at gunpoint, arrest them and then spend several entirely sleepless days marching them forty-five miles over gumbo and mud to the sheriff? Would you take your chance with Red Headed Mike Finnegan?

If a drunken bully menaced you in a bar, holding a loaded pistol in each hand, and everyone else was cowering and flattering and trying to avoid eye contact, would you stand up and try to knock him out with a punch on the snout?

I'd just wet my pants and beg.   *7/28/07*

Kevin Locke Offers Hope in Songs

I had the enormous good fortune the other day to sit like a mouse in a corner and listen to two of North Dakota's artistic masters at work. Kevin Locke (Tokeya Inajin) is a Lakota flute player, hoop dancer, storyteller and educator, and David Swenson is the founding director of the award-winning Makoche Recoding studio in downtown Bismarck.

Locke, whose Lakota name means "The First to Arise," lives on the Standing Rock Indian Reservation, but he performs all over the world. Swenson, who lives in Bismarck, has spent the past eleven years recording American Indian songs and stories and encouraging the preservation and dissemination of traditional Indian oral culture.

They were talking about the sun dance that is held every year near the Sitting Bull camp on the Grand River at Standing Rock. There was something hushed and magical in their conversation about the central religious ceremony of the Lakota people, which was banned by the United States government between 1904 and 1977 (so much for the American constitutional guarantee of religious freedom for all).

Locke is as unassuming a man as you are ever likely to meet. He has a shy, "who, me?" soul, and every word that comes out of him comes from both his mind and his heart. He speaks with a gentleness that is intoxicating. And he makes it clear that he regards himself as the luckiest and least likely of men to have been gifted with the talents he shares—humbly and in good cheer—with the world. He's performed in eighty-five countries, so far.

As Locke described the sun dance, I could see the tall cottonwood embedded at the center of the dance circle, with a medicine nest in the upper branches, prayer bundles tied lower on the trunk. Around the dance circle, an elaborately constructed arbor. Outside the circle, drummers seated around a large buffalo-hide drum recreating the heartbeat of the planet.

Birds clustered in the cottonwoods nearby listening to the concert of drum, that high-pitched songline of the Lakota, and the eagle bone whistles. The dancers, fasting, sleepless, taking not even water during the four days of the ceremony, moving against the earth hour after hour. And on the periphery, food preparation for non-dancers, feasting, prayer, community, and—for some—courtship.

What makes Locke so amazing is that he is willing to talk about something this sacred, in a generous and open, albeit very careful way. You can see, as he plays out his sentences one by one, that he is saying that which is appropriate for outsiders to hear, but in a way that does not make them feel like outsiders. He is talking about something that does not belong to non-Indians, indeed at which non-Indians are not generally welcome, in a manner that would not upset the most separatist of Lakota insiders. That's a form of genius.

Swenson is one of those rare non-Indians who is not only permitted, but actually invited to take his place at the sun dance. After almost twenty years of quiet, deeply respectful work with Indian drum groups, singers, dancers and storytellers, Swenson has built up a large fund of goodwill in Indian country. He has credibility, in part because the Indian community knows that there is not an exploitative bone in his body.

On the walls of the Makoche studios, you will see photographs of Keith Bear, Annie Humphrey and Mary Louise Defender Wilson, but also Dylan and the Beatles. Swenson is part musicologist and part '60s rocker. He's best known for his Indian record label, but more recently he has begun to get attention as a talented videographer. He wants to make documentaries.

Locke is a world-class Indian flutist and he played a pivotal role in the early success of Makoche. Swenson regards Locke as "the greatest traditional Indian flute player in the world."

Locke played a couple of songs on two different flutes at the Makoche session the other night. They were hauntingly beautiful, partly because of the reedy-raspy quality of the Indian flute in the hands of a master.

I asked him how long the flute has been an important vehicle for plains Indian music. The journals of Lewis and Clark do not, so far as I know, ever mention flute music, though the expedition encountered more than fifty distinct tribes. He explained that the flute is an essentially private instrument, usually played by an individual who was stationed at some distance from the village. Lewis and Clark, he explained, would have been treated to more public music: drums, what the journal keepers called "tambourines," and rattles.

"Flute songs are a little like country-western music," Locke said. "Often enough they are about someone who loves a woman, but she actually loves someone else. A lot of flute music is about unrequited love." You picked a fine time to leave me, Lucille.

> "You can see, as he plays out his sentences one by one, that he is saying that which it is appropriate for outsiders to hear but in a way that does not make them feel like outsiders. He is talking about something that does not belong to non-Indians, indeed at which non-Indians are not generally welcome, in a manner that would not upset the most separatist of Indians insiders. That's a form of genius."

A handful of individuals come along from time to time who are really touched by grace. Locke is one of those exceedingly rare people who find the lyrical, the whimsical, the life-affirming all around them, in a world that it would be possible to see as horribly fallen. He has a bit of the Renaissance humanist Erasmus' "wise fool" about him, or Jack Kerouac's "holy goof," both of those terms being wholly positive in connotation. He smiles more than anyone I know and his laugh—ready, unrestrained and unforced—is one of the most restorative sounds I have heard.

Makoche Records has a CD of Locke playing historically important flutes at the Sitting Bull camp on Standing Rock. The album is called *The First Flute*. It's the recording for which Swenson seems most proud.

If you have never seen Locke's hoop dance, you have one of life's great experiences ahead of you. Accompanied by Lakota music, often enough the traditional drum, Locke gathers up hoops, one by one, with his feet alone, and then twirls them simultaneously on his arms, on his legs, on the balls of his feet, around his neck and torso, in elaborate lyrical choreography, without ever pausing or missing a beat in his Lakota dance.

He works with twenty-eight hoops, one for every day of the lunar cycle, and as the dance progresses he configures the hoops, now one, now four, now nine, now eighteen, to represent clouds, flowers, butterflies, the sun, moon, the eagle and other natural phenomena of the Great Plains. By the end all twenty-eight hoops are dancing (almost by their own volition) around his body as he dances on the prairie grass. It's as close to the literal meaning of "incredible" as anything I have seen.

Twenty years ago I had the honor of spending a full summer working with Locke in the Great Plains Chautauqua. He concluded each of his presentations with the hoop dance. The audience would gather in a big circle on the grass outside the tent.

It was marvelous to look around at a couple of hundred faces as he formed more and more sophisticated hoop figures in a dance that lasted ten minutes or more. People laughed in wonder, and cried the way you do when you see something profoundly authentic in life, and their mouths literally hung open in awe. At the end, in his self-deprecating way, Locke would clutch his knees and gasp, "Anyone know CPR?"

Great Britain has an ingenuous dual system of leadership. There is a prime minister to run the government (Tony Blair) and a monarch to represent the nation (Elizabeth II). In France, the prime minister manages legislation, but a president handles the ceremonial functions of the nation.

This would be a good system for North Dakota. Let Gov. John Hoeven (or Schafer or Heitkamp or Satrom) legislate, but let's nominate Locke as Chancellor or First Citizen of the sovereign state of North Dakota. If he were our ambassador-at-large to the planet, North Dakota would get loving attention wherever he went, and our image in the world's arena would soar.

Think of it: a gifted, graceful, wise, and extraordinarily articulate Lakota artist as the poster child for who we are and what we prize. *1/27/07*

THE GREATNESS OF NORTH DAKOTA

GOVERNOR WILLIAM L. GUY

Last Tuesday marked the fortieth anniversary of the Kent State Massacre. Next weekend marks the fortieth anniversary of the peace march on the ABM missile site at Nekoma, ND. On May 15–16, 1970, approximately 1,500 people, mostly college students, gathered at the Stanley R. Mickelsen Safeguard complex to protest nuclear proliferation, the escalation of the Cold War, and—of course—Vietnam.

William L. Guy served as the governor of North Dakota between 1960 and 1972. The ABM protest march happened on his watch.

For that we have reason to be enormously grateful.

> "Peaceful demonstrations are in the best tradition of this country's democratic process."
>
> —William L. Guy

On May 12, a nervous and hostile US Justice Department sent out a riot control team to meet with Guy and other North Dakota officials. Guy regarded the federal agents as high-handed and patronizing, but-in his calm and competent way—he assured them that he would take adequate steps to prevent things from getting out of hand at Nekoma.

The shootings at Kent State brought America to a kind of collective nervous breakdown in the days and weeks following May 4, 1970. Hundreds of colleges and universities were simply shut down for the rest of the semester. The largest student strike in American history erupted across the nation, one million protestors for each of the four dead in Ohio. The war had come home to the American heartland. Every thoughtful American wondered—what next?

A few days before the march, Guy issued a statement of several hundred words to the people of North Dakota about how he intended to handle the situation. "I do not expect violence in this week's demonstrations," he said, "especially by those who point to the destructive waste of violence and war."

"Peaceful demonstrations are in the best tradition of this country's democratic process," he said. Guy explained that he was putting the North Dakota National Guard on "strategic weekend drill status" in northeastern North Dakota, but that the guardsmen would not be carrying ammunition.

The ABM peace march occurred less than two weeks after the catastrophe at Kent State. It is a study in contrasts. It reminds us of how important it is to elect leaders worthy of the sometimes-grave responsibilities with which we entrust them.

In Ohio, Governor Rhodes, campaigning for the US Senate as a champion of "law and order," went out of his way to condemn the Kent State students who were protesting President Nixon's invasion of Cambodia, thus widening the war he had pledged to wind down in the 1968 election. "They're worse than the brown shirts and the communist element and also the night riders and the vigilantes," Rhodes said.

In Ohio, John Rhodes (1) wrested control of the situation from the administration of Kent State University and informed university officials that he, not they, would handle the crisis; (2) demonized the protestors, ordered them not to demonstrate, and called them un-American; and (3) called out the National Guard, instructed them to take a hard line, and put bullets in their guns.

In North Dakota, Bill Guy (1) refused to demonize the protesters or condemn the demonstration, which he publicly defended as in the best tradition of American democracy; (2) made sure the National Guard was nearby, but instructed them, in his words, "not to interfere with the peaceful demonstration nor were they even to be present or visible along the assembly routes and at the ABM site;" (3) granted demonstrators permission to plant "peace trees" on the highway right-of-way near the ABM site; (4) and went to Grand Forks to meet personally with the students and faculty of UND, to listen to their concerns and to assure them that if they behaved responsibly they had nothing to fear.

Bill Guy listened rather than preached.

Because northeastern North Dakota was sodden from spring rains, Guy even instructed the National Guard to deploy two tow trucks driven by guardsmen in civilian clothes to pull vehicles out of ditches or farmers' driveways free of charge.

Civilian clothes.

Guy flew up to Grand Forks on May 13. He first met with about a dozen faculty members, who expressed their fears that the ABM march might spiral downward into another Kent State, then spoke with several hundred students in a UND dormitory complex. "The atmosphere," he writes in his memoir, *Where Seldom Was Heard A Discouraging Word ... Bill Guy Remembers,* "was tense and explosive." While he was at the lectern in the dormitory, a note was passed to the governor saying, "Attorney General John Mitchell wishes to talk with you." Guy assumed it was a joke, but immediately after the meeting returned the call.

You remember Attorney General John Mitchell, don't you? Mitchell (1913–1988) was Richard Nixon's campaign manager in 1968, then his tough-as-nails attorney general. The colorful champion of "law and order" later went to federal prison for his Watergate crimes.

When he got Bill Guy on the phone, Mitchell pressured the North Dakota governor to use the North Dakota National Guard to secure the ABM site. Guy flatly refused. It was a federal not a state facility, he said. Besides, he said, American citizens had a perfect right to engage in peaceful demonstrations.

The Attorney General then asked, "Do you plan to be at the demonstration site?"

Bill Guy replied, "Only if they need one more warm body to swell the crowd. You see, I too, protest the waste of tax money that the ABM represents."

At that the Attorney General of the United States said, "Oh my God," added an "expletive deleted," and hung up on the Governor of North Dakota.

The march on the Nekoma missile site was completely peaceful. The protestors planted trees, flew kites, and sat in a wheat field listening to poetry, free speech, and rock music. Nekoma had more in common with Woodstock than Kent State.

Experts who have studied that horrific month in American history say that our Gov. William L. Guy provided a "textbook case" of "precisely the right way to respond to a situation of this sort."

Thank you Governor Guy.   *5/9/10*

*I had the good fortune to make a documentary film on Bill Guy.
It was the work of the Dakota Institute of the Lewis & Clark Fort
Mandan Foundation. It's called* The Charisma of Competence:
The Achievement of William L. Guy.

IT'S NOT ABOUT ANY ONE RELIGION:

IT'S ABOUT FREEDOM OF RELIGION

I have great respect for freshman Minnesota Rep. Keith Ellison for taking the oath of office Jan. 4 on a Koran. Ellison, who was elected to represent Minnesotas 5th District on Nov. 7, is the first Muslim representative in American history. It's about time. There are more than 5 million Muslims in the United States.

And not just any Koran. In his private swearing-in ceremony, Ellison had the honor of placing his hand on a copy of the Islamic sacred text owned by Thomas Jefferson, America's greatest advocate of religious liberty. "I have sworn upon the altar of God eternal hostility against every form of tyranny over the mind of man," Jefferson wrote in 1800, after an election in which his own religious views were the subject of intense national debate. Jefferson was constantly accused of being an atheist. He was in fact a deist and a Unitarian. And he believed that it's none of your business.

There was a double solemnity to Ellison's oath-taking. Not only has he sworn to uphold the US Constitution on the book that matters most to his soul, but he has done so on a copy of that book owned by one of America's greatest individuals, the philosopher of the American dream, the religious thinker who gave us the phrase, "wall of separation between church and state."

The Koran was loaned to Ellison by the Library of Congress, which took delivery of Jefferson's immense private library (6,487 volumes) in 1815. Most of Jefferson's collection was burned in a Library of Congress fire in 1851. His Koran, fortunately, survived to play an important role in the ongoing debate about the place of religion in American public life.

Using Jefferson's Koran in his private congressional swearing-in ceremony was an act of real insight by Ellison, not to mention political shrewdness. In placing his hand on Jefferson's Koran, Ellison showed that he has a greater understanding of the fundamental values of the American tradition than do his critics, like Virginia Rep. Virgil Goode and talk show browbeater Sean Hannity, who argued that if you can take the oath on the Koran, how long will it be before someone wants to take the oath on *Mein Kampf*. It's only a matter of time, Sean!

Jefferson believed that religion is a purely private matter and that a person is entitled to believe anything she or he wishes if it does not lead to illegal activity. "It does me no injury for my neighbor to say there are 20 gods, or no god. It neither picks my pocket nor breaks my leg," Jefferson wrote.

Led by Los Angeles talk show host Dennis Prager, some American conservatives argued that if Ellison wouldn't take the oath on the Bible, he didn't deserve to be a United States representative. Writing in the *Wall Street Journal*, Prager declared, "Insofar as a member of Congress taking an oath to serve America and uphold its values is concerned, America is interested in only one book, the Bible. If you are incapable of taking an oath on that book, don't serve in Congress."

I'm glad Ellison didn't cave in to the demands of the narrow-minded. The whole controversy merely proves the poverty of evangelical conservatism. Ellison had the right to take the oath on any book he might choose: the Bible, the Koran, the *Bhagavad-Gita*, *Black Elk Speaks*, the Book of Mormon, or for that matter Ron Hubbard's scientological text *Dianetics*. No American law requires that the oath of office involve a book of any sort, much less the Bible.

The Constitution of the United States is quite clear on this question. It requires the incoming president to swear or affirm an oath of allegiance. Article II, Section 1 says, in its entirety, "Before he enter on the execution of his office, he shall take the following oath or affirmation, 'I do solemnly swear (or affirm) that I will faithfully execute the office of President of the United States, and will to the best of my ability, preserve, protect and defend the Constitution of the United States.'" Nothing more. No book specified.

The Constitution also says (Article VI), "Senators and Representatives … and all executive and judicial officers, both of the United States and of the several states, shall be bound by oath or affirmation, to support this Constitution; but no religious test shall ever be required as a qualification to any office or public trust under the United States."

Three things are immediately clear. First, the founding charter of the United States makes no reference to God anywhere in its text—no mention of providence, deity, the Judeo-Christian tradition, Jesus or the Bible. Second, the Constitution does not require that these oaths or affirmations involve a book of any sort. Third, insisting that Rep. Ellison take his oath on a Bible would constitute a "religious test," and that is explicitly prohibited by the Constitution.

Constitutional niceties aside, it might be useful to examine the idea of oaths from a purely rational point of view. If oaths have any actual value beyond ceremony, they are meant to bind an individual to a responsible course of action. If I—a Congregationalist—swore an oath on a sacred book that was not sacred to me (the Koran, for example), it's not clear how that text, which I neither know nor regard as authoritative, could shape my behavior.

Ellison's sacred book is the Koran. Which text is more likely to inspire Ellison to be a congressman of integrity: the Judeo-Christian Bible, which is a book about a religion that he does not subscribe to, or the Koran, which articulates his God's expectations for humankind? If you don't believe the book has divine energy in and about it, you may as well be taking your oath on a novel or a phone book. In other words, the very logic of swearing an oath on a book would seem to link Ellison with the Koran, not the Bible.

> 66Ellison had the right to take the oath on any book he might choose: the Bible, the Koran, the *Bhagavad-Gita*, *Black Elk Speaks*, the Book of Mormon, or for that matter Ron Hubbard's scientological text *Dianetics*.99

I think it's wonderful that Thomas Jefferson owned a copy of the Koran. How many of us do? Like his hero Francis Bacon, Jefferson took "all knowledge to be my province." It's not clear when Jefferson purchased the book or precisely why. Jefferson's copy is an English translation by the orientalist George Sale printed in 1764. He may have purchased it as part of his study of international law. He may have acquired it in the name of his occasional study of comparative religion.

We know that the Enlightenment had a kind of crush on Islam. Surveying mankind from China to Peru (as Dr. Johnson put it), the thinkers and reformers of the Enlightenment became fascinated by the different ways different peoples went about the business of life, from economics to constitutional settlements to religion. Scientific freethinkers like Jefferson, Madison, David Hume and Voltaire were frankly embarrassed by some of the Bible, by some parts of Christian doctrine, and by much of Christian history. Because the idea of the Trinity (three is one, one is three) particularly offended the Unitarian sensibilities of the rationalists of the Enlightenment, they turned with coy respect to Islam, which is more rigorously monotheistic. There was a kind of Islamic chic during the eighteenth century.

In his monumental *Decline and Fall of the Roman Empire,* Edward Gibbon wrote an appreciative chapter on Mohammed and the religion he helped to found. Jefferson would have been alienated by the militarism and imperialism omnipresent in the Koran and the history of Islam, but he was, to put it in simplest terms, fascinated by the idea that tens of millions of people could see the world in a way very different from his own.

And unlike today's nervous Nellies, who think that western civilization is so fragile that it has to be defended from all sorts of lovely variety and individual freedom, Jefferson kept his mind open to the idea that other traditions have a core of wisdom, just like ours.   *1/13/07*

I would have expected to get more criticism about this one. Even though we are constitutionally bound to separate church and state, a large number of Americans continue to argue, erroneously in my opinion, that we were intended to be a Christian nation. My response to that? Show me where in the founding documents that claim is made.

AND SO FAREWELL TO LEWIS AND CLARK

Last Sunday was a sad day for me. It was August 20, the bicentennial anniversary of the day Lewis and Clark left North Dakota forever. I spent the afternoon out at Fort Lincoln with Tracy Potter and about fifty others who had gathered to observe the denouement of Lewis and Clark's sojourn in North Dakota.

Given the endlessness of the Bicentennial (2003–2006), with nearly a decade of warm-up activities before that (*Undaunted Courage* by Stephen Ambrose, Ken Burns' splendid documentary, the blossoming of the Fort Mandan Interpretive Center), I did not expect to lament the passing of the historical commemoration of Jefferson's pet exploration project. Almost everyone I have talked with for the past year, including professional historians, has confessed to being "Lewis and Clarked out."

But I was overcome with sadness as I sat in the ceremonial earthlodge at On-A-Slant Village. Lewis and Clark were leaving us. Their boats were traveling eighty to ninety miles a day now, downstream. Their minds were bent on St. Louis. They were not coming back.

The Bicentennial has been extremely good for North Dakota.

The four strands of the expedition had re-entered what would become North Dakota between August 2 and 11, 1806, some by way of the Yellowstone and others by way of the Missouri River. All the strands reunited at Reunion Bay on August 12, 1806, one day after poor Meriwether Lewis was accidentally shot in the buttock by his otherwise trustworthy waterman Pierre Cruzatte.

August 12 must have been one of the most exciting days of the entire expedition. The strands had been separated since July 3, at the other end of Montana, and everyone had dramatic stories to tell. Sergeant Nathaniel Pryor had to report that all of his horses were stolen on the second day out by the Crow Indians. He's been forced to construct bullboats in which to float down to Dakota. Clark lost horses too, but his leisurely ride (almost a joy ride) down the Yellowstone had taken him through herds of buffalo so large that he despaired that anyone would believe his estimates. Collins and Colter had been "lost," that is, separated from the Lewis party, but they had lived like fur barons in the Edenic landscape of eastern Montana. As usual, Lewis had the most dramatic story of all. On the upper Marias River, July 26–27, 1806, he and three others had blundered into a skirmish with eight young Blackfeet men. At first light, after a night of tense talk and bivouacking, the young men made a grab for the expedition's rifles. Reuben Field had stabbed one of the Blackfeet to death, and Lewis killed another with his rifle as the young man attempted to abscond with Lewis's small string of horses. It was the only bloodshed of the entire expedition. Lewis and his three colleagues had endured a forced march of more than one hundred thirty miles on horseback in thirty-six hours to get out of Blackfeet country. They were fortunate to have escaped without injury, Lewis reported, and now to be shot by his own man ... !

Between August 14 and August 17, the expedition's leadership (now principally Clark; Lewis was nursing his wound and his humiliation) engaged in hectic diplomatic activity with the Mandan and Hidatsa people. As usual, Clark preached peace and commerce, but what he really wanted was a Mandan or Hidatsa delegation to accompany the expedition all the way to Washington, DC, to meet the curious and artful President Jefferson. In the end, after much persuading and the upping of the proposed compensation package, White Coyote, Sheheke-shote, agreed to make the immense journey, hoping, no doubt, that his participation would bring lasting benefits to his people. Sheheke-shote had been the expedition's principal Indian friend during its five-month residency at Fort Mandan, November 2, 1804–April 7, 1805.

August 17, 1806, was a day of farewells. The expedition said goodbye to the Hidatsa, to the Mandan, to the Charbonneau family, and to expedition member John Colter who had decided to return to the wilderness to try his luck in the beaver pelt trade. Clark paid Troussaint Charbonneau $500 and one-third cent for his interpreting services, plus payment for the use of a tipi and a horse. A few days later, Clark would express his regret that the US Army had no way of rewarding Sacagawea for her contributions to the success of the expedition. Clark had also fallen in love with Sacagawea's infant son Jean Baptiste (Pomp), and he was already proposing ways in which he could formally adopt Pomp, or at least supervise his education in St. Louis.

On August 17, the Mandan people said goodbye to Sheheke-shote, his wife Yellow Corn, their son, and Rene Jusseaume and his Mandan wife and two children. There was much crying and great grief. The Mandan were not sure they would ever see Sheheke-shote again. What Lewis and Clark were proposing was an epic journey to a faraway place, where no Mandan had ever been, and the journey began with a run through hostile Sioux country. The Mandan anxiety was only slightly misplaced. Sheheke-shote would be gone for more than three years. The US Army's first attempt to get him home (1807) would be turned back in northern south Dakota, not by the Sioux but by the Arikara, who had sent their trusted emissary off to see the Great Father, and he had died in the nation's capital.

> **"It is impossible not to wonder what was going on in the mind of Sacagawea as she stood on the shore on August 17, 1806, watching the Corps of Discovery prepare for departure."**

It is impossible not to wonder what was going on in the mind of Sacagawea as she stood on the shore on August 17, 1806, watching the Corps of Discovery prepare for departure. She had spent a year and a half with the expedition. She had crossed half the continent with Lewis and Clark. She had nursed her infant son all the way out to Oregon and all the way back. She had nearly died twice near the Great Falls of the Missouri in the summer of 1805, once in a flash flood and a second time from a bout of infection and fever. William Clark had helped to save her life both times. She had been reunited with her birth people on the Montana-Idaho border. The chief of the tribe, the Lemhi Shoshone, had turned out to be her brother Cameahwait. In the Shoshone village, she had met the Indian man to whom she had been betrothed in early childhood. At the Pacific Ocean she had seen a whale. On the return journey she had guided Clark's party over Bozeman Pass. Even Clark said that her presence had been a critically-important sign that the expedition had peaceful intentions.

Now it was over. She was back in the Mandan-Hidatsa world. Clark and the expedition were leaving forever. Charbonneau was staying behind. We would give anything to know Sacagawea's thoughts on August 17, 1806. Of course, she did not keep a journal. The expedition's six white male journal keepers were too busy that day to pause to describe her demeanor. Was she crying or laughing? Trying to keep her son from crawling into the boats or holding him quietly in her arms? Gravitating toward or away from Charbonneau? Reconnecting with her Hidatsa women friends or standing stoically alone on shore as romantic novelists like to see her? We don't know.

All we have is silence—and of course the marvelous Amy Mossett, who does not impersonate Sacagawea, but who has traveled farther into her soul than anyone who has ever tried.

Once all the hugs were exchanged, and all the tears of parting had been shed, and everyone in the descent party was on board the canoes, the expedition dropped down to the site of Fort Mandan. Clark had one more farewell in mind. He left the flotilla and walked up to the fort site. He discovered that Fort Mandan had burned to the ground. Only a small portion of the fort remained. Clark believed that the fire had been an accident—which means lightning or a prairie fire. There is something melancholy (and valedictory) in this picture of Clark alone at the charred remains of Fort Mandan. It had been a snug home, the site of the expedition's most successful relations with American Indians, and the location of the expedition's most reliable ethnographic study of plains Indian culture. Now it was a ruin.

On August 18, 1806, the expedition began its rush to St. Louis, eating the Missouri in great gulps. On the upward journey nine to fifteen miles was a good day. Now seventy-five miles was an unremarkable progress.

Clark paused long enough on August 18 to ask Sheheke-shote about the abandoned villages at the site of today's Bismarck and Mandan. Sheheke-shote, who grew up at On-A-Slant, told the story of the 1781 smallpox epidemic, and subsequent Sioux aggressions, and the story of the Mandan migration to the Hidatsa homeland at the mouth of the Knife River.

He also told the origin story of the Mandan people. And William Clark had the dignity and respect to cast the story in the journals in the phraseology and the cadence of the King James Bible's book of Genesis.

Two days later, the Lewis and Clark Expedition passed out of North Dakota forever.

We will miss them sorely. *8/24/06*

William Clark's visit to the ruins of Fort Mandan has always reminded me of the eighth book of Vergil's Aeneid, *in which Aeneas visits the future site of Rome. It is still a quiet pastoral village, but it is destined to be changed beyond recognition by Roman civilization. If I were writing a Lewis and Clark epic, I'd have Clark fall into a trance at the ruin of Fort Mandan and see the future of American civilization, good and bad, before returning (bewildered, sobered, struck silent) to the boats.*

JEFFERSON AND THE PRESS:

THE PARADOX OF THE UTOPIAN

Thomas Jefferson is properly regarded as one of America's foremost advocates of freedom of the press. His Second Inaugural Address, delivered inaudibly on March 4, 1805, contains what is possibly the finest paragraph ever written on this subject. But things are actually a bit more complicated than the Jefferson mythology suggests. Actually, James Madison is a purer—if less inspiring—advocate of freedom of the press than his political mentor. It was Jefferson, after all, who in his second term could call upon the governor of Pennsylvania to stir up a "few wholesome prosecutions" of the anti-Jeffersonian press in his state. It was Jefferson who, worn down by criticism, said in 1807 that hereafter all newspapers should be divided into four sections: truth, probabilities, possibilities, and bald lies.

For the record, the Second Inaugural Address really is inspiring.

"During this course of administration, and in order to disturb it, the artillery of the press has been leveled against us, charged with whatsoever its licentiousness could devise or dare. These abuses of an institution so important to freedom and science, are deeply to be regretted, inasmuch as they tend to lessen its usefulness, and to sap its safety; they might, indeed, have been corrected by the wholesome punishments reserved and provided by the laws of the several States against falsehood and defamation; but public duties more urgent press on the time of public servants, and the offenders have therefore been left to find their punishment in the public indignation."

It doesn't get any better than that.

On this question, as on most others, there are two Jeffersons. One is a nearly perfect figure of the Enlightenment, who articulated the principles of freedom of the press "in terms so plain and firm as to command assent," as Jefferson later said of the arguments of the Declaration of Independence. The other Jefferson was a thin-skinned political leader who was deeply disappointed when the press behaved in a way that did not seem to embody the civic ideals of the Enlightenment. In other words, one Jefferson can be counted on to trot out golden idealisms on virtually any subject (slavery, intellectual property, foreign policy, education, agriculture, etc. etc. etc.), and the other is a man who lived in the real world and did not like its political rough and tumble, though he managed to master that, too.

As a young man, Jefferson wrote, "The basis of our governments being the opinion of the people, the very first object should be to keep that right; and were it left to me to decide whether we should have a government without newspapers, or newspapers without a government, I should not hesitate a moment to prefer the latter." This is one of those lovely utterances that

Jefferson specialized in, wherein he says the best thing that could ever be said of a certain subject, and which continues to inspire our culture two hundred years after Jefferson's presidency. It's beautiful and noble and a little radical. But what exactly does it mean? More to the point, did Jefferson really mean it? Does he really believe that American civilization could exist without a government?

What Jefferson is pretending to mean is that self-government is about SELF government, that well-informed citizens who take their civic responsibilities seriously might be expected to restrain themselves and live according to the golden rule with a severely reduced government, but in order to behave in so exemplary a fashion they require lots of reliable information. Properly informed about the world around them, earnest citizens can constitute a republic without a formal government. But if they are un- or misinformed, they will have no capacity to make commonwealth decisions, and the society either collapses or finds itself needing a governing elite. Thus the vital importance of good newspapers in a republican society.

In Jeffersonian terms, the development of good citizens is more important than the existence of good government in a republic. This is probably true, but Jefferson has not crafted his argument in so reasonable a way. As usual he has articulated extremes—either to enforce his point or to enjoy the rhetorical effect. He seems to be offering us a stark alternative—you can have government or newspapers but not both—but surely he knows that there is a vast middle ground where the future of American life will actually be played out. So why the binary proposition?

> "What Jefferson is pretending to mean is that self-government is about SELF government, that well-informed citizens who take their civic responsibility seriously might be expected to restrain themselves and live according to a golden rule with a severely reduced government."

In other words, Jefferson is either actually advocating anarchy or he is making a point about the importance of a well-informed citizenry. If he really believes that no government is necessary in America, he's either an idiot or a wild utopian, which amounts to the same thing. No wonder John Adams found Jefferson exasperating. He is always writing something marvelous that presupposes a level of rationality, education, tolerance, self-restraint, modesty of spirit, and civility that has never characterized any society on earth. If he is merely saying that good newspapers are an essential element in a great civilization, and that the antidote to oppressive government is a citizenry that has the tools to think for itself about public affairs, then why has he overstated his case in such glowing, utopian terms?

This is what might be called the Paradox of Thomas Jefferson. John Adams could never take Jefferson very seriously, because he understood that any mature human being has an understanding of the imperfection (to put it mildly) of human nature and the imperfection of human institutions. For Adams, life is a messy business; people are not always their best selves; things tend to fall apart; and humans are actuated not by altruism but by naked self-interest or what Adams liked to call the "rage for distinction." Because Adams and the other Founding Fathers (George Washington, Benjamin Franklin, Alexander Hamilton—in short virtually everyone except James Madison and Thomas Paine) looked on life with a lens that was not rosy-tinted, they legislated for the world that is rather than the one they imagined in their dreams, and they did not say wild wonderful things about human possibility.

For some reason Jefferson thrived on those wild wonderful utterances, and he seems genuinely to have believed them and felt their intoxication. He seems to have believed—right to his core—that with the right habits and institutions in place, plus the vast unfinished continent of America, the United States might create the nearest-to-utopian civilization that ever existed on earth, and that it was not beyond the realm of possibility to believe that the great majority of humans might be able to be their best selves most of the time. Jefferson's vision is beautiful, if naïve, and it has had a huge inspirational effect on American civilization for more than two centuries. Virtually all newspapers, for example, regard Jefferson's government or newspapers bromide as a kind of institutional motto.

But there is a terrible problem in Jefferson's dream, one that has become the focus of Jefferson studies in the last two decades. It is one thing to quote Jefferson on these subjects. It is quite another to examine his behavior by the standards he himself set. Historians are increasingly struck by the gap between Jefferson's utterances and his actual deeds. Perhaps because we are in a period of historical disillusionment, scholars have not only luxuriated in the inconsistencies in Jefferson, or what they often characterize as his hypocrisies, but they have increasingly fixated on Jefferson's actual and often imperfect behavior to call into question, even discredit, the ideals he advocated. In other words, they have argued that the great ideals of the Enlightenment must be hollow—just words—because they have no anchoring in "the course of human events," not even for the golden boy who specialized in turning Enlightenment phrases.

The disillusionment has, in my view, gone too far. Jefferson was not a perfect champion of a "free marketplace of ideas," but he was better than all of his contemporaries except perhaps James Madison. He decried the Alien and Sedition Laws of the Adams administration, which he rightly regarded as a palpable violation of the Bill of Rights. He chose to look away from vicious assaults on his personal character, including such private matters as his religious sensibilities and the workings of his libidinous life, at a time when the American legal doctrine that public figures are fair game and thus unslanderable had not yet begun to develop. His character and his administration were actuated by a broad sense of tolerance and good sense. He truly believed that America thrived on a diversity of ideas, including political ideas, and that homogeneity is the death of a free society. He may, in extremis as an easily-wounded man, have welcomed a "few wholesome prosecutions" at the state level of his most obnoxious detractors (those who reveled in the Sally Hemings scandal, for example), but, unlike his predecessor, he steadfastly refused to use the national government over which he presided as a tool of censorship, and he knew that the ideal was a virtually unchecked press, even if he could not quite live up to that ideal when his own privacy and reputation were at stake. What he objected to was personal character assassination, not strongly-worded political opposition.

In other words, the focus on the imperfections in Jefferson misses the point of his essential commitment to unprecedented freedom of expression in what he regarded as an unprecedented society. Jefferson may seem naïve, but he actually believed that the only way to move towards Utopia was to invite people to live according to high ideals, to empower them to try, to avoid sneering at their lapses, and to check them as little as possible in their experiment in self-government. By those standards, John Adams is a mere grumpy pessimist. *10/2006*

I have spent most of my adult life thinking about Thomas Jefferson. I regard myself as a Jeffersonian. But my outlook, my view of human nature, is actually grounded more in St. Augustine than in Jefferson. I think Adams had a more accurate view of human nature than Jefferson. But I would not be an Adamsite for all the world.

THE BADLANDS SEIGNIOR AHEAD OF HIS TIME

The Marquis de Mores occupies a paradoxical place in the North Dakota consciousness. He lived among us only a brief time (1883–87), and he was as different from the overwhelming majority of Dakotans as it is possible to be, and yet he left a huge mythological imprint on the state. His twenty-six-room "chateau" continues to look down upon the rest of us, and the name "Medora," which belonged to his wife and which he gave to the village he built, is as evocative a word as exists in the North Dakota vocabulary.

His centrality in North Dakota mythology far exceeds his historical importance or his merit. In almost every respect, my grandparents and your grandparents did more for North Dakota than de Mores. They minded their own business, played by the rules, worked hard, formed realistic visions of what they could accomplish and did what they could to fulfill them. They treated the people around them as equals. Above all, they persevered.

De Mores swashbuckled his way through life. He carried himself like a feudal seignior, and he distanced himself from all those—the vast majority—he considered common folk. His visions were grand but unrealizable, and he bolted from Dakota as soon as it became clear that he could not accomplish his goals with money and will alone.

It was quiet, hard-working men and women, who chose not to call attention to themselves, who built North Dakota. De Mores was not one of them.

Theodore Roosevelt also was an aristocrat from another world who lived among us for almost exactly the same length of time. What distinguishes him from de Mores is that Roosevelt did not try to distance himself from the cowboys and frontiersmen he encountered here. He got down in the dirt, wrestled cows, felled trees, turned his fists rather than dueling pistols on those who tried to bully him, and he did everything in his power to overcome not the people he met, but his own privileged eastern education, style, and presuppositions. De Mores's aristocratic bearing deepened in the Badlands. Roosevelt's ebbed away. It was his capacity to humble himself and come to terms with the common man in himself that makes Roosevelt a great man, and transformed him—here, at the Elkhorn Ranch—from the eastern punkinlilly and four-eyed dude to the man who became president of the United States.

De Mores made terrible mistakes here. He was not an admirable man in a frontier democratic society. He is, in the world's if not in North Dakota's history books, a nonentity, while Roosevelt must be regarded as one of the greatest men who ever lived.

But I still find plenty to admire in de Mores. He said once that he was a man of great insight who instantly grasped situations that took others a long time to figure out. The problems he wrestled with here are, in fact, the perennial problems of Dakota. And though he did not succeed in overcoming them, his instincts were all correct. He was in many respects a man ahead of his time.

Take, for example, his main business venture, the slaughterhouse, the chimney of which still stands like a monument to his ... er, ego near the entrance of Theodore Roosevelt National Park. De Mores's idea was a good one. Instead of shipping live cattle off to slaughter in Chicago or beyond, why not slaughter them here and ship dressed beef to eastern markets? Since 60 percent of a slaughtered cow was at that time worthless, and cattle lost weight on the long journey to faraway abattoirs, de Mores reckoned that he could save shipping costs and preserve the quality of the beef by doing the processing here, taking advantage of the emerging technology of refrigerator cars.

Thus he was a pioneer in trying to overcome two perennial Dakota problems: remoteness and economic colonialism. The essential challenge of North Dakota has been to overcome its isolation from population centers, capital, and markets. De Mores's attempt to use state-of-the-art technology to level the playing field is no different from recent attempts to wire the state for easy access to the information superhighway, so that human resources and intellectual capital grown here can compete equally with the same resources in major population centers. If, as Thomas Friedman says, the world is flat, North Dakota (in theory) has equal access to the profit centers of the world as does the research triangle in North Carolina or a techno-university in New Delhi. De Mores also understood that if we do the value adding here, rather than ship mere commodities to faraway markets, we keep more of the final sale price of any resource we have. This is a lesson North Dakota relearns every generation.

> "The problems he wrestled with here are, in fact, the perennial problems of Dakota. And though he did not succeed in overcoming them, his instincts were all correct. He was in many respects a man ahead of his time."

De Mores wanted to "connect" the Badlands to a larger world. The Northern Pacific Railroad made that possible, but of course its owners lived elsewhere and were quite happy to exploit the isolated and politically weak plainsmen of Dakota. So de Mores created the Medora to Deadwood Stage Line, owned by himself, for the purpose of cornering the lucrative Black Hills freight and passenger market at a time when no direct rail line extended from Chicago, Denver, or Minneapolis to the gold fields of the Black Hills. De Mores understood the importance of connectivity. His stage line was just a very low-tech attempt to connect the backwater Badlands to the world it wished to supply. Horse-boat-stagecoach-railroad-diesel truck-airplane-Fedex-now the Internet. De Mores was as high tech an entrepreneur as the engineering of his time permitted.

De Mores also wanted to grow cabbages in the Badlands, employing as fertilizer the offal from the slaughterhouse. Thus he would be turning those otherwise worthless byproducts of beef production into a vital ingredient of a related agricultural industry. This sort of zero-waste manufacturing is now a standard feature of well-run industrial systems.

His scheme to create a Badlands pottery industry is being revived as the twenty-first century begins. He rightly understood that by turning Badlands clays, which were essentially free for the taking, into finished pottery, he was creating wealth in the purest sense of the term. He realized that North Dakota commodities (beef, grains, earth, coal, etc.) are heavy and therefore expensive to ship, but that when they are processed here they are much more profitable thanks to the value added in the field, not in faraway factories.

Probably his most forward-looking scheme was to ship fresh salmon from Portland to east coast markets. Today the best restaurants boast of their "fresh catch," and happily explain to customers that the salmon or mahi mahi was just flown in from the coast that day or earlier that week. De Mores's genius consisted of a triple insight. First, he understood the implications of the transportation revolution represented by the transcontinental railroads (in this case the Northern Pacific, completed in 1883, just in time). Second, he understood the novelty appeal of getting fresh salmon across the continent to dining rooms literally three thousand miles from the great Pacific rivers. In other words, he realized that scarce delicacies bring premium prices. Third, he saw half-empty trains pass through Medora from west to east every day, and realized that in getting fresh fish to Chicago and New York, he did not have to invent the logistical infrastructure, but merely take advantage of a system already put in place by other investors.

These and other schemes reveal the genius of Antoine Amedee Marie Vincent Amat Manca de Vallombrosa. Had he been a nicer man, had he called himself Tony Manks instead of "the Marquis" and shaved off that ridiculous moustache, had he possessed infinitely better diplomatic skills, had he taken a lesson in democratic gumption from that other aristocrat Theodore Roosevelt, above all, had he shown more perseverance, de Mores might have shaped and not merely decorated the history of North Dakota.
4/1/06

ROOSEVELT AND THE

CRADLE OF AMERICAN CONSERVATION

Last week, I heard a thoughtful man say that the Badlands of North Dakota were the "cradle of the modern conservation movement." That sounded so good I just wanted it to be true. I wanted North Dakota to be the cradle of something—other than of the children we raise and export to the rest of the world. His idea was that Theodore Roosevelt's great work as a conservationist had its roots in North Dakota, at the Elkhorn Ranch thirty-five miles north of Medora.

Then, unfortunately, I got to thinking about the claim, and wondering if it were really true. Can experiences that began in 1883, three hundred years after Jamestown, and more than a century after the Declaration of Independence, really constitute the cradle of conservation? That's pretty late in the game. We know that Roosevelt was an important conservationist, but does the idea that he was somehow a part of the birth of the modern conservation movement really make any sense? How important was the North Dakota sojourn (1883–87) to the development of Roosevelt's conservation ethic?

Historians of American conservation tend to write little about Roosevelt. He is usually regarded as a man of action, not of contemplation, and even his remarkable presidential achievement in conservation is usually seen as having been inspired by others, like his gifted US forester Gifford Pinchot. There also is the Roosevelt "problem." As one of America's foremost big game hunters, who killed so many large mammals in Africa (1909–10) that even he was embarrassed, Roosevelt, gripping a Sharps rifle with one foot on the corpse of a white rhinoceros, does not look like a poster child for American conservation.

It's the cradle issue that makes me skeptical.

Wasn't Walden Pond the cradle of American conservation? Thoreau, who died when Roosevelt was just three years old, lived at Walden Pond near Concord, Massachusetts, from July 4, 1845, to Sept. 6, 1847. His amazing journal—one of the greatest ever written—and his book *Walden* (1854) are among the most important texts in the history of the conservation movement. For many, they constitute the bible of American conservation. In the great journal, Thoreau wrote, "I have just been through the process of killing the cistudo (a tortoise) for the sake of science; but I cannot excuse myself for this murder, and see that such actions are inconsistent with the poetic perception, however they may serve science, and will affect the quality of my observations. I pray that I may walk more innocently and serenely through nature." On another occasion he wrote, "I saw a muskrat come out of a hole in the ice .... While I am looking at him, I am thinking what he is thinking of me. He is a different sort of man, that's all."

Imagine what Roosevelt would have said about these two sentences from Thoreau!

Two of Roosevelt's contemporaries would seem to have better credentials than his for birthing the modern conservation movement. Both of them influenced Roosevelt's thinking about the natural world.

John Muir (1838–1914) was, among other things, the founder of the Sierra Club. He became the leading American advocate for "preservation" rather than mere "conservation" of what remained of American wilderness. Muir loved untrammeled nature for what it offered to the human spirit, not for the resources that could be extracted from it. In 1903, he spent three days in Yosemite National Park with President Theodore Roosevelt—a primitive encampment with no Secret Service men or handlers. Roosevelt regarded the Yosemite interlude as one of the greatest experiences of his life. One of the first things Muir said to Roosevelt was, "Mr. President, when are you going to get over your infantile need to kill the animals you see in nature?"

When we think of Muir, we don't see a gun and a trophy. We remember the day he climbed a one hundred-foot Douglas fir in the Sierra Nevada Mountains, where he rode out a mountain storm. "Never before did I enjoy so noble an exhilaration of motion," Muir wrote. "The slender tops fairly flapped and swished in the passionate torrent, bending and swirling backward and forward, round and round, tracing indescribable combinations of vertical and horizontal curves, while I clung with muscles firm braced, like a bobo-link on a reed."

The one-armed Civil War veteran John Wesley Powell (1834–1902) ran the canyons of the Green and Colorado rivers with wooden boats in 1869. His ten-year immersion into the culture and geography of the Colorado Plateau and the Great Basin taught him that arid lands could not be developed according to the methods employed in Iowa and Indiana. In his famous *Arid Lands Report* (1878), Powell virtually rewrote the land use policies of the United States for the lands beyond the 100th meridian. He was the first prominent American to predict that water would be the issue of the American West, and that the sooner we began planning for the conservation and just distribution of the West's scarce water supplies, the healthier and more successful our western communities would be.

Other pioneers in the conservation movement include Mary Austin (1868–1934), the author of *Land of Little Rain*; John Burroughs (1837–1921), who spent a fortnight with Roosevelt in Yellowstone National Park; Roosevelt's friends and collaborators Gifford Pinchot (1865–1946) and George Bird Grinnell (1849–1938); and Aldo Leopold (1887–1948), whose *Sand County Almanac* is regarded by many as one of the primary texts of American conservation. Nor should we forget Thomas Jefferson in trying to find the "cradle of American conservation."

All of these individuals played a more important role than Roosevelt in developing an American philosophy of nature and resource conservation. Several of them were actually TR's tutors on conservation matters.

But that's not the end of the story. In this arena, Roosevelt was a statesman, not a philosopher. During the course of his seven-year, 171-day presidency, Roosevelt set aside 230 million acres of the public domain of the United States for conservation purposes. He added 100 million acres to the National Forest system. He doubled the size of the National Park system from five to 10 units, one of them—Sullys Hill—in North Dakota. He signed the Newlands Reclamation Act in 1902 and designated the first 24 national irrigation projects. One of them, the Lower Yellowstone Project, was set partly in North Dakota. He signed the Antiquities Act in 1906 and designated the first 18 national monuments. He convened the first White House Governor's Conference in 1908 for the explicit purpose of discussing conservation of the nation's resources. And he invented, by executive order alone, the National Wildlife Refuge System (1903). TR designated the first 51 federal bird sanctuaries, two of them—Chase Lake and Stump Lake—in North Dakota.

This magnificent conservation achievement is matched by no other president in American history. A professor friend of mine who is a great expert on environmental history says that TR's presidential action is "an almost unbelievably important accomplishment" in the history of conservation.

Was this stupendous achievement born at the Elkhorn Ranch? I'll address that question next week   *9/8/07*

This one caused some trouble. Some very powerful people were asserting that the Elkhorn was the "cradle of American conservation," and they did not appreciate my seeming diminution of Roosevelt's achievement. The phrase found its way into Douglas Brinkley's Wilderness Warrior: Theodore Roosevelt and the Crusade for America.

WHAT ROOSEVELT LEARNED

AT THE ELKHORN RANCH

The acquisition of the Eberts-Elkhorn Ranch by the US Forest Service is a great moment for North Dakota, a great moment for the United States and a great moment for the legacy of Theodore Roosevelt.

Roosevelt never owned an acre in the Little Missouri River Valley. He was, as he freely admitted, an open range squatter in the last years before fences (and legal deeds) transformed the open range into fixed property.

In his 1913 autobiography, he says he "took hold of two cattle ranches," the Maltese Cross, seven miles south of Medora (1883), and the Elkhorn (1884), thirty-five miles north of Medora. He regarded the more remote Elkhorn Ranch, which he chose personally in June 1884, as his primary Dakota Territory home.

The Elkhorn was a large ranch, whose informal "boundaries" were set by the custom of the Little Missouri country. Roosevelt was "entitled" to a range that extended four miles upriver from his headquarters and four miles downriver, and from the river bed all the way out on both sides to the sources of the feeder creeks of the Little Missouri.

The original Elkhorn Ranch, what we might now call the "Greater Elkhorn Ranch," thus extended eight miles along the Little Missouri (roughly south to north) and from ten to thirty miles east of the river and an equal distance toward the west.

Theodore Roosevelt National Park manages just two hundred eighteen acres on the west bank of the river, where the ranch house and outbuildings were located.

In other words, the national park, on behalf of all the people of the United States, owns and manages only the ranch headquarters, not the entire Elkhorn Ranch.

The sale of the Eberts Ranch to the U. Forest Service, and the sale of the adjacent Mosser Ranch to a private individual with a strong conservation interest, means that the viewshed from where the veranda of the Elkhorn Ranch once stood will be protected forever from adverse economic activity, from the formation of subdivisions or ranchettes and from resource extraction of a noisome variety.

In my opinion, the Elkhorn Ranch ought to be considered a national shrine—in the same short list that includes Walden Pond in Massachusetts, Mount Vernon and Monticello, the battlefields at Gettysburg and Shiloh, the Little Big Horn, the grave (if we can just determine where it actually is) of Sitting Bull, and the location in Arches National Park where the great Edward Abbey parked his ranger trailer.

I love it that the Elkhorn Ranch is remote, a little difficult to get to, unserved by any tourist amenities (unlike Walden Pond) and entirely unimproved. There are no plans to rebuild the 30-by-60-foot ranch house. The signage at the site is minimal and tasteful.

Appropriately, when you go there you cannot see, but you definitely do feel, Roosevelt's presence, and his reason for locating his ranch in that stretch of the river is immediately apparent.

In 1883, Roosevelt came to Dakota Territory to kill a buffalo. In the course of a buffalo hunt so difficult that it amounted to an ordeal, Roosevelt fell in love with the Dakota Badlands and impulsively invested $14,000 in the Maltese Cross Ranch. Or, as the late Stephen Ambrose put it, "He got his bull and lost his heart."

In the late spring of 1884, Roosevelt returned to the Dakota Badlands a grieving and possibly broken man. After his wife Alice and mother Mittie died on the same day, Valentine's Day 1884, Roosevelt returned to the Little Missouri River Valley to seek solitude.

That's when he scouted downriver for a second ranch far from the traffic lanes near Medora and the Northern Pacific Railroad. With the help of Howard Eaton, he found what he was looking for thirty-five miles north of Medora, and he named the new ranch for the interlocked horns of two bull elk he found at the site.

Roosevelt wanted solitude, and he found it.

We all know that Roosevelt went on to become the greatest conservationist in American presidential history: national parks, wildlife refuges, one hundred fifty new national forests, federal game preserves and much more. The great bulk of this was done publicly—during his nearly two terms as president and often enough by executive order—but he played an important private role in the history of conservation, too.

Roosevelt learned at least two critically important conservation lessons during his Badlands sojourn. First, he recognized that the Little Missouri River Valley, like most of the arid West, was much more fragile than it seemed. He realized that the grass was being overgrazed, and he correctly predicted that under a perfect storm of conditions—drought followed by a very severe winter—disaster was likely to follow. It did, in the killing winter of 1886–87.

Second, Roosevelt got one of the last two thousand or so buffalo in North America in mid-September 1883 and was mighty glad to display the head in his trophy room at Sagamore Hill for the rest of his life. But he realized that the majestic buffalo was in danger of extinction, along with other large mammals, unless humans worked in cooperation to sustain and rebuild the herds.

Roosevelt didn't write much about conservation in the books and articles that he published about his Dakota years. They are about adventure and the intense glory of the vanishing American frontier and about his own transformation from eastern dude to authentic American cowboy. They are, in my opinion, the best prose that has ever been written about the Badlands of North Dakota.

"The viewshed from where the veranda of the Elkhorn Ranch once stood will be protected forever from adverse economic activity, from the formation of subdivisions or ranchettes, and from resource extraction of a noisome variety."

Roosevelt understood the spirit of this place. All of his senses were on high alert. He was fully alive, completely present in a way that jumps off every page of his Dakota books and the magnificent Dakota chapter in his autobiography.

But almost the minute he got back to New York, he formed a friendship with one of his reviewers, George Bird Grinnell, and together, in 1887, they founded the Boone & Crockett Club, which played an extremely important role in the development of the modern American conservation movement.

It is not an exaggeration to say that the survival and revival of the buffalo owes as much to the Boone & Crockett Club as to any other entity, and that not only the existence of the national parks but the way we revere them as uncommercial sanctuaries for game and solitude owes as much to the Boone & Crockett Club (and therefore Roosevelt) as to the national government.

Even more to the point, Roosevelt's Boone & Crockett Club pioneered the concept of hunters cooperating to maintain sustainable game populations for the long run—enlightened hunters as our best game stewards—that has an incalculable legacy in Ducks Unlimited, Pheasants Forever and other conservation organizations.

Some of this conservation consciousness, surely, was born on the veranda of the Elkhorn Ranch. It is therefore fitting that the Boone & Crockett Club has played a key role in the US Forest Service's acquisition of the Eberts-Elkhorn Ranch.

The Elkhorn Ranch should be regarded as a national conservation shrine. More importantly, in my opinion, it should be regarded as a shrine to one of the most amazing men of American history, Theodore Roosevelt, who lived and learned and evolved here, and who, among other great achievements, went on to earn his place on the Rushmore of American conservationists, together with Henry David Thoreau, John Muir and Aldo Leopold. *9/15/07*

The quotation is from Roosevelt's book Hunting Trips of a Ranchman, *one of three books he wrote about his sojourn in western North Dakota.*

HAPPY BIRTHDAY, MERIWETHER LEWIS

My life can get so hectic that I nearly forget who I am. I was driving pell mell from Fargo to Bismarck on Tuesday night when it suddenly struck me that it was Meriwether Lewis's 235th birthday. Jefferson's protege was born on Aug. 18, 1774, within sight of Monticello.

There was a time in my life, and not long ago, when I lived and breathed Lewis and Clark. Now that remarkable adventure (1803–06) has slipped to the second tier in my cluttered-up garage or attic of a mind. I felt a twinge of sadness and shame that I have let Lewis and Clark slip a little. It's like very nearly forgetting your best friend's birthday.

The '60s poet Rod McKuen wrote, "The mind is such a junkyard. It remembers candy bars but not the Gettysburg Address, Frank Sinatra's middle name but not the day your best friend died." Indeed. I can remember a couple dozen plotlines of *The Andy Griffith Show* and even *Charlie's Angels,* but this morning, at dawn, I was trying to remember the Labors of Hercules and I couldn't get past four. That's terribly saddening. But it also tells you something about the power of television.

At any rate, happy birthday, Meriwether Lewis. Not that he would be glad to be so greeted. Though American mythology remembers Lewis and Clark as cheerful, more or less interchangeable heroes in buckskins, they were actually remarkably different men. Clark fits the stereotype pretty well, but his friend Lewis was a tightly wound, self-critical, brooding, often melancholic man who took himself, his transcontinental mission, and life very seriously. During the two years he lived with the immortal Jefferson in the White House prior to his expedition, the cheerful, even-tempered and Pollyanna-esque president noticed what he called "sensible depressions of spirit." He also noticed that Lewis drank, sometimes to excess.

That, at least, was Jefferson's retrospective assessment in 1813, four years after his protégé committed suicide.

Yes, suicide. I remember the moment when I first learned that the leader of the Lewis and Clark Expedition, the Neil Armstrong or John Glenn of his time, killed himself just three years after his return to civilization, after leading an amazingly successful 7,689-mile scientific expedition from St. Louis to the Pacific Ocean and back again, by way of our own Missouri River. He was thirty-five at the time of his death. He put a gun to his head and another to his abdomen at a lonely trailside inn in Tennessee. When I read that for the first time, in a book by David Freeman Hawke, I was in the office of the late, great Everett C. Albers, director of the North Dakota Humanities Council. "Did you know Lewis committed suicide in 1809?" I asked. Ev, who believed that the humanities are the elixir, the sorcerer's stone, the key to a complete and satisfying life, said, "No. Why did he do it?"

I have been trying to answer that question for the last twenty-five years. And not with much success. Suicide is always a profound mystery, even when the perpetrator and victim leaves a suicide note, which Lewis did not. I have hunches about Lewis, based on repeated and thorough sifting of the evidence, reading and re-readings of the large and growing literature on the subject, including Lewis's journals, endless meditation, research into the troubled returns of other explorers, including the fascinating contemporary case of the second man on the moon, Edwin "Buzz" Aldrin, and careful readings of case studies of the suicide phenomenon, beginning with John Donne's *Biathanatos* (the first-ever defense of suicide), and ending with the Johns Hopkins psychology professor Kay Redfield Jamison, whose book *Night Falls Fast: Understanding Suicide* has a chapter on Lewis saying that he is just the sort of driven, high-strung, self-castigating man who fits the profile.

In the end, the survivors never really know why anyone committed suicide, including someone they have known intimately for a lifetime. The mystery abides, deepens, perplexes, and eats away at one's sense of the rightness of things. For most of the history of Christianity, definitively since St. Augustine's masterpiece *City of God* (A.D. 410), suicide has been regarded as a sin and a crime. I'm with John Donne: judgment is easy, understanding hard, almost impossible, and that it is in our interest always to be charitable about something so intensely personal and inexplicable. I know this, too: That a suicide, any suicide, is like stone dropped into a very wide pond, creating a permanent (multi-dimensional) ripple action that gnaws at all the survivors and creates a crisis of meaning and identity for everyone who knew the person in question.

I have been writing about this as if Lewis's suicide, though ultimately a mystery, is an unquestioned fact of American history. That is not quite so. Though Lewis's two closest friends, Thomas Jefferson and William Clark, were shocked but not surprised when they heard the news in October 1809, and though all the evidence we have points to suicide, a dedicated cadre of diehards believes—hook, line and sinker—that Lewis was murdered on the Natchez Trace (murderer unknown) and that some sort of conspiracy was undertaken by those around Lewis to call it suicide instead. The murder theorists are loud and fiercely determined, and they are trying to get poor Lewis exhumed so that forensic experts can examine the skull. This has a kind of "second gunman, grassy knoll" feel to it. My hope is that the National Park Service, which maintains the burial site at Hohenwald, Tennessee, will continue to refuse to extricate Lewis's bones.

> "A suicide, any suicide, is like a stone dropped into a very wide pond, creating a permanent (multi-dimensional) ripple action that gnaws at all the survivors and creates a crisis of meaning and identity for everyone who knew the person in question."

My own deep prejudice is that documents, near eyewitness accounts, and historical analysis are a better tool than shovels in making sense of the richness and complexities of Meriwether Lewis.

Lewis celebrated (well, observed) his thirty-first birthday on the Idaho-Montana border near Dillon, Montana, on Aug. 18, 1805, not long after he bestrode the source waters of the "mighty and heretofore deemed endless Missouri River." After acknowledging that he had lived about half the time he expected to dwell in "this sublunary world," Lewis fell into dark self-reflection. "I reflected," he wrote, "that I had as yet done but little, very little indeed, to further the happiness of the human race, or to advance the information of the succeeding generation. I viewed with regret the many hours I have spent in indolence, and now sorely feel the want of that information which those hours would have given me had they been judiciously expended."

Well, I can certainly relate to that. I find myself in the midst of a much less articulate, but similarly self-critical, look in the mirror about once a week, and I'm now way beyond the halfway point of my time in "the sublunary world."

Even so, like Lewis, I always conclude my self-flagellation with resolute optimism. Said Lewis, "I resolved in future, to redouble my exertions and at least endeavor to promote those two primary objects of human existence, by giving them the aid of that portion of talents which nature and fortune have bestowed on me; or in future, to live for mankind, as I have heretofore lived for myself."

Rest in peace, Capt. Lewis. *8/23/09*

The Labors of Hercules:

Slay the Nemean Lion.
Slay the nine-headed Lernaean Hydra.
Capture the Golden Hind of Artemis.
Capture the Erymanthian Boar.
Clean the Augean stables in a single day.
Slay the Stymphalian Birds.
Capture the Cretan Bull.
Steal the Mares of Diomedes.
Obtain the girdle of Hippolyta, Queen of the Amazons.
Obtain the cattle of the monster Geryon.
Steal the apples of the Hesperides.
Capture and bring back Cerberus.

THE MAN WHO DEFINED THE HUMANITIES FOR NORTH DAKOTA

Can it be two years since Ev Albers died?

Everett Charles Albers died on April 24, 2004, in his home in Bismarck. He was sixty-two years old. He died of pancreatic cancer, against which he had been struggling for several years. As the poet Dylan Thomas demanded, he raged, raged against the dying of the light. But as Ev would be the first to remind you, death is an appointment that nobody fails to meet.

Everett was for thirty-one years the director of the North Dakota Humanities Council. Before that he taught humanities at Dickinson State University. He grew up on a dairy farm near Hanover. He was born during the Great Blizzard of 1942. He loved blizzards all his life. The worse the storm or the cold snap, the more he'd say, "It's a great day to be in North Dakota."

If his name doesn't immediately ring a bell for you, it is because he wasn't that well known in the community of Bismarck and Mandan. Everett was a workaholic who holed up in what can only be called a grotto deep inside the offices of the humanities council, which was located then on east Boulevard. It was almost impossible to spelunk your way into the sanctum sanctorum, through stacks of books, the wrecks of discarded electronic gadgets, old darkroom equipment, an array of three or four computers he had hot-wired together for the big publishing projects, a maze of Radio Shack cords (like the world's largest ball of twine), and piles of notes he had written to himself about pressing deadlines. It was an office a slightly sinister Dr. Seuss might have designed, and somewhere in the heart of it, in the dark, Everett could be heard typing madly or muttering under his breath about the limits of currently available software. He wasn't aloof. He was just busy—from dawn to late in the evening, every day for thirty-one years.

Everett was not one to call attention to himself. He preferred to inspire, enable, and encourage the work of others.

You may have seen him Sunday afternoons at the auditorium of the Heritage Center, greeting the public, making sure that the featured scholar (usually a historian) was properly introduced, fussing with the AV equipment, handing out humanities tabloids (a form of publication he actually invented in the United States).

The Crosby Journal once called him a "shaggy buffalo" of a man. He was a big man with a bigger soul and a heart that filled every room he entered. When he laughed, he invaded your personal space and put his glinting glasses and mischievous moustache about two inches from your nose and didn't pull back until you laughed out loud with him.

He drank coffee in oceans.

And he shaped the lives of a whole generation of humanities scholars. Most of them worked in North Dakota, but some sought his wisdom from across the nation. His mantra was that the great disciplines of the humanities (literature, philosophy, law, anthropology, history, religious studies, art history) are the best tool we have in our struggle to make sense of life, to endure pain and loss and self-doubt, and to place our little trials in the larger context of human history.

This sounds pretty heady, but there was nothing pretentious about Ev Albers. He never forgot his farm roots in Oliver County. He had a healthy Germanic earthiness about him. You were more likely to see him eating fleischkeukle than hors d'oeuvres, drinking Diet Coke not Dom Perignon. He believed that the Three Stooges were worth studying as closely as the poetry of William Butler Yeats, or his great favorite, North Dakota's Tom McGrath. He was not afraid of big ideas—he loved to spend hours at a time in the bathtub reading big books that purported to explain everything—but he didn't think that the life of the mind was the exclusive enclave of the social elite. Ever.

Ev changed the face of the public humanities in the United States. That can be said of only one or two other state humanities council directors in the country.

He invented Chautauqua, the traveling humanities tent show that features historical characters like Herman Melville and Booker T. Washington and

Abigail Adams. Chautauqua started its life back in 1976 in a tiny tent, which was driven to twenty towns per summer by Chautauqua's great tentmaster, Ed Sahlstrom of Dickinson, and a young college student. Now the Great Plains Chautauqua travels in five states every summer. This year, in North Dakota, it will visit Enderlin July 28–Aug. 1 and Grand Forks Aug. 4–8.

When he invented Chautauqua, officials at the National Endowment for the Humanities expressed concern that it was "history lite." Executive directors in other states shook their professional heads, raised their academic eyebrows, and often openly sneered. Now Chautauqua has a presence in more than twenty-five states. It's the most widely practiced public humanities format in America. Now the NEH praises and encourages Chautauqua without hesitation. Thanks to Ev.

> "When he laughed—which he did every day of his life—he invaded your personal space and put his glinting glasses and mischievous moustache about two inches from your nose, and didn't pull back until you laughed out loud with him."

Everett was the midwife to the film *Northern Lights* (1978), a North Dakota docudrama about the first triumph of the Nonpartisan League in 1917.

The film started as a proposal for a standard, thirty-minute documentary film. Ev at once saw the potential of the film and the cinematic talents of its directors Rob Nilsson and Jon Hanson. He coaxed more money from the humanities council, and worked with Nilsson and Hanson for several years to help them transform a journeyman project into a major work of art that won the Golden Camera Award at the Cannes Film Festival. If you haven't seen *Northern Lights,* you can order it on DVD in all the usual ways. It's one of North Dakota's supreme works of art, and it probably wouldn't exist were it not for the genius of Ev Albers.

He created the Larry Remele fellowships, in honor of one of his favorite humanities scholars. He printed the Bill of Rights on grocery bags. He found a way, somehow, to get money into the hands of every worthy humanities project that came to his attention.

He was a gifted short story writer, a brilliant letter writer, and a hilarious conversationalist.

In his last months, Everett wrote an online diary, which won him new friends, in the flat land of cyberspace, from all over America. Part memoir, part nostalgia for the North Dakota that is no more, part debriefing, and always an exploration of the ways in which the humanities can shape, enliven, clarify, dignify, and enrich our lives, Everett's journal is in some ways the best thing he ever did.

As his dear friend Jean Waldera put it, Everett lived his life in the humanities and he faced death through the lens of the humanities.

If ever there was a doting father, it was Everett. If ever there was a loyal friend, it was Everett. If ever there was a man who read the world through books, it was Everett. If ever there was a man who took himself seriously, but never too seriously, it was Everett. If ever there was a person who understood that the most redemptive tool we have is laughter, it is Everett.

And now he is dead, these two years. For almost everyone who knew him, life is a smaller thing without him.

His daughter Gretchen is a brilliant young humanities scholar at the University of Calgary. She's going to publish great things about the Great Plains and, unlike her father, spell every word right too. His son Albert is a fine musician and software expert, living in Madison, Wisconsin, and Albert's wife Bobbi is about to have Ev's first grandchild. How he would have reveled in that.

He'd be thinking about creating a tabloid to serve as a birth announcement.
4/29/06

Quiet Leaders

Who Make Difficult Decisions:

Let Us Now Praise

Those with the Courage to Lead

Kudos first to novelist Louise Erdrich, who quietly turned down an honorary degree from the University of North Dakota because she objects to the nickname "Fighting Sioux." Erdrich is one of North Dakota's greatest artists.

In a letter to UND President Charles Kupchella, Erdrich explained that she felt deeply honored to be offered the honorary degree and would certainly have accepted, had it not been for UND's insistence on retaining the moniker "Fighting Sioux" in the face of a series of NCAA rulings requiring UND to change its nickname to something less offensive to the American Indian community.

"I hate to do something like this," Erdrich told the *Minneapolis Star-Tribune.* "It goes against my grain. But I do feel strongly about this symbol."

There is nothing of the grandstander in Erdrich. In her humble and thoughtful way, she just keeps writing wonderful novels: *Love Medicine* (1984), *The Beet Queen* (1986), *Tracks* (1988), *The Master Butchers Singing Club* (2003), and *The Painted Drum* (2005), among others. Many of her novels explore the contrasting destinies of Indians and non-Indians on the North Dakota prairie. In other words, she knows whereof she speaks. Erdrich, who is an enrolled member of the Ojibwe (Anishinaabe) nation, grew up in Wahpeton.

The leadership at UND needs to be made to understand that it will realize that the price for clinging stubbornly to a nickname that both the NCAA and tribal leadership in North Dakota and beyond have denounced as insensitive. It is quite possible that eminent scholars will refuse to be re-cruited by UND until the name is changed to something more benign, that celebrated writers, both Indian and non-Indian, will refuse to attend the annual UND writers' conference, and that some foundations will refuse to make grants to UND given its intransigence on an issue so peripheral to the outstanding intellectual work that occurs there.

At some point, the leadership at UND will realize that the prize for poor sportsmanship and illiberal stubbornness is simply too high.

It wasn't easy for Erdrich to refuse so great an honor from the pre-mier educational institution of her home state. It took quiet courage. Who knows? Her courage may inspire others.

Kudos, too, to Ken and Norma Eberts, who persevered against almost impossible odds for more than four years and finally were able to sell their 5,200-acre ranch on the Little Missouri River to the US Forest Service. The controversial Eberts sale and a private conservation sale involving the adjacent Mosser Ranch mean that the viewshed from Theodore Roosevelt's beloved Elkhorn Ranch will be protected against adverse industrial or eco-nomic development. This is great news for lovers of Roosevelt, for the fu-ture of the Badlands and for the people of North Dakota.

Still, the Eberts story proves that no good deed goes unpunished.

Ever since they began quietly to initiate the sale of their ranch to the National Park Service or some other national government entity, the Eberts have been treated savagely by many of their neighbors in the Little Missouri River Valley. They have been ostracized by the ranch community, shunned even at their church, and publicly denounced. Their motives and character have been impugned, and their careful and humble statements of purpose have been deliberately distorted for political gain.

Why? Because they are perceived to have a cozy attitude towards the great Badlands bogey—the federal government. Yes, that's the same fed-eral government that saved the Badlands during the Depression and Dust Bowl catastrophes by buying up bankrupt and eroded ranches with the express purpose of leasing them right back to the ranchers who had been operating them. Yes, that's the same oppressive federal government that subsidizes leasing rates on BLM and National Forest acreage at well below the fair market leasing rate. Yes, that's the same intrusive federal govern-ment that Billings County is counting on to help pay for a bridge or cross-ing over the Little Missouri River somewhere near the Elkhorn Ranch.

Of course the federal government can sometimes be high-handed and insensitive. Of course it sometimes tries to impose blanket regulation regimens across the American West without really understanding the nuances or the heritage of specific regions. But by any rational measure, the federal government has been a fair, generous, and even deferential supervisor of our public lands in the Little Missouri River Valley.

We sometimes fail to remember that they are our lands, which we have sensibly leased to Badlands ranchers because we understand that they are good stewards, and because we all want to preserve and protect the family-agricultural heritage of North Dakota's most colorful cattle country.

The Eberts sold their ranch to the US Forest Service not because they love the federal government (that's none of our business), but because they believe the ranch is of great historical importance to the legacy of Theodore Roosevelt in Dakota Territory (1883–87).

The Eberts Ranch is what you see from the 218-acre Elkhorn cabin site across the river.

What we call the Eberts ranch was once an integral part of Theodore Roosevelt's principal Dakota home. The sale effectively knits together two segments of the heritage Elkhorn Ranch: the ranch headquarters (administered by the National Park Service) on the west bank of the Little Missouri and the Elkhorn cabin's viewshed on the eastern bank of the river.

Thanks to many people, including Joe Satrom, Keith Trego and David Pieper, of Bismarck; Lowell Baier of the Boone and Crockett Club; and especially Sen. Byron Dorgan, the deal was finally consummated on April 25 in Dickinson.

The other day I wrote to Ken and Norma to congratulate them on the sale. Their reply was characteristically modest.

They said they couldn't have persevered were it not for all the support they have received from friends and perfect strangers.

They were just trying to do the right thing, and they had no idea when they began that their cooperation with the feds would ignite so much controversy. They said they were and are very uncomfortable with the way they have been dragged into the public arena, and by the ways in which they have been lauded and criticized by people they have never met.

Finally, kudos to President Lee Vickers of Dickinson State University, who announced his resignation last week, effective early in 2008.

Vickers has done wonders for Dickinson State University.

Under his watch, DSU has enjoyed eight years of growth, increased prestige and a flowering of academic achievement.

What impresses me most has been Vickers's commitment to regional outreach. It used to be, even in places as modest as Dickinson, that academic institutions behaved like fortresses of learning and wisdom. Their message to the outside world was, "If you want enlightenment, ascend to our citadel and we'll see if there is anything we can do for you."

Vickers rejected that attitude as elitist and stagnating. Under his watch, DSU has reached out to southwestern North Dakota—from the Fort Berthold Indian Reservation to Bowman and Regent, from Killdeer all the way to Bismarck. In other words, DSU is taking its services on the road, and its attitude is not "jump through these hoops," but "how can we best serve you?"

That's a revolution in higher education.

Thanks to this entrepreneurial service agenda, DSU recently received a huge grant from the Bush Foundation. It also is the home of one of North Dakota's Centers of Excellence, which will be dedicated to the economic revitalization of what has come to look increasingly like North Dakota's "empty quarter."

Vickers's wife, Deanna, is without question one of the most active, intelligent, and productive university presidents' wives in the history of North Dakota—and beyond. She has essentially redefined the role of the presidential spouse.

Lee Vickers will be regarded as one of the best-ever presidents of Dickinson State University. He has set a standard that his successors will find it difficult to maintain.

It cannot have been easy for Vickers to announce his resignation at a time of such success and opportunity at Dickinson State. He did it because he has other worlds to conquer. *5/5/07*

Since I wrote this column, a plebiscite on the Spirit Lake Indian Reservation (April 2009) endorsed the continuation of the nickname and logo by a two-to-one margin (774–378). UND is now committed to retiring the name and logo, with support from the State Board of Higher Education, even though a large and vocal percentage of North Dakotans continue to seeks ways to perpetuate the name. Every time I have thought that this issue was resolved, nickname supporters have found ways to revive the controversy. At some point in the course of the protracted drama, it seemed to me more sensible just to let the nickname stand. As Indian nicknames go, it was far from the most objectionable.

STUMBLING INTO THE WAR

BETWEEN ONE BAGGAGE CLAIM AND THE NEXT

Here's an Afghanistan war parable. I stumbled into a war zone this afternoon.

By the merest chance, I happened upon the return of the 188th Air Defense Artillery Battalion's Security Forces (SECFOR) unit, which has spent the last year in Afghanistan. The soldiers arrived at the Bismarck airport at approximately 12:37 p.m. Friday, March 30, 2007. The Iraq-Afghanistan war hasn't come home to the American people, except for those who have fathers, daughters, brothers, nephews, sons, mothers, friends, lovers, and grandchildren over there, and for them it is a raw thing. The rest of us can turn away. They cannot. They will not. While the rest of us shop, talk, watch TV, and sleep in our comfortable beds, our service men and women are posted halfway around the world, now wedged into a civil war that we cannot possibly put to rest, and the country back home for the most part has lost its will to continue the war, a war that most of the country never really registered as ours. I had read that the 152 soldiers were returning this week, and I had thought then that it would be something to witness that, but, like most of America, I went about my business and kept the war meagerly out along the periphery of my life. For me it has been a current events theme, a thing to read, talk, argue about. For them it is the pivotal story of their lives. Four members of the 188th did not come home. Their families were there, with brave proud grieving faces, standing next to the governor and David Sprynczynatyk. Their hearts were broken in a whole new way today.

Because my outbound plane was late, thanks to the sleet storm, I stood in the crowd and waited for the mayhem to erupt when the soldiers walked through the doors into the airport lobby. I expected to be moved, but "moved" doesn't cover it. I stood against the rail overlooking a sea of love and pain and expectation and dread and I wept like a baby. It was the largest crowd in the history of the airport. It was the most intense concentration of human emotion I have ever seen. My dumb business trip to California now seemed like utter frivolity and self-indulgence. I've never served my country, not once.

More than five hundred people crowded into the baggage claim area of the airport, waiting, waiting, holding up posters, wearing welcome home and solidarity t-shirts, sporting armbands, clutching balloons and flowers and gifts. It was a mass of expectation. I saw mothers who would not breathe fully again until they gripped their sons and daughters in their arms, fathers glancing around nervously, stoically, bursting with pride and sorrow and anticipation. There were girlfriends in sensible clothes and girlfriends in hot clothes and young children everywhere, a few of them babies who had never met their fathers. Rumors moved through the crowd like the "wave" at sporting events. "They are within range." "They will be coming through the door over there." "They may have to regroup outside the plane first."

Many held flags. Some were draped in flags. The posters said, "You're Our Heroes," "Welcome Home You Knuckleheads," "God Bless the 188th," "We love our Troops," "We are Proud of You 188th," and the one that broke my heart, "Welcome Home Standing Chief."

> **"A number of Dakota citizens stood like a gauntlet and shook each man's, each woman's hand and held the grip as long as the soldier would permit."**

Then the first cheer blew the roof off the airport, and the soldiers walked through the door, home, alive, some limping, touched to the bone by their experience in the desert and now blinking around, overwhelmed by the welcome they were receiving. They scanned the crowd for their loved ones. No need. Their loved ones jumped them like the woman on the tarmac in the famous "Vietnam soldiers return" photograph.

Some of the home folks laughed. Some cried. Most fought back tears. Women whooped. Extended family cheering sections roared the arrival of the one so long awaited, so viscerally welcome now. The crowd was a sea of small flags waving frantically, look, look over here. The crowd clapped slowly and with a reverence never seen in the theater through the twenty-minute parade of veterans. An Indian drum began to thunder through the building and the high keening voice of Mandan-Hidatsa-Arikara singers deepened the intensity of the homecoming. An elder from Mandaree stood in perfect pride. Tears dampened his cheeks. "When I landed in San Francisco in 1968, it wasn't anything like this," he told me. "This time we're together. We're cohesive. This is how it is supposed to be."

In single file, a little uncertain, the returning men and women walked slowly to the escalator and stairs, which were lined with comrades in arms who have not yet gone, or who have gone and already returned. A number of Dakota citizens stood like a gauntlet and shook each man's, each woman's hand and held the grip as long as the soldier would permit. A few of the soldiers cried. Some looked as if they would rather have returned to a quiet and empty terminal. Some were shy. The pride was almost too intense to watch, though some wore it mutely and others on their camouflaged sleeves. Many of the soldiers looked as if they hardly dared relax into the sheer joy of stepping foot on North Dakota soil again. That would come later. When I come home after a weeklong visit to Florida or Chicago, I often find myself singing out to myself, "I'm home I'm home I'm home in North Dakota." My idea of a rough trip is a cab at dawn or an hour-long flight delay. You could see in the eyes these young men and women the power of the idea of home in North Dakota. For the moment, Afghanistan seemed far far far away, but we all know that such an experience cannot be shrugged off like a trip to New Orleans or Las Vegas. And what happened in Kandahar does not stay in Kandahar.

As the crowd began to thin, I went through security. The TSA folks were subdued, and it was clear that some of them had been crying.

I'm sure not all of these young men are heroes. Most of them wouldn't like to be talked about in that way. But I know this: they have served their country in ways that most of the rest of us have not and really cannot understand, and whether we like this war or not, we all owe them an enormous amount of gratitude. More than that, because they have served us and indeed served in place of us, we now must serve them with the fullest local, state, and national respect: with the best health care America offers, with education, with whatever programs are needed to ease their re-entry.

We have not, in my view, done enough for our American troops at any stage of this conflict, from the gear they needed and asked for or the troop members the generals sought, from real respect for the service traditions of the National Guard and the Reserves to real candor in our national leadership about the purposes and causes of the war, and the outlook for its eventual end. All this is outrageous, but it is not scandal. The scandal is at Walter Reed Army Hospital. The scandal is political posturing while our most fervent citizens are in harm's way.

As I drove to the airport, all I could think about was a memo that is overdue, a book I forget to pack, a call I need to make, the hesitation of drivers in a sleet storm. Then I stumbled into what was, without question, the most intense experience I had since I returned to North Dakota. I would not have missed it for the world, even though, in my indifference and selfishness, I almost did.

As I fly away now to Denver and beyond, I sit in a stew of admiration and guilt. I feel shame in several directions—but most of it points straight home at me. *Unpublished, 2007*

The famous photograph is called "Burst of Joy." It was taken by AP photographer Sal Veeder at Travis Air Force Base on March 17, 1973. The deplorable conditions at Walter Reed Army Medical Center were reported in the Washington Post in February 2007.

Happy birthday, Arthur A. Link.

The former governor of North Dakota (1972–80) will celebrate his ninety-fourth birthday Saturday.

Thank goodness for your longevity, Gov. Link, and thank you for the quality of your leadership, before, during and after your time in office.

Thank you for the phrase "one time harvest," which reminds us that if stewardship is not at the center of our basic outlook on life, we are selling our birthright for a mess of pottage. Thank you for insisting in 1973 that reclamation of coal strip mines was both possible and affordable—even though the captains of the coal industry insisted that reclamation would bankrupt them and leave North Dakota out in the cold. We owe a lot of our topsoil to you. Thank you for your "go slow" approach to energy development—that's why we are North Dakota and not Gillette, Wyoming.

> "The son of an immigrant from Sudetenland goes on to become the governor of North Dakota. That's the meaning of America."

Art Link grew up on a farm near Alexander in McKenzie County. That's the key to his character. His formal education ended with the eighth grade, but he has continued to read and study and cogitate for the subsequent eighty years. He had the wisdom to see that we North Dakotans live on a broad and fruitful prairie whose highest purpose is the production of food. And he had the moral courage to stake his governorship on that principle when it would have been so easy to get on board with the draglines.

We are a better place—more truly North Dakota—for his leadership.

Art Link has become virtually a mythic figure in the North Dakota consciousness. Back in the spring of 1946, he was called to public office from across the creek that flows past his house in McKenzie County. The creek was in flood. Link was at work on the farm. A committee of Democrats came to draft him to run for the Legislature, but they couldn't get to the house. So they shouted their summons across swollen Antelope Creek. It's the story of Cincinnatus (from ancient Rome) set in northwestern North Dakota.

Think of it. He is the living child of a man who immigrated to the United States in his youth in the year 1900. Art Link is a first-generation North Dakotan. The son of an immigrant from Sudetenland goes on to become the governor of North Dakota. That's the meaning of America.

Immigrant and pioneer John Link lived with his son Art and daughter-in-law Grace in the North Dakota Governor's Residence in the 1970s. Art Link tells the story of playing pinochle with his elderly father in the residence while trying also to keep one eye on the evening news. Keeping up with the news is, after all, part of a governor's job. But John Link was having none of it. Finally he blurted out, "Look, either play cards or watch the news, but don't try to do both." The governor of North Dakota turned his attention to pinochle.

As a congressman in Washington, DC, (1970–72), Rep. Link changed his own oil in the family car—using Farmers Union oil. This is the stuff of myth.

And, of course, in 1973—on Oct. 11, to be exact—he gave what is widely regarded as North Dakota's "Gettysburg Address." At a rural electric cooperative meeting in Mandan, waiting to be introduced after the meal, Gov. Link suddenly decided to jot down—right from the heart—a few sentences about coal and our future in the margins of the speech his staff had helped prepare for the event. The governor's speech is known now by the profound subordinate clause by which it begins: "When the landscape is quiet again."

"Events now beginning to unfold in the North Dakota energy crescent will tell us whether we intend to let the landscape be quiet again, or whether we'd rather pocket the rip and roar."

Just stop and meditate that phrase for a moment. "When the landscape is quiet again. . . ." Does anything encapsulate what is best in North Dakota better than that?

The governor went on to say: "When the draglines, the blasting rigs, the power shovels and the huge gondolas cease to rip and roar, and when the last bulldozer has pushed the last spoil pile into place, and the last patch of barren earth has been seeded to grass or grain, let those who follow and repopulate the land be able to say, our grandparents did their job well. The land is as good and, in some cases, better than before."

Gov. Link, you did your job well.

The question he asked, thirty-five years ago, is how much can we disrupt our prairie landscape and still be North Dakota? His answer was: Err on the side of caution. Art Link embodies something very deep in the North Dakota experience and character. He represents what we have been for most of our heritage. He is elderly now. Some entrepreneurs of the current generation regard his views as quaint. Events now beginning to unfold in the North Dakota energy crescent will tell us whether we intend to let the landscape be quiet again, or whether we'd rather pocket the rip and roar.

I have had the opportunity to spend some time with Gov. and Grace Link during the last year. It has been one of the great honors of my life. Whenever I leave one of our meetings, I am happier to be alive, prouder to be a North Dakotan, more eager to do the right thing, and more sure that North Dakota is at its best when it is a land of agriculture.

One afternoon, I heard their son Harvey talk about how much the governor loves Grace's plum dumplings. I drove immediately to the grocery store, bought supplies, and did my best to make my first-ever batch of plum dumplings. They were mediocre, but I felt the way you do after you vote in a close election or participate in the wheat harvest. Those poor plum dumplings were a kind of tether to the hardscrabble farms of the west river country—to the distant Sudetenland—and to what we must not let slip away in North Dakota life.

Happy birthday, Gov. Link. *5/19/08*

Arthur A. Link died in Bismarck, North Dakota, on June 1, 2010. He was born on May 24, 1914.

CHUCK SUCHY: THE VOICE OF NORTH DAKOTA

Last Saturday night I rode with friends south of Mandan on ND 6 to hear the Suchy family's fifth annual Bohemian Hall outdoor concert. Over the years I have heard the great Chuck Suchy sing alone on many occasions, but I have never heard them all—Chuck and Linda, and their children Andra and Ben—in their Von Trapp family mode. This year's concert had special significance because it commemorated the one hundreth anniversary of the Bohemian Hall. Approximately four hundred people turned up, with blankets and lawn chairs and food and drink, and found their places on the prairie between the road and an amazingly healthy corn field.

I cannot recall ever being at so perfect a concert "hall" on so perfect an evening. The Suchys schedule the event on the August Saturday that is closest to a full moon. The moon was just short of full on the 25th, and it rose on schedule from the southeast in the middle of the concert. The low stage was set up against the north wall of the weathered old hall. A slightly garish, lighted artificial palm tree standing next to the stage added a little funk to the evening, along with an old mustard-colored VW microbus and a wee steeply domed aluminum trailer. The sunset was exquisite. Everyone started out in shirtsleeves, but by the end of the night, everyone was wearing every garment they could get their hands on. What could ever be better than that?

Since Chuck Suchy's music is so deeply rooted in place, in fact in this very place, it is wonderful that he and his family performed outdoors, as it were in their own backyard. Andra Suchy, whose voice is as pure as a meadowlark's, sang a song she has just written about Little Heart Creek, which meanders toward its mother tributary just a few miles south of

Bohemian Hall. Chuck sang "Saturday Night at the Hall," from his *Dakota Breezes* album, which celebrates Bohemian Hall, "built by the good of an old brotherhood," "where the highway runs down just south of our town." There we were, as the song says, on a beautiful moonlit night, fulfilling Suchy's lyrics: "No matter the season they sure find a reason for Saturday night at the hall."

What impressed me most about the evening was its quietness and calm, which may sound odd considering that it was an amplified music concert. There was none of the usual event hassle in the makeshift parking lot. People just found a spot to park with no jostling for position. The crowd was gentle and extremely appreciative. Many sat holding hands. Everyone knew it was one of the last great nights of the summer, and there could be no better place to spend it.

The great mandolin artist Peter Ostroushko came out from Minneapolis to join the Suchys on stage. Ostroushko, who is perhaps best known from his countless appearances on Garrison Keillor's *A Prairie Home Companion,* either is—or for us pretended to be—jaded and weary of the world. He played several mandolins with his usual virtuosity, including one that Chuck Suchy inherited from his great Aunt Lou via his cousin Art. The banter between Ostroushko and Chuck, and Ostroushko and Linda, was obviously the public surface of a very deep private affection. Ostroushko's presence itself was a tribute to the Suchys, and his occasional citified jabs at Chuck's prairie earnestness only made that earnestness more pure and attractive. Ostroushko's best moment was his long rendition of a song, written by Keillor, about a man who has sunk into a Barcalounger squalor and self-pity after having been left by his woman, and maybe just likes it there! Ostroushko managed to sing it in a way that pulled the Keillor bitterness right out of it.

It was a love fest. The volunteers who brought the food and attended the informal gates wore none of the usual beleaguered expressions of event volunteers. They were glad to contribute kuchen and bars, and it was clear that they all love the Suchys and feel honored to be allowed to help out. The Suchys' organic, grass-fed beef was delicious. And the Suchys themselves were so clearly a happy and harmonious family, each one tolerant of the musical and sartorial styles of each other, that I'm guessing every person in the audience thought, "That's what a family should be."

We North Dakotans are so fortunate to have Chuck Suchy among us. He is truly a state (regional, even national) treasure. He's an extremely talented singer and songwriter. He's a working farmer, which means that when he sings of the satisfaction of the harvest or celebrates a trusted old piece of farm equipment, or the joy that can be found even in the grimy weariness after a hard day's work, his listeners can literally hear the authenticity. He's humble, self-effacing, self-depreciating and self-amused, and he never

> **"We North Dakotans are so fortunate to have Chuck Suchy among us. He is truly a state (regional, even national) treasure. When he smiles his broad "ah gosh" smile, the whole crowd smiles back, as if involuntarily."**

misses a chance to make sure those around him get their chance to shine. When he smiles his broad "ah gosh" smile, the whole crowd smiles back, as if involuntarily. He so clearly loves this place, its history, heritage, its people, its quirkiness, its muted west-river landscape beauty, that he can really be called the voice of North Dakota.

His son Ben Suchy, who performs Monday nights at Casper's East Forty in Bismarck, has an edgy, gravelly sound, more evocative of jazz and blues than of his lyrical father. He plays a number of instruments, including the harmonica, extremely well, and he is clearly establishing his own identity, based on, but away from Little Heart Creek.

The highlight of the evening, for me, came when Chuck and his daughter Andra sang (he says for only the second time) his song, "Just One of Those Days." It was a surpassingly lovely moment: The blending of their voices, hers as thin and pure as a flute's, his still earnest in middle age. The love that passed between them, father and daughter, on stage, at home, in their eye contact, was as life-affirming as anything I have seen in many a day.

As we drove home, I thought, in sweet melancholy, "Summer's over now."
9/1/07

ARTHUR A. LINK: THE LAST AGRARIAN

The passing of Art Link Tuesday was the death knell of one phase of North Dakota history.

We will not see his like again.

He had just celebrated his ninety-sixth birthday. At ninety-six, death can be a release, but I know for a fact that Art Link was not ready to go. I had the joy of spending a couple of hours with him ten days ago.

He was as vital and engaged with the world as someone half his age. He spoke of the future like a man who expected to see it. In his last days, his voice had taken on a piping quality. A severe thunderstorm forced us to go down into the common room of the facility where the Links live.

I asked Art if I could push him in his wheelchair. With some reluctance, like a parent turning over the car keys for the first time, he agreed. I made the rookie mistake of approaching the elevator head on. The governor barked out the proper wheelchair protocol. "Back in! Back in!" he cried, and "Line up straight so you don't scrape the door sill." We laughed hard at my ineptitude.

In that same evening, just a week before his death, after almost a century of good life in North Dakota, Art Link expressed his concerns about the energy boom that is unfolding up in his home territory in northwestern North Dakota. He talked about his sweetheart Grace, who served cake and coffee and shook her head and laughed at his courtliness. He shook hands like a young farmer.

What was the meaning of his life?

He was the son of an immigrant who went on to be the governor of North Dakota. Just stop and think about that for a moment. We are unlikely ever to see that again. His life exemplifies the story of North Dakota. In the last years of the nineteenth century, tens of thousands of Europeans took the risk of migrating from their homelands to the heart of the American steppe.

They worked incredibly hard and most of them prospered in a modest sort of way. Their greatest achievement was that they made it possible for their children to have better lives than they did, less burdened with hard physical labor. Art Link had natural gifts that elevated him into public service, but his story nevertheless epitomizes the North Dakota chapter of the story of the American Dream.

He was actually called to public office. That's extremely rare. The story is part of the Art Link legend. There is a surprising amount of Art Link mythology (stories that are true but have a kind of winsome larger than life quality).

It was the spring of 1946. The Nonpartisan League of McKenzie County was holding its annual caucus. The creek in front of his farmhouse at Alexander was flooded, so Art Link could not get to town.

That afternoon, a car drove down the hill toward the farmstead, inching as close to the edge of the creek as the driver dared. When Art approached, a man representing the NPL called out, across the creek, "I just stopped, Art, to tell you that we nominated you for our candidate for the Legislature up at the caucus today."

For North Dakota, that little creek was a Rubicon.

He was as authentic a man as you will ever meet—plainspoken, artless, straight, earnest, grounded. And yet he had an exquisite sense of humor and a playfulness and a lust for life that made it impossible not to cheer up in his presence.

> "He so represented what we thought we were."
>
> –Mike Jacobs.

In my opinion, he represented the very best of the North Dakota character—the humility and strength of a man of the soil; a profound, usually unspoken, belief in the nobility of the agrarian way of life; a solidity of character and principles that made him impervious to inessential things; passionate, usually unspoken, love of the quiet landscape of North Dakota; a belief in the redeeming power of hard work; an unwavering unposed allegiance to family, place, nation and state.

> **"He was the son of an immigrant who went on to be the governor of North Dakota."**

When the great test of his leadership came in 1973, when North Dakota might have become an energy sacrifice zone, he reached deep into his core to coin words that changed the nature of the energy debate. We will cooperate fully with the need for stepped up energy development, he said, but we cannot permit that industrial activity to be a "one time harvest." Those words resonated with the core values of the people of North Dakota.

We did not shrink back from our destiny as one of the leading energy producers in America, but we shifted gears thanks to the leadership of Art Link. "Slow, orderly development," he said. Could there be any greater wisdom than that?

His creed (and his legacy) is perfectly articulated in the speech he delivered in Mandan, on Oct. 11, 1973, "When the Landscape Is Quiet Again." That poetic expression of the primacy of stewardship in North Dakota life should be memorized by every North Dakota schoolchild. It should be given as a welcome wagon gift to every new North Dakotan, particularly those who come to work in the energy corridor.

A while back, Mike Jacobs of the *Grand Forks Herald* explained to me what Art Link had meant for North Dakota. At the close of a long and remarkable interview, Jacobs said, "He so represented what we thought we were." In a mere eight words, Jacobs—as usual—nailed it.

Notice that he did not say, "He so represented who we are" or "who we were," but "who we thought we were." There is deep insight and a smidgeon of disillusionment in that sentence, spoken by another North Dakota leader with deep agrarian roots.

In 1893 historian Frederick Jackson Turner wrote a famous essay about the significance of the frontier in American history. In 1890, the US Census Bureau officially declared that the American frontier was closed. At the end of his masterful essay, Turner concluded, "And now, four centuries from the discovery of America, at the end of a hundred years of life under the Constitution, the frontier has gone, and with its going has closed the first period of American history."

The death of Art Link has closed the first period of North Dakota history. Our agrarian phase lasted from 1889 to approximately 1989. What we will be in the twenty-first century we are still to determine.

Unfortunately, we will not have Art Link to help us remember who we are.
6/6/10

I had the great good fortune to make a documentary film about Art Link for The Dakota Institute: When the Landscape is Quiet Again: The Legacy of Art Link.

WHERE I LIVED
AND WHAT
I LIVED FOR

The Heart Leaps Best

in the Beautiful Badlands

I think this was the best Valentine's Day of my life. And yet I exchanged no kisses.

My dearest friends and I drove out to Theodore Roosevelt's Elkhorn Ranch site on the Little Missouri River between the two main units of Theodore Roosevelt National Park.

It was a perfect day. Our leader called it an April day in February. As we sat in the sun overlooking the Little Missouri, there were moments when the day actually felt warm. The light was achingly beautiful—perfectly clear air, illuminated by a waxen yellow sun, which made every feature of the landscape stand out in sharp relief. North Dakota has hundreds of beautiful places, but I think the Elkhorn Ranch site may be the most beautiful of them all. Add Roosevelt to this mix, and you have a magic place. Sacred ground.

> **"I felt chills run up my back and neck because I could picture TR looking around—in his thick glasses and his grimace—as he crafted each phrase and weighed the effect of each adjective he chose as he told the world about this remarkable place."**

We had the best possible guide to the Elkhorn Ranch, Bruce Kaye, chief of interpretation at Theodore Roosevelt National Park. Kaye has been at the park for eighteen years. He knows the history of the Badlands as well as anyone alive. He is a quiet and gentle man with an unending fund of information, and it is clear that he has a special love of the Elkhorn Ranch that transcends his job description.

"This is the Walden Pond of the American West," he said.

We sat where the 30-by-60-foot cabin once stood, and we talked in quiet tones about Roosevelt's sojourn in this place. Roosevelt established the Elkhorn Ranch in 1884 just a few months after the sudden death of his mother, Mittie (49), and his first wife, Alice (22), on the same day. Those terrible deaths occurred in New York City on Feb. 14, 1884, and now we six were in the place of solitude where TR came to recuperate, precisely 122 years after the hardest day of Roosevelt's life. We might have celebrated Valentine's Day anywhere. We chose to spend it here, in friendship and in love with North Dakota's imperiled Little Missouri River valley.

We spread a splendid picnic on the prairie grasses, cheeseburger soup, fried chicken, salami, strawberries, sharp black coffee, and wine for those who wished it. We broke homemade bread together.

Kaye read to us TR's descriptions of the Elkhorn Ranch—the cottonwoods, the shape of the bluffs, the meanderings of the great little river through its half-mile-wide valley, the colors and the contours of the countryside—and while he read those words written more than a century ago, the rest of us looked around and saw that TR's description still captures the place perfectly.

I felt chills run up my back and neck because I could picture TR looking around—in his thick glasses and his grimace—as he crafted each phrase and weighed the effect of each adjective he chose as he told the world about this remarkable place. Earlier in the day, we had seen at the national park visitor's center an ink bottle found by archaeologists at the Elkhorn site. It is not unlikely that TR dipped his pen into that ink well as he described his ranch to family and friends.

We were all visibly affected to be in this place with this guide reading these words on this occasion. I think we all felt the same thing: that our most immediate heart's desire, this Valentine's Day, is that the greater Elkhorn Ranch site—the existing 218 acres administered by the National Park Service and the few thousand acres of viewshed over to the east—will be preserved forever from industrial scars, vanity McMansions and adverse economic "development."

Nobody wants to take it from anybody. This is a story that doesn't involve confiscations. The people who own one of the two principal ranches across the river—the Eberts family, Norma and Ken, Jennifer and Allen, Jeannette and Dennis—desire of their own free will to sell their ranch to the United States government—that is, to the people of North Dakota and the United States. They are going to sell their ranch to somebody, but they prefer to sell it to America for the best and noblest of all possible reasons. They feel that the ranch they have been blessed to own is so beautiful and so historically important that it should join the existing 218-acre Elkhorn site as a permanent shrine to TR. The Eberts look west across the Little Missouri at TR's cabin site. But from his veranda, TR looked east at his Elkhorn rangeland—at what is now the Eberts Ranch—and that view, by any rational standard, is at least as important as the ground on which he sat.

There are no shenanigans here. We have a willing seller and a willing buyer, and the price is reasonable and competitive.

Call me naïve, but I thought that was the very idea of private property in the United States. That a person who owns a piece of property can sell it to the buyer of his choice, without his fellow citizens meddling in something that is none of their business. And yet the Eberts have been criticized by some and vilified by a few, for wishing to cooperate with the United States government. In my opinion, they should be celebrated. They have the vision to see that the future of this small corner of the Badlands is as much thoughtful cultural tourism as grazing. Or both at once.

The Elkhorn Ranch matters as much as the two larger units of Theodore Roosevelt National Park. In my opinion, more. The whole bowl of the site, the cabin site and the bluff-enclosed view to the east should be preserved forever as close as possible to the way Roosevelt found it in 1884 and the way that he left it a decade later. If the US government obtains title, the loss of tax revenues to Billings County would be minor, and it is quite possible that they would be directly recompensed every year from the national treasury. The Elkhorn Ranch site, properly protected in its magnificent solitude, will in the long run prove to be a much greater economic engine for Billings County than cattle and oil, and it is quite likely that the site will still be grazed by cattle if it becomes part of the National Forest system. We should preserve the Greater Elkhorn Ranch irrespective of economics, because this is the most important Roosevelt site in America, certainly in the American West. But the fact is that the economics favor Billings County.

> "Call me naïve, but I thought that was the very idea of private property in the United States. That a person who owns a piece of property can sell it to the buyer of his choice, without his fellow citizens meddling in something that is none of their business."

Our governor and our three-member congressional team need to get this thing done now. This is not some precedent-setting slippery slope of federal intrusiveness. This is a unique situation—the preservation of the homestead, indeed the heartstead, of one of the greatest men in American history, one of the top four or five of the forty-three presidents of the United States, a larger than life man who chose to dwell among us and who combined a deep love and respect for ranching and frontier life with a firm belief in wise-use conservation of our natural resources.

On the long drive home, I called my eleven-year-old daughter in Kansas. She had received the flowers and the helium balloon, and she discovered she has a secret admirer who sent her a gift and a Valentine's card. Today, perhaps, her heart leapt in a certain way for the first time. This summer, before it is too late, I will bring her to the Elkhorn Ranch.   *2/18/06*

The US Forest Service purchased the Eberts Ranch in 2007. It would have been better had it been purchased by Theodore Roosevelt National Park, but the Forest Service (National Grasslands) will protect the site and some day it may graduate to National Park or National Monument status.

Waking up Chilly and Oh So Alive

Oh, what a difference a year makes.

Last night, I woke up at around 4 a.m. because I was cold. I sleep with the windows open, and so far this summer a thin sheet has been plenty of cover. Sometime before dawn today, a cotton sheet was not enough, even after twenty minutes of experimenting with variations of the fetal position and sheet wrappery.

Perfect North Dakota August weather. We live in so marvelous a place.

I laughed out loud in my kitchen this morning as I battened the windows, when I recalled that exactly one year ago this week I was coming off the Little Missouri River at the North Unit of Theodore Roosevelt National Park, after seventeen days of hiking and camping. They were amongst the hardest and most satisfying days I can ever remember. There were no chilly nights.

I had started at Marmarth on July 31, bear-hugged, fed and ridiculed by my old friend Patti Perry, the mayor. She is not the kind of person who worries much about the fate of geeks in the Badlands, but this time her farewell lecture at the U.S. Highway 12 bridge consisted of three propositions, one of them uncharacteristically serious. First, she said, only a fool would hike the Little Missouri River Valley under any circumstances. Second, anyone who hiked the Badlands in an August as hot as 2006 was taking unnecessary risks and might actually suffer or perish. Third, as I walked off, she turned to my dear friend and driver and said, "There goes pure insanity."

It turned out to be a blisteringly hot summer adventure. I would call it an ordeal, but for all of the heat, dehydration and fatigue, it was as glorious as anything I have ever experienced, and never once did I consider bailing out. The temperature never dipped below 85 degrees at night, and by 9 a.m. the next morning, it was usually well over 90. There was only one day in which the afternoon temperature did not top 100 degrees, and always well before noon. On the hottest day, it was 109. My rule was "nine by noon." If I could lug my 65-pound pack and my middle-aged body nine miles by noon every day, I reckoned, I could proceed on at least 12 or 13 miles a day and thus complete my hike. Under normal weather conditions, I could expect to hike up to 25 miles per day, but in extreme heat anything over 10 was a triumph.

An adventure of this sort, as Thoreau taught, reduces us to lowest terms, what in *Walden* he calls "grossest groceries." My seventeen days consisted of eating beef jerky (homemade) and freeze-dried food, and moving from random flowing well to random flowing well. Each time I blundered upon a well, I doused myself with water, like a child running through the sprinkler, and forced as many ounces of that water (good, bad and indifferent) into my stomach and my water bottles as they could possibly contain. Then I rested for a few minutes, topped off my waterlogged stomach and lurched off with determination to the next water source, all day every day for more than two weeks.

On previous treks in the Little Missouri Valley, water had never been an issue. This time, because of the heat wave, it was the issue, and on a few occasions I actually worried about whether I would get to the next cattle trough in time or whether I would be reduced to drinking from the Little Missouri itself. I tend to regard that as a fate worse than death, but Patti Perry says—in her wise but scoffing way—that it is, in fact, just the reverse. Not knowing just where the next well might be added to the anxiety and adventure of the hike.

When my friend Jim picked me up at Juniper campground in the North Unit of Theodore Roosevelt National Park in mid-August, he stopped for gas at the convenience store on the south end of Killdeer. We separated as he paid for the gas, and I strolled along the aisles, shaking my head at what capitalism can stock in a quick shop. Eventually he found me, mesmerized, drooling, before a rack of powdered doughnuts, Twinkies, Ho Hos, Cheetos, and Hostess cupcakes. I felt like Chevy Chase (as Clark Griswold) in *National Lampoon's Vacation* after his solo hike across the Arizona desert. When, half dead, he finally staggers up to his family at a roadside gas station, he hugs his son Rusty and cries out, in his shrillest and most neurotic voice, "Hey! Shall we get a pop?"

A few weeks ago, I hiked up White Butte near Amidon with a good outback friend to see how things looked from the highest point in North Dakota. The view is magnificent. It was a hazy day, but we saw at least twelve prominent buttes from the summit, and the sense of standing on the top of the world, even at a mere 3,506 feet above sea level, was delightful. It was the hottest day of this summer. As we hiked up with our lightly-loaded day packs in the oven-like afternoon, I actually said, "What kind of idiot would do any serious hiking in this kind of weather?"

And then I realized. Oh, my kind of idiot. As usual, Patti Perry was right.

Last summer, let us hope, was an anomaly. This summer is how I think of North Dakota. Spells of seriously hot weather, with just a few nights in which the temperature does not drop to comfort levels, surrounded by long stretches when it rises into the 90s by day, but drops down to about 68 at night. Add to this some gray days in which the temperature does not nearly reach eighty degrees and a cool, at times almost chilly, breeze perfects the morning. All that has been missing this summer are appallingly beautiful thunderstorms.

> "We separated as he paid for the gas and I strolled along the aisles shaking my head at what capitalism can stock in a quick shop. Eventually he found me, mesmerized, drooling, before a rack of powdered donuts, Twinkies, Ho Hos, Cheetos, and Hostess Cupcakes."

I love waking up cold in my bed, summer, spring and autumn, and seeking out a blanket to pull up and huddle under. There is only one thing more pleasurable: waking up slightly cold in a sleeping bag in the Little Missouri country when the breeze is performing a sweet rustling symphony in the cottonwoods overhead. *8/18/07*

THE JEFFERSONIAN JOY

OF A GARDEN AT SEASON'S END

My garden now has a rangy, Halloweeny look. The pumpkin and cucumber leaves have withered and turned gray-black, and the depleted corn stalks now stand like brittle scarecrows on the west edge. I don't know whether there has been a hard frost at my house, but I think not.

Tomatoes are surely a more reliable guide than Daniel Gabriel Fahrenheit (1686-1736) and Anders Celsius (1701-1744). I counted 337 tomatoes this morning, including several bushes gravid with cherry tomatoes. Some are overripe. Most are still far too green for late September. Fully one hundred are perfectly ripe and need to come out of the garden today. It's a miracle. It's also Miracle Grow.

My hero, Jefferson, got it right when he wrote to his friend Charles Willson Peale in 1811: "No occupation is so delightful to me as the culture of the earth, and no culture comparable to that of the garden. Such a variety of subjects, some one always coming to perfection, the failure of one thing repaired by the success of another, and instead of one harvest a continued one through the year." Right, as always. Jefferson was such a lovely, serene and exquisite man. He took all knowledge to be his province. He was a perfectionist with a deep commitment to making sure everything around him was as beautiful and harmonious as possible. In Shakespeare's term, "there was a daily beauty in his life." He said once, "There is not a sprig of grass that shoots uninteresting to me." If genius is "an infinite capacity for taking pains," Jefferson was a genius.

> "When you reach the phase of your life in which you're frying up bacon for yourself, bypass surgery cannot be far behind."

Jefferson kept five daily diaries: a farm book, a garden book, a letter log, an account book and a weather journal. He possessed and was possessed by a rage for order perhaps greater than that of any other American. He worked out the dimensions of the buildings he designed to three, sometimes four decimal points. He took down weather data twice a day (dawn and mid-afternoon) virtually every day of his adult life. He invented a library classification system for his books—based on Francis Bacon's belief that products of the human mind can be put into three basic bins: reason, memory and imagination. He wore a crude pedometer to chart his daily mileage and he tried to convince America to adopt a decimal metric system.

The first entry in Jefferson's Garden Book, begun in 1766 (when he was 22), tells us who he was: "March 30. Purple hyacinth begins to bloom."

"The failure of one thing repaired by the success of another," Jefferson wrote. My tomatoes were good, but not great this year. (Last year, they were spectacular). Perhaps because of the late May freeze, my fifty-one tomato plants bushed out rather than climbed this time, and I spent a fair amount of time devising support structures to keep the fruit off of the ground. But my onions, garlic and sweet corn were perfect, especially the corn.

The best nights of my summer had the simplicity of Thoreau. I'd walk out to the garden and dig up three potatoes with a tined shovel, pull up an onion, twist off a cucumber and pluck a softball-sized tomato, and with a sense of deep satisfaction walk back into the house. Then I cut up the potatoes, fried them with onions and garlic from the garden, and made myself a little Greek salad with the rest of the onion and the cucumber and tomato. Once, I even home-made the dressing from my grandmother's cookbook. At least twenty times this summer, I ate raw tomato sandwiches. I'm waiting for my friend Jim to appear so I can make tomato and bacon sandwiches. The bacon seems a little decadent for one dining alone. When you reach the phase of your life in which you're frying up bacon for yourself, bypass cannot be far behind.

> "If you do not feel the grace of God in a garden, or the sheer fecundity of nature, or the pertinacity of the life principle, you have not sat down in the earth and drunk it in."

What I love about potatoes is that you don't know how many or how large they are until you dig them up.

I walked through the garden this morning to see how things are faring as North Dakota makes the turn from summer to autumn. Three large pumpkins have emerged from the shriveled foliage. They are still partly... well, pumpkin-colored, and still partly green. When I saw them squatting there big as basketballs, two little detonations went off in my noggin. First, my soul soared the seven hundred-odd miles to my daughter, who was probably walking to school at this very moment. She would be delighted to see those pumpkins and she would propose, because she is still one-part a child, that we carve one up tonight and save the rest for October. My impulse would be to resist that idea—but why?—and in the end we would carve and find a candle and make hot chocolate and luxuriate, until the chill came, on the deck.

It reminded me, too, of one of the greatest of the parables of Jesus, the parable of the mustard seed. I quote from my favorite gospel, the book of Mark: "And he said, Whereunto shall we liken the kingdom of God? It is like a grain of mustard seed, which, when it is sown in the earth, is less than all the seeds that be in the earth; But when it is sown, it groweth up, and becometh greater than all herbs, and shooteth out great branches; so that the fowls of the air may lodge under the shadow of it." If you do not feel the grace of God in a garden, or the sheer fecundity of nature, or the pertinacity of the life principle, you have not sat down in the earth and drunk it in.

One of the best moments of my summer came about three weeks ago when I was awakened at 6:13 a.m. by a phone call. I was fast asleep, as I tend to be at that hour (funny, I get some of my best sleep at night). It was the Burleigh County sheriff's office. Calvinist that I am, I immediately began to try to imagine what I had done to deserve the rare dawn arrest. The deputy identified himself and then said, "I hope I haven't woke you up or nothin'." "No," I lied. Most of us do this when we are awakened by a call, but of course we invariably sound like heavily sedated deep-sea divers talking on a tin-can telephone from Davy Jones's locker. "No, been up for hours!"

He explained that the cows had gotten out of a nearby ranch and rampaged the neighborhood and they had spent some time eating my garden, had knocked down about half of my corn and trampled other stuff. How he knew this I don't know. It was still pitch dark. He wanted to know if I would like to file a report so that I could seek damages from the rancher. "I don't know," I said. "Perhaps AFTER THE SUN RISES! I will walk out and survey the damage."

What I didn't tell him, not wanting to cloud his dream of a tort, is that it delights me mightily to think that I live where the cows can still vandalize a town now and then. I ate the remnant ears of my sweet corn with a special joy thereafter—because scarcity heightens all human experience—and I will be so very sorry when Bismarck eats the ranch that nurtures the grass that grows the cow that climbs the fence and eats the corn that lifts my life. *9/22/07*

> *This is one of my favorite columns. I'm sorry to report that it is no longer possible for neighborhood cows to decimate my garden. The biggest mistake I made in moving home to North Dakota was not anticipating the explosive growth of Bismarck.*

A Time to Till, a Time to Plant,

a Time to Hope for Timely Rain

A year ago, my mother gave me a rototiller as a housewarming gift. A week ago Saturday, on a moderately warm perfect afternoon, moderate breeze, meadowlarks singing, I tilled my garden.

On Thursday, I saw my first crocus (pasqueflower). Last Sunday evening, I witnessed my first thunderstorm of the year. It was an odd, tentative, unintegrated thunderstorm, sharply powerful in bursts but not quite sure of itself.

Tally: First meadowlark of 2008, March 25. First pasqueflower, April 17. First thunderstorm, April 20.

Spring has sprung. The grass has not riz. One of my neighbors is already watering. That's a very bad sign.

It took me about an hour to start the tiller. Note to self: Next year, don't leave it out for part of the winter. I yanked the cord enough times to propel an Apollo capsule all the way to the moon. If I did not quite dislocate my shoulder, I certainly dislocated my heart. At one point, I thought of just pouring gasoline over the entire machine, tossing a lighted match from a safe (?) distance, and seeing what happened. By that time, I knew I could live with the outcome, either way.

In the end, of course, the tiller started, just at the moment when the Barcalounger region of my brain was saying, "Well, you don't really need a garden anyway. They're a lot of work. It's cheaper just to go to the farmers market. If you think about it, you'd be doing a lot of earnest vegetable growers a favor. Fresh food is overrated." And so on.

After that little crisis of slothfulness (No. 4 of the seven deadlies), I tilled happily, even blissfully, for the next five hours. I'm an obsessive tiller—deep, thorough, and many more passes than necessary. Every twenty minutes or so, I'd idle the tiller and run about moving the hose along the line of ponderosa pines. By sunset I had created—with a little help from the industrial revolution—a beautiful, rectangular, black earth garden plot. I took my shoes off and walked through it with winter-tender bare feet, just to feel the warm earth, the consistency of coffee grounds, between my toes. It's so beautiful that I almost hate to plant it.

Thomas Jefferson was right: "Those who labour in the earth are the chosen people of God, if ever He had a chosen people, whose breasts he has made his peculiar deposit for substantial and genuine virtue." I would never try to pretend, even to my susceptible self, that I "labour in the earth." I labour, if labour it can really even be called, in the coffee shop and the library and the airport concourse. But my dalliance in my garden is the sanest, most stabilizing and most re-connecting thing I do.

Photo Gallery:
Clay Jenkinson's North Dakota

Clay began his career as a photojournalist, first at the Dickinson Press, then the Wahpeton Daily News. When he left for college in 1973, he intended to study journalism. But when he discovered the humanities in a Shakespeare seminar at the University of Minnesota, he changed course and never looked back.

The photographs in this special portfolio represent "Clay Jenkinson's North Dakota"—not the round bale and red barn Dakota of tourism calendars and glossy magazines, but a vast, windswept, and open plain at the heart of the North American continent. Clay's goal, in his newspaper column and in all else that he does, is to celebrate North Dakota as it actually is, in all of its moods, on good days and bad, in serenity and in disarray, rather than as it appears when the camera is focused selectively on what Clay calls "the state's thirty perfect days per annum."

Self-portrait by the author on the third day of his 173-mile solo hike along the Little Missouri River. This photo was taken a few miles south of Bullion Butte.

The incomparable Sheila Schafer at Buck Hill, her favorite place in Theodore Roosevelt National Park.

The fabulous prairie crocus (technically pasque flower) on Bodmer ridge overlooking Fort Union and the confluence of the Missouri and Yellowstone Rivers.

The quintessential Great Plains quadruped—eighteen pronghorn antelope thunder off to the horizon for no good reason.

The "famous triathlete" Melanie R. Carvell teaching her dog Fury how to lope the plains. For Melanie, there is no shutter speed fast enough…

Sunset at Bohemian Hall, with an assembly of the enlightened, listening to North Dakota's troubadour Chuck Suchy.

The Little Missouri River country in the big oxbow around Bullion Butte.

East Rainy Butte at dusk. Clay's fascination (obsession?) with the buttes of North Dakota is inexplicable.

The superintendent of Theodore Roosevelt National Park, Valerie Naylor, finishes an inspection tour of the Little Missouri River near Wind Canyon.

The North Unit of Theodore Roosevelt National Park. North Dakota has landscapes as beautiful as any on earth.

On the seventh day of their attempt to recreate the Lewis & Clark Expedition, the author and his friend David Borlaug were reduced to eating pine bark.

Mama in her element, on the porch of her wee cabin near the portal of Yellowstone National Park. With Boz her faithful Schnauzer. It's July 4, but that's a fire in the fireplace.

North Dakota's infamous winters seldom disappoint. Loving North Dakota is loving it in all of its many moods.

Former North Dakota Governor Arthur A. Link at Old Settler's Days in Alexander, North Dakota. "That oil's not going anywhere," he said. "We don't need to be in any hurry to bring it to the surface."

The future of North Dakota? The industrialization of the Great Plains south of Clay's beloved Marmarth.

Out where the Jeffersonian rectangular grid breaks down. From the air southwest of Dickinson. Wheat fields in arid country, the triumph of hope over experience.

In the midst of the largest energy boom in northern plains history, family farms are the forgotten core of North Dakota life.

The sensuality of the agrarian in open country. November, on the road to Grand Forks, before the landscape goes flat.

King Wheat near Hebron. On the Fourth of July, fully 25% of the surface of North Dakota is carpeted with hard red spring wheat. Eat that, Kansas.

There is nothing quite so exhilarating as a punishing lightning storm. This photo was taken from the author's deck.

On those handful of days in August when I gather every item of my evening meal fresh from the garden, and do little more than scrub it before eating it slowly, like a sacrament, with a glass of wine by my side, I feel that my life has meaning. I feel a kind of redemption.

But on a spring Saturday afternoon as I tilled, the wind picking up at the rate of a few more miles per hour every hour, I realized how very dry the land is this year. It tilled too easily, and what little moisture there was in the earth evaporated within minutes of my turning it over. Immediately, the veneer of my garden blew away to Minnesota. Trouble ahead, unless some soaking rains visit the earth in the next month or so.

I met a brand new adult North Dakotan this week, just transplanted from Missouri, and naturally I asked her how she likes it here. "Great," she said, and then without pause, "Is … it always this windy here?" One never quite knows how to answer that one.

I love North Dakota in all of its moods. I'm not fond of the "perfect summers and often great autumns" argument. And though some of my good friends are snowbirds who maintain winter homes in Arizona and Florida, I dislike the phenomenon. I prefer my North Dakota raw and un-apologetic. If you don't like to be made aware of your fragile temporariness in the cosmic scheme of things, you shouldn't live here. To be a North Dakotan is to get wind-whipped with some frequency. The sky matters here more than elsewhere, and it does like to get in your face, to blow you off the walking path, to make you concentrate hard while driving, to pit your windshield and your siding, to rattle your serenity, to wreck your picnic, to scatter your laundry to king-dom come, and to blow stuff over that you thought was well secured. Now add some driving snow and January temperatures that kill and appall, and you have a formula for a sparsely populated place.

> "I asked her how she likes it here. "Great," she said and then without pause, "Is … it always this windy here?" One never quite knows how to answer that one."

To ease my new friend's mind, I photocopied a page from the State Historical Society's book *A Vast and Open Plain: The Writings of the Lewis and Clark Expedition in North Dakota* and sent it to her.

Lewis and Clark left Fort Mandan on April 7, 1805, almost immedi-ately after the ice broke up in the Missouri River. They were headed up "the heretofore deemed endless Missouri River" in search of its source. The winds were just what we've been experiencing lately, but even more pronounced in the wind tunnel of the Missouri River. For days the expedi-tion could make no forward progress whatsoever, or they would start out in a 20 mph wind and then just give up—for all of their puissance—by 11 a.m. when things really got to blowing. Eventually, Meriwether Lewis, who regarded himself as the first white man ever to see that country near Williston, actually had to wonder, "is it always this windy here?"

On April 23, 1805, he wrote, "Set out at an early hour this morning. about nine A.M. the wind arose, and shortly after became so violent that we were unabled to proceed, in short it was with much difficulty and some risk that I was enabled to get the canoes and perogues into a place of tolerable safety, there being no timber on either side of the river at this place. these hard winds, being so frequently repeated, become a serious source of detention to us."

The winds eventually attenuated. Lewis and Clark did reach the Pacific. And they grew to love the buffalo plains of North Dakota.

If these 2008 winds ever die down, I'll plant potatoes.   *4/26/08*

I've got to stop writing about the day in August when I first harvest an entire evening meal in my garden. But it is so nearly a perfect pleasure that I cannot help it.

Rain is Good,

More is Better,

Lightning Sublime

The rains of the past week have been modest, but for the moment, at least, they have changed the face of North Dakota. They also have put smiles on people's faces. The prospect of a summer wherein the grass never greens up, in which the plains start out yellow and wind up tan-gray was making me—and everyone else—fretful.

Flying back into the state in May, I looked down every time on the rolling plains of North Dakota and saw a tawny grassland with widely scattered patches of dull green, mere hints of a stalled spring. It should have been Ireland green in the second half of May. We landed one evening in gale-force winds. My friend Jim took me out for supper. "Everyone's grumpy," he said. "The whole state's grumpy. We're tired of the wind." We ate quickly and without much pleasure.

Since then, we've had a little relief. You can see it in people's eyes.

It's still windy and it's still fundamentally dry, dry to the point that the US Forest Service has ordered grazing cuts in the Little Missouri National Grasslands, but the modest rains we've had have brushed a patina of green over the land. Everyone is grateful and now hopeful, though not quite free of anxiety. Keep it coming—maybe a three-day soaker.

We live in a semi-arid place. Like it or not, this is the norm.

I went out for a long walk the other night and got caught in the best rain of the year so far. It had been a bright and clear, but windy, afternoon. By the time I got into walking shoes and found a book, a storm front had moved in out of nowhere. It was only 6 o'clock but it suddenly felt like dusk.

I love that. If you live in North Dakota, you perforce have a relationship with the sky. Think of the American Indians who lived here, but essentially lived here outside. No wonder they were so spiritually alive.

The front edge of the vast cloudbank hovered over the Missouri River between Bismarck and Mandan. Sudden gusts of violent wind scattered loose papers on my dining room table. I thought of taking a slicker, but I reckoned it was a front without any moisture in it, and that the rain would be measured in mere hundredths.

I was wrong.

By the time I had walked half a mile, the raindrops had begun to assemble into clusters. The individual drops were dense and cold and hard, as if they really would have rathered be hail, and they began to penetrate through my work shirt onto my skin. Turn back? No way. I felt the chill, but it was in that wonderful borderland between agreeable and disagreeable. It seemed wrong to yearn for rain and then to be turned back at the first sign of deliverance.

When you live in dry country, getting soaked can be a satisfying experience. At first the rain was so half-hearted that I reckoned the evaporation rate would keep up. Not so. My shirt got wetter and heavier and it began to cling to my skin. Rivulets began to run their traceries down my face and blear my eyes. I could feel myself smiling, a rain dope. Huge drops hit the walking path and bounced a little, carrying up a little detonation of dust. Suddenly, the sky had an aroma—that magical smell of life and renewal and clarity. I walked by a lilac bush and took a deep breath. It's enough to make you almost faint to smell the lilacs at full bloom.

> "If you live in North Dakota you perforce have a relationship with the sky. Think of the Native Americans who lived here, but essentially lived here outside. No wonder they were so spiritually alive."

Then the lightning came. The sky had been rumbling in a distant kettledrum sort of way, and the thunderheads had lit up like cartoon clouds, but it had all been heat lighting until now. Now, suddenly, classical streaks of vicious zig zag lightning hurtled from heaven to earth, and split the whole sky in the aftermath. I counted the seconds between lightning and the appalling crack of thunder—thunder that began slowly as if the sky gods were unzipping the heavens and grew to an explosive crescendo that makes you actually jump from the ground.

Perfection of nature! We live on so interesting a planet. Imagine a planet without dramatic weather. What would be the fun of that?

You find yourself doing a bit of probability analysis in such situations, assuring yourself that the chances of being struck by lightning are really very low. You inspect the soles of your shoes and try to determine whether plastic or leather is the superior insulator. You walk more deliberately, picking up your feet to make sure you are not shuffling up static electricity.

I tried to imagine what it would be like to be struck by lightning. We've all read stories about individuals who have been struck—a few of them repeatedly through life as if their body chemistry somehow made them human lightning rods. Would it blow off my toenails? Would it weld the pen in my breast pocket to my ribs? Would I bear a zig zag stigmata down my back for the rest of my life like Harry Potter? Would I suddenly start receiving FM radio and, if so, could I choose NPR rather than rap or acid rock? Would I be split open like an over-cooked bratwurst and left to smolder through the night?

There have been times, later in the summer, out in the Little Missouri River country, when I was literally the highest object on the landscape. In the worst (actually, best) thunderstorm I ever experienced, I was so frightened that I threw myself face down on the plains grass in a kind of hollow and felt that even then I was the highest object on the landscape. On that occasion, and a few others, I believed it quite likely that I would be killed. That's not a very comforting experience, and yet there is an exhilaration in it too, a heightening of consciousness and a presence that we seldom achieve as we go through the motions of life.

Last week's lightning spared me for another time. When I got home, I stripped my clothes off in the entryway like a summer child, took a long, long hot shower, and discarded my sodden book.

There are lots of books. *6/7/08*

I am a sucker for a lightning storm. When I was young I used to drive out into them and do everything but hold up a five iron. It made my mother very nervous. When I lived away, in Reno, Nevada, I missed two things particularly: the smell of agriculture and thunderstorms.

Suddenly, The Light Has Gone Away:

Canning Tomatoes in the Dark

Suddenly, as if out of nowhere, I am lamenting the loss of light. I'm not meteorologist enough to understand it, but between June 21 and some point in early September, the evenings linger endlessly in a way that feels constant and uniform—and perhaps permanent. Then one late summer or early fall day—as if out of nowhere—it's getting dark at 7:45 p.m. There is some moment at which a switch seems to have been thrown, and our summer revels are declared over, and the summer light is packed up with the boat and the family-size tent. It makes me literally want to cry out in anguish.

> "I pressed the juice through a French colander with a wooden pestle. I filled each jar to the proper mark with warm—almost hot—thick tomato juice that was so sensuous, so magically red, so pregnant with the earth's fertility, that I had an impulse to bathe in it."

Now we begin that gloomy and inexorable slide toward existence in the dark: children heading off to school in the dark, darkness awaiting us as we return home at the end of the work day. Even the lowering winter clouds seem to signify that the hidden sun has been switched to "energy saving" mode.

I do not mind the cold, no matter how cold. But, like Dylan Thomas, I want to rage, rage against the dying of the light. The sole compensation for this loss is the little seed of knowledge that half a year hence the evening will come when I look around the prairie like a pronghorn antelope on alert and say, out loud, "The light's back!" I'll be outside, trying to untangle the hoses from the heaps that I tossed unceremoniously into the garage the day the first big freeze was announced this fall, and I'll suddenly notice—in a recognition of pure joy—that light has returned to the world.

The recent freeze near Hettinger was a shock that threw me into tomato processing. Some sort of creature has been taking one bite out of each of my beautiful tomatoes, so I decided to make tomato juice to preserve what they did not eat. I bought a dozen new jars and lids, sterilized them in the way that my grandmother taught me long ago. I washed and trimmed the tomatoes and then blanched them, all to the tune of Handel's *Largo*.

I pressed the juice through a French colander with a wooden pestle. I filled each jar to the proper mark with warm—almost hot—thick tomato juice that was so sensuous, so magically red, so pregnant with the earth's fertility, that I had an impulse to bathe in it. Then I wiped the tops of the jars with a paper towel, placed the rubberized lids on top of the jars as carefully as if I were docking the space shuttle, and then spun the brass screwtops into place with a kind of flourish, like a '50s DJ.

The rest was simple: Lower the jars into the mottled canning pot, make sure they are covered with an inch or more of water, boil slowly for forty minutes, extricate carefully, cool slowly. Voila.

I know I am making a big deal out of something many of you do with cool efficiency year after year, but for me it is a very big deal. I have now stored up a handful of jars of tomato juice against the apocalypse. It's the first time I have ever canned all by myself, and—frankly—the second time I have ever canned. My life mostly has been about hectic consumption and wastage. Now, in mid life, home where my heart always has been, I have finally turned a corner and begun to exhibit a teeny glimmer of stewardship. For me, canning those few jars of food I have actually grown in my own garden was a sacrament as powerful as baptism. I have more jars and many more tomatoes and I am going to try to see this through—for a change.

The jars I have already "put up," as my grandmother used to phrase it, are on the shelf in my front entry, glowing with the life force, right next to the lone jar of pickles she granted me when we canned a dozen quarts of her prize cucumbers together twenty years ago. I have carried that jar of pickles from house to house and town to town across America since that day in her linoleum kitchen in September 1988, when she was still in her late prime, still storing up produce against the lean times. Every time I have moved, I have attended first to that jar of pickles, wrapping it carefully in big fresh sheets of packing paper, then in towels, and placing it in the center of a big box marked "FRAGILE."

The ancient Romans had something called Penates—the household gods unique to each family—which they treasured up in the most important place in their homes. The Penates were a little like American Indian medicine bundles. They protected the household and the sanctity of the family. The word Penates actually derives from a Latin word for "provision of food." I have my Penates now, in Bismarck, in North Dakota, at the center of the North American continent, presided over by Rhoda Straus's alpha jar of cucumber pickles. Every day when I walk by those jars of tomato juice, I feel a wave of pride and also a sharp rush of loss.

The softer fall light, glowing rather than shining through air clarified by the recent rains, has made North Dakota's countryside a paradise. The fall light somehow brings the buttes and the coulees and the ridgelines into greater relief. It's as if "flat" North Dakota is being rendered into 3D. I have discovered buttes I never bothered to see before. Each time I see something as if for the first time, I say to myself, "I'm going to climb that butte and see what the world looks like from up there." Soon, while there is still light.

The other night, I went out walking the trail near my house with a good book. There is almost nothing I enjoy more than that. Before I could turn back for home, I was squinting in the dusk to read about events that happened long, long ago and far away in a world that never could have conceived of North Dakota. By the time I stumbled onto my home street, there were a million stars and Jupiter bright and proud in the southern sky. There are compensations for the loss of light.

I am making two resolutions, one of which I know I will keep. First, on Dec. 21, the darkest day of the year, I'm going to uncork the first of those jars of tomato juice and drink it. Second, I'm going to roll up my hoses properly this year. Really. *9/13/08*

Actually, you can see only about two thousand stars on a clear night in an isolated place. Bismarck is no longer that place, but you can get to one within half an hour no matter where you live in North Dakota. That's one of the prime reasons to live here. So my claim that there were millions of stars visible by the time I got home would seem to be a whopper.

Fort Union in the Footsteps of Karl Bodmer

When Lewis and Clark visited these parts in 1804-06, they brought along a blacksmith and a carpenter, a sign language interpreter, and a mapmaker (Clark), but they did not bring an artist. It was a military reconnaissance mission into unknown and potentially dangerous territory and there was literally no room for nonessential personnel.

The captains needed every ounce of every man's thew and sinew to propel the Corps of Discovery to the Pacific Coast. I don't know how many Evinrude outboard motors would be required to propel a clunky keelboat and 30 tons of baggage up against the pre-dam currents of the Missouri River, but since not even steamboats existed in 1804, Lewis and Clark crossed the continent on behalf of President Jefferson on the backs and thighs of their doughty men. Even expedition commander Meriwether Lewis had to double up as specimen collector, celestial navigator, diplomat, and field scientist.

A good visual artist was a luxury Lewis and Clark could not afford. Not that they weren't aware of the gap this left in their record of the journey. After he "discovered" the Great Falls of the Missouri River on June 13, 1805, Meriwether Lewis—who was an outstanding writer—did his best to pen a description of the principal waterfall of the Missouri River, "which has from the commencement of time been concealed from the view of civilized man."

Today's readers know he succeeded, but Lewis was convinced that he had failed to capture the essence of what he called "this truly magnificent and sublimely grand object." He lamented that he did not have the talent of a good landscape artist like the seventeenth century painter Salvator Rosa. Even at that moment, when he felt like a complete failure, Lewis does not say he wished he had brought an artist on the journey—he wished instead that he had artistic talent.

> **"Bodmer's Overlook is one of the half dozen most magical places in North Dakota. The vastness and openness and endlessness and treelessness and windsweptness and end of the universeness of that lavishly rolling grassland in that outlier corner of North Dakota is almost unbelievable."**

One generation after Lewis and Clark, the Enlightenment ethnographer Prince Maximilian of Wied-Neuwied in Germany (1782-1867) visited the Upper Missouri. He was self-consciously traveling in the wake of Lewis and Clark, with their journals and maps in his rucksack. Unlike Jefferson's muscular proteges, he was a traveler, not an explorer. He was not opening new country but buying a ride on a fur-trade steamboat on a transportation infrastructure that was well established. Payload was not an issue. Cottonwood-powered steam was doing the work. He had the luxury of bringing an artist into the wildest country of the continent.

That artist was Swiss-born Karl Bodmer (1809-1893), arguably the greatest artist ever to paint the Missouri River and the Great Plains. You can see his artwork in books or online, or (better yet) at the Lewis and Clark Interpretive Center at Washburn, where all eighty-one of Bodmer's magnificent aquatints are on display this year.

Last Sunday, I had the pleasure of taking a group of about forty history lovers on a loopy bus journey to faraway Fort Union, the reconstructed American Fur Co. trade fort located on the confluence of the Missouri and Yellowstone rivers, twenty-five miles southwest of Williston. Although Fort Union was at one time one of the most significant outposts in the North American fur trade, it is now isolated and lonely. It's one of those places you have to want to go to, because nobody just bumbles into it on the way to somewhere else. The giant, splayed-out rolling hills and breaks country around Fort Union is to the rest of North Dakota what North Dakota is to … say, New York or Massachusetts.

Our goal was to climb to something called Bodmer's Overlook, recently developed by the Fort Union Trading Post National Historic Site. At the summit of a bosomy hill a mile or so north of Fort Union, you can literally stand where Bodmer stood in 1833 when he painted his famous watercolor of the confluence of the Missouri and Yellowstone rivers.

It was a gray but sometimes luminescent day, blousy, bordering on windy. Big sky—bigger than Montana's, for all the PR boasting of our bully neighbor to the west. The clouds pillowed the whole sky from horizon to horizon without a single blue break or oculus, big dramatic but not threatening clouds, clouds so prominent and beautiful that they force themselves into your view and refuse to be mere backdrop.

The sky toyed with drizzling a couple of times, but nobody got even slightly wet. The temperature was somewhere around forty degrees—chilly but by no means cold or even disagreeable. The endlessly receding grass was still brown and gray after the brutal winter, but you could see (actually it was more like feeling than seeing) that it was about to pop into Ireland green.

On the bus from New Town to Fort Union, we kept saying, as helpless as Meriwether Lewis, "Welcome to Bodmer's America." It's as if God borrowed Bodmer's aquatints when he fashioned the landscape.

It takes about thirty minutes to climb the trail to the summit. After establishing a base camp on the first knoll, we distributed a dram of chocolate to each pilgrim and made the final ascent.

Bodmer's Overlook is one of the half dozen most magical places in North Dakota. The vastness and openness and endlessness and treelessness and windsweptness and end of the universe-ness of that lavishly rolling grassland in that outlier corner of North Dakota is almost unbelievable.

Even to a North Dakotan who loves big open "empty" country, it's foreboding and a little frightening. It feels like it might swallow you up. In fact, it does swallow you up—in a way that makes you feel thrilled and apprehensive at the same time. You cannot be there and not be made aware of the "littleness of man," and temporariness of your existence. It's a buffalo commons where even buffalo might glance around a little uneasy.

Everyone went silent as we gazed down on two of the world's great rivers as they folded into each other. Our corps of discovery moved instinctively together into a little cluster on that remote hill, which is at once the center of North America and the edge of nowhere. From where we stood, the fort on the brink of the river looked like a popsicle stick model in a diorama the size of Wyoming.

It was a perfect moment in a perfect place on a perfect day. I'm planning to return again and again as long as I can hike, and like Coleridge's ancient mariner, I've been singing the praises of Fort Union country to anyone who will listen.

This is why we live here. *5/2/09*

The occasion was the last day of a cultural symposium on Maximilian and Bodmer hosted by the Dakota Institute of the Lewis & Clark Fort Mandan Foundation.

AND SO, ONCE MORE TO THE RIVER
BEFORE THE LEAVES BLOW AWAY

After a so-so summer, we have been given the gift of an absolutely magical autumn. It has been a variable autumn—now drizzly and gray, now windswept, now perfectly still and sun-drenched like an immortal tableau of the savannah, now hot and dusty like August, now tiptoeing on the lip of the first serious freeze.

We even had that remarkable autumn thunderstorm a couple of weeks ago. It was somehow distinct from the typical transient, masculine, blow-hard summer storm. It was gentler without being less spectacular, and there was clearly a kind of summer curtain call in it. I stood out in it until I was drenched.

A friend of mine, who lives north of town overlooking the Missouri River, said he has never seen the five elements—grain stubble, the late lingering green of the prairie grasses, the fall sky, the Missouri River and the irradiating gold of the cottonwoods—look more beautiful than in the last ten days.

"Wish we could just freeze frame it for a few months," he said and then immediately sighed, because he knew that the glory of a perfect autumn day is the awareness, never far back of the joy, that it cannot last, that sharp winter is hovering on the northwestern horizon, and that the months of what Theodore Roosevelt called "iron desolation" are queuing up to pound us into submission.

There have been a number of days in September and early October that for some reason we call "Indian summer"—these are the days we live for. These are the days when the light is gentler than summer light, and the plains stand out in bas relief, when the warmth of the afternoon air is somehow borrowed heat, and when there is change in the air, however subtle. There also have been mornings that are clearly the advance agents of grim winter on the northern plains. When I wake up to leaden sky and stiff, scuttering wind, I think: Brace yourself.

It's the variety that makes this time of year so attractive. I love North Dakota in all of its moods.

After a series of meetings in Dickinson the other day, I had pressing business back in Bismarck. I drove my car up to the Interstate interchange fully intending to hurtle home and eke out a life of duty. But when I got to the interchange and gazed out onto the buff butte country to the west, I just gave up and turned the car west toward the Little Missouri River. I felt like Lot's wife (Genesis 19:17).

For me, there is only one irresistible place in North Dakota. It is more or less anywhere between Marmarth and the Long X Bridge on U.S. 85 south of Watford City. The oftener I stick my foot in the lonely Little Missouri River, the saner and happier I am. For me, it is really that simple.

One of my close friends lives out there and is willing to go hiking on short notice. So we thermos'd up and drove into Theodore Roosevelt National Park.

From the Wind Canyon overlook, the valley of the Little Missouri River was as beautiful as I have ever seen it. If you close your eyes and imagine it, you can see it far better than I will be able to describe it. The air was perfectly clear and lucid. It felt as if we had been glaucomic all of our lives, and suddenly we'd had Lasik surgery. The sky was vast and embracing and endless in every direction, the best blue you ever saw, about 15 percent of it dashed with scattered thin autumn clouds.

> "And then, as we sat there in speechless wonder, a herd of eighteen pronghorn antelope sprang up in perfect unison on the plane just below us, and charged off towards the river as if this were the pronghorn Olympic trials."

We stood on the ridge of broken country and we looked off at broken country in every direction, but it did not feel at all hostile or forbidding. It felt miniature in scale and welcoming and timeless. (Ah, but time is catching up with the Badlands. We all know that.)

There was more than a breeze and less than a wind. For the most part the breeze was precisely the same temperature as the day, but every forty seconds or so it carried a momentary column of chill air. We almost shivered, but then didn't, because it was not disagreeable after all and it passed on almost as soon as we felt it.

And in the middle of that circle of land and sky before us was the magical improbable Little Missouri River ambling along in lazy S-curves, blue as God, sheathed in the most perfect trim of golden cottonwoods you have ever seen.

The leaves of those bordering trees were the color yellow squared or cubed, and in places a tawny golden so sensuous that it made our knees buckle a little to gaze upon it. The river cut cliffs where it made its turns, ribbed with dull coal and red-pink scoria heaps, and bentonite caps of shattered, marble-sized, dry gray mud, like a thick berber carpet.

And then, as we sat there in speechless wonder, a herd of eighteen pronghorn antelope sprang up in perfect unison just below us, and charged off toward the river as if this were the pronghorn Olympic trials. They kicked up a low thin cloud of dust as they belted across the sage flat, driven apparently by the sheer exuberance of their quadruped lives.

It was as superlative a moment as I can ever remember.

We walked down along the ridge to the river. We did not need to bushwhack because the buffalo had already trampled out a rutted path about the width of a suburban sidewalk right down to the river. The game trail followed the contours of the Badlands with perfect equipoise. It was as if a buffalo with a Ph.D. in engineering had designed the road after months of careful triangulation, studying geographical information systems' maps and taking core samples along the ridge. It was not the ancient Romans who invented road building, but the game herds of the Earth.

When we got to the river, which was clear and less than a foot deep on a chip-rock bed, we didn't even discuss it. We just walked into the river fully clothed, shoes and all, and tramped around for more than an hour. We had expected the water to be cold but it wasn't. Here and there we sank into little pools up to our knees, but for the most part we were walking on water in a perfect place at a perfect moment.

We found two large flat sandstone rocks in the middle of the river, each a foot above the surface, about twenty feet apart. We lay down on them, on our backs, and gazed up at the perfect sky. In the course of half an hour, each of us dozed a little. We were silent mostly, but from time to time we spoke with a simplicity and authenticity you'll never see in a committee meeting.

Have I mentioned that we live in paradise? *10/11/08*

This is one of my favorites. My goal, as a writer, is to try to put you in the scene, to notice the details that make you feel as if you were there too. Walking into the Little Missouri River fully clothed is a surprisingly satisfying experience, which I recommend to everyone.

Oh Please

Let the Rototiller

Be in the Garage

Mountains of snow. The roads are narrowing. Valley Drive as it crests Ash Coulee has been reduced almost to a single lane. At what point does it start to feel like driving through snow tunnels? I feel sorry for the mailmen and women this year, both those on foot and those who do drive-by deliveries.

No matter what I do, I cannot keep my mailbox unobstructed. The plows roll through in the middle of the night (beep beep beeping as they back up), and though they do a superb job, they invariably leave a ridge along the line of mailboxes on my street. Whenever I think of how this must complicate my mailman's job, I go out and hack away at the ridge, but it is getting harder and harder to keep up, and my mailbox is actually now in danger of being buried by the sheer accumulation. Is there a point at which snow could actually paralyze the city?

No end in sight.

As far as I'm concerned, it's the best winter ever, but then I am not feeding cattle or trying to keep a small business parking lot clear.

I bought cross-country skis a week ago in Fargo, for there were none to be had then in Bismarck, and I pulled out from a deep recess in my garage a never-used pair of snow shoes. The cross-country ski trail at Riverwood Golf Course is absolutely spectacular. When you stop to gaze at the charcoal smudge of the tall riverside cottonwoods against the almost unbearably pure white canvas of the snow, you drink in the magic of North Dakota in a whole new way. Everyone you meet on the trail wears an expression of joy and wonder and "who knew?"

When I look out at my garden as it slopes up west of my house, now covered literally with eight feet of snow, I have four thoughts of about equal potency. First, this is going to be my best garden ever. Second, did I leave my rototiller in the garden that great November Saturday? I hope not. Third, my house is almost certainly going to flood. I don't know whether to just shrug my shoulders and hope for the best or to start stockpiling cubits of gopherwood and pitch. And fourth, I cannot wait to see Lake Sakakawea rise up to the something like its normal pool level.

Imagine the waves of phone calls that Sears, Menards, and Lowe's are getting as people who were hoping to gut it out give up and seek the help of the internal combustion engine? Apparently there isn't a snowblower for sale on the Great Plains right now, and the few that turn up are fought over like Super Bowl tickets. I've heard a rumor that a few otherwise good and perfectly healthy individuals have been reduced to playing the "sob story, elderly shut-in" card. Fortunately the salesmen have been trained to detect such lies. (So, I'll try another strategy). Actually, I'm beginning to think that all snowblowers are just toys in a winter like this. I'm thinking "Bobcat."

Everyone who is old enough is now talking about the blizzard of 1966, which left drifts up to the roofline of our house and killed five people in North Dakota. My family lived in Bismarck then, in a bungalow over on the east side, about a mile from a little ma and pa grocery store on Broadway. Either the roads were closed or the cars wouldn't start, and our neighbors began to run out of food. Finally, Mrs. R. (the Beret Hansa of this story) told her strong but dunderheaded husband Mr. R. that he would have to take one of the children's sleds and fight his way through the storm to the little store to buy enough basic supplies to get them through.

This, by the way, is a true story.

Mr. R. bundled up in all the coats, mittens, and scarves he owned and silently knelt down to buckle up his overshoes. It was a solemn moment when he kissed his wife and children goodbye. Stoically, he threw his weight at the front door and forced it open, and thrust himself out into the raging storm in that instant before the door slammed shut again. He was immediately swallowed up by the blizzard. We could hear him singing some kind of brave heart song, but we could not see him five feet from his front door. It was fearfully cold, and the wind was blowing unobstructed from the North Pole to New Mexico. There was real danger in his venturing forth. Once he was gone, we gathered up all the snow that had blown into the entryway when he opened the door and ran it down the sink. We played Monopoly and shared a can of Spam.

Mr. R. was gone for a very long time.

We were beginning to get worried.

Finally, near dusk, we heard a muted thump on the front door. We were not at first sure whether it was our hero returning or a mere trick of the appalling wind. When we forced open the door, there was Mr. R. looking like the abominable snowman—with iced eyebrows and snot stalactites, stiff and numb as an oversized snowman, but with a huge grin on his face. We pulled him into the house, sled and all, and excavated him from the stiff layers of winter clothing in which he was now fused.

He could not speak for some time.

Then. and only then. we turned to the sled.

Here is a precise inventory. It contained a loaf of bread, a case of Hamms beer, and two cartons of cigarettes.

It took many years for Mr. R. to live down that story. Somehow the Spam and bread got us through, KFYR regained its network signal, the plows made the roads passable, and that year's wheat harvest was spectacular. *1/17/08*

The story about Mr. R. is true. He and my father worked together at a small loans company in Bismarck. I remember that wild storm as if it were yesterday. The NBC network was down for several days, and KFYR had a copy of a film called The Thing from Another World, *starring James Arness as the Thing. My memory is that it was shown many times during that crushing storm. The reference to gopherwood and pitch comes from Genesis 6:14.*

EMPTY, GLORIOUSLY EMPTY, AND GOD AWAITS

Gertrude Stein wrote, "In the United States, there is more space where nobody is than where anybody is."

I wish Stein (1874-1946) could have seen North Dakota in the early twenty-first century.

This is not another lament about rural outmigration. Au contraire. My theme is how gloriously empty most of North Dakota is. I'm calling attention to the happy flip side of the outmigration coin. Most Americans regard North Dakota as an empty place in the Empty Quarter. They are right. But what they don't know is what population we have (635,867) is mostly huddled in a few places in North Dakota, and the really empty part is, well, really, really empty. Scary empty. Magically empty.

The cliche is that the Great Plains is godforsaken country. But my sense is that God likes empty places, and we have a better chance to wrestle with God out on the "emptied prairie" than more densely settled places.

North Dakota ranks forty-seventh in population density. That means that only Montana, Wyoming and Alaska have fewer people per square mile. New Jersey ranks first in population density with 1,138 people per square mile. (Weighing the quality of life, including crime statistics, hmm.) North Dakota provides only 9.3 people per square mile. If you organized them in pairs and spread them out on a section of land, it would be like a five on dice (a quincunx), with one loner in the middle. They'd be able to see each other—barely. Of course, at any given moment, they would not be out, manning their stations. They'd be indoors, watching *American Idol* or reruns of *Friends* or checking corn futures on the Internet. If they were out at their stations, they would almost certainly not be standing at attention, but slouching in their pickups, listening to Rush or NPR.

We live mediated lives, and at any given statistical moment, we see nature, if at all, through a stout pane of glass. Even farmers, come to think of it.

At a time when there is more clamor in America for open space than ever before, we North Dakotans have open space in glorious, stupendous abundance, almost in infinite supply. If I were the state tourism department, that's what I'd try to sell to the rest of the world. Come to North Dakota to have it "all to yourself." Commune with "Nature and Nature's God" (as Jefferson formulated it). In the great circle of land and sky that is North Dakota (America's true Big Sky Country), you can stand alone between the Earth and the end of the universe and … pray, shout down the gods, dance to the music of the spheres, listen to the wind, rehearse your proposal, cry for your losses, put your fingers in the ground, recall (or reinvent) your life. But if you just shut up and look around in wonder, the sheer vastness of the Great Plains will swallow you up in all the right ways, and you will ask some big questions before you get back to town.

> "The cliché is that the Great Plains is godforsaken country. But my sense is that God likes empty places, and we have a better chance to wrestle with God out on the "emptied prairie" than in more densely settled places."

So we rank forty-seventh, with 9.3 people per square mile. That's a misleading statistic, of course, because the population of North Dakota is not evenly distributed. Pitiful little Slope County (my favorite, home of Marmarth) has only 713 people, while at the other end of the state, Cass County, which is not significantly larger, has a population of 132,525. Thus, Slope County has .6 persons per square mile. I happen to know Point Six. Her name is Patti Perry. And I'd put her in the scale with any 20 urbanistas.

Cass County has sixty-nine people per square mile. That, interestingly enough, is just a little more than the Minnesota average, which confirms my dark suspicions. Nearly one in five North Dakotans lives in Cass County. Only one in nine hundred lives in Slope County. And, I can hear Patti Perry vociferating, "That's the way we like it!"

People don't diffuse themselves evenly over landscape. They tend to cluster. It's not at all surprising that people accumulate along the main transportation hubs. But that means that the rest of the countryside is almost unbelievably empty. A third of our population lives in the Red River Valley. The biggest chunks of the rest of it live along the I-94 corridor. Those counties-Cass, Barnes, Stutsman, Kidder, Burleigh, Morton, Stark, Billings, and Golden Valley—have a combined population of 292,519. That's 46 percent of the North Dakota population.

As the twenty-first century begins, thirty-six of North Dakota's fifty-three counties are now regarded in demographic circles as new "frontier" counties, meaning that they have fewer than six people per square mile. So in those thirty-six counties, our quincunx consists of singletons, not couples, or perhaps one on the middle of the section.

I wonder how many North Dakotans live more than thirty miles from a four-lane road? It would be possible, if a little tedious, to work this out from U.S. Census statistics. My answer, which is not altogether technical, is: not many.

Last week, I flew out of North Dakota toward the east. It was a magnificent, perfectly clear day. I had a window seat. I was able to study the landscape and look for things I recognized all the way to Minnesota, where clouds obscured the view. I felt that strange patriotic surge as we flew over North Dakota's unusual Capitol building. I was able to pick out my house, perched (for the moment) right on the edge of the gigantic prairie. A little later, I saw Long Lake, and soon Jamestown Reservoir, which looked rather menacing from thirty-five thousand feet.

There was a dusting of snow east of Jamestown, which did not cover the ground, but accentuated the section lines in a wonderful way. I sat entranced by the vastness of the place we call home and its amazing beauty, and I did not mind its emptiness one bit. In fact, I gloried in how big and free our place is, so far from the corridors of trouble. By now, we were angling southeast toward Minneapolis, but I was able to spy the Sheyenne and the Wild Rice and then the Red River. In the distance, I could just make out the brown smudge (not so large, really) that is Fargo.

I wanted to be down on the plains walking somewhere I have never explored before. And I resolved, on Easter (today), to venture out into the middle of nowhere (Genesis 32) somewhere west of the Missouri River to wrestle with God. *3/22/08*

All this is changing, fast. Still, North Dakota will always be a mostly empty place. The depopulated central counties—Sheridan, Foster, Kidder, Pierce, Logan, Wells, etc.—are becoming more attractive to me now that we are degrading the region west of the Missouri River.

THE EMPTY PRAIRIE IS A GOOD PLACE TO LIVE

We need to take a deep breath. The furor over the January issue of *National Geographic* is almost as silly as the article it contains on rural decline in North Dakota. The article, written by Charles Bowden with photographs by Eugene Richards, is melodramatic and arguably biased. It lacks balance and context. But the central premise is irrefutable. Rural North Dakota is being abandoned.

This can hardly be called news.

"The Emptied Prairie" belongs to a journalistic genre known as the "dying town story." In this case, it is more of a "dying state story," which is one reason why folks here are all stirred up. Dying town stories are a staple of Great Plains journalism. They are expected to have a kind of haunting elegiac feel and to emphasize words like "windswept," "forlorn," "stark" and, above all, "vanished." In this regard, "The Emptied Prairie" does not disappoint.

It's a formula. Find the last guy in the last cafe, the old man walking along the railroad tracks, the crib in the abandoned farmhouse with a wind-bleached doll lying on its side.

I was really glad to see one of my closest friends, Patti Perry of Marmarth, quoted in the article. I feel certain she'll whup Bowden if he ever dares to turn up again in Marmarth's delightful Pastime restaurant. Not that she would disagree with his thesis, but I can hear her saying, "Geez, stop wringing your hands and talking about tragedy and saying asinine stuff like 'something in the earth and the sky mutinied against the settlers.'"

The actual argument thesis of Bowden's article is that although the overall population of North Dakota is stable, the rural districts are undergoing rapid and seemingly irreversible depopulation. Who can refute this? Divide County, population 2,092 in 2006, down 8.4 percent since 2000. Billings County, population 829, down 6.6 percent. Slope County, population 713, down 7 percent. Bowman County, 2,991, down 7.7 percent. Golden Valley County, 1,691, down 12.1 percent. Adams County, 2,332, down 10.1 percent. Hettinger County, 2,564, down 5.6 percent. Dunn County, 3,443, down 4.4 percent. Burke County, 1,947, down 13.2 percent. Renville County, 2,425, down 7.1 percent.

Very bad, but listen to this. Stark County (home of Dickinson), 22,167, down 2.1 percent. Ward County (home of Minot), 55,207, down 6 percent. Williams County (home of Williston), 19,456, down 1.5 percent.

Half of the population of North Dakota now lives east of Carrington. Almost 40 percent of the North Dakota population now lives east of Interstate 29. Bismarck, Mandan, Minot, Grand Forks and, above all, Fargo, are thriving. The villages, especially those west of the Missouri River, are "drying up and blowing away," as Bowden might put it. Our towns are struggling. We've become an urban state, a vast landscape punctuated by thriving "city states," with an increasingly abandoned countryside. And the great migration is not nearly over.

I do regard this phenomenon as a very sad thing. I believe North Dakota was a better place when our population was more evenly diffused across the landscape, when the towns had vibrant business districts, when people shopped locally, when farms were defined by the number of acres rather than the number of sections they encompassed. I believe that something essential in the North Dakota character is being lost—forever—as our agrarian, our small town, heritage ebbs away. I worry about what North Dakota will be when we have filtered our lives through Best Buy, Bed Bath & Beyond and Starbucks as thoroughly as everyone else in America.

> "I believe that North Dakota was a better place when our population was more evenly diffused across the landscape, when the towns had vibrant business districts, when people shopped locally, when farms were defined by the number of acres rather than the number of sections they encompassed."

Easy for me to say. I live in Bismarck, not Epping. I shop at Best Buy. Most North Dakotans, indeed most of my friends, are far less nostalgic for the heritage of North Dakota than I am. A few of them declare—with some acerbity—good riddance to all that. What Bowden failed to realize is that even those North Dakotans who lament what has passed and is still to pass, have largely come to terms with it. That's why they are annoyed by his pose of mawkish bewilderment.

Here's why Bowden's article upsets us. First, nobody can deny that tens of thousands of North Dakotans have departed for more promising places in the past half-century, but for most of those who are still here, things never have been so good. We have more money, better jobs, better and more reliable vehicles, greater comfort, greater mobility, dramatically more variety in our food and almost infinitely better access to the fruits of life as Americans define their pursuit of happiness. Hey, Charles Bowden, don't rain on our parade. The irony of this, of course, is that the amenities boom in North Dakota is largely an urban phenomenon, made possible by the abandonment of those farmhouses Richards loves to photograph.

Second, this is a time of unprecedented prosperity in North Dakota. If we were experiencing rural depopulation and economic depression at the same time, we might lose more sleep. But as long as good times continue, North Dakotans seem willing to find a way to deal with the demographics.

Third, it offends us when people like Bowden assume that rural depopulation is inevitably a sign of failure, broken dreams, and "abandoned human desire." Maybe it's a sign of good sense and intelligent life-planning. It offends us, too, when people like Bowden suggest that those who still live here are yokels who are too stupid to join the parade, to get their jalopies on Route 66 in search of a better life. Contrary to Bowden's suggestion, the suicide rate in North Dakota is comparatively low.

Most of us like it here.

Here's some consolation. A misguided article in *National Geographic* is not going to change the nation's perception of North Dakota. No couple in Tampa or Portland with the moving van full is going to pause at the onramp and say, "Gee, honey, now that we've read this article, maybe we should rethink our plan to become new North Dakota pioneers."

Patti, get your gloves on and whup him.   *1/12/08*

The offending article appeared in National Geographic *in January 2008. Many North Dakotans worked themselves into high dudgeon, wrote to NG to denounce the article, sponsored essay contests in which young people could explain what is right with North Dakota, etc. This seemed a little thin-skinned to me, another sign of our state insecurity. I hoped Governor John Hoeven would get himself invited onto the* David Letterman Show *to give the Top Ten reasons why North Dakota is an empty place. In other words, turn the incident into a good humored marketing opportunity.*

EASTER:

AMONG OTHER THINGS,

THE RETURN OF THE LIGHT

Because we've had a sockdolager of a winter—long, windy, often bitterly cold, perhaps unprecedentedly snowy—most of us are feeling a little cabin feverish. Our North Dakota spring is finally showing signs of shaking off slumber and trying to get in sync with the "official" spring season, which began twenty-three days ago (March 20).

Have you noticed how deeply the returning light has cut into the long dark winter night of the northern Great Plains? If I had a fatted calf, I'd sacrifice it now to the returning light. Theodore Roosevelt's "season of iron desolation" is at last ending—although at this point, it would not surprise us much if nature threw one or two more cheap shots at us as we lean on our knees fighting for air.

The Christian meaning of Easter is the more profound for its echo of festivals of return, renewal, and "resurrection" that predate Judaism by untold millennia.

Time for first sightings of the pasqueflower (the crocus) and the erotic dance of the prairie chicken.

I love the light. I love the annual return of light. But can we please slow down the locomotive of the summer equinox (June 21, 12:45 a.m. CDT) this year and linger in late spring just a little? Some of the best moments of the North Dakota year come on the evenings of the next month when we find ourselves commenting, out loud, in shirtsleeves, a little chilly but not quite willing to fetch a jacket, on how late it is light, how the sunsets are creeping up toward 9 p.m., how the day seems willfully to be holding out against the darkness.

Because the winter has been so formidable, I have felt pretty disconnected from the landscape of our homeland. For months it has been hard to get out, hard to get around, hard to stay out very long. Last Tuesday, to my mind, was the first truly magnificent day of 2009: fifty-some degrees, a spring breeze this side of wind, open skies, wild decibels of light. It would have taken shackles to keep me indoors.

My friend Leon and I have been talking about a project involving buttes (of all things) for more than a year. On Tuesday, when cabin fever and spring fever converged, we dropped everything and flew over southwestern North Dakota in his single-engine airplane. He's a pilot, an artist, and a lover of North Dakota's back country.

We flew from the Mandan municipal airport to magnificent Marmarth and back again, at 3,000 feet, zipping from butte to butte as in some absurd connect the dot project. We circled the bigger, more dramatic buttes to photograph them from every possible angle.

Our headset conversation, aside from a sliver of air traffic compliance, and "Could you circle that one again?" was like a Chatty Cathy on steroids, hepped up on the glory of North Dakota. "Wow." "That is an incredibly beautiful butte." "Can you believe the quality of light today?" "I don't think I have ever seen the countryside look so gorgeous." "Oh my goodness, would you mind zipping over to that one?" "Look at the way the snow brings that butte face into relief?"

Our madcap itinerary took us from Crown Butte (2,321 feet high) to the Schollaert Hills (near Almont) to Heart Butte (2,509—never more beautiful) to Pearl Butte (2,828, south of Lefor) to East and West Rainy Buttes (North Dakota's most classical buttes, 3,356 and 3,347) to White Butte (at 3,506, the summit of North Dakota). Then to Black Butte (3,465), Pretty Butte (stunning, in spite of its inadequate name, at 3,182), and of course, the butte of buttes, the mother of all buttes, the butte that changes the course of the Little Missouri River ...

Bullion Butte.

If there were only one butte, it would have to be Bullion (3,336). We circled it until we were dizzy. We were effectively too close to do it justice with photography, so huge is its footprint, so wide its reach, so complex its system of feeder and tributary buttes. We gazed in ecstasy at the sharp Teepee Buttes that are a part of its massive south face. We buzzed my favorite North Dakota resort, the Logging Camp Ranch, nestled into North Dakota's sole pine forest. We flew in awestruck silence over the endless elongated tight looping oxbows of the Little Missouri River as it searches for a way to get around Bullion Butte and resume its northerly journey to the mainstem Missouri near Halliday. We saw—and grappled, up close and personal—with the geology of the alluvial plain of the Rocky Mountains.

> "The Little Missouri is the sinuous signature of God."

It just felt fabulous to be alive on such a day in such a place.

We noted a score of places we intend to visit by car, by four-wheel drive, on foot. Always in part, at least, on foot. Because of the long Laura Ingalls Wilder winter, I plan to make this the most intensely active summer of my life—at least since, when the world was all before me at the age of eight, I built forts and played sandlot ball with my boyhood pals, eons ago in Dickinson. I plan to picnic on public access buttes, to lie in the grass of flattop buttes and gaze indolently into the sky, to "loaf and invite my soul," as the poet Walt Whitman phrased it.

We formulated a handful of observations from 3,000 feet.

North Dakota is anything but flat, especially west and south of the Missouri River. It is, in fact, a jumble of rolling broken land, a maze of complex contours, punctuated by spectacular box buttes. Thus far the human footprint on the land is relatively modest. The plains landscape is not what it once was, but there is a seemingly infinite array of country all spread out in every direction. The ribbons of scoria, blacktop and concrete roads are a slender gossamer, the farmsteads and villages and industrial structures are widely diffused, and—frankly—not very intrusive.

There are a dozen unnamed buttes for every one with a sobriquet.

There is still a lot of snow to melt. This is going to be one of the greenest summers ever, and the grass will flourish until we cry in joy.

The Heart River is a really beautiful stream, much underrated as plains rivers go.

But the Little Missouri is the sinuous signature of God.

Happy Easter. *4/11/09*

State Fruit: Chokecherry—
Official Greek God: Aelous

Canoeing the Little Missouri River last weekend on a windy (and I mean windy) afternoon, I asked two of my closest friends how many "perfect" days we have per annum in North Dakota. My friends—a couple—are deep, insightful, ideal North Dakotans, lifers, who love this place with all their hearts. They get it that North Dakota has a raw and at times brutal climate, and it doesn't bother them much. They'd never be snowbirds, even if they won the lottery.

It would be interesting to know what percentage of our population would flee the harsh months if they had the means. It would be equally interesting to know what percentage of the population actually does bolt for Florida, Arizona, and California sometime after Halloween when the season of "iron desolation" comes to the northern Plains. Then compare those percentages to Colorado or Hawaii. Or even Nebraska.

What is a perfect day in North Dakota? That, of course, depends on the eye of the beholder, but we can all agree that it means something like: blue in the sky, clarity in the air, nothing that could be called a wind, and temperature not a factor. That allows for perfect winter days, when jackets or coats are necessary, along with proper gloves and footwear, but Aeolus, the Greek god of wind, has tied up all the winds in his leather bag. I've experienced a handful of perfect days at 15 below zero—so long as there is no perceptible wind, not even a tendril or a whiff—when a kind of cosmic peace has come to blanket the Great Plains and you could stand in

Pembina and hear a beer can drop in Marmarth. Actually, those are among my favorite North Dakota days.

Answering my question in the middle of the wind-stymied Little Missouri River, one of my friends said, "thirty perfect days per year." The other, "No, that's too few." Then the conversation broke down, as we fought like Argonauts to keep our canoes in the river against a wind that was determined to throw us up onto the shore. This is not an exaggeration. We literally spent the day doing everything in our power to keep our canoes in the river. At any given time, one of our four canoes was careening into the riverbank, while its churning helpless paddlers cried out in protest like Job.

In North Dakota, you have to factor in the possibility that the June wedding, the August family reunion, or the fall picnic will be ruined by wind or a sudden cold front. Any given day in the calendar can be appalling, including during the North Dakota summer. No ceremonial function or event can be planned here with assurance that the "weather will cooperate," as we like to put it. The Fourth of July can be magnificently hot, bright, brassy and blue—on the river or at the lake—followed in perfect slow motion by a sweet gentling of the light and heat around sunset, so that you sit around the fire or grill in the ever-so-slight chill, sipping something in animal contentment and eating just one brat too many as you wait for fireworks. On nights in the heart of summer when the tangerine and charcoal dusk lingers for a couple of hours, you want almost to swoon with joy. Those are the nights you truly wish would never end.

Just as often, Fourth of July can sandblast you right over into Minnesota like a tumbleweed, with a gusty, thrumming, incessant, blasting wind that propels you into a sour mood, especially when your mother or brother—whoever is in charge of holding things together—says, "Well, let's just make the best of it. Put those cinder blocks on the corners of the table cloth."

It's really all about the wind. I'm always amused when my fellow North Dakotans say, "I like everything about this place except the wind." That's like saying, "I like everything about church except the sermon," or "I like everything about coffee except the taste." If you don't like wind, you don't really like North Dakota. If you live for those few days per year when North Dakota's weather is limpid and perfect—we all love those days and store them up in our souls—you really love the "California" in North Dakota rather than the "North Dakota" in North Dakota, if that makes any sense.

North Dakota is a stark, windswept, treeless place where on any given day, chosen at random, the temperature is probably between twenty and sixty degrees, when there is at least a breeze and just as often a gale force wind, The most significant factor in North Dakota life is that you can never allow yourself to forget climate and weather. There is no day in the year when you might not need a coat. When you start out on an auto trip any time between October and June, you have to consult the paper or almanac, then gaze around at the sky and wonder what might blow in when you least expect it. More than most other folks, we North Dakotans live in nature and pay it the respect it demands.

> "North Dakota is a stark windswept treeless place where on any given day, chosen at random, the temperature is probably between twenty and sixty degrees, when there is at least a breeze and just as often a gale force wind."

That shapes us in really important ways. There is grit and pit on our windshields and our souls.

Without wanting to seem like Pollyanna, I like to look at our rawboned climate through the other end of the lens. How many undeniably awful days do we have per year, when the wind blows like a son of a gun and makes it impossible to think straight, when you find yourself getting frustrated and emotionally exhausted whether you wish to or not? On how many days do you huddle inside listening to the grit pitting your windshield or the windows of your house? Odd though it seems, I love to listen to that insect-like Dakota sandblast of snow or sand, as long as I'm inside, though it always makes me wonder how well my property values are holding up. On how many days does the inside of your car howl and whistle (like a trumpet) no matter how good the door and window seals?

In my calculus—or mythology—there are approximately 325 perfect days per year in North Dakota. I like my North Dakota visceral, not a scene out of Bride's or Sunset Magazine.

Besides, when our canoe trip finally came to an end, a splendid Badlands ranch couple was waiting with wine and cheese and the best beefsteaks you ever ate.

Half of their savor came from the wind.   *5/9/09*

This is one of my favorites. When I write that "if you don't like wind, you don't really like North Dakota," I am perfectly serious. One of my goals is to convince my fellow Dakotans that North Dakota is lovely because it is a windswept place with a violent climate, not in spite of that.

And So Once More to the River:

Is It True You Cannot

Walk into the Same River Twice?

In two weeks and one day my mother will drive me to Marmarth. We will have a meal at the Pastime restaurant. Then we'll drive to the bridge over the Little Missouri River. My friend Patti Perry, the former mayor of Marmarth, will drive over from her house three blocks away. There will be some hugs. Patti will call me a damn fool. Then I'll shoulder a fifty-five-pound pack and walk north (downriver) a couple of miles and camp.

From July 31 to August 17, my plan is to walk the Little Missouri River from Marmarth to the North Unit of Theodore Roosevelt National Park. I need hardly say solo.

I'm writing this so I cannot weasel out of it at the last minute.

The Little Missouri River starts at Oshoto, Wyoming, near Devils Tower. It slides along the northwestern edge of the Black Hills, then enters North Dakota where the Dakotas and Montana come together. Just north of Marmarth, it starts to flow through badlands. By the time it gets to the North Unit, it has cut what can plausibly be called the Grand Canyon of the Little Missouri. In other words, the scenery will look more dramatic every mile I walk. My increasing debilitude and spiritual exhaustion will unfold in ever more sublime landscapes. In its total run of 560 river miles, the Little Missouri passes through the village of Oshoto, Wyoming, Alzada and Albion, Montana, Camp Crook, South Dakota, and Marmarth and Medora, North Dakota. The largest of these towns is Medora, with a year-around population of about ninety. There are far more cattle than humans in the Little Missouri River Valley. Note: Medora now has a Starbucks. I'm counting on a hundred-shot latte to propel me to the Elkhorn Ranch site.

This journey has been three years in the making. I conceived it as my way of closing my Lewis and Clark bicentennial and, at the same time, undertaking a homecoming adventure in the part of North Dakota I love best. That's why the trek has to start in Marmarth. The hardest challenge was to carve out seventeen days of free time. I would have preferred thirty. As 2006 began to shape up, I took what I could get. Even at that, I've upset my professional world in forcing this mini-sabbatical. One of my purposes in doing the hike is to declare war on the insane pace of our lives, my life. When we were young, we could slip into adventure mode more or less at will. As we grow older and start buying insurance, we find less and less time and engage in tamer and more cautious jaunts. Then one weekend we realize we are watching the bowling channel from a La-Z-Boy recliner and wondering if we have the strength to find a phone to order a pizza.

It's now or never time. This may not be, as Roosevelt explained his South America rivers expedition in 1913, "my last chance to be a boy," but on a good day, when my left shoulder is hurting and I am sleepwalking through my life, I can almost, just about, see darkness at the end of the tunnel.

I want to walk off the grid, if only for a couple of weeks. I don't really even know who I am any more. I certainly don't know what I am capable of. It has been a very long time since I tested my body and soul against anything that wasn't climate controlled. My spiritual being has been so thoroughly neglected that it is a mostly-spent ember that I am hoping the winds of the Dakota plains will make glow again. The software I have been running for the past twenty years still works, but it is essentially inadequate to the tasks it is now being asked to perform. And, at fifty-one, my hard drive is so pitted that whole sectors are hard to access. (Look, I'm speaking in industrial metaphor—that's how far gone I am).

> "Turns out I did meet with the species *pricklius landownerius*, but not until after my return."

Seventeen days is not enough to bring on the metamorphosis I'm talking about. But it is a start. Nor, by big wilderness adventure standards, is this much more than a stroll. The gear is now so marvelous that it is almost lightweight enough for me to carry it 250 miles along the banks of the Little Missouri. In my imagination, this feels like a raw back-to-nature trek, so low-tech as to be a little alarming, but by any rational analysis I am only able to make the journey because I am carrying equipment produced at the apex of the vast industrial pyramid. I may feel self-sufficient, but I'm not really walking off the grid at all. Rather, I'm taking a kind of synthetic portable grid with me. I refuse to take a cell phone (sorry, mom), but I am taking a GPS unit (for later mapping the route). I'm not carrying an iPod, but my Leatherman knife is so amazing that Jim Bridger would have gathered furs for a whole year to get one. My tent weighs two pounds because it is made of—oil. And the freeze dried food—Sesame beef with shallots and slow-cooked curried chicken with red potatoes—I don't really even want to know.

As the trip approaches, and I feel more and more anxiety in the pit of my stomach, I have spread out all of my equipment on my living room floor. In June I made thirty pounds of beef jerky, in different flavors. Thirty-four packets of freeze-dried food are grouped into four provisions boxes. Packets of Kool-Aid and Crystal Light wait for their moment in trying to flavor the dubious waters of the flowing wells I'll encounter. Water is the biggest issue on this journey. The poet Coleridge is right: water water everywhere, and not a drop to drink. Patti Perry says you can drink right from the Little Mo—if you get thirsty enough.

I've been getting ready by walking five to ten miles per day in my new high-tech boots, which will permit me to walk through the river ten to twenty times per day and drain dry when I am back on land. North Dakota's marvelous triathlete Melanie Carvell has been my trainer. That's like getting Michael Jordan to teach your child to dribble or Mozart to give me piano lessons. Melanie starts her day at first light with a thirty to fifty mile bicycle ride, then works all day at the Women's Health Center at Medcenter One, breaking only to swim across the noon hour, then goes home to cook oppressively healthy food for her husband and children, and then—as a kind of postprandial saunter—walks me into the ground! It's perfectly absurd. She's a BMW, I'm a Ford Fiesta. She's titanium alloy. I'm Mr. Schwinn. She goes home and reads Ben Hur. I go home and search for Ben Gay. But I am immensely grateful. I think she is conducting a scientific test: can a schlump be made to carry his own weight? *7/4/06*

"When we were young, we could slip into adventure mode more or less at will. As we grow older and start buying insurance, we find less and less time and engage in tamer and more cautious jaunts."

People stop me on the street to tell me that of all my columns, they liked the ones on my hike the best. It turned out my mother could not drop me off at Marmarth—her calendar was already full! Melanie Carvell did the drop—and stole my Cloverdale Tangy Summer Sausage just to torture me. She denies the crime. If she can live with that answer, I can.

No Time to Weasel Out Now:

Crossing the Rubicon at Marmarth

Tomorrow I embark on my seventeen-day trek on the Little Missouri River. By 7 p.m. I will be lumbering north along the banks of the river. My plan is to walk four or five miles and then camp. This is what is known as a Hudson's Bay start. That way, if I discover that I have forgotten anything important—my sleeping bag, matches, my knife—it's not too late to turn back and regroup.

I haven't been this excited in many, many years.

I haven't even thought about weaseling out.

My secretary Nancy has added her voice to a chorus of others who insist that I take a cell phone. I've tried to explain that some things have to be done without a net. The whole point of this trek is to walk off the grid, to go out and test my body and my soul, to go face myself without a lifeline, for the first time in many, many years. Besides, what do you think the chances are that there will be a cell signal at just the remote spot where I become the first victim of the mountain lion counter-offensive? No. No cell phone.

I did write a last will.

The gear is good. It is spread all over the living room floor, gleaming, unscratched, full of new gear smell. It's so bright and marvelous that I almost hate to use it. Three weeks from now it will be grungy. New gray internal-frame pack. One-man tent. Featherweight sleeping bag. Air mattress?—Still deciding. Freeze-dried food, homemade beef jerky, baker's chocolate, Crystal Light. Miniature cookstove. Titanium-alloy pans and utensils: ruinously expensive. Leatherman knife set. First aid kit. Shirt, jacket, extra socks, Little Mo baseball cap. Camera, GPS unit, voice recorder. Journal, pens. Maps. Batteries. Miner's headlamp. Aspirin.

I'm taking four books, though not all at the same time. The first and primary text is Henry David Thoreau's *Walden* (1854). *Walden* is my desert island book, the one American book I would choose if it were the only book I could keep while all others disappeared forever. I've read it perhaps fifteen times in the course of my life. As with all classics, I expect it to be marvelous in both familiar and new ways. If I get through that (unlikely), I'll read Edward Abbey's *Desert Solitaire,* Kathleen Norris's *Dakota: A Spiritual Geography,* and Ian Frazier's *Great Plains. Desert Solitaire* is in some respects the *Walden* of the twentieth century. It's about Utah, but Abbey's conservation ethic is about Dakota, too. Besides, it's grumpy about the industrialization of the West, and I expect to see things I'd rather not see along the Little Missouri. Norris' and Frazier's books both rubbed me the wrong way when I first read them, but I consider them important books about our place and experience, and I'm starting over.

I have been asked by a number of people what I expect. My daughter wanted to know if there were bears in the Badlands. My former wife asked me if I were aware that I am fifty-one years old. A dear friend, yesterday, asked, "Aren't you afraid of being alone with yourself for all that time?"

Yes, a little.

We're a radically over-stimulated people. The bombardment is relentless. It comes from every direction. It cheapens life. The trivial, banal, vulgar, and demeaning overpower all that is genuine in us. We become numb and we slip into a kind of autopilot. We stop actually living life and merely go through the motions. Our sense of wonder is deadened. It breeds cynicism. It's a kind of sleepwalking, and I am one of the worst offenders. It's toxic, and it is so effective that we forget that we are toxic.

> "Wondering, as we must on such occasions, why does civilized man seek out opportunities to revert to a kind of Cro Magnon primitiveness, and feeling a little scared, as we always do when we are alone in a little zone of light in the outback, with darkness and mystery just beyond the precinct of the fire, eager to swallow up the fire?"

For a couple of weeks carved with difficulty out of my hectic life, I want, as Thoreau put it, "to reduce life to its lowest terms." My hope is that if I simplify things and get into a meditative hiking rhythm, clear some of the crap out of my soul, and listen to the river and the wind, I might be renewed. Reinvigorated. Rejuvenated. Released. Returned.

It takes about three or four days to clear all the noise. Then, if all goes well, I'll wake up and smell the—freeze-dried Southwestern chicken. I so want to wake up, in North Dakota, my home, along the Little Missouri, "my" river, and experience the world with a renewed sense of wonder and possibility. Is it possible in middle age? I really don't know. I'm a little worried. What if I sleepwalk the Little Missouri?

It satisfies me to think that, no matter what else is true, I am going to slow time down to a crawl for seventeen days. Or maybe I'll be doing the crawling. I'm going to earn my forward progress one step at a time. I'm going to sleep under cottonwood trees on the banks of a Great Plains river, a man alone walking across the circle of land and sky with a billion stars overhead, and some fierce thunderstorms, I hope.

The moments I am most looking forward to are these:

First, sitting literally in the Little Missouri River for an hour or two in the searing heat of the afternoon, sitting in the current on a gravel bar in five or six inches of water, reading and looking around at the cottonwoods and the hills and musing on where all the water comes from and where it goes. Not much gets read, but the book adds to the moment, and one or two sentences can serve as a provocation to minutes or hours of meditation.

Second, squatting on my haunches by a cottonwood branch fire just after dusk (if the burn ban is lifted), feeling a little alone and a little eerie, with occasional snaps and glowing chip bursts from the fire, and the dull soft sound of the firewood collapsing and subsiding as it consumes itself. Wondering, as we must on such occasions, why does civilized man seek out opportunities to revert to a kind of Cro-Magnon primitiveness, and feeling a little scared, as we always do when we are alone in a little zone of light in the outback, with darkness and mystery just beyond the precinct of the fire, eager to swallow up the fire?

Third, the tenth or fifteenth mile of hiking in late afternoon or early evening, when the heat of the day has broken, and there is a crystalline clarity in the landscape, and the body is a little tired but not weary, and you gaze around at the world of the American West as if for the first time, and you reckon you could walk a dozen more miles with ease.

You realize, you rediscover, that you live in America, which, because of its vast empty and wild places, is still, even now, fundamentally different from France and England, Germany and Italy, those domesticated lands that lost their Edens, and you are filled with wonder and joy and gratitude, and you just hope that it will always be this way, that our grandchildren will not find that we tamed the wildness out of our place too.

Fourth, lying on my back and looking up at the stars and wondering. Wondering. Wondering. And finally losing the battle against sleep.

Some of this I am sure to experience—if my middle-aged body holds up, if I don't panic, if I am still who I like to think I am. But we cannot be sure. Anticipation is a great magical elixir, and yet almost all of our expectations miscarry on the reef of real life. T.S. Eliot said, "Between the idea / And the reality / Between the motion / And the act / Falls the Shadow."

Time and 250 river miles will tell. All I know is that I am immensely glad to be making this journey, immensely glad to be a North Dakotan and delighted that in some sense you are along for the voyage. *7/29/09*

I only read through Walden. *The other books I never cracked. My copy of* Walden *was a lovely little red hardcover, smaller than an old-style paperback. The trip turned out to be all that I anticipated, and more. To think back on it now, six years later, gives me a deep sense of melancholy. I am going to do it again.*

A GREAT THIRST ON THE LITTLE MISSOURI

Today, Aug. 6, I reached the halfway point of my Little Missouri trek. At about 3 p.m. I walked into Sully Creek State Primitive Park. Hey, it has water, so it is not primitive to me. Thoreau said he went to the woods to reduce life to its lowest terms. That's what's happened to me. Food. Tent. Good shoes. Above all, water. It has been so hot that, for the first time in my life, I cannot keep enough water in me. I'm drinking a couple of gallons a day, but there are times when all I can think about is water.

The Little Missouri River is surprisingly clear this year, but I'm not ready to drink out of it, not with cows standing in it and eliminating their wastes into it. It may come to that in McKenzie County, but I hope not. So I essentially travel from artesian well to artesian well. An artesian, as I am sure you know, is a well you tap rather than pump. The pressure is supplied by gravity. There's water in the hills along the Little Missouri. For the last 125 years, those who have tried to live here have spent a great deal of time attending to water. It is not much of an exaggeration to say that almost every bottom, every bench of grass between the river's S-curves, has or had a flowing well. My job is to find as many as I can. And fill up. I can't say my life depends upon it, but at times it feels that way.

These wells take several forms. Some are old tractor tires sealed up at the bottom. I've stopped at several made of concrete and several of heavy iron. Most these days are brown or blue fiberglass or plastic. A pipe comes up from the ground and spills glorious (often cold) water into the trough. Sometimes the water has a mineral taste. Sometimes it smells like sulphur. Sometimes it has a rusty look. But in no instance have I rejected any water from any well. Nor has the well water had the slightest ill effect on my body. A few ranches just let the trough fill, spill over the lip and create a spongy mess that makes it hard to get close enough to get the water. Most create a safety valve that draws off the excess and channels it into a draw, or down toward the river.

This is probably more than you ever wanted to know about artesian wells, but for the past week this has been just about the most important thing in my life. At 2 p.m. with the temperature at ninety-six degrees and not the slightest breeze, my eyes are scanning the territory for a water trough. I'll walk half a mile out of my way to get to one. I'll wade the river, climb up the opposite bank to get to one. At almost one hundred yards, I can usually tell whether they are running or not. When they are, particularly when I can see the glint of running water in the sun, it's a kind of ecstasy. I frequently move into a kind of trot as much as that is possible for a tired fifty-one-year-old with a fifty-five-pound pack. When the well turns out to be dry, it is a little heartbreaking. There have been moments when I felt like crying. But, a couple of more miles, a few more oxbows, and there will be another opportunity. That is the faith by which I walk the Little Missouri River.

Starting Aug. 5, I have been removing my shirt and soaking it in every well, and where that is not possible, in the river itself. This has a double use. It's a simple form of laundry. And it cools me from the outside in, rather than from the inside out, which perspires away my internal water supply. With this regimen, and perhaps a couple of comparatively cool days ahead (eighty degrees is paradise), I should make it.

So far, this has been a glorious and clarifying journey. When it is too hot to walk, I hole up and read *Walden*. When it is too hot to read Thoreau, I just sit in the river and doze. Needless to say, the scenery is sublime (or supply your highest term of appreciation). The moon has been so bright that it casts an eerie night shadow. And the coyotes have provided their evening concert just before dusk. I have walked into only one rattlesnake, a huge old Badlands veteran, and it chose not to strike. I have had just four encounters in a long week, Marmarth to Medora: with a pleasant rancher on an ATV; with the marvelous Robert Hanson of the Logging Camp Ranch, a charming, graceful philosopher of the Little Missouri River Valley, who stirred up some pink lemonade and asked whether it would violate my code to be invited into his kitchen; with a young, aggressive absentee landowner, who offered me bottles of cold water and explained that everything ("I mean absolutely everything") in the world is for sale; and Aug. 5, with a very startled woman in a golf cart. "Hi, mind if I hike through?"

> " ... the marvelous Robert Hanson of the Logging Camp Ranch, a charming, graceful philosopher of the Little Missouri River Valley, who stirred up some pink lemonade and asked whether it would violate my code to be invited into his kitchen."

I've shed some weight and some notions. I've made some plans and reset the priorities of my life. I've thought through some situations that were tripping me up. I've dreamed—awake and asleep. But the best thing is that I've spent hours and hours just being. Just sitting on a bluff, or sitting in the river, or lying with my head on my pack, saying to myself, "So, this is life."

The phrase that keeps recurring to me is that this is a humbling form of confidence building, and a confident form of humbling.

One more word on the wells, each one an oasis in this semi-desert country. Robert Hanson, who has been out here for at least half of the settlement period, and who never says a thoughtless word, explained to me that almost every well represents a former homestead. A low log cabin built more than a century ago, with a corral and a well, on a bench of grass in an oxbow of the river. You've seen them on postcards of the old Badlands, so squat and low-tech and romantic. Hundreds of small ranch homesteads were here once. Every one was a monument to the American dream. Today, there are only twenty-three ranches on the river between Marmarth and Medora, and almost all of them are occupied. You can still see a few slumping shacks here and there in the valley, and some ancient corrals. But mostly the wooden structures are gone, and what remains is the well alone. What once provided water to a pioneer family now waters cattle. There is something beautiful and melancholy in that. As I fill my water bottles, and splash cool water on my face and neck, I try to imagine the people who proved up here in the decades after Theodore Roosevelt and the Marquis de Mores left. Who were they? What brought them here? What were their lives like? When did they move on, and where did they go? What was their final assessment of this land?

I am drinking with ghosts. *8/12/06*

I wrote this column in my journal, in block print. My friend Charles Carvell took it back to Bismarck in time to meet the Tribune's deadline. This is the only column that I "filed" the old fashioned way, the way in which all newspaper articles found their way to print until about 1985.

The Lesson of the Little Missouri:
The Authenticity of Earning Every Mile

It was the hardest adventure of my life.

My trek along the banks of the Little Missouri River ended in the North Unit of Theodore Roosevelt National Park on Monday, Aug. 14.

I've showered three times now, first shower in fifteen days, and eaten fresh tomatoes and onions from my garden. Fresh tomatoes!

When I woke up this morning, in a soft bed on crisp fresh sheets, surrounded by books, with a thunderstorm lingering outside, I almost wondered if I had made the journey at all.

Civilization eats us up again so quickly and so completely.

Two nights ago I huddled in my tent in the middle of nowhere as the lightning slashed and punished the prairie bluff on which I was camped, and I literally wondered, not in abject terror, but in rational anxiety, if I would survive the night. In a moment of comic self-awareness, I actually composed my obituary on what I named "Electric Ridge," envisioned myself found by a rancher, two months from now, middle-aged bleached white male in pale blue boxer shorts bloated up like a pork sausage, hair still standing on end, a miner's headlamp flashlight fused to his head, clutching a pen and a journal. In the morning, when I woke up, I found almost two inches of rainwater in the bottom of my cooking kettle.

Then I began to worry that the river would rise to engulf me on the last day of my journey. I packed up wet (extra weight), put on sodden socks, and slushed into waterlogged shoes. By noon my gear was dry as ash.

You go out there alone, with no possibility of easy egress to the car, the basement, the shelter, or the ranch house 4.82 miles away, and it means you face what nature decides to throw at you. You become aware, early, of your utter vulnerability.

Nature no more cares whether I live or die than it worries the death of the bighorn sheep whose carcass I stumbled over north of the Elkhorn Ranch. You're on your own, and the only way to get to the egress point is to put one foot in front of the other. That's why I went. To earn it for a change. To see if I had the right stuff to carry my own weight for a change.

To put it in a nutshell: I hiked alone 173 miles along the banks of the Little Missouri River from Marmarth to the North Unit. I averaged 2.7 miles per hour, according to my GPS unit, which I will today download onto USGS topo maps of the badlands.

My pack weighed 55 or 60 pounds. Actually, I was walking down hill. At Marmarth the elevation is 2700 feet above sea level. At the North Unit, it is 1975 feet. I descended 725 feet in 173 miles. No wonder it was so easy!

Everything I needed to survive I had to carry on my back. As with all such journeys, there was a payload paradox. If I took what I wanted, I would be unable to lift the pack. If I took what my back was willing to carry, I would be on severely Spartan rations.

What you want, of course, is an outfitter that meets you at the end of a strenuous day of hiking with cold beer, crab hors d'oeuvres, shrimp salad and pork loin, with wine breathing in anticipation of chocolate at dusk. But that entirely defeats the purpose of the journey. So you carry what you can heft. My friend had squirreled a baggie of red nib licorice in a side pouch on my pack. I ate two nibs a day, and brought most of the bag home to Bismarck.

I lost twenty pounds without ever thinking about it. I'm pondering a national television infomercial: "The Marmarth radical weight loss program—a new body in just seventeen days—just don our patented Bow-Trek Pack Module and hike alone through knee-deep grass in one of the most isolated places in North America! Call now, 1-800-B.A.K.S.T.R.A.I.N."

For reasons I don't remember, I have a golf-ball sized welt on the back on my head, and some pretty raw chafing sores on my right hip and the small of my back. Some sort of spider bit me about thirty times on my left thigh. Somewhere north of Bullion Butte, I lost my left big toe nail. Beyond that, I feel better, stronger, younger, healthier, humbler, clearer, more virile, more sober, more authentic, more alive, more confident, more optimistic, more resourceful, more integrated and happier than I have in twenty years.

I feel completely renewed. In some important ways, I feel reborn. On the eighth day of the journey, I realized what my purpose for living is for the next 10, 20 or 30 years. I discovered what I want to explore, what I want to achieve and what I have to contribute to North Dakota's cultural life.

On the night that I slept within the chalk lines at Theodore Roosevelt's Elkhorn Ranch cabin, I recognized who I am now, at fifty-one, and what I live for. Before my journey ended, I made some careful but very firm resolutions about the rest of my life. They are not of the "write the great American novel" sort. They are the resolutions, I hope, of realistic mid-life maturity.

It was the third most important thing I have ever done. First, my child, daughter of the Little Missouri. Second, I moved home to North Dakota eleven months ago. Third, I hiked the Little Missouri alone.

It was impossible to keep track, but so far as I can estimate, I waded across the river between 10 and 20 times per day, so more than 150 times total. There is no trail along the banks of the Little Missouri. The sensuous S-curvings of the river actually force you to slosh across every time the bluffs encroach to turn the flow of the river. Roosevelt counted 23 mandatory crossings between Medora and the Elkhorn.

The grass is really dense and tall this year, though as dry as Melba toast or hundred-year-old newspaper, so a fair amount of each day's hiking was a kind of bushwhacking. I tripped scores of times on the cottonwood trash, the fallen branches of the big glorious cottonwoods of the Little Missouri, covered by grass. Three times, I fell on my face with my pack adding insult to the injury. Once I sank waist-deep into the muck of a side creek. That was terrifying. Near the Maltese Cross, I walked into a hole in the river and went in up to my nose. My digital camera died that day.

It would have been a hard journey in the best of fortnights, but this was the hottest summer that the ranchers I met could remember. The heat was unrelenting. It was like walking through an oven. The dry, usually wind-less, midday heat was not only searing and at times extremely uncomfortable, but it sapped the energy right out of me. After four or five days of trying to ignore the heat and concentrate on forward progress, I realized that I really must hole up in shade for a few hours every afternoon or I wasn't going to make it.

My rule was "nine miles by noon," which meant getting up before sunrise and walking purposefully as the temperature rose from seventy to one hundred degrees. During the hottest period of the day, I rested, read, wrote, or just dozed and dreamed, and drank in the some of the most beautiful landscape of America. About 4 p.m., when the heat felt slightly less dangerous, I lumbered on for a few more miles.

The only book I read was *Walden,* but it proved to be the perfect text for my trek. Thoreau's sojourn at Walden Pond (1845-46) was in many respects an experiment in getting rid of unnecessary baggage. Thoreau wonders what our "grossest groceries" really are. Answer: water.

He was engaged in what he called a "voluntary poverty" that was designed to inspire spiritual richness. I started with as little as possible, but three times in the course of my journey I jettisoned a couple of pounds of gear that proved to be entirely unnecessary. My heart is still out there at a bend in the Little Missouri River, near dusk, with a breeze just picking up, some licks of heat lightning off towards the horizon, a few scattered ponderosa pines in the near distance, and the cottonwood leaves beginning to rustle over my little tent.

A sip of water, and then I'm crawling in.

I won't write about this in this space again.   *8/19/06*

People have asked me why I so sternly announced that I would not write about the trip again. The answer is that I don't want my newspaper column to be about me. It is, of course, about me, since I am the one choosing the topics, engaging in the adventures, reading the books I write about, commenting on the weather and the seasons, taking the walks, analyzing the public events of North Dakota life. But I try always to write about the world through me rather than about me in the world, if that makes any sense. Besides, anyone who reads my column regularly knows that I never let more than a few weeks go by without getting myself into the Badlands.

RECENTERING THE SOUL

WHILE STANDING ON OLD BULLION BUTTE

Does life ever just overwhelm you or bombard you from so many directions at once that you think your head is going to explode? On Tuesday morning I was completely out of sorts, soul congested, in part because the morning paper reported that the North Dakota Legislature had indeed passed its trigger-happy anti-abortion law. Meanwhile, it was reported that the Republican leadership in the Legislature was more interested in determining who's Alpha Male than doing the people's business. My own life was coming apart at the seams on several fronts. I wasn't feeling well. Several deadlines were coming at me like a freight train.

"The world is too much with us," wrote William Wordsworth exactly two hundred years ago, in another post-agrarian place.

And to top it off, I had a hiking date in the Badlands. For a few shameful minutes, I thought about trying to weasel my way out of the hike, which had been scheduled for two months. But then I decided that the only thing worse than doing it would be to flake out.

So, bleary and bickery, I drove out to Medora and caught up with a good friend who had never climbed Bullion Butte. We coffeed up, topped up the gas, shyly compared lunch ingredients, made sure we had plenty of water, and headed south on West River Road, toward what I regard as North Dakota's premier butte.

It is literally the case that once we hit scoria, I began to cheer up. The vast emptiness of western North Dakota swallows the little dramas of humanity like airplane peanuts. We drove slowly with the windows open much of the time, engaging in catch-up conversation, venting conversation and compare notes conversation, but carefully postponing the big rich conversations we had been anticipating until we got up the butte into the really fresh air. Some conversations you have to earn with your legs.

Deer sprang around in the hollows along the muted orange and pink scoria road. Meadowlarks shot their perfect songs into the cab of the SUV—perfect in length, perfect in pitch, so much more interesting than the "hooo, hooo" or "kaw kaw" of other common plains birds. We each confessed that we desperately want to see a mountain lion, even if it winds up eating us, and we grumbled for a while about the new Game and Fish protocols that will result in more lions being killed for no good reason in North Dakota. It didn't take us long to realize that we were the wisest people who ever lived, and if Gov. John Hoeven, George Bush, President Ahmadinejad and the United Nations would just give us a call, we'd have the whole planet singing "It's a Small World after All," within hours.

> "The vast emptiness of western North Dakota swallows the little dramas of humanity like airplane peanuts."

That's Square Butte off to the southwest, and the outlier of Sentinel Butte way over to the right, and you can see Five Point Butte way off on the Montana line. We stopped to take pictures from time to time, especially as we skirted the west end of Theodore Roosevelt's Maltese Cross ranch. I pointed out Chimney Butte, which was the name Roosevelt tended to use for the ranch, and we had a short debate about whether Roosevelt ever climbed it and, if so, whether he rode to the top or parked his horse and scrambled up the "chimney" portion. We decided that Roosevelt would not have been able to resist the climb.

All the while we gabbed and laughed and gazed about at North Dakota's finest (and most fragile) landscape, Bullion Butte grew and grew out the left side of the windshield, and its sheer mass began to dominate our excursion.

We were going to park, adjust our packs, and then climb up to the top of the world to see what we could see.

What's your favorite butte? Many people I have asked this question have looked at me with a certain, shall we say, "detachment," as if to suggest that it is possible that I have far too much time on my hands. People have favorite books, favorite movies, favorite songs, even favorite places, but most of them, even North Dakotans who love the outdoors, do not seem to have taken the time to rank our buttes.

Bullion Butte is not the highest butte in North Dakota, but I believe it is the largest. At 3,336 feet above sea level, it is 170 feet lower than the highest point in North Dakota, White Butte, a few dozen miles to the southeast. Bullion is certainly the most geologically influential butte in North Dakota. If you look at a map of North Dakota, you will find it northwest of Amidon, right at the center of the big sweeping oxbow detour of the Little Missouri River. The Little Missouri tends north and slightly east as it travels through North Dakota. The crazy erosions of the Badlands remind us that the Little Missouri knows full well how to carve out its path. But Bullion Butte proved to be too much for the Little Mo. At some point tens or hundreds of thousands of years ago, the river just gave up and walked around the butte to the east, humbled but in no great hurry to discharge its silty load. The Bullion Butte detour is the largest diversion the Little Missouri makes between its source near Devils Tower in Wyoming and its mouth near Twin Buttes.

For the record: Bullion Butte, Black Butte, Pretty Butte, Killdeer Mountain (south), East and West Rainy Butte, Sentinel Butte, Square Butte, Little Heart Butte, Lone Butte. Some just because they are beautiful, others because I have had winsome adventures atop them. Your list?

We parked the car on a two-track road on the southwest side of the butte. Even though most of the Bullion Butte district is publicly owned, part of the Little Missouri National Grasslands, we left a note on the windshield saying that we were harmless geeks without guns or fire just climbing the butte to look around.

The temperature was absolutely perfect at about sixty-five degrees. There was just enough breeze to dry the sweat we worked up climbing the butte, which is steep enough in places to make you hold your knees and puff. We stopped three times to rest before we reached the summit. Total climb time: approximately ninety minutes. The top of the butte is a flat carpet of lush grass, with a bright rim of purple and golden cap rock all the way around the perimeter. Huge slabs of the cap rock have sheared off over the last thousands of years, and tumbled down the butte slopes, where they now lie like giants, waiting for the time when they will tumble lower and crumble and dissolve and head for the Gulf of Mexico.

By the time we settled in a grassy hollow on the eastern rim of the butte, in the words of Huckleberry Finn, "all my troubles was gone."

We opened our packs, pulled out food made delicious by the climb, opened a small bottle of what my hiking companion called "camping wine," and toasted the empty redemptive wildness of North Dakota. There was just enough breeze to fill us with wonder when we went silent, as the landscape encouraged us to do for long stretches of time. From any edge of the butte, you can see the glorious, improbable Little Missouri River threading its way, glinting blue in the sun, the lifeline of the Badlands country.

There were thousands of purple pasqueflowers in full bloom at Bullion Butte last week. The bitter chalky chocolate was perfect dessert. We talked endlessly. At last we climbed down with some sadness that so perfect a day had to end. We prayed, in a secular way, that this magnificent magical place will remain just what it is: empty, windswept, a paradise of grass and spiritual restoration. Roosevelt said it best: "Leave it as it is. The ages have been at work on it and man can only mar it." *4/28/07*

THE MAGIC GATE

TO NORTH DAKOTA'S

PETRIFIED FOREST

I don't remember the first time I went to Theodore Roosevelt National Park. It was when I was very young. My father worked for a bank in Dickinson. The annual bank picnic was held in the park. At that time we were the kind of family that experienced the Badlands mostly from the overlook at Painted Canyon. My father was a brainy and decidedly indoors sort of man. He did not hunt. He did not hike. He did not fish. He did not camp. He did not play ball. His very limited interest in nature was satisfied by a jaunt along the loop road in the national park once a year.

His favorite way to observe wildlife was through the window of his car. On the one occasion when we went camping—against his better judgment—in the South Unit of Theodore Roosevelt National Park, he spent the first part of the evening cursing the day we had purchased a heavy green canvas Montgomery Ward pup tent, which he couldn't figure out how to erect. At bedtime, he actually changed into pajamas before inserting himself, feet first, into the tent. The mosquito netting snapped rather than zipped shut, and he fretted endlessly about the possibility of a nocturnal raid by bugs, prairie dogs, skunks, vermin, or snakes, which he seemed to regard as inevitable. He was, in short, a wilderness moron.

The tent collapsed on my parents sometime in the night and that was the end (as well as the beginning) of our family camping history.

My father sincerely believed that the whole point of civilization was to emancipate us from ever again sleeping on the ground. He used to say to me, "Look, ten thousand years of slow human progress has brought us beds, refrigerators, ovens, couches, electric lights, and hygienic toilet facilities. Why would any rational being turn back the clock on all those conveniences, and pretend to enjoy it too?"

Fair enough. I know a lot of people who agree with him, more or less.

A few days ago I had the joy of taking a very different family of three from Illinois for a hike in the national park. The parents are historians with an interest in Theodore Roosevelt, and their son is the brightest and most agreeable whippersnapper I have met in a very long time. I gave them options: the loop road followed by ice cream (the Charles Jenkinson option); a hike somewhere in the park; a serious venture down West River Road to Bullion Butte and possibly on to magical Marmarth; a trip to the Petrified Forest.

They jumped at the Petrified Forest.

We drove west of Medora and north on West River Road. If you follow the tiny brown TR icons on the ranch and forest service roads (gravel), you get to the parking lot for the Petrified Forest in about half an hour. To get into the park, you have to bend over and crawl through an ingenious little gate in the park fence. The gate was designed to let humans in but not let buffalo out, but it has the droll effect of reminding you that you are entering a magic kingdom, like Harry Potter's Hogwarts or Alice's wonderland. Probably nothing could have induced my father to take that plunge.

> "My father sincerely believed that the whole point of civilization was to emancipate us from ever again sleeping on the ground."

The Petrified Forest is one of the handful of best places in North Dakota. After a short and delightful hike you crest a hill and come upon hundreds, perhaps thousands of petrified trunk and stump sections of ancient trees, thought by geologists to be between 55 million and 67 million years old. They are grand, stark, gnarled, massive, and weirdly strewn about as if by a disorganized petrified giant who gathered materials for a building project and never quite saw it through. Some of the stumps, which are thought to be primordial cousins to the cypress, are plunked on the side of nearly vertical cliffs in a manner that seems to defy gravity. The lingering stupid boy in me wanted to run up and try to dislodge a couple of them so that I could watch them tumble down into the valley. I resisted the urge to be a reverse vandalizing Sisyphus.

The petrified trees pop out like colossal mushrooms where the Sentinel Butte and Bullion Creek formations are exposed in the Badlands. As you scramble around the dry, scarred landscape, it's not easy to appreciate that the zone where we were hiking on an absolutely perfect North Dakota June afternoon was once a subtropical forest at or near an Everglades-like swamp. As you stand next to a petrified stump five to ten feet wide, the remnant of a tree that was at least one hundred feet high tens of millions of years ago, your brain tries to wrap itself around the concept of geological time. But what's actually right in front of you is too amazing and magnificent, too present and commanding, to turn away from toward some animated diorama of the geological imagination.

TRNP Superintendent Valerie Naylor says the Petrified Forest is thought to be the third largest in the United States.

All I could think was: this treasure is in North Dakota. My guests are happy, relaxed, and enchanted. They are seeing one of the wonders of the world in a place where they would never have expected to see it. They will not forget this day, when they sauntered through an ancient forest ruin surrounded by the greenest grassland you have ever encountered, the grass strewn with the most beautiful wildflowers you could ever happen upon. Temperature sixty-eight degrees and only a gentle breeze to remind us that we were hiking on the Great Plains. This will be their memory of North Dakota. Splendid satisfaction.

My remarkable father could have told all of us how a petrification works—how the organic fibers and structure of the tree are gradually replaced by local minerals, so that petrified wood is not wood at all, but rock that has become a simulacrum of a tree that has vanished from the earth. He would have loved to explain that process—over a thoroughly civilized meal and a fine glass of wine, indoors. *6/20/10*

The staff of Theodore Roosevelt National Park, in their infinite wisdom, have replaced the Magic Gate with a clunky, boring gate. They have all sorts of "good reasons" for doing so, but the net result is to lower the magic of the Petrified Forest. As usual Thoreau had it right: "As with our colleges, so with a hundred "modern improvements"; there is an illusion about them; there is not always a positive advance. The devil goes on exacting compound interest to the last for his early share and numerous succeeding investments in them. Our inventions are wont to be pretty toys, which distract our attention from serious things. They are but improved means to an unimproved end, an end which it was already but too easy to arrive at."

Meandering Along

the Loneliest Country in America

Last Saturday evening, I had the enormous pleasure of driving on U.S. 85 from Belfield to the Black Hills. Then a shag carpet roadside motel. The next day, I drove S.D. 79 to Hot Springs, then U.S. 385 (marvelous road) to Sidney, Neb., and on over into northwestern Kansas.

U.S. 85 from Belfield to the Black Hills is my favorite Great Plains highway. It is hard to think of a better plains highway anywhere (please let me know if you have nominations), though U.S. 212 and U.S. 12 through eastern Montana are spectacular, as is I-94 along the Yellowstone River, even though it is an interstate. What I look for on a Great Plains highway is a vast and open sweep of grassland in every direction, the kind of rolling plains country that just swallows up whatever you thought was important, punctuated not too often and not too seldom by buttes, breaks, pine ridges and gravel roads leading off to some even more remote place that you will probably never see. Every half hour or so you cross an unspectacular plains river; unspectacular, that is, until you get to the Platte.

And antelope. The pronghorn antelope (*Antilocapra americana*) is the quintessential Great Plains creature. There are a bunch of them in south-western North Dakota. In Wyoming and South Dakota, they are as common as prairie dogs, but of course infinitely more graceful, lithe, whimsi-cal and magnificent. My, how they run.

From Belfield to a few miles north of Amidon, U.S. 85 is a nonde-script Great Plains highway. Then, without warning, the road curves (no, it sweeps) into the West, and things suddenly get very interesting. White Butte, Black Butte and its outliers (Tepee and Slide), the two majestic Rainy Buttes far off to the east, and Bullion Butte dominating the Little Missouri River valley over your right shoulder. I stopped every few minutes to take pictures. Every time I got out of the car, a meadowlark sang to me and an 18-wheeler thundered by and nearly blew me off the road. The temperature was perfect. The quality of light was simply exquisite.

The Twin Buttes just north of Bowman would be so much more beauti-ful if Bowman weren't parked just under them.

I have a terrible confession to make. The butte country of northwestern South Dakota is even more beautiful than the butte country of southwest-ern North Dakota. It wasn't God, of course, who sliced Dakota Territory horizontally, but politicians. If the territory had been sliced vertically, the west river state might have been called Les Buttes or Godforsakia or more appropriately Lakota. Probably it is good that North Dakota gets its Fargo,

South Dakota its Sioux Falls, to serve as counterweights to what otherwise would have been an impossibly marginal west river state. But from Pretty Butte (north of Marmarth) or the Slim Buttes (near ... well, nothing), Fargo is a meaningless idea.

I mean no disrespect to Fargo, our cultural "capital," but when I am in the crescent between West Fargo and Grand Forks, I never once have thought, "Thank God I live here," but I find myself literally saying those words, out loud to the sky, between the Sheyenne River and Helena. Granted, Fargo-Moorhead has Thai food, a lively arts community and even some ethnic diversity, but the Red River Valley corridor feels to me like a poor cousin to Maple Grove and St. Louis Park, Minnesota, while the butte corridor between Bowman and Billings and Killdeer and the Scottsbluff isn't the poor cousin to any landscape in North America. There is something undeniably authentic about the country around Ludlow, Reva, and Buffalo, S.D., that makes access to Old Chicago Pizza and Macy's less necessary to the pursuit of happiness. I have heard people in Bismarck say, recently, "Finally, we have a few restaurants worth eating at." To which I say, "Hey, don't be dissing Kroll's Diner and the Seven Seas," and "Is it really about food?"

> "I have a terrible confession to make. The butte country of northwestern South Dakota is even more beautiful than the butte country of southwestern North Dakota. It wasn't God, of course, who sliced Dakota Territory horizontally, but politicians."

Almost the minute you cross over into South Dakota on U.S. 85, the country splays out dramatically, the buttes get more lonely and towering, and the pines appear more often on the crests of ridges. It's just bigger country. There is less till agriculture. There's no (aptly named) New England to suggest Midwestern gumption and boosterism. The great South Dakota buttes, Haystack, Castle Rock, Owl, Deers Ears and others, are somehow more romantic than their North Dakota counterparts.

In northwestern South Dakota, you really are in the middle of nowhere. A Cenex sign is like an oasis. Whenever I make that drive, I feel that all is right in America. So far from everything, bin Laden seems like a figure out of a Manichean comic book. Does anyone out here really care whether Tom Cruise is gay? This is a landscape where even red America seems too cosmopolitan.

Well, that's how I see it and some others. But not everyone. I'm sure Paris Hilton would rather be in the L.A. County Jail than out here. A couple of years ago, my daughter and I, after Thanksgiving, drove U.S. 85 and stopped for the night at a Holiday Inn in Spearfish. It had been a magnificent day with a dusting of bluish snow and the most purely blue skies you can ever see. By the time we checked in, I was euphoric from the combination of daughter and the landscape and the freedom of a road trip. The young woman who checked us in was unusually friendly and generous. She asked me where we had come in from. I rhapsodized about our drive from Bowman. "Oh yeah," she said in a perfectly friendly way, "that's like sitting in a room staring at wallpaper all day long." OK, not for everyone.

Inevitably, on U.S. 85 between Bowman and Buffalo, you find yourself saying, "Boy, I hope we don't break down out here." The phrase may be more meaningful than it seems. Somewhere north of Buffalo once, at 11 p.m., my father, who was not fond of the open plains, got a flat tire and the jack didn't work. I do not exaggerate when I say it took him months to get back to equilibrium, and it really was our last family vacation ever, mostly for that reason.

One of the joys of U.S. 85 and other roads in the western Dakotas, Nebraska and Kansas is that you drive across what Plains writer Mari Sandoz called the "ladder of rivers" that are the west river tributaries of the Missouri. Better yet, you drive across them at or near their sources when they are still intermittent rivulets. In North Dakota these rivers are the Heart, the Cannonball, the Cedar and the Grand. In South Dakota, the two Moreaus, the Belle Fourche, the Cheyenne and the White. In Nebraska, the unbearably beautiful Niobrara, which cuts what only can be called a grass canyon as it snakes its way toward Vermillion. And then there is the Platte, which, with its indeterminate width, its braidings, its sand and its shallowness, fills me with awe every time. Every time I see it, I wonder what it would be like if Nebraskans hadn't turned it into an irrigation feeder.

I so wanted to wander west into the Cave Hills, linger at the historically important Crow Buttes, or venture seven miles west of the highway to the true "Center of the Nation" to get re-centered.

But I had promises to keep. *6/23/07*

U.S. 85 is sublime, especially south of Bowman, ND. But S.D. 79 is one of the greatest highways on the Great Plains, too.

THE BUTTES *of* NORTH DAKOTA
CLAY'S TEN FAVORITE

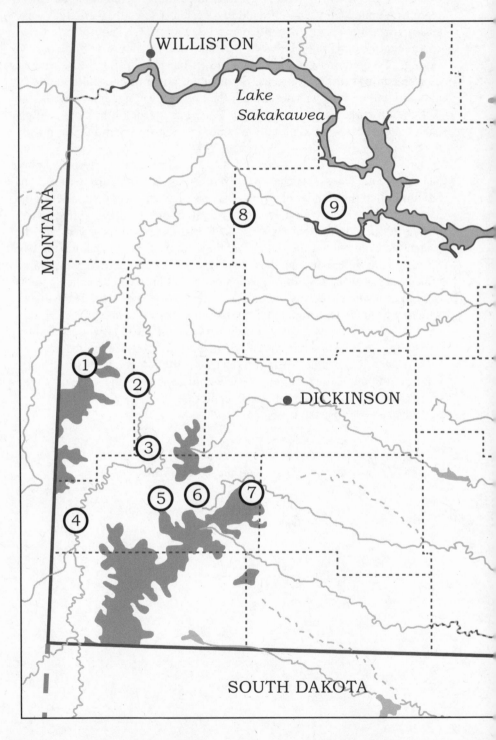

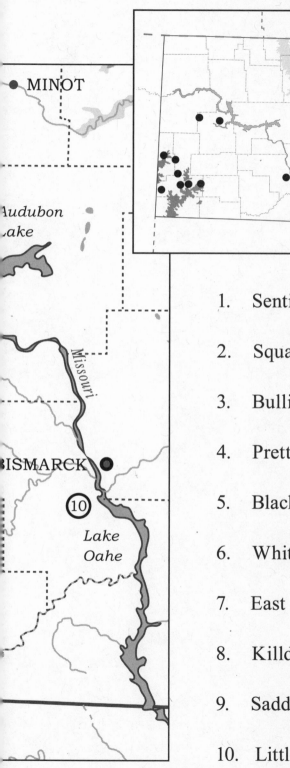

1. Sentinel Butte

2. Square Butte

3. Bullion Butte

4. Pretty Butte

5. Black Butte

6. White Butte

7. East and West Rainy Butte

8. Killdeer Mountains

9. Saddle Butte

10. Little Heart Butte

FAMILY

Last Thanksgiving at the Farm

Thanksgiving is my favorite holiday. Christmas is so buried in the rubble of commerce that finding joy in all that chaos is difficult and finding serenity nearly impossible. The Fourth of July is all boats, bottle rockets, and beer. Besides, I'm usually working. But Thanksgiving is wonderfully free of merchandize and, unique among holidays, it always delivers the essence of what it is about. It's a harvest festival. It's about fecundity. Its measure is gratitude. It gets at the essence of the American experience, nature's abundance, but it ties that abundance to thankfulness and family love. The traditional Thanksgiving meal reflects the New World's agricultural gifts to the world: pumpkins, potatoes, including sweet potatoes, beans, cranberries, and turkey. Thomas Jefferson wanted the turkey to be the national bird of the United States.

I have vivid memories of several dozen Thanksgivings, including a purely absurd one my friend Douglas and I attempted in Great Britain, which does not celebrate Thanksgiving and therefore does not readily sell the fixins. But the greatest Thanksgiving of all was the last one we spent with my grandmother Rhoda Straus on the farm.

My grandparents had lived for decades on a modest dairy farm just south of Fergus Falls, Minn. The farm had no more than 110 acres, a third of which was pasture, the rest divided among oats, silage corn, wheat, flax, hay, and barley. Twice a day, year after year, they milked sixteen cows together. As a child, I had come to consider one of the Holsteins my own. I called her Pal. She was all white with black spots around her eyes. My grandparents sold the farm to the city of Fergus Falls in the late 1970s, but part of the deal was that they were permitted to live on the home place for the rest of their lives. Grandpa died in 1981. Grandma stayed on, baking bread twice a week, maintaining a vast garden, and canning and preserving hundreds of quarts of produce per year. By now she was frail, almost doubled over from osteoporosis. She was ninety.

My father Charles loved holidays, which meant for him staying in his pjs all day, shuffling about in slippers. It was he who suggested that we celebrate one last Thanksgiving on the farm. We all knew that Grandma was by far the best cook in the family, and the best baker, and that a holiday meal there was synonymous with delicious abundance. Grandma was a human cornucopia. We could plan on retiring from the Thanksgiving table miserable with satisfaction.

My family and I salivated our way across the 350 miles from Dickinson to the farm, each nominating that portion of the feast for which we felt the deepest anticipation. Would it be a twenty pound turkey, or the rarer twenty-eight pounder? Would there be enough mashed potatoes for fried potato patties the next day? Would there be two pies or three, and would they all be pumpkin? Mother hoped for beets. I could not wait to taste homemade dill pickles. I asked mother if she would consider making a turkey pot pie with the leftovers. Homemade rolls. We were all ecstatic.

Alas.

A widow for a decade, in declining vigor, Grandma Rhoda had reached that stage in her life when she tried to cook not an ounce more than would be consumed at any meal. Accordingly she had purchased a seven-pound turkey. She had expected to feed six with that slender bird, and now, thanks to her last minute impulse invitations to cousin Marvin the pig farmer and his wife Corinne, and Aunt Marge and her daughter, there were ten of us around the great old table in the dining room. Each place was beautifully set with Straus family china.

> "It was not a picture of abundance. No cornucopia this, the turkey looked like a Cornish game hen as my father addressed it with the antique carving knife, which suddenly wore the grandeur of a scimitar next to the scrawny bird."

My father Charles was to carve. This was, in fact, the only role that my grandparents had ever assigned him in the forty years of his marriage to my mother, their eldest daughter. He knew nothing about agriculture, and cared less. He was a man of great gifts in some arenas, but he was completely out of place in rural America, and he was a dork with a pliers. My grandparents knew this. They kept him away from power equipment. Still, he could carve a turkey with some proficiency.

The great moment came at last. We were summoned to the table. And then my mother walked in from the kitchen with a huge wooden trencher on which sat ... well, a shriveled little seven-pound turkey.

It was not a picture of abundance. No cornucopia this, the turkey looked like a Cornish game hen as my father addressed it with the antique carving knife, which suddenly wore the grandeur of a scimitar next to the scrawny bird. There was visible anxiety on each guest's face as the modest slices began to make their way around the table. The turkey wasn't an entrée. It was a mere hors d'oeuvre. Thanksgiving is one meal of the year in which one can fairly play the glutton, when one deserves to pig out, and we had gathered from five states at the old family farm to celebrate the great harvest festival of the Pilgrims and of America, and now we looked upon the prospect of exceedingly meager rations, the slimmest pickings of any Thanksgiving meal in our family since, and maybe including, the Great Depression.

There was one further complication: my aunt Susan. Susan was mentally handicapped. She was born with Down's Syndrome. She was high-functioning, but she could not quite read, and her every daily activity required supervision. She had lived on the farm her whole life. She was perhaps the most amazing person I ever knew. Susan brimmed over with love and laughter, joy and creativity, and a huge lust for life. She slurred her words. She was hard to follow in conversation. Like many people with Down's Syndrome, she was seriously overweight. She was forty-some years old. She also had a gargantuan appetite. It is not an exaggeration to say that she could have polished off that pathetic little turkey all by herself. We all eyed her with misgivings.

My father controlled the distribution of turkey, but somehow Susan got hold of the mashed potatoes first. She shoveled two massive heaps onto her plate, and poured off 75 percent of the gravy onto a vast, plate-full sea of potatoes. The rest of us were appalled, even angry, but there was nothing to be done and little to say. Nine of us would have to share the mashed remnants of two or three potatoes with a thin varnish of Grandma's magnificent gravy. And so we loaded up on beets and green beans with vinegar and bacon bits. And homemade rolls.

I wish I could say that, as in the great parable of Jesus, Rhoda Straus had been able to turn that puny little meal into loaves and fishes sufficient for an assembled multitude. Fortunately the pies were more abundant than the meal proper, and my mother rustled up a gallon of Cass-Clay vanilla ice cream from the massive freezer in the dark little basement. Later, we made several batches of popcorn.

Everyone lived.

It was Thomas Jefferson who said, "No man ever regretted having eaten too little."

And yet, for all of this, it was the loveliest and most memorable of Thanksgivings. I wouldn't trade it for all the twenty-eight-pounders in Christendom. Partly because it reminded us all that not everyone in the world—or in America, or for that matter in Otter Tail County—shared our general abundance, it inspired a special piquancy as each of us, at Grandma's urging, intoned, some in choked and self-conscious sentences, those things for which we were especially thankful that year, the last Thanksgiving with Rhoda Straus, that marvelous German gardener and dairy farmer of Fergus Falls, Minnesota. I knew as we nibbled our turkey bits that we would never sit around that farm table again.

God bless America. *11/21/05*

Just before this book went to press, my mother informed me that the City of Fergus Falls has now torn down the old farmhouse and built a twenty-first century landfill infrastructure where Dick, Rhoda, and Susan Straus farmed.

Killing a Red Fox While Driving to Kansas

I hit a fox last week while driving to Kansas. It was late in the evening, just before sunset, and I was a few miles north of Newell, S.D. My daughter was with me in the passenger seat reading Nancy Drew. We came up over a hill and there it was, a red fox (Vulpes vulpes), sitting serenely in the right lane of the highway.

I remember thinking how tremendously beautiful it was sitting there at full alert in the roseate light of sunset. We had been driving for hours. I was in the zone wherein you feel you could drive forever.

At first, when I saw the fox, I did not know what it was. Then my brain registered that it was an animal. Then it came to me that it might be a fox. The world went into slow motion. I could not get over how beautiful it was, sitting there, in classical capital-A formation, as if the highway had been created as a dais for its feral majesty. I remember wondering, what is it doing sitting there, of all places. Then it dawned on me: I'm going to run over it.

I swerved as much as I dared, but I hit it square. There was a terrible thump and jolt, and on we went to Rapid City, where we ordered a pizza and my daughter watched an hour of Disney sitcoms.

It has haunted me ever since.

In the moments after the accident, I forced myself not to over-react. My daughter is twelve, and I was afraid that she might dissolve into a "poor Bambi" reaction and that my sense of horror might just make things worse. She was philosophical. "There was nothing you could do, Daddy. I just hate that noise when a car hits an animal."

We drove on. I did not dare look back. I knew I should stop the car and make sure it was dead (it was, of course, dead) and pull it off to the side of the road. But I could not bear to see its crushed back or shattered skull, at least not with my daughter squatting next to me over the still-warm corpse.

She got over it and moved on and went back to her book. But she wasn't the driver. Now I cannot stop brooding about it. A few days before that drive, I had been out camping and hiking on the Little Missouri River, where I was likelier to be victim than predator. Every rancher I met asked me if I were afraid of being breakfast for a mountain lion. I saw a red fox near Bullion Butte, but from a long distance, and I remember hoping that someday I would see one up close.

How could a fox, that quickest and wiliest of creatures, that epitome of alertness, just sit there on Highway 79 and not jump out of the way of an oncoming car? The highway between Newell and Hettinger is a lightly traveled road. It was an unusually still and beautiful sunset. The asphalt was radiating the accumulated heat of the day. My Audubon Society Grasslands guidebook says, "Even when fairly common, the red fox may be difficult to observe, as it is shy, nervous, and primarily nocturnal (though it may be abroad near dawn or dusk or on dark days)."

It's a mystery.

If I had run over a child walking along that road, there would be an investigation and an arrest and a trial and my life would never be the same. I think of that whenever I drive. The village of Newell would have held memorial services, and a community fundraiser for the grieving family, and the story would have been remembered for a whole generation. But if I hit a red fox in the prime of its life, and snuff out its existence instantly and forever, "it's just one of those things" and we drive on and order a pizza.

I get it that there is a distinction between running over a fox and running over a child, but the gap of response and responsibility seems too large. Is the divide between humanity and the rest of creation that wide, that fundamental? The Humane Society of America estimates that the daily road kill in the United States runs to at least 1 million creatures. Hunters kill 200 million game animals per year, and 100 million lab animals are killed in the name of medical progress and better cosmetics, but the roadkill estimates are close to 400 million per year.

Last year, 47,000 Americans died on America's highways, a national crisis, we were told by the AAA.

When he walks onto the stage carrying his dead daughter Cordelia, King Lear asks, "Why should a dog, a horse, a rat, have life and thou no breath at all?" I ask, in whose eyes is a red fox expendable in a way that a human life is not? Is it God's hierarchy—or just man's? I get it. I am not suggesting parity. I'm with Hamlet that we are the "beauty of the world, the paragon of animals," but I don't understand why manslaughter is so profoundly graver than animal slaughter.

I've never hit a deer (or shot one for that matter). In some ways, that would have been easier to handle, because deer kill is so common. Everybody knows somebody who has hit one. The damage to the car in some way takes over the story and those unpleasant logistics (towings and body shops) help to keep the dead deer at bay. The sheriff takes charge and offers soothing words. Over the years I have hit my share of birds, porcupines, snakes, jackrabbits and field mice. Once, in Dickinson, rushing through town to rescue a friend whose car had broken down near New England, I hit a cat. Two things seared into my memory that night as I knocked on doors to find out whose pet I had killed. The cat twitched grotesquely on the road for a few minutes - I shudder to remember it thirty years later. And there was a teenage boy on a bicycle at the scene, who laughed sadistically as I looked around in horror.

We all draw the line somewhere. I don't lose sleep over a thousand mosquitoes on my windshield, or even the thump of a skunk or porcupine now and then, but a fox, a deer, a coyote, or a hawk or eagle would bring on grief and lost sleep.

My former father-in-law, a Kansas farmer, used to swerve, not to avoid, but in order to hit badgers, raccoons, skunks and other small animals. He regarded them as vermin who dig holes and destroy crops. He was completely intolerant of their existence. He used his big car as a blunt instrument with which to kill small quadrupeds. He would not have run down a deer, of course, but he did not hesitate to dispatch a fox or coyote.

Once when I swerved dramatically to avoid killing a raccoon, my former wife rebuked me severely. "You're going to have to learn to run over animals on the road. It's a shame, but better they die than both of us."

I get it.

Still, I find the nonchalance and the arrogance of humanity deeply troubling, not because I am beyond it, but because I live right at the heart of that worldview. And like the rest of us, I find the death of a Somalian or a Sri Lankan or an Iraqi or, for that matter, a Texan much less upsetting than the death of my friend from Mandan.

The great William Stafford wrote a poem called "Traveling through the Dark," about coming upon a roadkilled deer "on the edge of the Wilson River road." (It's worth Googling). "It is usually best to roll them into the canyon," Stafford wrote. The doe was dead, but he discovered there was still a living fawn in its womb. "Her side was warm; her fawn lay there waiting, alive, still, never to be born." Stafford's narrator hesitated. "Around our group I could hear the wilderness listen."

"I thought hard for us all—my only swerving—then pushed her over the edge into the river."

Some things you never forget. *9/9/06*

GIVING THANKS IN A TIME OF UNEASE

Maybe I speak only for myself, but Thanksgiving this year has a special piquancy. The world feels less stable than it did at this time last year. It feels as if the forces of chaos are gaining strength and the world just might spin completely out of control any day now.

Everything I observe around me feels fragile all of a sudden. If you've ever walked out on ice over a body of water before it's really safe, putting one foot forward very tentatively, then another, and listening hard for the sounds of stress, holding yourself ready to scramble backward at the first indication of collapse, that's how things feel to me this year.

The economy, from the price of a loaf of bread to the instability of the stock market. Foreign policy and entanglements. America's threadbare sense of itself. The war that won't go away, at ruinous cost to our treasury, our military morale and our standing in the world. Civil strife, insurrection, military adventurism across the globe. Raving dictators in North Korea, Venezuela, Iran, elsewhere. Terrible setbacks to democratic progress in Russia, in China profound indifference to the world's hard-won standards of environmental and product safety. It feels like we're edging toward the abyss.

It's as if the world is spinning under a permanently full moon.

I'm going to eat my turkey and cranberries with a special relish Thursday, but also with some melancholy. It seems like a paradox, but Thanksgiving in a disintegrating and uncertain world is more meaningful than one that merely celebrates abundance, stability, and prosperity. Abundance is not automatic, even for those who work hard and play by the rules. My grandparents knew that as the central fact of life. My parents knew it enough to be cautious. My generation has known only reckless abundance.

Actually, Thanksgiving against the odds, Thanksgiving in spite of the evidence, is firmly grounded in American history.

The first American thanksgiving (1621) was a sacrament of gratitude to celebrate the Pilgrims' hard-won toehold on a vast and largely inhospitable continent. Thanksgiving as we now celebrate it dates to Oct. 3, 1863, at the darkest time of the Civil War, when President Lincoln proclaimed Thanksgiving a permanent national holiday. Through most of American history, designations of days of thanksgiving were coupled with a call for prayer. We've been so prosperous and stable for so long that we've forgotten how fragile our lives really are.

I've known some of this fragility in my own experience, and I can always sense it burbling just below the surface as I try to glide through life. Over the past couple of years, I have witnessed the proximity of the abyss among my closest friends. Loss of loved ones in their prime—inexplicable, harrowing, crippling loss—the horror of siblings or grandchildren debilitated with disease, a serio-comic episode with the game warden (all the more hurtful for its essential innocence), bewildering setbacks in professional life, a humiliating standoff with overzealous lawmen, a child arrested in the night, a sudden wearying regimen of blood transfusions, the car accident on the county line, the job that went to someone else, a sharp quarrel with a mere stranger about ... nothing.

We like to think that life runs by a software that shelters us from chaos, but it is not so. We can increase the odds of stability by working hard, practicing thrift, and living with integrity, but there are no guarantees. One day, we are planning an extension on the house, and the next day, we are diagnosed with pancreatic cancer. We always rolled our eyes and laughed when my grandmother said anything can be endured as long as we have our health. It does not seem so silly any more.

I'm going to dig up the last of my potatoes this week and serve them for Thanksgiving. That will give me more pleasure than almost anything else. My daughter, who is just thirteen, called me last night and asked me to UPS her a plastic container of my cranberry sauce. "Don't tell her, but yours is better than Mom's," she said. I didn't have the heart to say I just follow the recipe on the back of the bag. Against the odds of spillage and perishability, I will send the cranberry sauce.

The events in Pakistan (Islam's only nuclear power) terrify me, whenever I look up from Sudoku or Patriots' games long enough to gaze around. Burma (Myanmar) is coming undone, in spite of the best efforts of one of my heroes, Aung San Suu Kyi, winner of the Nobel Peace Prize.

I do not believe, with Gloucester in Shakespeare's King Lear, that "we have seen the best of our time," but I ruminate about this proposition now more than at any previous time of my life. At $95-a-barrel oil and talk of air strikes against Iranian nuclear facilities, it's hard not to feel pessimistic. Probably we will edge away from the abyss. Humankind's capacity for muddling through is enormous. That alone is abundant cause for giving thanks.

On Thanksgiving, surrounded by family in the midst of so much abundance, we ought to remember three less fortunate groups. First, there are our troops spread across the planet, many of them in harm's way. More than a quarter of a million Americans, mostly young, will be a world away from their loved ones this Thursday eating MRE's. Half of them are in Iraq.

Then there are the millions of people, some of them in North Dakota, who cannot afford to spread cornucopia across the dining room table come Thursday. The price of food is sharply higher this year. The number of poor for whom the cost of gas, of fuel oil, and of food has bitten painfully into their lives is sharply higher. Finally, there are those for whom personal losses in 2007 have made this Thanksgiving a bittersweet charade.

I believe in grace, and I want to live in joy. For all of these disquieting notes, I know we have much to be thankful for, in some sense now more than ever. I am immensely thankful for my friends, some of them new friends in 2007. I am so thankful to live in North Dakota, which understands Thanksgiving better than any other place I have lived. I am thankful for the opportunities I have to do satisfying work. I am thankful for my mother. We're no longer a "nuclear family": we're just a hydrogen atom these days, a single electron spinning around a proton nucleus. It's hard to know just who is the electron. She travels almost as much as I do.

Above all else, I am thankful for a winsome thirteen-year-old who is the greatest blessing of my life, and without whom my life would be a dry shard, and who is now waiting for a package at the other end of the Great Plains.

At the grocery store the other day, I bought a giant turkey, at least three times bigger than I need for mother and me. It was like a statement of defiance against the times. And now I need to buy more cranberries and a really high-end piece of Tupperware. *11/17/07*

A New Year and a Petrified Forest

To cap a wonderful Christmas, my daughter and I ventured out to the petrified forest in Theodore Roosevelt National Park on New Year's Eve. The superintendent of the park, Valerie Naylor, offered to take us to the remote and seldom visited site. To my surprise, my thirteen-year-old daughter jumped at the chance.

> "I measure my happiness and my mental health by the number of days per year I get to spend in the Badlands."

If there was ever a time in my life when New Year's Eve signified dressing up, drinking heavily, questing for conviviality and eros, and finding a crowd with whom to sing in the new year, that era is decidedly over. It's a rare New Year's wherein I actually see the clock reach twelve. Starting the new year with a hangover has always struck me as an odd way, in Thomas Paine's phrase, "to begin the world over again."

What better way to start 2008 than in the Badlands, on foot, in a wilderness area, in pursuit of 50-million to 60-million-year-old trees? That, like Shelley's poem "Ozymandias," puts one's New Year's resolutions into perspective.

I measure my happiness and my mental health by the number of days per year I get to spend in the Badlands, or rather in what Lewis and Clark called the "black hills." The explorers used that term to designate the pine-dotted country east of the Rocky Mountains and north of the Platte River.

Once, when I lived for a summer near Salisbury in England, I asked the well-traveled patriarch of my host family what he liked best about America. He paused and then said, "Egg McMuffin." It was a typical British cheap shot, but he probably meant it. Today, as I drove my daughter from Dickinson to Kansas, feeling the melancholy of the closing of the holiday interlude, I looked out at the distant contours of the Cave Hills and realized that what I love best about America is the fact that we have a West. A big empty quarter of essentially uninhabitable land punctuated by geological splendors like Devils Tower and Arches National Park. England doesn't have that. France and Germany don't have that. Japan doesn't have that.

America means continental vastness, an array of landscapes that look as if John Wayne or Shane might still ride through them, the presence or echo of American Indians, and an almost unbearably beautiful symphony of sky and untrammeled nature.

That's the American West. And we need to keep it empty if we can.

We parked the car up off West River Road at the portal of the petrified forest. The sun was shining wanly. The day seemed milder than it actually was. Every two or three minutes, a strong raw wind sprinted through from the northwest. At those moments it was bitingly cold. We mummified my child in all the scarves, hats, mittens, and leggings we could scrounge up in the SUV. I could see that she was nervous. It was simply the case that she had never before undertaken a winter hike on a potentially dangerous day in what seemed to her the middle of nowhere. She wanted to know just how far it was to "this petrified forest." Valerie said she had hot chocolate for later.

We crawled through the fence and began to hike the mile and a half to the ancient trees. My daughter asked if the forest was intact—in other words, a full, tall, freeze-dried magic forest with roots, trunks, branches, and leaves, perfectly preserved. It's a fair question, which reminds us of how open the universe still is to a thirteen-year-old. I asked myself where the tallest intact tree petrification can be found. Yellowstone, I think. Now Valerie and I worked to lower her expectations without cutting into her sense of wonder and curiosity. Not easy.

My deepest hope as a parent is that my daughter will craft a life of integrity, character, achievement, and good humor.

My second deepest hope is that my daughter will be a true child of the Great Plains, preferably the northern Plains. If she chose to cast her destiny with North Dakota, I would feel that I had really accomplished something in my life. So far, she exhibits a very limited interest in the Great Plains. She humors me when I take her to the Little Missouri River. Custer, Lewis and Clark, the Indian wars, the artistry of Karl Bodmer are so far pretty ho-hum to her. As we drive the Plains, I say, "Look at that butte, isn't it wonderful?" She looks up in a pro forma way and puts me out of my misery with as few words as necessary, then returns to her book.

This could change. I didn't come alive to the magic of the Great Plains until I was sixteen, and then it was not my parents who took the lead, but a remarkable mentor.

At last we reach the petrified forest. Scores of petrified trees (OK, tree pieces) grace a landscape that is not what you see from the Painted Canyon overlook, but more like the little Badlands south of South Heart or the truly wild gumbo and sandstone country north of Marmarth. Sections of trunks lie at odd angles against the gray soil, like segments of columns in the ruins of an ancient temple. Wholly intact stump and root structures, the size of ATVs or VW bugs, some perched on surprisingly delicate pedestals, stand out from the barren land in every direction.

> "I realized what I love best about America is the fact that we have a West. A big empty quarter of essentially uninhabitable land punctuated by geological splendors like Devils Tower and Arches National Park. England doesn't have that. France and Germany don't have that. Japan doesn't have that."

It is one of the most amazing places in North Dakota. Indeed, it is one of the most amazing places I have ever seen anywhere. Fifty million years and there they are. That won't be said of St. Peters of Rome.

As we examine the grain structure of one magnificent stump, I do my weak best to explain that this was once a semi-tropical place where cypresses (or their ancient cousins) grew, that what we are touching are not trees hardened into rock, but rocks formed by water percolating into the cellular structure of trees, that under every hillock in sight there are probably other petrified trees yet to be excavated by the processes of erosion … Yadda yadda yadda. I look over at my daughter. Her eyes have a wild look. She gets it. No words are necessary. In fact, they are really just noise here.

We all go silent. That's what the West is for. Each in her (or his) own way drinks in the place to her heart's content. We sit on the leeward side of the giant cypress stump and drink hot chocolate in silence.

Then, on the ridge half a mile to the south—suddenly—several hundred elk appear. They form an astonishing silhouette against the southern sky. Like all herds—from ants to geese—they move with some kind of group brain that is more than the sum of its parts. For a few minutes they do not see us. Their movements, therefore, are unselfconscious and, to us, magical.

Were it not so cold, were the wind not sharper with each sprint, were the thermos not empty, it would be hours before we ventured back to the new year and the car and all that represents. *1/5/08*

I attended a lecture at the University of Colorado once, in which an entomologist said that ants do not so much have individual brains as anthills represent a kind of group brain. In other words, when you are looking at the anthill you are looking at the antbrain. Any individual ant is just a moving bit of that brain.

Ozymandias

I met a traveller from an antique land
Who said: "Two vast and trunkless legs of stone
Stand in the desert. Near them on the sand,
Half sunk, a shattered visage lies, whose frown
And wrinkled lip and sneer of cold command
Tell that its sculptor well those passions read
Which yet survive, stamped on these lifeless things,
The hand that mocked them and the heart that fed.
And on the pedestal these words appear:
`My name is Ozymandias, King of Kings:
Look on my works, ye mighty, and despair!'
Nothing beside remains. Round the decay
Of that colossal wreck, boundless and bare,
The lone and level sands stretch far away."

—Percy Bysshe Shelley

Rites of Passage in Two Places

The great American winemaker Robert Mondavi died last weekend in Napa Valley. He was ninety-four years old.

More than any other individual, Mondavi carried the California wine industry onto the world stage. He was one of America's greatest winemakers and he was unquestionably American wine's greatest ambassador.

In the 1960s, he literally traveled the world to see how the best wines were made, stored, bottled, and marketed. He brought that knowledge, and his own fierce commitment to mastery, back to Napa Valley. His message to California was simple and at the same time profound: We are going to become one of the world's best wine-producing regions.

Although he was one of the most cosmopolitan men of the twentieth century, Robert Gerald Mondavi was actually born in Hibbing, Minnesota, on June 18, 1913. He was the son of Italian immigrants. His father was a miner, and his mother ran a boarding house.

Mondavi believed that wine is not an alcoholic beverage but a work of art.

I had the opportunity to do some research for Mr. Mondavi a few years ago. He wanted to know about Thomas Jefferson and wine. He had heard that Jefferson wrote, "No nation is drunken where wine is cheap and none sober where the dearness of wine substitutes ardent spirits as the common beverage," and he reckoned he wanted to know more about such a man.

Jefferson was America's first great wine connoisseur. He never produced wine at Monticello, but he knew what there was to know about wine. He became the wine adviser to the other four of the first five presidents of the United States.

Like Mondavi, Jefferson understood that wine is exquisite, delicate, and temperamental. Genius, by one definition, is "an infinite capacity for taking pains." That's Jefferson. It was also Robert Mondavi.

I dined with Robert and Margrit Mondavi and their longtime friend and wine historian Nina Wemyss a year ago in St. Helena, California. He was terribly frail, but all the old passions still glowed through the wreck of his body. He could barely eat, but there was mischief in his eye, and he still drank his wine with a relish that was part peasant and part world citizen.

We all knew it was the last time we'd be together. I was melancholy when I left for my hotel, but also immensely glad that I had had the opportunity to spend time with such a man. No one who ever met Robert Mondavi left his presence without wanting to live more, see more, do more, be more.

At the other end of the spectrum, my daughter Catherine Missouri graduated from eighth grade in a small village in Kansas last week. My life is often logistically chaotic, but to get there I had to scramble in an unprecedented way. It exhausts me even to think about it.

When I finished eighth grade decades ago, we merely cleaned out our lockers and walked home for the summer, but these days in rural Kansas, graduation is a very dramatic occasion. The girls wear prom dresses. Every graduate has a personal profile booth in the cafeteria as if this were a science fair or MySpace in 3D. Extended families imported from all over rope off sections of chairs in the gym hours before the ceremony. There were thirty graduates and two hundred video cameras on tripods.

She had been confirmed earlier that week in the United Methodist Church. My mother, who drove down 781 miles from Dickinson, gave her a Bible for confirmation and a dictionary and thesaurus for graduation. I still have the red-letter Bible my grandmother gave me when I was confirmed. When I hold it in my hands looking for Matthew 6:5, I am transported to a dairy farm in Fergus Falls, Minnesota.

Three pairs of students reminisced in the "remember when Brett belched really loud during the math test" and "Tyler accidentally wore two different shoes" manner. There were prayers—because this part of rural Kansas is so remote that it apparently regards itself as beyond the jurisdiction of the First Amendment. The middle school band played "Pomp and Circumstance" with excruciating earnestness.

The ponderousness of commencement exercises always reminds me of Woody Allen's "My Speech to the Graduates:" "More than at any other time in history," he intones, "mankind faces a crossroads. One path leads to despair and utter hopelessness. The other, to total extinction. Let us pray we have the wisdom to choose correctly." That pretty much covers it.

Graduation speakers like to tell young people that the "best is all ahead," that "there is nothing you cannot do if you set your mind to it," and "today is not an end but a beginning." Fine words, but the fact is that lives miscarry in all sorts of ways for all sorts of reasons. Grace, good fortune, and a carefully regulated upbringing stand between every successful life and the abyss.

> "There were prayers—because this part of rural Kansas is so remote that it apparently regards itself as beyond the jurisdiction of the First Amendment."

I didn't have time to cry at her graduation because everything was so hectic—I was dispatched to the modest local grocery store at the last last minute for buttermilk and margarine, batteries and wrapping paper. But the bittersweetness of the occasion has been percolating in on me every day since she walked, half shy, half proud, across that freshly waxed stage.

My role is to come to terms with the fact that this spark of creation that once lay on my lap enveloped by a couch pillow is now a young woman. She is not so much my child any longer as she is my daughter. I welcome this as one welcomes the harvest, but oh how I already miss the lyrical, innocent, unselfconscious child.

My dream is that she will master all she does, but belch, too, and laugh till the soda runs out of her nose from time to time before it's too late.
5/24/08

THANKS AND ANTELOPE IN THE EMPTY QUARTER

Mom Christmas, Dad Thanksgiving. Anyone who says that divorce is not a cataclysm is in denial.

I had all the time in the world to think about things this year, because I drove to Kansas to get my daughter, who is now fourteen. It's a trip of over seven hundred miles across the loneliest stretches of highway in America. The combined population of the Dakotas, Nebraska and Kansas is 5,986,497. These four large rectangular states contain (for the moment) approximately one-sixteenth of the US population, but we all know that the overwhelming majority of Plains people live east of the 100th meridian, indeed east of the 98th meridian. Grand Forks, Fargo, Aberdeen, Sioux Falls, Omaha, Lincoln, greater Kansas City and Topeka have a combined population of 1,930,411. They all lean yearningly into the states to the east.

I was driving out in the empty quarter on the other end of the plains. That alone is reason for thanksgiving. My route took me through Dickinson, Bowman, Marmarth, Camp Crook, Belle Fourche, Rapid City, Hot Springs, Chadron, Alliance, Sidney, Ogallala and Imperial before I entered Kansas airspace just south of Benkelman, Nebraska. Add up the population of those towns, with the exception of Rapid City, and the descriptors that begin to pile up are desolation, wind-swept, isolated, dilapidated, and forlorn. My favorite part of America.

Here's what I saw.

South of Marmarth, on the western banks of the Little Missouri River, on the old Camp Crook road, almost unbelievable amounts of oil development. Enough to make your jaw drop. I took photographs of everything I could see from the road—it made for a very long thirty-five miles to the South Dakota border. This is some of the least-visited country in North Dakota, and most beautiful too. It's as isolated as any place on the Great Plains, and it has been transformed from a kind of magic outback into an industrial landscape. Because almost nobody goes there (you have to want to go there), all this oil extraction occurs below the radar. Oil development is a fact of life. It is in some respects reason for thanksgiving—look at the North Dakota budget surplus—but it also is a jarring, scarring, marring assault on the magnificence of the rolling hills and butte country that we choose as our homeland.

> "We take the Great Plains for granted, but every hour or so I wake up and look out at something that takes my breath away."

I try to take a different route to Kansas every time I go see my daughter. No matter which route I choose, I have to eat up the northern half of the Great Plains to get there. It's a very long way between decelerations. The only stop signs are at correction lines and major road intersections. It's really easy—and delightful, and a little dangerous—to go into a semi-trance. We take the Great Plains for granted, but every hour or so I wake up and look out at something that takes my breath away. A pine-dotted ridge halfway to the horizon, a butte shaped by the butte god for pure butte perfection, a sluggish S-curved plains river (creek) carving out little half-hearted Badlands here and there in its journey, pyramidical sand hills barely holding their thin veneer of wispy grass, sensuously contoured rolling hills that seem to drift off to the end of the Earth in every direction, Bear Butte from twenty miles away, barely visible in the haze.

The variety of the Great Plains is remarkable. As with great books, you have to read the Plains again and again to see the subtleties. On this trip, I saw ridges and isolated hills that I had never noticed before. At least five times in two days, I wanted to turn off the pavement and head down the gravel roads to explore and maybe get lost or stuck or saved. It cost me something to keep on the straight path—I know my Robert Frost, that I might never be back—but the young whippersnapper at the other end of the journey was where my joy and thanks overwhelmingly reside, and I would hack my way through bin Laden or a desert of thorns to get to her.

The skyscrapers of the Great Plains continue to be grain elevators, including the big clusters of concrete giants. This fall they were all full to bursting, with rail cars lined up to haul all that grain away. Up and down the plains I saw at least fifty vast mountains of wheat next to the tracks in a perfect Hershey's Kiss pattern, rust tawny. The world economy may be in slow-motion collapse, but the sheer abundance of the harvest, the glut of grain so great that it could not be stored or carried away, made me fall in love with America all over again. Everywhere, I saw farmers combining in the yellow brittle corn rows with huge semis at the edge of the field, hastening to get the crop in before winter blows in earnest. I wondered if they would have to combine through Thanksgiving this year—if they did, think of their sense of weary, but intense satisfaction at the end of the day when they came in to see that mountain of food spread across the rarely used dining room table.

We sometimes forget: Thanksgiving is a harvest festival. It is a celebration of the grace of American abundance. That abundance is best seen not at Best Buy, but among the heartland's towns and fields.

And when you least expect it, driving to beat the band up over a hill, a herd of thirty pronghorn antelopes grazing by the side of the road, the quintessential Great Plains animal on a stunning autumn Great Plains day. They pause for a second or two before they storm the next ridge, and then pause again to stare and maybe return nonchalantly to grazing. Is there anything more beautiful than an antelope, a quivering still or charging San Juan Hill?

Finally, stiff and brain-numb, I pulled up in front of my daughter's school, got out and shook the shards of Doritos off my jeans, and signed her out. She came down the hall at the fastest clip that accords with teenage detachment. Her smile, when she got within range, filled me with love and thanks and happiness right through the roof. I banked it up like grain.

In a few days, I get to drive her home, by a different route, at $1.85 gas. My chief thanks in life is to be her father. My second thanks is to live on the Great Plains. My third is that so few others wish to crowd our homeland.
11/29/08

Searching for Christmas Spirit

in All the Wrong Places

If your experience is similar to mine, "the Christmas spirit" is not something that comes automatically on the heels of Thanksgiving. In fact, as I grow older, I find that getting into the Christmas spirit is a bit like getting into the clothes you wore to the senior prom. It can be done, but at serious cost to the human spirit. And don't look in the mirror.

This year, I feared that I would never get into the spirit.

We all know the truth. Christmas is better when it is simpler and less materialistic. When we slow down and smell the cinnamon. When somehow the birth of Christ gets to stay somewhere in the equation. When we give ourselves the gift of singing. When we sit by the light of the fireplace or the Christmas tree and talk in quiet sincerity with those we love.

So, just to make sure we don't become complacent with that serene picture of love and family and Christ, we Americans have somehow transformed Christmas into a month-long decathlon of shopping, partying, decorating, shipping, drinking, cooking, baking, gift-wrapping, gift-delivering, gift-exchanging and gift-returning, not to mention re-gifting. Forty percent of all retail commerce occurs around Christmas.

Perhaps because this Christmas season began with a man being trampled to death in a Long Island Wal-Mart on the day after Thanksgiving, I had a particularly hard time getting into the festive mood. I've been unusually busy this fall, and by the time I started to get serious about Christmas, it was bearing down on us like a freight train. The only thing worse than the Christmas rush is the Christmas desperate scramble.

In a moment of madness, I decided to make most of my gifts this year. That always sounds so wholesome and enlightened at the moment of conception. Then, on the 20th of December or so, you find yourself pacing the canyons of Wal-Mart alone at 3 a.m., looking for replacement glue sticks and glitter paint, and asking a bewildered nocturnal stock clerk whether Goop or epoxy is better for gluing a baby food jar Christmas tree into place on green-painted plywood. By the time I had finished my gifts, my whole house had been transformed into a small but inefficient industrial assembly line. There was no need for egg nog—I did not want it to interfere with my glue and varnish buzz.

When it was all over, in the light of day, all those homemade gifts looked really ... homemade.

A few days before Christmas, I drove down to northwestern Kansas to see my daughter, who is now fourteen. It was 15° below zero as I turned south at Sterling. The day had begun with a jump start and a new Die Hard "double-extreme, Arctic Blast" battery, and bloody knuckles, too, because I had perversely refused to let the Sears crew install it. It warmed up two degrees every hundred miles of the trip, but the wind was a grim, grinding constant for all 751 miles.

The wind was so violent and unrelenting that it felt as if the entire Great Plains were about to be overturned, like a tumbleweed, into the Midwest. I had to grip the steering wheel with both hands just to stay on the road. When I met the big 18-wheelers on the narrow stretches of the highway, I had to prepare for the double wallop, first when the big rig created a temporary wind screen for my car and nearly sucked me into the vortex of the trailer, and then when it cut me loose, like a sledge hammer, back into the storm.

By the time I got to my daughter's village, I was brain-numb from the road, and my arms were actually sore from fighting the wind.

My daughter is a freshman in high school, now in the era of Paris Hilton. On most days she is still three parts girl to one part young woman, but she is definitely no longer the child of my Christmas fantasy, breathlessly waiting for the thump of Santa Claus on the roof, leaping out of bed like a Seuss character to see what's under the tree. She has been proficient on a computer keyboard since she was six. She spends as much time on the parallel planet of Facebook as I do checking my e-mail. She has never known a world without media saturation. When I try to explain to her that when I was a child we had only two television stations and no cable, she can almost comprehend it, but when I tell her we had to get up to change the channel—well, she's just not buying that. She has reached that moment in her life when toys are no longer acceptable gifts. She wants clothes. She wants makeup. She wants iTunes credit lines. She wants a Netflix account. Ho ho ho.

> "We all know the truth. Christmas is better when it is simpler and less materialistic. When we slow down and smell the cinnamon. When somehow the birth of Christ gets to stay somewhere in the equation."

Whenever I walk past an Easy Bake Oven, I just want to throw it into my jumbo shopping cart. Why can't I buy Legos or a red wagon or even Barbie doll accessories anymore? Clothes? Who wants to buy his beloved child clothes? Or makeup? Why would I encourage the advent of the makeup phase of her adolescence? I don't know much, but I know this much with certainty: Any clothes I purchase without having been given the precise size, color, and catalog number are going to be unceremoniously exchanged on Dec. 26 for what she really wanted. And if I am merely the credit card for items precisely specified and pre-inspected by her, how is that Christmas in any meaningful sense of the term?

On the evening of my arrival in Kansas, after what seemed like endless hours on roads that were not icy, but—much worse—intermittently icy, my daughter and I were informed that we wanted to go to the Christmas program at the church. Given my exhaustion and the limited amount of time I had to spend with my child, I was not eager to attend the service.

We attended the service.

It was an evening of singing, readings from sentimental Christmas stories and skits. At times it felt like a cross between a Christmas pageant and a karaoke evening at a non-alcoholic community center.

But then my niece Mara and her friend Audra stood up in front of two hundred people in a Methodist church in a village in Kansas and sang "O Holy Night" a cappella.

Before they were two lines in, I burst into tears. Their pure thin voices, the magnificent lyrics of the hymn, that lovely elusive idea of human redemption, the solemnity of the church, the sudden memory of my grandfather Diedrich singing "Silent Night" in German in a church in Fergus Falls, Minnesota, when I was seven and life was still magic—all that simply trumped the secular insanity of the season and restored me to life.

I took out the pew Bible and opened to Luke 2:1. "And it came to pass in those days that a decree went out..."

Now I was ready for Christmas. *12/27/08*

AND THEN THERE WAS SKYPE

My daughter lives in northwestern Kansas. She is fourteen. Her life is as busy as it could possibly be. Whatever my tired heart has to give, has been freely given to her, and there is no other child, no other claimant.

So I live and breathe for her, which is of course insane, for she is fourteen, and she was born, like every other child in the world, to pull away in her second decade of life. The pain of this would be unbearable, except that I know she cannot become the adult I am so eager to meet unless I hold open the door and call after her to wear mittens and phone home whenever she can.

> "My letters are little more than a continuous attempt to find new ways to say I love you and I am thinking about you today."

We see each other at least once a month, without fail. I call her (cell phone to cell phone) every day, 350-plus days per year, often several times per day, and we now text too, which is just a high tech and inexpensive way of telegraphing a wee message of affection.

It's amazing how a "Hey, Papa, 'sup," can make my day and keep me from drifting into the backcountry of despair. I write her a couple of actual letters per week, hand- or typewritten, and send them in a big white envelope, with something called a postage stamp. It's very odd, this phenomenon.

For about 50 cents, I can get a trained professional to come to my house and pick up a very small item and then carry it seven hundred miles to a young woman far away. She infallibly gets the little package in three or so days—for less than 50 cents!

As you can see, I regard the US Postal Service as little short of a miracle.

My daughter, however, looks upon my letters as a quaint Paleolithic affectation, a very late and low-tech echo of something you might read in *Little Women* or a novel by Charlotte Bronte. She senses, I think, that I write these letters as much for me as for her. Maybe she is right.

It always settles my heart to put a blank sheet of paper in front of me and take half an hour to compose a letter to her. It means that, for that half hour, I am thinking solely about her. I try to guess what it would please or comfort her to read from her absent papa. It gives me a chance to try to imagine the rhythms of her life, the moments of unreserved laughter, the many plaguing anxieties of adolescence, the little feuds and misunderstandings with equally constipated classmates, and the first waves of possibility that come in these years and fill a young person simultaneously with eagerness and dread.

I went underground when I was fourteen. I literally moved into the basement, and much that was most compelling in my life never again found its way to the dinner table. Where is she with the subterranean, I wonder, and look up from the page with my own wave of anxiety.

She gets it that my writing actual letters to her should be regarded as something special, and she puts them, when she is not too rushed with "practice" and Scholar's Bowl or the game against the hated cross-county rival, in a special little box.

Perhaps someday she will read them through in a single night, looking for clues, remembering the days of her childhood, taking a transfusion from the unmistakable, unceasing expressions of love they contain. My letters are little more than a continuous attempt to find new ways to say I love you and I am thinking about you today.

In the mythology of my life, actual letters-in-an-envelope are one of the supreme pleasures. I don't receive many letters anymore and don't write many either, given how easy it is to stay in touch by other and more efficient means. We can lament this as much as we please, but it is not likely to change. I fear the day when the last piece of traditional mail is delivered in America and the last newspaper thumped up on the porch at dawn.

The best letters I ever received came from my mentor and closest friend. I keep them treasured up in a special box. I open the box and glance into them now and then, but I cannot really read them, because they are too raw with soul. I used to write and receive love letters when I used to love.

My father, who lived at the other end of the loquacity spectrum, for many years sent me what I called "terse notes." He somehow expressed all he wanted to say in a couple of bone-lean paragraphs. I reread those terse notes now and then and smile and sometimes laugh out loud, but mostly I just miss him and wish he were around so that I could share this portion of my life with him, and put my daughter at his feet.

My daughter doesn't understand this meaning of letters—and really why should she? That was then and this is now. It's like asking her to enjoy old time radio drama or the Grand Ole Opry. She has been typing since she was six, and she has never lived without access to a computer.

When I was struggling to produce a PowerPoint lecture a couple of years ago, I called to say goodnight, and wound up discussing my frustration. "Oh, Daddy," she replied, "let me walk you through it." Which she did.

Now we have discovered Skype. Skype is an Internet communications technology created by a team of software developers based in Tallinn, Estonia. It allows free online phone calls (ho hum) but also video conversation. Now a few times a week my daughter and I "Skype up," as she puts it, and talk for a few dozen minutes face-to-face across seven hundred miles.

It's so magical that it is scary. Last night, she "called" pretty late and I had to shake off my bleariness because of course I was "on camera." She wanted to talk about Homer's *Odyssey,* but also about her friend Jess who is being a brat.

To see her mouth quiver just a bit, almost imperceptibly, as she tried to brazen it out and say she didn't care if Jess "ever, ever" apologized, was worth all the postage stamps ever printed.

We live in a fabulous time, and we must embrace the new world that is bursting like fireworks over our heads. But I'm still going to write those letters. *1/31/09*

Things were soon patched up with Jess, probably before this column went to print. When my daughter says she will "never, ever" talk with someone again, I know enough to stay tuned.

Gardening as a Poem of Filial Respect

My grandmother Rhoda Straus planted a garden every year all her life, until her osteoporosis became so bad that she literally could not crawl through the black earth any more.

She lived her whole life in or near Fergus Falls, Minnesota. Until some time well after World War II, her life was a very hard one. A faraway accountant just looking at the figures would have called it poverty.

If there was plenty of food (and not much else), it was because Grandma gave a significant portion of her life energy to food production—milking cows, feeding steers, separating cream, churning butter, baking bread and pies, canning, freezing, drying, and curing cottage cheese on the stovetop.

Not to mention driving the grain truck. She baked bread twice a week from the age of eight to ninety-two.

That toast was the best toast I ever ate.

She saved every plastic bag she ever got her hands on, from the day when the newfangled first plastic bag appeared in northwestern Minnesota in the 1940s to the last few years when it no longer mattered.

The moment any plastic bag had served its primary purpose, however firm or flimsy its construction, she smoothed it out on the counter with her strong calloused hands, folded it twice as if it were agricultural origami, and placed it like lace in a drawer in her kitchen.

In those early years, the bags were clunky. When you pulled one out to put a sandwich in it, decades later, you'd see the fault lines of its construction, and the accumulated mottling from use after use after use.

When Grandma died in 1993, my parents and I converged on the farm to clean out the house. My mother, who left the farm, went to college and never looked back, not once, opened that drawer, made a little sound of appreciative disgust, and dumped her mother's lifetime plastic bag collection unceremoniously into the trash. How Rhoda would have clucked at that.

> "Grandma's left thumb was pitted and grooved like an Edison recording cylinder or an old cutting board—which is precisely what it was. I don't suppose there is any way of knowing how many potatoes she peeled in the course of her life, but I think "infinite" is the correct technical term."

Grandma's left thumb was pitted and grooved like an Edison recording cylinder or an old cutting board—which is precisely what it was.

I don't suppose there is any way of knowing how many potatoes she peeled in the course of her life, but I think "infinite" is the correct technical term. I have her favorite knife. It has been sharpened countless times over sixty or seventy years (though never by me) until it's literally about half the size it was at the time of its purchase. It's curved like a scythe from the way Grandpa honed it.

I used it yesterday to cut up seed potatoes. When the dull edge slashed through the first potato, to my uncalloused, consumerist thumb, whose principal encounters are with the space bar on my laptop, a wave of pride and an inrush of sorrow passed through me into the black soil of my garden where I sat. A meadowlark sang its liquid song like Chanticleer, just over in the prairie grass.

> "My grandmother Rhoda is the person I admire most. The parts of my character I admire all come from her. The parts I don't admire come from someone else."

Some very large part of me believes we have lost more than we have gained.

She made patchwork quilts all her life from remnants of cloth left over from sewing projects. You could, if you wished, "read" one of her quilts: that one's the shirt she made for Grandpa the year the cultivator fell on his leg; that's my sister's nightgown for her fifth birthday; that's the drapes that still hang in the dining room; that's the year her church circle went nutzoid over cowboy kerchief throw pillows; that's that sky blue corduroy jumper you can see in the family studio portrait from 1968, when rural Minnesota was time immemorial and the rest of the world was coming apart at the seams.

In my twenties, I made half a dozen quilts at the farm, with Grandma's advice and consent. It was like working with an inscrutable Zen master. It always felt as if she might suddenly thwack me with a stick for a dropped stitch, or blindfold me and say, "Tie the yarn with your heart, not your fingers, grasshopper."

Because I had no heritage basket of fabric scraps, I bought a yard of this and a yard of that to make a special quilt as a wedding gift. When we set up the card table in the living room of the old farmhouse and I pulled out those gleaming, unscathed yards of cloth, Grandma looked at me in disappointment and a hint of contempt. I could hear her thinking, "You may be intelligent, but you are not very smart, are you?"

When I was studying in England, she used to send me journal letters on crinkly onionskin paper (to save on postage), five hundred words one day on the hail damage from the big thunderstorm, one hundred words three days later on the good sermon at church.

Her beautiful penmanship (the Palmer method), in several colors of ink on the same page, flowed through gift pens from the grain co-op or the veterinary clinic or insurance adjuster.

I remember one evening opening a lean airmail envelope with four sheets of onionskin in it. The first line read. "Today I put up 42 apple pies." I thought: "Great, I read act two of *King Lear* and spent three hours with my friend Douglas in a coffee shop."

A life radically misspent.

When I moved into my house here, the first thing I did was hang a photograph of Grandma on the wall leading into my kitchen, carefully positioned so that I would see it every single day.

The snapshot was taken in 1980. She is standing behind a large wooden picnic table on the worn concrete slab that jutted out from the one-story farmhouse. The table is covered with ripe tomatoes—every square inch, every square millimeter from tip to tip in both directions. The red tomatoes are so neatly nested against each other that to add a single cherry tomato would require starting a second tier. She stands behind that part of her tomato crop in a thin faded cotton farm dress.

My grandmother didn't like being photographed, and she understood from her scarred thumb to her work-weakened knees that pride goeth before the fall. But if you look carefully, there is a glorious, unmistakable, though barely perceptible, intimation of smugness in that portrait.

You could say that I plant a garden, now that I have returned to the heartland, in Grandma's honor, but that would not be quite accurate. I plant a garden because the almost buried, nearly spent, barely glowing ember in me that is Rhoda Straus's grandchild is the best of me by far.   *3/23/09*

A LONG DAY'S JOURNEY INTO ADULTHOOD

I've been thinking about journeys lately, partly because the North Dakota Humanities Council has been conducting a fascinating journey stories initiative, partly because I have been writing a long essay about journeys (the *Odyssey, Huck Finn,* Kerouac's *On the Road*) and partly because I just made a loopy auto journey of 4,895 miles with my daughter. She's now a genuine American teenager.

My vehicle averaged a miserable 18.3 miles per gallon. That's 267.48 gallons. The price of gas hovered around $2.75 per gallon. Not to mention motels, souvenirs, entrance fees, emergency toothbrushes, ice for the cooler, appalling quantities of soda and chips, daily ice cream treats and value meals at all the major fast food outlets, at every one of which we were urged to order the big-calorie version of whatever it was that we wanted. The geographic zone we explored was bounded by Detroit Lakes on the east, Yellowstone National Park on the west, Washburn on the north, and darkest Kansas on the south.

We saw a grizzly bear. The Yellowstone River was running as full as I have ever seen it. It was green as Ireland for almost the entire journey. Only on the return, in the marvelous Custer State Park in South Dakota, did the grass have the bleached and tawny look of summer on the Great Plains. I took a photographic portrait of my daughter at Mount Rushmore, to enlarge and hang next to the one I took of her there when she was nine.

Actually, she'd like that earlier one retired to a closet.

We played miniature golf. We talked about God and life and books and colleges and boys(!) and family and "the course of human events."

She predicted that the mountain carving of Crazy Horse will never be finished. We attended the Medora Musical. We hiked. We drove over Beartooth Pass and wandered through obscure canyons in Wyoming that would be national parks anywhere east of the 100th meridian.

There are no words to explain the immense joy of wandering America with the person you love most in the world, sitting together in the car, drinking it all in, laughing endlessly, talking in lovely bursts of memory and revelation, and gazing out in silence for long stretches on the endless highways of the West. Drifting past distant pine ridges you would love to visit and never will. In Deadwood, S.D., as Simon and Garfunkel voiced it, "She said the man in the gabardine suit was a spy." As with all good journeys, we discovered things about each other and about ourselves that we did not previously know.

We made a sweet pilgrimage to my grandparents' farm just south of Fergus Falls, Minnesota. It was her idea. She had never before been to the farm, which is no longer owned by our family. Nor had she ever visited the graves of her maternal ancestors.

No one lives on the farm now. The house was locked, the barn boarded up, silo and granaries empty, the humans and livestock all gone, the flower beds overgrown with weeds. Still, we could feel the souls of my grandparents there, and though we did not talk about it much, I could see that it was an important rite of passage for my only child.

Her great-grandparents are mythological creatures in her consciousness. She never met them. She has been told they were giants in the earth. She wanted to see the ground that made them strong. I told her beautiful, wry stories about her mother's first visit to the farm. She was gratified to see us all together, even if only in my narrative.

Eventually, all journeys must end.

I dropped her off at her mother's house in northwestern Kansas on Father's Day. We all shared a quick meal. Then I turned the car north and started for Dakota.

It was about 8:30 p.m. Exquisite light, no wind, an open road straight to the vanishing point, my heart full of love and joy and biting sadness. With the radio off and windows down, I cruised along at a deliberately unhurried pace.

The wheat down there in Kansas is ready for cutting. It's going to be a bumper crop.

The sky was that serene blue of late June. Temperature seventy-two degrees. It was the first day of summer, the longest day of the year, in the season of endless dusk. The car seemed to drive itself through that improbable Van Gogh landscape: section-sized fields of yellow wheat, oppressively green corn, a flawless blue sky, antelope drifting the ridges and the charcoal ribbon of backroads highway. Somehow to me it was more beautiful than the Rocky Mountains or Yellowstone National Park.

> "There are no words to express the immense joy of wandering America with the person you love most in the world."

In that wonderful numb state we get into at the end of a very long day of driving America, I tried to imagine my daughter's re-entry into her world after two hectic weeks with Papa. She would be telling her mother stories of our adventures, showing off her new clothes, queuing up journey photographs on her laptop (no need to send film to the developers any more), repeating strong and amusing bits of her grandmother's conversation, describing moments that would make little sense to her mother out of the context of the trip. She also would be trying to determine the minimum quantum of time she needed to spend with her mother before she could call her best friend to catch up on a world much more real and significant than the one her faraway father inhabits. I felt no self-pity in that. Life is what it is.

She was to start driver's training the next day. It occurred to me that in our immense journey she had never once consulted any of the maps or atlases in the car. For perhaps the last time in her life—she will be fifteen soon—on her summer vacation of 2009, she put herself wholly in her father's hands. She had assumed (erroneously, in the way of our children) that he knew what he was doing. It suddenly struck me, in the afterglow of that long, long Great Plains day, that there will never be another auto journey with my daughter in which I do all of the driving.

My heart broke—right there on Kansas Highway 27.

I wanted to hoist her life (and mine) up on blocks and put the vehicle into reverse and race back the odometer, like the shadiest used car dealer in the country.

No, grasshopper and gray-haired wanderer, the journey is always forward.
6/28/09

Jenkinson's Rites of Spring

in Four Movements

One

An hour before sunset the other night, I was sitting out on my deck reading and musing and dozing. Sound travels long distances in the clearness of evening. Down the street, in the next block, a father was teaching his son how to mow the lawn. They were too far away to see clearly, but the father was in his thirties and the son not yet ten. Their yard was a bursting square of Ireland green against the subtler windswept green of the prairie behind them. The father spoke to his son with gentle firmness—it is power equipment, my son—and the son so wanted to be handed the mantle of responsibility of mowing that lawn for the first time himself. "Now here's how you back it up. You have to be really careful. That's right; that's exactly how to do it. Good job."

It was heartbreaking, not only because this is an important rite of passage in suburbia, between father and son, but also because six years from now that same father will discover that nothing but the direst threats will induce his son to mow the lawn.

It reminded me of when I taught my daughter to ride a bicycle. She was so whimpery and scared—of falling or failing. Over and over, she exacted from me iron promises never to let go of the bike under any circumstance. Of course we both knew that I was going to betray that promise and let go of the bike, and that she would wobble and nearly fall and then ride and, after that, never look back for the rest of her life.

Two

By now I have rototilled my garden within an inch of its life. I like garden dirt to have the consistency of coffee grounds. The black earth looks so rich and Jeffersonian out back of the house that I almost hesitate to plant it. The garlic is up in two neat rows. So far I've planted only onions and potatoes, but I have a plastic toolbox full of unopened seed packets, string, marking pens and row label sticks. Last year was my first garden in more than twenty years. Mixed results, prodigious tomatoes. This year I have tripled the size of the plot. My rhubarb has exploded into the spring light. Two falls ago I transplanted it from my grandparents' farm in Fergus Falls, Minnesota. When I make rhubarb crumble, I think of Grandma Rhoda Straus, the bread-baking, produce-canning, pie-making, quilt and crochet artist of Fergus Falls. When I dig in the garden on quiet evenings, the meadowlarks sing to me in their full-throttled way. The other night I planted more than forty trees, some of them possibly in violation of city regulations.

Three

Last night I was driving east on Century Avenue around sunset. In the lane next to me there was a man driving a classic Chevrolet, watermelon red, hauling a modest fishing boat. He was, like me, a middle-aged man, a man in sunglasses and a sporty shirt behind the wheel of a great car hauling a boat on a perfect May evening. He had the faraway look of spring fever in his eyes. It was the night when, after supper, he said, "You know, maybe I'll go get the boat and bring it to the house. That way—" and off he went to a storage facility or perhaps a farm in the country, where a friend or cousin had agreed, perhaps reluctantly, to store the boat.

Now, here he was at the stoplight, revving the engine just a little, and probably listening to the Beach Boys. I couldn't tell because it is North Dakota, not California, and his windows were up against the growing chill of evening. I felt that when the light turned green we should perform a little middle-aged drag race, right there on Century Avenue, but I was in a four-cylinder Honda and he was hauling a boat, and it was Bismarck.

The light turned green. We drove off slowly. All the rest of the evening, I hoped that our summers live up to the impossible expectations born of such spring excursions at dusk.

Four

My daughter went to her first important dance the other night. She is twelve. This was the celebrated end-of-seventh-grade dance, and apparently no rational being would think of attending in anything but a new dress. She technically had a "date," but she informed me a bit defensively that it is a date of mere convenience and that she and the boy agreed to burst apart to opposite ends of the gymnasium the minute they arrive. Oh, she'll dance with the poor fellow a couple of times, "but none of the slow dances, Dad." Works for me.

In Denver ten days ago, I took my daughter dress shopping. In retrospect I see that I was suckered into this by her mother, who assured me that our child knew precisely what dress she wanted and it was merely a matter of getting to the correct mall shop, a twenty-minute operation followed by dinner at Macaroni Grill. So off we went.

It turned out to be a long day's journey into night. Altogether we went to five malls, spread across the sprawling metropolis of Denver, and we entered at least twenty stores. We found the shop in question right away, but they didn't have the intended dress, and that somehow proved to be worse than starting from scratch. Now call me an idiot, but in the space of five hours I saw many, many dresses that seemed not only adequate, but splendid. It was soon made clear to me, however, that I understand nothing about dresses, and that she would know she had found the right dress when she encountered it. That seemed a little Zen to me.

My beloved daughter is just crossing the threshold of puberty, and I'm not supposed to know about this, so there were—in shopping for the perfect seventh-grade dress—many hidden landmines involving straps, necklines, levels of opacity, clinginess, etc., that I was supposed to "get" without ever mentioning. All I could think, through the endless afternoon, was, "There are some things a father is not really equipped to do."

We ate Cinnabons and pretzels and Orange Juliuses, and I managed to be allowed to buy one teeny electronic gadget through the course of the dress quest. How I wished that I had brought a book as I sat in the causeways outside fitting rooms, feeling as uncomfortable as a registered sex offender at a parent-teacher conference. I was required to weigh in on every dress, but not allowed to inspect the fit or ask any useful questions. My "that looks great, honey, shall we buy it and call it a day?" routine was patently inadequate even to me.

> "Over and over, she exacted from me iron promises never to let go of the bike under any circumstance. Of course we both knew that I was going to betray that promise and let go of the bike, and that she would wobble and nearly fall and then ride and, after that, never look back for the rest of her life."

It was a long frustrating day and, in the end, there were tears.

But she told me to get a grip on myself, and at last we (I mean she) found not the perfect dress, but a very fine dress that cost, thanks to globalization, less than the gas we used to find it.

After dinner we drove four hours to her farm village in northwestern Kansas. Along the way we had a long-delayed, extremely important, and oh-my-goodness difficult conversation about drugs, alcohol, shoplifting, cars, peer pressure and the ways of boys. Finally, we got to the subject of subjects.

"Do you know anything about sex?" I asked. "Not much, Daddy."

"Me either." But on we talked until we reached an understanding.

So off she went to the big dance. Only she and her mother know with whom she slow-danced. I think of her leaving the house with curled hair and all that anticipation and trepidation, nobody holding the bike this time, carrying a loaner cell phone (today's emergency dime in the pocket), standing awkwardly next to Poindexter with a rural Kansas corsage.

Two things I want to cry out.

"Come back, Shane. Come back." Come back, my innocent girl. Linger in your childhood just a little longer.

But also, Godspeed, my daughter. *5/12/07*

In Which

Your Faithful Correspondent

Goes to the Prom

I flew to Denver at the crack of dawn last Friday to see my daughter. I did my best to doze in the little space into which I was boxed. When we arrived in Denver, it was still dawn. I rented a car, stopped to buy a gift for my child, and then drove east toward her village in Kansas. It's a four-hour drive through some of the biggest, openest landscape of the Great Plains. I love the drive, because it is the path to my principal happiness.

Saturday was prom. Prom is so monumental in her little Mott-sized town that, grammatically speaking, it doesn't even require a definite article. We don't go to the prom. We go to prom.

A father is not the best aide de camp on an occasion like this. So much of a girl's prom prep involves grooming and tucking and hitching and hooking. There is a vast array of things a father never thinks about with respect to his adolescent daughter, because his heart still sees her as a four-year-old sitting in a heap of Legos or a six-year-old hugging him unhesitatingly in a thunderstorm.

I don't ever want to be asked whether a strap shows because I do not want to be that observant in a world that, in the most important sense, is none of my business. When she asks, "Does this look all right?," the only sane answer is "yes" unless she realizes that you are humoring her, in which case you are toast. But if you are ever foolish enough to say, "no," you are in for a long afternoon, because you are going to be expected to justify your answer before a hostile jury, and your response is going to prove that you are a moron, and an insensitive one at that. When your daughter asks, "Dad, which looks better ... ," it appears to us like Identical X versus Identical Y, but if you give the wrong answer you can throw a whole fifteen-year-old solar system out of equipoise. It's best to stand around like Fred MacMurray with a credit card, ready to run last minute errands.

My daughter and I have a wonderful relationship, full of laughter and joy and adventure. We approve of each other. But ... she's fifteen. We have reached the point in which I am, at best, a superfluous and at worst an annoying person. Most of our time together is splendid, but when we are in the presence of her peers, particularly boys, my job—if I only will stick with the script—is not to do something appalling. The problem is that almost anything can be construed as appalling, including (apparently) existence. It's a minefield and there is no map or rulebook.

Nincompoop that I am, I did not realize that preparing for the prom is a daylong affair. Late morning: two full hours with a local hairdresser. My urban bias made me wonder if I had cash enough to cover the appointment, but the total, with tip, came to $20. Hail to thee, rural America! Then she took the world's longest bath. Then we went to Taylor's house for makeup.

How can I draw an accurate picture of that fascinating rite of passage? Eight girls in T-shirts and team mascot sweat pants, all wearing flip-flops, chewing gum as if their mouths were generating the electricity for the curling irons and hair dryers. All of them simultaneously gabbing, gossiping, primping, dissing, eating, laughing, questioning, bickering, suggesting, comparing, fussing, crying, and texting—while listening to music and watching TV. All in various stages of Big Hair.

> "I felt like one of those creatures in a dinosaur movie. As long as I remained perfectly mute and immobile, the pack of Pubesaurians were unaware of my presence."

On the long kitchen island, boxes of congealing pizza and a dozen half-eaten Subway sandwiches, big bags of chips, a dozen liter bottles of soda. Cans of heavy-proof, industrial strength hairspray on every flat surface. Half a dozen mirrors propped up spa-like on tables and counters, behind each of which one or two girls grimacing and striking Vanna White poses. I felt like one of those creatures in a dinosaur movie. As long as I remained perfectly mute and immobile, the pack of Pubesaurians was unaware of my presence.

Although each one had had her hair thrashed back into the 1980s by a trained professional earlier in the day, it turned out that each girl's hair needed to be redone in some essential way before she could possibly face the world.

Finally, there was just enough time to go home and dress before a young man in a pickup would appear at the door, as if from the future. I sat in the living room awkwardly, book on my lap, fretting with my camera and my Mount Sinai lecture. The boy came right on time, slicked and gussied, after a prep time of approximately half an hour. He came for my child and left with a pretty young woman. I hardly recognized her as mine.

I went to the Grand March, locally known as the "Promenade," and took enough photographs to earn a "Daaad!!!" glare-frown. Then I slunk back to my hotel where, for the next six hours I had only one thought. May there be no glitch, no setback, no hurt feelings, no disappointment, no fracture in my beloved child's romance with life—not tonight.

She slipped in deep into the night and woke me up just long enough to say that it had been "perfect." I would have cried had it not seemed so pathetic, so Hallmark channel. The next morning I found a heap of thirty-seven sprung bobby pins, a "diamond" studded hair clasp, and a cloth pink rose, all excavated from her hair at 3:15 a.m. before she flopped down into sleep. I put them into a baggie and brought them home to Dakota. I'm going to give them to her on her thirtieth birthday with a photograph of her at the Promenade.

The next afternoon, we spent three hours together shoveling pig manure out of the stall where she is keeping her three 4-H hogs. The irony of our trajectory from prom to pig pen in twenty-four hours was not lost on either of us. We were in perfect harmony. But she texted a lot. *4/25/10*

I'm the luckiest man alive.

Only Daddy Thinks He Knows Best

My daughter is knocking at the door of puberty. She is twelve. I'm a wreck.

Puberty is such an unpleasant word. It sounds like a health condition rather than one of the most magical and important rites of passage in life. The word puberty does not even begin to capture the mystery, the sense of new and often dark possibilities, the wanderings of the spirit (in class, in church, in 4-H, at the dinner table), and the dawning, often disenchanting, realization that life is a many-layered experience and that people and things are seldom what they appear to be on the surface. It's agonizing and exhilarating and it's coming to my child, whether I like it or not.

My daughter looks on its approach with wary fascination but with genuine eagerness. For me, it is bittersweet to the bone. I do look forward to meeting my adult daughter, to having long literary talks with her, hiking the Little Missouri River together, traveling the world as adult companions, father and prized daughter. But I do not wish to relinquish the child in her. Not yet, not ever. I do not want to let that little girl go, the one who laughs without inhibition, who snorts soda through her nose when something suddenly delights her, practices her school cheers in the aisles of the grocery store, who informed me not long ago that it was unnecessary for her to brush her teeth before we went to a party "because I brushed once today already," and who exhibits a Huck Finn-like reluctance to shower. Her love is pure, uncomplicated, unreserved, unself-conscious. Her lens on the world is so far innocent. She is unashamed. She is entirely positive about life.

Puberty is the fall. It is when we discover that we are—somewhere near the center—sexual beings, and that the tincture of sexuality will stain almost everything that happens, perhaps not forever, but for a very long time.

Puberty comes from the Latin words *puber* (adult), and is related to the word *pubes* (pubic hair). An adult, in short, is somebody with pubic hair—and frankly I don't want to talk about this any longer!

In their retirement correspondence, John Adams asked Thomas Jefferson if he would agree to live his life over again. Yes, said the eternal optimist Jefferson, again and again, as long as the Creator offered it to me, but with this condition. Never again from one to twenty-five, for no rational being would want that.

Adolescence is a perilous time. It's like walking through a field of land-mines but without a map of any sort. Almost nobody gets through without getting hurt. Some of the scars last forever. (Have you been to a high school reunion?!) Sex, drugs, STDs, emotional and developmental setbacks, violence, brushes with the law, a growing sense that adults are aliens or hypocrites, the abandonment or slippage of school performance, and all the dangers attendant on teenagers in automobiles—these and other perils are just lurking out there in the night, waiting for my little child to stumble by on her way to adulthood. And now the Internet with its gigantic capacity for predation.

> "I want so desperately to protect my daughter as she makes this journey. And I know how to protect her, if she would only take my lead."

I want so desperately to protect my daughter as she makes this journey. And I know how to protect her, if she would just take my hand. The horror is that she won't be turning to me for help. In school projects, yes; in the great project of adolescence, not much. Her mother will be blessed with all those late-evening conversations. "Do you think I'm pretty?" "Do you think Tyler likes me?" "What was it like on your first date, Mom?" "How did you and Daddy meet?" "What do you do when you sort of like a boy, but one of your best friends … ?" It's heartbreaking. I want in on this precious set of conversations. I promise I will never laugh. I will never condescend. I will never fail to realize that these little dramas are, at that moment, the whole world to my child.

She went to her first dance a few weeks ago. Apparently, she spent most of the day trying to figure out what was precisely the right outfit to wear: not too dressed up, not too casual, not quite what the other girls were wearing, but not too different either, wanting desperately to look pretty, but not wanting to call too much attention to herself. Then there was makeup. She needed enough to acknowledge that it was her first dance, but not enough to be turned back at the door by her mother, the killjoy of eye shadow.

When we next spoke by phone, the day after the dance, she answered my eager questions with studied monosyllables. I got nothing. I wanted to say, "Tell me every detail. Please, don't cut me out of the circle, my child." A couple of days later, her mother gave me the scoop. The boys mostly stood around being obnoxious and infantile, the girls mostly giggled and looked impatiently over at the boys, who were engaged in burping contests and putting their hands in their armpits to simulate the sounds of flatulence. To the extent that there was dancing,at all at the dance, the girls mostly moved about in small clusters with each other, but in the course of the evening, she did dance with boys three times. Unfortunately, in compliance with the iron law of adolescence, the boy she wanted to ask her to dance never did, and the boys she wanted most to avoid were the ones who slithered up.

I remember my own summer of puberty. I was over-the-moon enthralled by a girl named Patty, who of course barely knew that I existed on Earth. For her benefit, at a picnic in the Badlands, I tried to jump over a barbed wire fence to fetch a stray baseball. An hour later, after I had been taken to a first aid station to bandage the four puncture wounds in my leg and determine whether I needed a tetanus shot, I returned to the picnic where, paralyzed in shame, I could not even look in Patty's general direction, much less look her in the eye. I still have a scar on my leg from that adventure, and when I notice it in the shower, I smile queasily.

She lived a mile or so from my house, and many times that summer I would walk over toward (not to) her house at dusk, and from a few hundred yards away gaze for an hour at her world. I don't know what exactly I was expecting, but I found myself again and again swimming into her orbit by the gravitation of adolescence. I never knocked on the door. During those years, when I left the house, my mother would ask me where I was going. "Out," I would say. Eventually she went Guantanamo on me. "Are you going out, or just out?" she'd say. "Just out," I'd bark back, offended that she would ask such an unreasonable question. But somehow she knew I was a virgin and would be for a very long time, so she shrugged her shoulders and let me wander about town like a moonstruck nitwit.

My daughter and I were together at a formal dinner in Virginia the other night. She looked very grown up in a long skirt, lacy black tights, a white blouse, and a formal little jacket, and through the long (somewhat tedious) dinner she was a perfect companion. Her conversation was civil and even grammatical. She exhibited better table manners than many of the adults. She pretended not to hear those things children ought not to hear. She was, in every respect, a young woman, and one whom I was immensely proud of.

Fortunately, when we got back to our room, and the door had been shut on the formalities of the evening, she let out a belch worthy of a longshoreman, got out of her stuffy clothes and into a T-shirt and shorts, and turned on the Disney Channel.

As I watched her devour a bag of Cheetos, her mouth turning more wonderfully orange by the minute, I prayed, please, please, my child, just linger here on the brink a little bit longer. *10/25/06*

Father's Day, It's Not About the B-List Tie

When I was first married, and full of "how could we responsibly bring a child into this muddled world?!" nonsense, my friend George Frein gave me the best advice I ever received. "If you are tempted to forego any of the great rituals of life, do not let it be becoming a parent." My own father, who faced the world through irony, gave me only two pieces of memorable advice: "Never kill a cop." And "never buy oats for a dead horse." Fair enough. The first has been easier to comply with than the second.

For almost twelve years now I have been a father. I was in the hospital room when my daughter made her grand entrance on August 10, 1994.

> "My father belonged to the eye-brow raising paradigm of parenthood, not the water balloon school. I'm trying to reverse that pattern with my child."

It was 3:17 p.m. The doctor let me cut her umbilical cord. Then I got to hold her in my arms. As I looked into her little searching eyes for the first time, I stepped off a chasm of love so deep that it remains a helpless freefall more than a decade later.

Who knew? Who warned me that it would be this strong? Where is it written that it will be the most intense, purest, most redeeming, most humanizing, and humbling thing that ever happens in the whole course of our lives? One day you live for skiing or stamp collecting or fishing. Then your child is born. Now your fishing tackle is a heap in a box in the garage and you find yourself in heartache and close conference over the little tragedies of the schoolyard.

It has been said that we don't love our children; we fall in love with them again and again.

Who could have known, back when the heart was still an open, exploring, yet unscarred muscle, and gender chemistry was the brine that flavored almost my every move, that I would never know what infinite-and-yet-still-growing love was until I became a father? I love my mother greatly, but I would not jump in front of a bus to save her life. But I would do so unhesitatingly, instantly, in order to save my child. If someone hurt my daughter, I would have no trouble performing manslaughter and then standing up straight and proud in the courtroom docket. In daily life, normally I cannot be trusted to cross the street to mail someone's letter, but I would walk across the planet in high heels to help my daughter in an emergency. She's the only trump card in my world.

It's hard not to feel a little disappointed that the mother-child relationship is so emotionally tight, so celebrated, while father-child relationship exhibits a fair amount of detachment. We all get it that the mother-child relationship is a mammalian biological imperative, while that father's role, especially now that women are taken seriously in the law and marketplace, ceases to be biologically essential at conception. When my child needs support (in several varieties) she often comes to me. But when she needs that most basic form of human comfort, she invariably gravitates to her mother, even when they are at odds on other fronts.

In some ways my relationship with my daughter is more successful than the one she has with her mother, but it is not nearly as strong. She does not seek me out to talk about her interior life—her feelings about her friends, about boys, about her doubts and secret aspirations. Her mother, who is my good friend, provides sanitized reports of some of those marvelously intimate and soulful conversations—in part to torture me—and I find myself on the outside looking in and feeling sad that I am not entrusted with all these delicacies. It was the same in my childhood. I needed my mother's love and I never doubted its immediate availability, but I wanted to please and impress my father. I thirsted to tell him what I had accomplished, not what my heart murmured. He was the first person I called when something went spectacularly right in my world. Mother was the first person I called when things went fundamentally wrong.

My child need only say "daddy," in a certain tone and I melt into my best self. There is no action, project, conversation, or event that I will not instantly suspend when she utters that talisman: "daddy." That one word has the power to refill the pool of good will instantly. When she says it ("daddy") in order to get my full attention, like Pavlov's papa I surrender myself wholly to her. For that instant, all is right with the universe. It's a form of magic.

Of course, she is a keen observer, and she is not above playing that card from time to time just to maneuver the doting one (soon to be dotard). But even when I know I am being bamboozled, I find it hard (ok, impossible) to resist her.

Father's Day. It's not about the B-list tie. It's the day we men get to reflect on the greatest joy we will ever know.   *6/14/06*

"For unflagging interest and enjoyment, a household of children,
if things go reasonably well, certainly makes all other forms of
success and achievement lose their importance by comparison."
Theodore Roosevelt

How Could We Have Forgotten
the Batteries and Scotch Tape?

The day before the day before Christmas.

The airport waiting lounge is full. It's OK if the planes are late (a little late) today, because that deepens the anticipation. This is the time when the expatriates come home for one of their two annual visits. Oh how they love North Dakota, how much they want to see their aging grandparents and to take a walk on the curving earth with the dog, but they don't quite see how they could live here. I've been on those planes. Now I wait for them.

All over North Dakota, red and green Jell-O is being poured into tree, wreath and Santa molds, with miniature marshmallows as a garnish. My mother puts celery and carrot slivers in hers, I guess so we can call Jell-O a health food. It's surprisingly good.

I'm going to make my Grandma Rhoda's apple cake (really apple bread), a recipe that came from Germany more than one hundred years ago. It's never very good when I try to make it, from a recipe in my grandmother's pure Palmer method handwriting, but Mother appreciates it and my daughter humors us. Since my grandparents have been dead these many years, the smell of the yeasty dough, the cinnamon and the bubbling, baking apples somehow brings them into our house and doubles or triples the spiritual joy of Christmas. I make apple cake, not because I really want to eat it, but because it is a family tradition. It reconnects us to a pioneer world, to farm life, and to the immigrant heritage of Minnesota and Dakota. It's part of our family's Christmas liturgy. It makes us feel a little less like over-stimulated, credit-card-wielding materialists in a disenchanted, globalized world.

All over America, UPS employees are home today bracing for Monday. It will be, I imagine, an exhausting but nevertheless exhilarating Christmas Eve for them. Think of the number of people who will be looking anxiously out their kitchen windows Monday, waiting for the UPS truck and hoping against hope that that gift they should have ordered much sooner arrives. "Oh, thank goodness," they will say when the brown truck stops. The UPS delivery folks will hear expressions of authentic relief and genuine gratitude all day. It would be fun to count the number of times they will hear the words, "Boy, am I glad to see you."

It also would be interesting to know how many times today, across the vastness of America, someone somewhere will say, "If you don't settle down right now, there isn't going to be ...." How unfair it is to ask people to settle down who still believe in the magic of life.

I'm with Theodore Roosevelt, that strenuous lover of rambunctious family life, who said he could not really trust a man who had not been something of a rapscallion as a boy. I would give anything to be bursting with anticipation for a wagon, for my first BB gun, for a Commodore computer—actually, for anything this world has to offer.

Here is what I remember.

Flannel jammies, bounding down the stairs as fast as sleep-warm little feet can churn, and finding—with a yelp of pure joy—a Texaco gas station all set up at the base of the Christmas tree. Years later, it was revealed that my father (who was quite happy to be inept at all such things) had stayed up until 3 a.m. trying to determine how flange 18c fit into support bay C, and that as he came to terms with the phrase "some construction required," he had uttered strings of words at the other end of the spectrum from "Hallelulah" and "Good will to men."

My grandmother sewed pajamas for my sister and me fourteen years in a row, until we began to open them with disappointment and a shrug. Then I asked my mother to ask my grandmother not to give me pj's anymore, because she sewed them without a fly and, as everyone knows, a "man" has to have pj's with a fly. Now I would give anything to have any pair of those diminutive flannel pajamas with their airplane or train or cowboy or snowman patterns, the bottom and knees more worn than the rest. I'd take them out today and hold them in my hands, and then fold them neatly and put them carefully away in a drawer.

> "How unfair to ask people to settle down who still believe in the magic of life."

There is a scene in the brilliant *National Lampoon's Christmas Vacation* in which Chevy Chase gets stuck in the attic for the day. He finds a box of grainy old 8mm movies and a working projector (there's the fiction). He watches holiday movies from his childhood when his mother was young and a sled was the best thing that ever happened. The tears just run down his cheeks as he watches his childhood and aches for all that is gone. It's one of the best Christmas moments in American culture.

My grandmother saved all the wrapping paper. She clucked in dismay when our excitement led us to rip the paper off a package. At the end of Christmas morning, she gathered the mottled paper and smoothed it out and folded it neatly. She used every bit of it in later years, but never in gifts to us. She was that frugal and that thoughtful.

One year, early, it was a stuffed animal: Huckleberry Hound. Later it was a G.I. Joe with dynamite and a pill box. As I opened it, everyone turned instinctively toward my grandfather Dick Straus, the Minnesota dairy farmer, to see how he would react to a ten-year-old boy getting a doll for Christmas. Answer: not well.

We all know in our hearts that it is not about the gifts or the value of the gifts, but about the "value added" of thoughtfulness or special generosity or sacrifice. And yet the malls are full to bursting. The hand-painted, ceramic Christmas tree candy holder my daughter made me five years ago is my favorite of all the gifts she has ever given me.

The best Christmas gift I ever received was used, not new. I still have it. I keep it in a special drawer. I take it out and turn it in my hands from time to time when I am trying to fathom the meaning of life. It was a modest 35mm camera, before 35mm was widespread. It changed the destiny of my life. Even more important, I know that my parents struggled to afford it and wanted me to know that it was special without wanting me to be burdened by that knowledge.

> "I'll know my daughter is no longer a child when she bursts into tears, too."

I'm fixin' to read my daughter the Christmas chapter from Laura Ingalls Wilder's *Little House on the Prairie*. I read it every year and she endures it with patience. You know, the one where Mr. Edwards swims across the swollen creek to bring Laura and Mary gifts from town, and Pa's eyes get moist and he cannot talk for a while and when he does his voice is husky. The girls each get a shiny new penny and a tin cup and a candy cane (Mary savors hers, of course, and Laura, well, you know what Laura does), and a small square of cake made from white flour.

I'll know my daughter is no longer a child when she bursts into tears, too.
12/22/07

CONSERVING
OUR HOMELAND

AN ELEGY FOR HISTORIC BEAR BUTTE

Bear Butte is a lonely spur of the Black Hills. It rises from the plains in majestic relief a few miles northeast of Sturgis, South Dakota. If you squint just right, it can be seen to resemble a recumbent bear. For centuries it has been regarded as a sacred place by the Indian peoples of the Great Plains. If you hike up the trail to the top, you will see thousands of small colorful prayer bundles tied to trees and shrubs all along the way. Indians from throughout the region—and beyond—come here to pray, fast, dream, dance, renew and find solidarity with other pilgrims.

Bear Butte is a sacred mountain. It also is a South Dakota State Park. And it is close enough to Sturgis to be a victim of the annual motorcycle festival, which attracts hundreds of thousands of visitors from all over the world.

There is something powerful at this place. If you go silent and stand still there, you can feel something in the grass, hear something in the wind. On my lists, Bear Butte ranks as one of the five most magnificent places on the Great Plains.

I drove past Bear Butte (on South Dakota Highway 79) recently on my way from Rapid City to Dickinson. My goal was to photograph the butte in the November morning light. In the past twenty years, I have driven past Bear Butte a hundred times, and stopped to climb to the top on more than a dozen occasions. Whenever I have something really important to ponder or work out, I drive to Bear Butte and climb up to the top of the mountain (technically a volcanic laccolith 4,422 feet high, 1,253 feet above the surrounding plains) to brood while gazing off at the vastness of the Great Plains. I never drive past it in the daylight without stopping to take photographs.

The other day about 9 a.m., I came up over the rise expecting to see the stark and lonely magnificence of Bear Butte as it always has been and always will be. But what I saw instead was a scar as red as lipstick that marred, perhaps even ruined, the view.

The scar is a biker bar.

Last summer, a man named Jay Allen built a twenty-two thousand-square-foot, three-story roadhouse bar two and a half miles north of the base of the butte. It's called the Broken Spoke. Its garish red metal walls shout down the subtle drab pastels of the plains. It's an eyesore. It's an open affront to American Indians. The parking lot looks like one you would find at a baseball stadium or special events center. Allen plans to carve out a thirty thousand-seat amphitheater at the site where he will host rock concerts during the annual Sturgis rally. According to press reports, one regular feature of the Broken Spoke will be a Best Breasts contest. You get the picture.

From a beer, biker and boobs perspective, it makes perfect sense. It would be hard to imagine a Great Plains bar with a better backdrop. According to the protocols of American free enterprise, Allen has a perfect right to buy private land anywhere he wishes and do with it anything that is permitted by law. He saw opportunity, invested heavily, and expects to prosper. It's the American way. It's important to remember, too, that many of the bikers who gravitate to Sturgis feel an affinity with American Indians, especially the defiant Crazy Horse, who visited Bear Butte in 1857, and vowed to devote his life to resisting the white invasion of Oglala Sioux country. Hundreds of bikers each year climb Bear Butte to experience its medicine power and exhibit their respect for American Indian culture.

But the Great Plains are a big platform, and Allen could have built his biker bar in any number of places close to Sturgis without offending Indians or impairing the Bear Butte viewshed. He chose to locate his bar in the shadow of Bear Butte for the express purpose of using the magnificent mountain to extract money from the pockets of the bikers who flock to Sturgis every August. In other words, he believes he will earn more money at a roadhouse that fronts Bear Butte than one located on the undifferentiated plains directly east of Sturgis. In doing so, he is appropriating something that belongs to the American Indian community, something sacred, for his personal profit. He is extracting beer sales from Bear Butte, just as surely as the Homestake Mining Co. extracts gold from the Black Hills. It's a very old pattern in American history.

The Lakota and Cheyenne, among other tribes, exerted what influence they could to dissuade Allen from building his roadhouse so close to a place so important to their historical traditions and their religious activities. In choosing to ignore their passionate entreaties, Allen violated no laws, but he did commit an act of grotesque insensitivity. It would be like building a striptease joint near the foundation of St. Peter's Basilica at the Vatican in Rome, or a Wal-Mart at the base of Notre Dame Cathedral in Paris. Or, if you prefer a secular analogy, it would be like throwing up a waffle joint beside the Lincoln Memorial.

Civilization has chosen to protect the precincts of St. Peter's, Notre Dame, and the Lincoln Memorial from adverse economic development. So why do we show so little respect for the magnificent and sacred places of the American West?

Open a porn shop next to the new Lutheran mega church on north Washington Street and all of Bismarck would rise up to force the shop's relocation. Build a wet T-shirt bar in the precinct of the Indian "cathedral" of the northern plains and most of the white community shrugs its shoulders and gets on with life. We need a more mature and sensitive land ethic on the Great Plains. We need to designate the places that are unique or infused with natural or cultural heritage, and write reasonable laws to restrain insensitive economic development in their vicinity. What is so glaringly occurring at the base of Bear Butte also is unfolding in less dramatic fashion in the Badlands of North Dakota, near Devils Tower in Wyoming, at the base of Lewis and Clark's Pompey's Pillar in Montana, on the Missouri River north of Bismarck and Mandan—wherever there are scenic vistas to be seen through McMansion windows, wherever money can be made from a business's proximity to grandeur.

Respect and cultural sensitivity are not legally enforceable. They are habits of the heart. But rational zoning laws make sense, just as neighborhoods establish covenants about acceptable and unacceptable behavior.

Once you destroy the aesthetics of a place, there is no turning back in any human-scale timeframe. Now Bear Butte always will be impaired by the Broken Spoke, which could just as easily be located in Denver, Reno, or for that matter Rapid City. But Bear Butte only can be located here. And it has priority on every scale—except that of heartless capitalism. On the strength of Allen's precedent, other roadhouses are being planned for the shoulders of the butte.

The Lakota and Cheyenne Indians, together with sixty other tribes, discouraged and then fought the project and attempted to convince the Meade County Commission not to issue a liquor license to Allen. Their goal, which from their point of view is entirely reasonable, is to create a five-mile buffer zone around Bear Butte to prevent just such developments as the Broken Spoke roadhouse. The local tribes have been buying up land around the base of the butte—more than $1 million worth so far—but they were unable to purchase all of the requisite land before Allen started to lay down asphalt.

My Bear Butte experience the other day was a wake-up call. If this trend continues, the future of the Great Plains is not going to be decided by good sense and community consensus, but by the arrogance of money and power. It's going to be a battle royal. If you love the beauty of this place, you had better suit up for the fight. *12/2/06*

This is a Sanctuary, Not an Oil Patch

Billings County wants to build a bridge or low water crossing over the Little Missouri River somewhere in the vicinity of Theodore Roosevelt's Elkhorn Ranch Site, which is located thirty-five miles north of Medora. There isn't a single bridge between Medora and the Long X Bridge on U.S. 85 near Watford City. That's a distance of fifty eagle and seventy automobile miles.

Billings County wants to build the crossing mostly to facilitate the oil industry, but the project is mainly being sold to the public as a way to accommodate recreationists and enable emergency fire and ambulance vehicles to reach the remote homesteads of North Dakota's Badlands.

There is nothing wrong with wanting to increase the efficiency of the oil extraction industry. The world is hungry for oil. Western North Dakota needs the economic activity. A state that wrings its hands constantly about outmigration and depopulation needs to work hard to accommodate an industry that employs our young people and attracts workers from elsewhere to the "emptied prairie."

Still …

I don't feel strongly about most issues. I feel very, very strongly about this one. The Badlands and the Little Missouri River Valley are North Dakota's greatest natural treasure. Anything we do that degrades the beauty, the starkness, the pristinity or the quiet of that glorious swath of country between Marmarth and Lake Sakakawea is, in my opinion, a short-sighted and profound mistake.

It's not the proposed bridge that bothers me. It's what the crossing will enable.

> "The scenery of the Little Missouri River Valley is worth more to the human spirit, to our self-identity as North Dakotans and Americans, than all the minerals that will ever be removed from below our soil."

The scenery of the Little Missouri River Valley is worth more to the human spirit, to our self-identity as North Dakotans and Americans, than all the minerals that ever will be removed from below our soil. America's greatest conservationist, President Theodore Roosevelt, understood that "the live deer is more valuable than the dead carcass" to a western state's attractiveness. When we North Dakotans think of who we are and what North Dakota means, we invariably gravitate to the Badlands.

What makes the Little Missouri River Valley so charming, so compelling as North Dakota's premier tourist and recreational destination, is that it looks as if humans have agreed to leave it alone.

In the ideal world, there would be no new roads, bridges, oil rigs, recreational sites, or other industrial structures near or within the river bluffs that embrace the Little Missouri River. Even in the real (not ideal) world, it would be quite possible for all of us to agree to this standard of land stewardship and yet still enable oil development, traditional ranching, recreation, hunting, and even new ranchettes in the valley.

In other words, we don't want to stop "progress." But we need to work very hard and very carefully to insure that economic development in the Badlands is done in the least disruptive, least destructive and least disrespectful way. We have to get it right. We have to go forward in a way that shows that there are values that we regard as equal in importance to profit.

Of the Grand Canyon, Roosevelt said in 1903, "Leave it as it is. The ages have been at work on it and man can only mar it." That's precisely how I feel. That should be the official motto of the North Dakota Badlands. It should be printed in the first paragraph of every environmental impact statement for every proposed new development in the Badlands, and only if that standard receives the weight it deserves in the deliberations should new developments go forward.

The easy thing to do with the Badlands would be to shrug our shoulders and let things unfold with minimal debate and social planning. Let's do the hard thing instead. Let's find a meaningful way to create a real statewide dialogue about how to balance the values and the pressures at work in the Badlands, and then let's go out of our way to preserve the thing we love even as we find creative ways to extract the oil.

If there must be a crossing somewhere between the North Unit and the South Unit of Theodore Roosevelt National Park, I think we should all insist on two things. First, the No. 1 consideration should be that the structure be built where it will have the least possible impact on the Roosevelt Elkhorn Ranch Site and the "greater Elkhorn Ranch," which includes the former Eberts Ranch. In this regard, there are four impacts to worry about: dust, noise, visual impairment and the equally important but intangible "shattering of the spirit of the place."

As anyone who has camped in the Cottonwood Campground in the South Unit of Theodore Roosevelt National Park knows, noise travels far in the Badlands. From your sleeping bag at Cottonwood Campground, you can listen all night long to highway traffic on Interstate 94 and the coal trains that are hauling Wyoming and Montana bituminous to Midwestern power plants. I'm no noise expert, but I've listened to the oil trucks rumble through the Badlands all of my adult life. They have a way of disturbing the peace of the place.

The possibility of peace—the liturgical simplification of our scattered and distracted lives in a place that retains something essential of the pre-industrial magnificence of America—should take center stage at any discussion of the future of the Badlands, particularly where they approach the three units of Theodore Roosevelt National Park.

Second, we should insist that any new crossing—carefully located to minimize its impact on North Dakota's national park—be an actual bridge, not a bargain basement "low water crossing" consisting of box culverts overlain with a rough concrete road cap. Two low water crossings already mar the Little Missouri River in North Dakota: one south of Marmarth, the other the VVV (Triple V) crossing on the southwest face of Bullion Butte.

Low water crossings are nothing more than cheap and clunky ways to get vehicles across the Little Missouri River. On the spectrum of crossing structures, they are much closer to "leaky dams" than anything that could honestly be called a bridge. They are dangerous because they have no guardrails. A canoe or kayak can float under a bridge. A low water crossing requires a portage. That's enough to spoil a float trip. It also would seem to me to violate the idea that the Little Missouri is a "wild and scenic river."

The Elkhorn Ranch Site was the Dakota home of one of the most remarkable men of American history. It's an understated national shrine to intelligent conservation practices. Roosevelt believed in economic development, but he wanted to pursue it in a way that "conserved" our natural resources for future use and "preserved" places in the American West of extraordinary natural beauty, places that reminded all of us of what American meant in the era of Daniel Boone.

The Elkhorn Ranch is one of the most important sanctuaries in the American West. We should cherish it—to use TR's words—the way we would cherish and protect a cathedral or a Native American holy site.

Why would we ever let ourselves treat it like an oil patch?   *7/26/08*

The low water crossings really offend me. They represent a cheapness of the human spirit and a fundamental lack of respect for the Little Missouri River. As this book went to press, Billings County was proposing a proper bridge, no longer a low water crossing, but it was still targeted at or near the Elkhorn Ranch.

Who are We and Where are We Going?

This is a plea for help. Even though I am keenly interested in the future of North Dakota, I don't really know how to read the signs. Does the future of North Dakota look bright to you, or bleak, or somewhere in between? What do you think North Dakota will look like in 2025? How would you wish it to look?

With more than $500 million in surplus, booming cities, centers of excellence springing up across the landscape, more and more research initiatives taking root along the Red River, a gigantic energy boom looming in the heart of the state, and even a modest influx of new people, it seems as if North Dakota may be entering a period of economic opportunity and growth. Good news, right?

On the other hand, I have driven through Hebron, Hettinger, Towner, Lakota, and Velva in the past month, and they all look desperate and minimalist. If the state's population is barely increasing, and yet Bismarck, Fargo, Grand Forks, and Minot are growing dramatically, then most of this city-boom is from internal migration. Can we be a viable state with an essentially empty countryside, but with a series of five to nine prosperous "city-states"?

> "Thomas Jefferson might argue that a five thousand- to ten thousand-acre farm without livestock or even a vegetable garden is "agrarian" only in the narrowest sense of the term."

Another marginal western state that I know, Nevada, long ago decided that it could only survive if it embraced some odd economic engines: divorce, gambling, legal prostitution, and a blank check for the mining industry. It worked. All those things that seemed so sinful or uncivil seventy years ago have ceased to offend most Americans. Nevada is booming.

So, as cold, isolated, semi-arid North Dakota contemplates its twenty-first century economic options, which of them can we embrace and still be ourselves? Where do we draw the line? Who decides questions of this magnitude?

Are we, like Nevada, prepared to do whatever it takes, no matter how much that may violate the heritage values of North Dakota?

Do those values still really exist?

It seems unmistakable that we are moving toward a post-agrarian future. There probably always will be farms in North Dakota, but they are going to grow ever larger and more mechanized. Thomas Jefferson might argue that a five thousand- to ten thousand-acre farm without livestock or even a vegetable garden is "agrarian" only in the narrowest sense of the term, but at this point there is not much room for quaint thoughts about what my old friend calls "farmy farms."

Agriculture, like all else, is headed toward an increasing concentration of capital and energy: hog confinement facilities (hard to see the 4-H pig in this phrase, isn't it?), giant feed lots and dairies with hundreds of cows milked three times a day. North Dakota's surviving fifteen thousand to twenty thousand mega-farms are not going to support many towns. And farm families who have that kind of capital are not exactly what Jefferson or Lincoln or William Jennings Bryan would regard as a sturdy and independent yeomanry.

Is this OK with you? When a farm state loses its farm base, what does it become?

In the coming permanent world energy crisis, North Dakota is going to be one North American locus of intense industrial activity. We have abundant lignite coal reserves, and what is regarded as plenty of water to process that coal. That means liquefaction and gasification, and more coal-fired power generation plants.

We have oodles of wind. There may be a lot more oil in the Williston Basin than anyone knew. How do you extract it? You thrust new roads into remote places, drill deep and at a slant, and then pipe or truck the thick crude somewhere else.

Ethanol, biodiesel, hydrogen, and other emerging energy technologies will dot the landscape.

In the 1970s, led by agrarian Gov. Art Link, North Dakotans decided they preferred to engage in moderate and restrained energy development rather than the more enthusiastic variety in Montana and Wyoming. In other words, we decided that we wished to remain primarily a farm state with a subordinate energy industry. Do we have that option this time around? How about the political will?

On the one hand, it's exciting to think that we might be at the center of the next great wave of world energy development. If ever the United States is going to achieve energy independence, North Dakota is going to play a significant role in that drama.

That means billions of dollars of economic activity—much of it involving highly paid high-tech jobs in emerging technologies. If we can retain a fraction of a fraction of that gross economic product, we can fund all the remaining schools in North Dakota for the foreseeable future.

On the other hand, a big energy boom means new and larger strip mines, some in parts of the state so far left alone, gigantic consumptions of water, huge processing plants that will make the Mandan oil refinery look like the monkey bars at a schoolyard playground, and of course "effluents"—in our water, in our air, in our soil. And where, from Sutter's Mill to the Alberta tar sands, has a gold or energy rush ever been harmonious, civil and enlightened?

So far as I know, no North Dakotan now regards the "energy crescent" between Washburn and Beulah, the coal mine and power plant corridor, as the most beautiful landscape in the state. The landscapes we do prize are those in which the human industrial imprint is largely absent or essentially benign.

For many, it's the patchwork quilt of family farms, the villages that serve them, the vast, treeless, open spaces, the giant skies and the abundance of game that constitute the idea of North Dakota.

How much does it really matter that half of our population clings to Minnesota and the rest of the population is gravitating steadily toward cities and big towns? How much does it trouble you that most of North Dakota's villages are dying, that most of the towns are straining to hang on, that even the big towns (Jamestown, Dickinson, Williston) are merely holding their own? Cataclysm or shrug your shoulders?

The percentage of the North Dakota population that lives east of Valley City is surprisingly large. The percentage that lives east of I-29 is staggering. Meanwhile, Slope County, 709 people; Divide County, 2,149 people.

The state is tilting toward Minnesota.

That sounds bad, but maybe it just is what it is. Most of the population of Canada is concentrated on a one hundred-mile strip along the US border, after all. You can wring your hands about rural outmigration, but what good will that do? Maybe Montana east of Billings and Great Falls, and North Dakota west of Minot and Bismarck is just going to be a vast empty quarter dotted here and there with crossroads service centers and beleaguered towns like Glendive and Watford City.

> "Most of the valley people I know regard Bismarck as a long journey for... well, nothing, and if they could get away with it they would undoubtedly move the state capital as well as the waters of the Missouri River closer to their doorsteps."

The people I know in the Red River Valley don't regard this phenomenon as alarming.

Like the rest of us, they feel a certain nostalgia for the North Dakota that is passing away forever, but they have managed to come to terms with it.

Though they may feel an occasional pang of regret for the decline of rural North Dakota, they are thoroughly wedded to urban life and they frankly wonder why any rational being would live west of the ancient shoreline of Lake Agassiz.

Most of the valley people I know regard Bismarck as a long journey for... well, nothing, and if they could get away with it, they would undoubtedly move the state capital as well as the waters of the Missouri River closer to their doorsteps.

They see Fargo and Grand Forks as progressive, diverse and culturally tolerable. They regard Bismarck as a cultural and gastronomic backwater, and the rest—well, as the land of dearth and deterioration.

Maybe what I feel is just a self-indulgent nostalgia for a North Dakota past that is gone and never coming back. Perhaps I remember a past that never really was, a past that I have idealized because of the occasional farm experiences of my youth.

Call me a hopeless romantic, call me unrealistic, call me alarmist, but I freely confess that when I think about the future "character" of North Dakota, I ache. No part of me says, "hurray for our post-agrarian future!" *2/17/07*

THE EBERTS RANCH AND THE ELKHORN

The Eberts Ranch was finally purchased by the US Forest Service in 2007. That would seem to have settled the issue, but a Miles City, Montana, businessman who owns a percentage of Eberts Ranch mineral rights has repeatedly threatened to develop a gravel pit on the site. This has caused considerable consternation. My view is that we should call his bluff rather than pay him an exorbitant sum to convince him to do the right thing. If he can get the clearances to develop his gravel pit (which I very much doubt), have at it and let's get it over with.

WE OWN THE EBERTS/ELKHORN RANCH; NOW, WHAT SHALL WE DO WITH IT?

Now that the Eberts Ranch has been acquired by the US Forest Service, it might seem that the long struggle to protect Theodore Roosevelt's Elkhorn Ranch is over. Not quite.

The 5,200-acre Blacktail Creek Ranch (aka the Eberts Ranch) now belongs to the people of the United States, to be supervised by the US Forest Service. That's the province of Dave Pieper and Dakota Prairie Grasslands. Pieper has pledged to keep the Eberts acreage open to traditional uses, which include grazing, oil development and recreation. The ranch includes the 5,200 acres recently acquired, and the 18,000-plus acres already owned by the US Forest Service that were leased by the Eberts family.

Ranchers in the valley routinely own some property (including their ranch headquarters) and lease additional acreage from the public domain. This is the wonderful legacy of the Bankhead-Jones Act of 1937. When the ranches of the American West were in a state of economic and environmental collapse during the Dust Bowl years, the federal government purchased large portions of bankrupt ranches and leased the acreage back to the ranchers at highly advantageous rates so long as the ranchers agreed to permit modest federal supervision of grazing practices. What could be more generous or more fair?

The "greater" Elkhorn Ranch is of immense historical importance, and it deserves to be treated as a unique, not routine, property. It's former President Roosevelt's second home (after Sagamore Hill on Long Island). It's where he ceased to be a New York dude and became a small-d democrat. It's where he recovered from the death of his first wife, Alice Hathaway Lee. It's where he wrote part of one of his best books, *Hunting Trips of a Ranchman.* It's where he began to formulate some of the conservation policies that he would implement as the twenty-sixth president of the United States. It's where one of American history's most important men was renewed, and in some sense reborn.

It's a special place that deserves a special future.

The Medora Grazing Association would like the Eberts acreage, one parcel of the 290,000 acres of National Grasslands in Billings County, simply to be divvied out to area ranchers for traditional grazing purposes. This makes a kind of sense. The two traditional economic "uses" of the Badlands have been grazing and mineral extraction. In other words, it's cattle and oil country. If Dakota Prairie Grasslands is serious about continuing to support traditional uses of the land, why not fill the vacuum left by the departure of the Eberts family by letting other ranchers lease the grass?

Such an outcome would not be the worst thing that ever happened. But there is a much better use for the land in question, and it would be a terrible mistake not to take advantage of this historic moment on this historic property to take public grazing in North Dakota to the next level of thoughtful conservation and wise management. Instead of simply parceling the acreage out and letting it slip below the public radar, Pieper would like to turn the Eberts-Elkhorn acreage into a grassbank. The grassbank idea is relatively new (1990s), which is the main reason some people find it threatening.

A grassbank is an acreage where grass is banked (like a grass savings account) for use in extraordinary circumstances. Instead of merely parceling the Eberts Ranch out for routine grazing, the grassbank would be available to ranchers throughout the region in times of drought, or after devastating fires, or while individual ranchers rest part of their lease acreage to restore creeks or rehabilitate stressed pastures. A grassbank can provide habitat for stressed or endangered species and for wildlife restoration on public lands. A grassbank also is a kind of grassland experiment station where new practices can be tested for the good of the entire region, with limited economic liability to any individual grazer. A grassbank is a kind of grass co-op or a grass safety valve. It doesn't diminish rancher access to the public lands. In fact, it may have the effect of increasing access (and productivity) through the intelligent incorporation of new stewardship practices.

In other words, Pieper does not want to lock up the Eberts-Elkhorn Ranch. He wants to graze it, but in the most sensible and enlightened possible way, not for the benefit of the few, but for the general benefit of all of the ranchers in the Little Missouri River Valley.

The ranchers' concern is that the Eberts-Elkhorn deal increases federal control in the Little Missouri River Valley, that it effectively reduces the number of cattle in Billings County, that it is just a hint of a large long-term and hidden agenda to diminish or destroy the ranch industry and transform the Badlands into something else. These are legitimate concerns that must be addressed in the most respectful and honest way. It will take time.

> **"If traditional ranchers ebb away and the designer-wear faux ranchers take over, it will be one of the greatest social disasters in North Dakota history and one of the greatest blows to the state's unique character."**

None of us can know what the Little Missouri River Valley will look like in one hundred or even fifty years. We can surely expect greatly increased oil and gas extraction—together with a labyrinth of new roads, low-water crossings, and a noisy and ugly industrial infrastructure. We can expect subdivisions and other "Aspenization" and "Telluride" effects in the valley, particularly south of Medora. We can expect the replacement of traditional family ranches with highly-capitalized vanity and hobby ranches, where all the buildings, fences, and vehicles gleam while a few cattle are grazed by tenants or overseers for tax purposes and for show. We can expect paved roads along both sides of the river deep into what we now regard as the Little Missouri outback. We can expect dramatically less public access to the public lands thanks to clever and subtle blocking mechanisms set up by wealthy (and often enough, absentee) landowners.

In my opinion, it is in everyone's interest to preserve the existing family ranching community in the Little Missouri River Valley. If the traditional ranchers ebb away and the designer-wear faux ranchers take over, it will be one of the greatest social disasters in North Dakota history and one of the greatest blows to the state's unique character. To prevent this from happening, we are going to have to cooperate in an unprecedented way. We are going to need extraordinary leadership from the governor, our congressional delegation, the Billings, Slope, and McKenzie county commissions, local, state and national conservation groups, and enlightened citizens. We're going to have to come together and talk it through, no matter how difficult that is, and put aside some of our differences. The goal is to conserve family ranches on thriving public lands where the energy industry has ample access, but not at the expense of the aesthetic grandeur or the long-term integrity of the place, and where a range of recreationists will not only be tolerated but welcomed as the natural allies of an enlightened cattle industry.

Pieper's proposed Elkhorn grassbank in no way threatens that vision or the existing ranch community. Just the opposite. At the Elkhorn grassbank, the future can be envisioned, discussed and experimented with in a place once occupied by one of America's most visionary—but extremely pragmatic conservationists. *10/13/07*

> *David Pieper retired in 2011. Some ranchers in the Medora Grazing Association believe that, when the Eberts Ranch was purchased by the US Forest Service, they were promised that the grass would be parceled out to existing commercial ranches. Pieper disputes this claim.*

A MODEST AND EXTREMELY IMPORTANT WILDERNESS PROPOSAL FOR NORTH DAKOTA

An ad hoc group, known as the North Dakota Wilderness Coalition, has put together a sensible and modest proposal to designate some sixty-eight thousand acres of public lands in North Dakota as permanent wilderness.

It's a purely wonderful idea whose time has come. If we don't act now, it's an idea whose time will be soon be gone forever. As far as I can determine, there is no rational reason to oppose the proposal. Nobody's ox is gored.

The proposed Prairie Legacy Wilderness will not be a contiguous unit. The coalition has designated six parcels for wilderness status, five diffused across the Badlands of western North Dakota, and a sixth in the Sheyenne National Grasslands southwest of Fargo. Why scatter the parcels in this way? Alas, we have so thoroughly domesticated all the rest of the wild lands of North Dakota that these are more or less the only remaining primitive islands in a sea of development, mostly oil development.

In the early 1970s, North Dakota possessed more than five hundred thousand acres that were deemed by the US Forest Service (the National Grasslands) as suitable for wilderness. By 1977, that number had been cut in half. Today, there are about forty thousand prime, suitable for wilderness acres left. Time is running out. As we stare over the brink toward an energy boom—an oil, coal, natural gas, wind and uranium rush—that will dwarf the three or four that have come to North Dakota before, we need to select a few precious acres of what is left and say: Not here!

The proposed wilderness areas are Bullion Butte in Billings County (9,720 acres), Kendley Plateau in Billings County (16,810 acres), Long X Divide in McKenzie County (10,670 acres), Twin Buttes in Golden Valley and Billings counties (13,590 acres), Lone Butte in McKenzie County (11,510 acres) and the Sheyenne Grasslands in Ransom and Richland counties (5,410) in southeastern North Dakota.

North Dakota is already graced by a few slivers of wilderness land. Chase Lake and Lostwood National Wildlife Refuges each contain a few thousand wilderness acres. The two units of Theodore Roosevelt National Park embrace a little wilderness, too, on the west bank of the Little Missouri River. These little parcels of already designated wilderness represent merely one-tenth of 1 percent of North Dakota's land base. If the coalition's humble and thoughtful proposals become law, another one-tenth of 1 percent of North Dakota will become wilderness.

Can we stand that much wildness in our midst? One-fifth of 1 percent of our total land base?

Our neighbors all have chosen to protect more wilderness than we do. South Dakota contains 77,570 acres of wilderness in two units; Montana 3,443,038 acres in 15 wilderness areas; Minn. 816,268 acres in three units; Wyoming 3,111,232 acres in 15 units; Idaho 4,005,754 acres in six wilderness units; and Colorado 3,390,635 acres in 41 units.

Think of what this proposal really amounts to. A handful of little patches of wild land would be preserved forever as prairie, plains and Badlands remnants, as reminders of what the northern Great Plains once were. Why would anyone oppose a wilderness plan so intelligent, so well thought through, and so carefully targeted?

And yet there are people who will oppose this proposal not on its merits, but merely because they cannot stand the idea that the conservation community would win a little victory in the land use wars of North Dakota and the American West. I hear the phrase "damned environmentalists" almost every day of my life. Some will oppose the plan because the word wilderness is such a loaded term at this dispirited, resource-hungry moment in American history. Look how this single, profoundly American word makes North Dakota's political leaders squirm. Some will oppose the proposal because it violates the seemingly sacred American notion that nature exists to be exploited, extracted, developed, and improved. Or because it is somehow disturbing that we could decide just to leave a parcel of our land alone, forever, just for the sake of leaving it alone.

Why do we need wilderness? Here's why.

On a tiny percentage of our public lands, we need to remind ourselves of what America looked like before we began to slice and dice it with our industrial tools. A century ago, Theodore Roosevelt called upon us to preserve some bits of the America of Daniel Boone and Lewis and Clark. He wanted Americans of every generation to have a chance to reduce life to its lowest terms and sleep on the ground out where the wind rustles through the trees at dusk.

Forever.

We need to protect a few scattered sanctuaries where we can go to refresh the human spirit without being reminded of the amenities and the infrastructure and the daily hum and drum of our lives. It can be argued that we don't need much such space, but we certainly need some. Roosevelt called American wilderness places our cathedrals our Notre Dame, our St. Peter's, our Parthenon, and he insisted that we treat them as lovingly as Europeans maintain their sacred grounds.

Above all, we need to show, even if only in this modest and symbolic way, that we have the capacity to restrain ourselves as we come to terms with the landscape on which we have chosen to live. Acts of restraint, as every theologian knows, dignify our experience, and bring a greater measure of purpose and integrity to everything we do. Fully 89 percent of North Dakota is farmed and ranched. Only 2.7 percent is owned by the federal government. Over in our neighbor Montana, the feds (that is, we the people) own 29.9 percent.

> "As we stare over the brink towards an energy boom—an oil, coal, natural gas, wind, and uranium rush—that will dwarf the three or four that have come to North Dakota before, we need to select a few precious acres of what is left and say: Not here!"

This seems to me like a proposal that everyone can support, if only because it is so extremely modest. There are no takings here. Some state lands would have to be transferred to federal jurisdiction; a few acres of private inholding would need to be purchased to secure the integrity of the parcels. Nobody's barn has to be torn down. Carefully regulated grazing and hunting still will be permitted on the wilderness acreage. If there is oil under these small parcels, it can almost certainly be reached by slant drilling.

Nobody can argue that this proposal represents a slippery slope or a Trojan Horse designed to open the door to bigger, wilder proposals that will follow if this one is successful. There is almost no land left in North Dakota that can qualify as wilderness. If this proposal succeeds, it's the end of the wilderness story: just two-fifths of 1 percent of North Dakota, while the other 99.6 percent can continue forever to be not wilderness.

At this point in American history, most wilderness proposals require real sacrifice. They represent hard choices that have to be made in our attempt to balance the magnificence and sublimity of the American West against other important values like economic development and the sanctity of private property. This North Dakota proposal, to redesignate sixty-eight thousand acres already in the public domain as wilderness rather than roadless is as painless a wilderness plan as ever has been advanced.

Let's get it done. Now. While there's still time. *8/23/08*

Nothing has so far come of this proposal. Time is running out.

THE MISSOURI RIVER

Long River, Moderate Volume,

Impossible Demands

For North Dakota, I believe, the two great stories of 2006 will be energy and water. Energy news is going to pervade our lives—well, at least the pages of this newspaper. It's going to be as if America woke up and discovered coal all over again. The future of North Dakota's water resources, though less dramatic, is an even more important story, in my opinion, and one that is likely to slip in under the radar.

Everything I read says that the water is going to be the oil of the twenty-first century: the finite and over-subscribed resource that drives economies, national and international politics, war, and the law.

I want to start with the Missouri River.

We tend to take it for granted. And yet it is one of the world's great rivers. Combined with the Mississippi, it is one of the two or three longest rivers in the world (at 3,710 miles, just behind the Nile and the Amazon), and it flows through the heart of North Dakota from west of Williston to just south of Fort Yates. The Missouri is one of the most heavily industrialized (perhaps a better term is engineered) rivers in the world: party for flood control and hydropower generation, partly to maintain a shipping channel between Sioux City and St. Louis. Irrigation, for all of its former promise, plays a minor role in the Missouri basin outside of Montana. It may seem ludicrous to talk about the "integrity" of a river that has been dammed seventy-five times and has been metamorphosed into a chain of slack water lakes between Fort Benton, Montana, and Yankton, South Dakota, but somehow, no matter how much concrete and steel technology we throw at it, the Missouri retains some of its romance and some of its riparian character.

In a purely rational world we would be asking certain questions about the future of the Missouri River. 1. Does America need barge traffic on the lower Missouri? 2. Is the cost of making the river capable of supporting barge traffic worth paying? 3. How many dams do we really need on the Missouri? 4. If there are more dams than needed to achieve flood control, would it make any sense to breach one or more of them, especially in an age of energy scarcity? 5. If so, which dams should be demolished? 6. How much could the river (and its backside life) recover if we restored the spring and summer "rise" of the Missouri? How long would it take? What would be the cost? Would this create any danger of flooding? 7. How important is reservoir recreation likely to be on the Missouri in the twenty-first century? 8. What diversions of water from the Missouri are reasonable and healthy? 9. Is trans-basin diversion ever healthy? Who should control the destiny of the river and the peoples and other creatures that live along its meanders?

> **"**It may seem ludicrous to talk about the "integrity" of a river that has been dammed seventy-five times and has been metamorphosed into a chain of slack water lakes between Fort Benton, Montana, and Yankton, South Dakota, but somehow, no matter how much concrete and steel technology we throw at it, the Missouri retains some of its romance and some of its riparian character.**"**

Or, to put it in a much broader perspective, what would we like the Missouri River to be and to look like in the year 2050 or 2106? And what do we think our relationship with the river ought to be in the twenty-first (as opposed to nineteenth and twentieth) century?

At the moment the Missouri River is operated like an engine, what the historian Richard White calls an "organic machine," the purpose of which is to maintain a nine-foot navigation channel below Sioux City. The problem is that the Missouri is a shallow wide river that does not wish to maintain so deep a channel. To make barge traffic possible the lower river must be continually dredged, rip rapped, and channelized. In a sense, that's their business. But to maintain nine feet at Sioux or Jefferson or Kansan City, virtually the whole of the upper basin's water reserves have to be thrown downstream every year to float grain and gravel along a corridor that has an Interstate highway and a major rail line. This is, in my opinion, purely idiotic and it continues to occur, continues to dominate the Missouri River, merely because of politics. In a free market economy, it would simply not be feasible. It is, in a nutshell, socialized federal aid applied by the army (the US Army Corps of Engineers) to promote lower basin grain trafficking at the expense of the upper basin. Your taxes and mine help pay for a grain-transportation system from which we get no benefits whatsoever and which hurts the vital recreation industry in North Dakota.

Meanwhile, the cities of the Red River Valley want to tap the Missouri River to stabilize their municipal and industrial water supply, and anticipate population and economic growth. They say they only want a trickle. Nobody with any sense of the history of water diversions elsewhere should believe this. Once the precedent is established—when the first slender little straw starts to run water out of the Missouri and into the Red—it will become enormously more difficult to prevent further, much more dramatic diversions.

Transfer of water from the Missouri to the Red River Valley seems reasonable for two reasons, both erroneous in my opinion. First, it seems like a small demand on the infinite water resource. The giant reservoirs and the popular mythology of the "infinite Missouri" make every demand on the river seem like a mere pinprick. The key to understanding the Missouri River is to understand that it is a long river with a moderate volume of water. The Missouri is subject to brief bursts of big water years surrounded by long periods of low water years. There is not as much water in the Missouri as we like to think. Just drive south of Bismarck on Highway 1806 something this winter. As the multi-year drought continues, you will be shocked to see how little is left on Lake Oahu between Bismarck and Fort Yates.

Every diversion, no matter how seemingly insignificant, is a serious drain on the Missouri.

Second, we North Dakotans cannot get the failed promise of Garrison Diversion out of our minds and (what is worse) our hearts. We want our massive federal water project! We regard it as an unfulfilled entitlement, our compensation for Garrison Dam, and we are bitter that it never came to pass. If it no longer makes sense to divert for irrigation, what if we resurrected (that's the key word) the Garrison Diversion project to provide municipal water for Fargo and Grand Forks? That's part of the subterranean logic that the planners of this diversion are counting on to get you to agree to it.

It's time for all of us to think about water, to read books about the Missouri River, to engage in a statewide conversation about the future of North Dakota's water resources and the future of the Missouri River, the Sheyenne River, the Little Missouri River, and the Red. We need a series of public forums based on history and geography, not just policy. We also need true (not pro forma) policy debates throughout the state. The Canadians need to be at the table. I suppose the barge barons need to be there. And the Corps. And the environmental activists. And most certainly the Lakota, the Mandan, the Hidatsa, and the Arikara.

I believe this issue, more than any other, is going to determine the future of North Dakota. I don't presume to know the answer to the water problems we face. But I know a few of the questions, and I'd love to help organize the forums. *Unpublished, 2006*

I wrote this early in my life as a columnist, and I paid an enormous price. A Fargo legislator went after me with a vindictiveness that I would have thought alien to North Dakota life. He threatened to cut funding to organizations for which I work. He refused to sit down with me to discuss the issue, after I wrote a sincere apology. He did his best to convince fellow legislators to denounce and dismiss me. One of my close friends, a federal wildlife guy, wrote to say that, in talking about water and the Red River Valley, I had touched "the third rail" of North Dakota politics.

I continue to believe that there are in-basin solutions to Red River water problems.

Notice at the end of the column I wrote that I "don't presume to know the answer" to these issues, and that what I was advocating was a statewide public discussion of water issues. In other words, let's talk about it.

A WATER BIBLIOGRAPHY
FOR NORTH DAKOTA

John R. Ferrell. *Big Dam Era: A Legislative and Institutional History of the Pick-Sloan Missouri River Basin Program.*

Bill Lambrecht. *Big Muddy Blues: True Tales and Twisted Politics Along Lewis and Clark's Missouri River.*

Michael Lawson, et al. *Dammed Indians Revisited: The Continuing History of the Pick-Sloan Plan and the Missouri River Sioux.*

Patricia Limerick. *A Ditch in Time: Denver, the West, and Water.*

Marc Reisner. *Cadillac Desert: The American West and Its Disappearing Water.*

Robert Kelley Schneiders. *Big Sky River: The Yellowstone and the Upper Missouri.*

Schneiders. *Unruly River: Two Centuries of Change Along the Missouri.*

John E. Thorson. *River of Promise, River of Peril: The Politics of Managing the Missouri River.*

Paul VanDevelder. *Coyote Warrior: One Man, Three Tribes, and the Trial that Forged a Nation.*

Donald Worster. *Rivers of Empire: Water, Aridity, and the Growth of the American West.*

Farewell to the Bridge of Our Youth

Last things matter.

On Wednesday I went up to the bluffs just west of Bismarck State College to watch the final two spans of Memorial Bridge come down. The implosion was scheduled for 10 a.m. It actually occurred a few minutes after 11.

A quiet crowd of more than one thousand was strung out along the ridgeline. Some people stayed in their cars, more stood or sat on the prairie grasses sipping coffee out of high-end Styrofoam cups. There were a dozen or so boats in the water half a mile upriver from the bridge, including a red canoe. The minute I saw it, I wished that I had taken my kayak down to the river in the morning and witnessed the bridge come down from the water's surface. A couple of folks were standing like sentinels on a slender sandbar in the center of the river. How I envied them.

> "Both of our colleges, BSC and the University of Mary, have buildings with spectacular views of the Missouri River. That is incalculably important in the education of our youth."

I was surprised and pleased that so many people came to watch the last gasp of Memorial Bridge. Implosions always draw a crowd, I suppose. The mood was festive in a muted sort of way. I tried to reckon what percentage of the crowd felt sad to see the venerable old bridge spans collapse into the river. Not many, I think. It was more about spectacle than loss.

BSC President Larry Skogen had invited folks to watch the implosion from the splendid new energy building on campus. The view from the fourth floor is magnificent. Both of our colleges, BSC and the University of Mary, have buildings with spectacular views of the Missouri River. That is incalculably important in the education of our youth—as important to the spirit of our place as the neoclassical colonnades are to the spirit of the University of Virginia at Charlottesville.

However much the Missouri has been compromised and degraded by industrialization, it is still—even in its Corps of Engineers straitjacket—one of America's greatest rivers. Not even the notorious Flood Control Act of 1944 and the Pick-Sloan Plan, which threw up six giant mainstem dams between Fort Peck, Montana, and the bottom of South Dakota, could quite destroy the romance of the Missouri River or its extraordinary heritage. North Dakota is fortunate to be bisected by what Meriwether Lewis called "the mighty and heretofore deemed endless Missouri River," even in its domesticated state. Try to imagine North Dakota without it.

When John Steinbeck came through in 1960 in his pickup camper, Rosinante, doing the field work that led to *Travels with Charley,* he instantly recognized the importance of the Missouri River. "Someone must have told me about the Missouri River at Bismarck, North Dakota," he wrote, "or I must have read about it. In either case, I hadn't paid attention. I came on it in amazement. Here is where the map should fold. Here is the boundary between east and west. On the Bismarck side it is eastern landscape, eastern grass, with the look and smell of eastern America. Across the Missouri on the Mandan side, it is pure west, with brown grass and water scorings and small outcrops. The two sides of the river might well be a thousand miles apart."

Sarcasts put it more rudely in my youth: "Mandan, where the West begins, and the East dumps its garbage." I have always loved Mandan, mostly because it is not Bismarck.

Memorial Bridge was the arched symbol of Steinbeck's line of demarcation. It was, with our unique Capitol building, the most widely recognized landmark in Bismarck. The three more recent highway bridges at Bismarck are efficient and structurally sound, but essentially invisible. You can cross them without really thinking about what you are doing, because they do not scare you or make odd humming noises or call attention to their engineering. Memorial Bridge was a kind of clunky twentiety century exclamation mark that said: "Hey, pay attention, you are now crossing one of America's major rivers, and it wasn't easy to build a crossing here, so don't ever take the Missouri River for granted."

Those days are now gone forever.

When I got to the energy building, I hesitated a second too long at the door, and discovered that I actually had no interest in going inside. I didn't want even a remarkable eighteen-foot-high pane of glass to stand between me and the bridge. Besides, it was just about as beautiful a late fall day as I have ever seen—fifty degrees (above!), a gentle breeze, a dry, breathtakingly clear sky, crisp as Halloween time generally is. It was jacket weather, just this side of chilly. It just felt glorious to be alive on such a morning, and everyone who gathered on the ridge knew: Not much longer now.

By Wednesday morning, I had long since come to terms with the fact that Memorial Bridge was going to be erased from the Bismarck-Mandan landscape. Like many others, I hated to see it go, because it so thoroughly represents my idea of Bismarck. Until the other day, it had never not been there, in the whole course of my life.

I believe the bridge should have been preserved as a monument to our past—the Capitol will be obsolete one of these days too, but I bet it will not be imploded to make way for some gleaming State Bank of North Dakota-like building. At least one span of Memorial Bridge should have been lovingly placed on a river ridge, like the old threshing machines that punctuate our lost homesteads. Or parked downtown as a pedestrian plaza, the way the old "Biggest Little City in the World" signs are preserved on

Reno's back streets. But there was no sufficient public outcry to save the bridge—or a chunk of it—and everyone understood the structural challenges it presented to those who maintain our infrastructure.

I made my peace with the loss of Memorial Bridge on the last day it was open for traffic, July 31. I drove across it twice that morning, half an hour before traffic engineers closed it, and I walked across it from east to west and back again. Only a handful of people walked the bridge that day, though hundreds queued up to make their last drive across the bridge, which opened for traffic in August 1922.

Still, I feel great loss, in a very personal way, the way one feels when one of the Beatles dies or a venerable president or movie star from the golden age of film. I can remember in my youth riding in the back of our Ford Falcon from Dickinson to my grandparents' farm in Fergus Falls, Minnesota. In my childhood the only way to get there was old Highway 10. The Memorial Bridge was the only way across the Missouri in this part of the world. It still had its steel mesh roadbed then—which frightened but fascinated my sister and me, and just frightened my phobic father. The hum of the car's tires on the bridge delighted us. Crossing the great bridge was an event then, a marker of the progress of our journey, perhaps because we were not in the back seat fumbling with iPods and Nintendo DS.

I am feeling old today. Some of my spans are showing signs of fatigue. Rest in peace, Memorial Bridge. You will be much missed. *11/1/08*

The new bridge is actually quite beautiful, the best of the "new" Bismarck bridges, except for the veterans' memorials on either end. They are important for a number of reasons, but not, in my opinion, very attractive in their perpendicularity.

The Lesson of Lewis and Clark in Montana

Every summer at this time for the past seven years, I have led a Lewis and Clark cultural tour somewhere along the trail between Fort Yates and the Pacific Ocean. This year our eight-day trek (July 22-30) was split between the White Cliffs reach of the Missouri River in eastern Montana and the Lolo trail between Missoula, Montana, and Lewiston, Idaho. We camp a couple of nights in a row, if you can call catered meals, fine wine, and someone else doing all the actual work camping, then check into historic lodges, such as the Grand Union Hotel in Fort Benton, Montana, for a shower and a bed, then camp again a couple more nights in another historically important place. We're on the Lewis and Clark trail but we're not exactly roughing it. It's fun for a few days to pretend we are a Corps of Northwestern Discovery, but if we had to push thirty tons of luggage against the current of the Missouri, we'd have quit after the first hour.

About this time every summer, cultural tour participants from all over the country gather at the airport town nearest the part of the West we wish to explore: to follow the trail of Lewis and Clark, to see what they saw, step where they walked, eat what they ate (except dog), and at times sleep where they slept. Some tour participants are buffs who can never get enough of Lewis and Clark. Others have never been west of the Mississippi River, and regard Lewis and Clark as those guys on the highway signs.

Evenings around the campfire I lecture and answer questions about every aspect of Lewis and Clark. There is nothing I love more than a campfire talk in the wild, wild West. Eventually the talk gives way to the stars and the beer, and around midnight we all slip off to our tents, tired but glad to be alive.

This year we put eight canoes into the Missouri River a few miles east of Fort Benton, Montana, and floated on down to Judith Landing, at the mouth of the Judith River, named (May 29, 1805) by William Clark for his future wife Julia Hancock. The current does most of the work, but we paddle in pairs in the 90-degree heat, with frequent stops for swimming, lunch, a little riverside geology, or some talk about travel in the age of Thomas Jefferson. Occasionally we get into our life jackets and float down towards the Gulf of Mexico, bobbing along in the surprisingly strong current. You cannot be in the Missouri river where it actually still flows without feeling its massive and inexorable strength. It's not as loud or coltish as a mountain stream, or as clear, but it is infinitely more powerful.

> "Wouldn't it be marvelous if somehow we could liberate just a bit of the mighty Missouri in North Dakota from its dull industrial drudgery, and let it work again on our souls?"

As I canoed silently in placid Missouri waters past the famous Hole in the Wall, gazing around at what Meriwether Lewis called "scenes of visionary enchantment" that reminded him of the crude masonry formations that might be produced by a race of giants in the earth, I was struck by the difference between North Dakota's Missouri River and Montana's.

Through much of Montana, from the Jefferson River at Dillon southwest of Three Forks, all the way to the backwaters of Fort Peck Reservoir, a distance of hundreds of river miles, the Missouri is a recognizable river that flows downstream, behaves like a Great Plains river, and provides a river's joys and diversions. It's not as natural as the Yellowstone, which is (somewhat inaccurately) known as the longest free-flowing river in the United States, and there are a few Missouri River dams in the Helena to Great Falls corridor, but none is large enough to break the paradigm of one's idea of what a river is and should be. Because of this, Montana's Missouri attracts lovers of rivers. They come from all over the country, even all over the world, to play in what Meriwether Lewis called "the mighty and heretofore deemed endless Missouri" in kayaks and canoes. They come precisely to take a break from the internal combustion engine.

It is probably a misnomer to speak of the Missouri River in North Dakota. What we have instead, thanks to the Pick-Sloan Plan of the 1940s, are two gigantic slack-water reservoirs, and two remnant stretches of "river" from the Montana line to Williston and from Garrison Dam to just below Bismarck. The eighty-mile stretch north of Bismarck can only be called the Missouri River in a very nominal sense. The banks are rip rapped and stabilized by the US Army Corps of Engineers. Thanks to the impoundment of the dam, the water is unnaturally clear and cold. Near Bismarck, the banks are as likely to display Kentucky blue grass and gazebos as willow, grass, and cottonwoods.

The forms of recreation that thrive on Lake Sakakawea and Lake Oahe— fishing, including ice fishing, water skiing, pontoons, shoreline cabins, jet skis, power boating—give people great pleasure and add greatly to North Dakota's economy. Almost everybody believes the dams are here to stay. After all, they have now been here for half of North Dakota's statehood.

Reservoir recreation is lucrative and it's a settled habit of North Dakota life, but it is not, I think, the way tourism is headed. The future seems to be heritage tourism—by which I mean finding a way to give people a chance to experience the American West the way it was before white folks arrived with asphalt, town plats, and power equipment. As the United States becomes more urban, more abstracted from nature's pith and rhythms, more bombarded by mediated experiences (from cable television to the Xbox to the ubiquity of cell phones), people are seeking ways to return to authenticity, to participate in experiences that focus on spirit of place rather than technological wizardy. There's a great book on this subject by Joseph Sax called *Mountains Without Handrails*.

The enormous success of the Lewis and Clark Bicentennial can be attributed to the window it opened to an American past that we admittedly romanticize, but nevertheless regard as an essential counterweight to our synthetic and oil-propelled lives.

We Dakotans love our lakes, but what people from around the country and around the world want to see are buffalo and antelope grazing on native grasses without visual noise in the picture. They want to see (and feel) rivers flowing in their primordial way. They want to walk on and listen to the grass. They want to see the West as Lewis and Clark saw it, as Custer and Sitting Bull saw it, as the Mandan and Hidatsa saw it before Verendrye arrived in 1738.

Not so far away, in Montana, in the White Cliffs corridor, as you sit in a canoe gazing in wonder at the un-industrialized landscape all around you, feeling the slow but massive tug of one of the world's great rivers, letting your mind dance around the bluffs without the drone of an engine from any direction, you feel more fully American not in a patriotic but in a primordial way. Wallace Stegner's great dream, "a society to match the landscape," captures the essence of the experience. It's a lazy afternoon, and hot, and the living is easy (thanks to the marinated buffalo we'll be eating with a glass of Merlot and a goat cheese salad just hours from now).

By any realistic standard, I suppose it is too late to contemplate a time when the Missouri will flow free again in North Dakota. But wouldn't it be marvelous if somehow we could liberate just a bit of the mighty Missouri in North Dakota from its dull industrial drudgery, and let it work again on our souls.

We'd be better off if we let the river flow.   *7/31/06*

July, Huck Finn and the River

A few days ago, I spent the afternoon and early evening in Washburn. Working like a demon. At about 8 p.m., weary as can be, I turned my vehicle for Bismarck. Distracted by all the numbing pressures of life, I had been planning to hurtle home on U.S. 83 on the soul's autopilot, and drink in as little of the experience as possible.

Unfortunately for my plan to pass through life rather than really live it, I glanced through the passenger window over to the west and there was the Missouri River, angling its way in no great hurry to St. Louis.

Just at that moment, the turnoff for N.D. 1804 materialized. I remember saying, "OK!" in precisely the same way one says "OK" when the kickoff finally occurs on Super Bowl Sunday or on Thanksgiving when your grandmother finally says, "Come to the table now." I took the turn onto N.D. 1804 at about sixty-five miles per hour, which, for a middle-aged man, is the equivalent of "peeling out."

The Missouri River. Meriwether Lewis called it "the mighty and heretofore deemed endless Missouri River." Think of that.

A very large ingredient of the romance of America, particularly the romance of the American West, is embodied by the words "Missouri River." Thomas Jefferson believed that the Missouri is the mainstem and the upper Mississippi a mere tributary joining the Missouri at St. Charles. That view, to which many scientists subscribe, would make the Missouri the longest river in North America and one of the three or four longest rivers on earth. It would mean that Huck and Jim were floating down the Missouri during their epic raft journey from slavery to higher law, not the Mississippi.

One of the things that bothers me about North Dakota is that we have so little actual respect for the Missouri River. In the menu of things the Missouri River could be to us, we prefer to think of it as hydroelectric power, municipal and industrial water supply, recreational platform, fish farm, straight-jacketed channel flowing benignly past my riverside house. Lake. All wonderful things, but none of them is what the Missouri River would be if we hadn't thrown the whole weight of the Industrial Revolution at it. Here's heresy: Every other state through which the Missouri River flows cherishes the now-raging, now-languishing Missouri of Lewis and Clark more than North Dakota does.

But back to the river, such as it now is, on an 85-degree evening north of Bismarck.

It was the bluest and most beautiful blue that blue can ever be, with tawny sandbars here and there, some of them in the center of the river, the shape of a single imperfect parenthesis. Where the sun glinted off the river, it was like an array of one hundred thousand diamonds, so brilliant that you wanted to but could not bring yourself to look away.

"A lazy July afternoon on a sandbar is as close as we can still get to the world of Huck Finn. There is no summer feeling more agreeable than the last hour of a long day on a sandbar, most sand between your toes, the plains country softening as it rolls away to the vanishing point."

I ambled south along N.D. 1804, windows open, at a speed so leisurely that it would have driven anyone behind me to distraction, had there been anyone. It was just stunning to observe the river make big sweeping curves in its effort to annoy the US Army Corps of Engineers. The key to the beauty of the Missouri River is sandbars. The river insists upon forming them, even when it is channelized and rip rapped, and—lower down the river—dredged.

A lazy July afternoon on a sandbar is as close as we can still get to the world of Huck Finn. There is no summer feeling more agreeable than the last hour of a long day on a sandbar, moist sand between your toes, the plains country softening as it rolls away to the vanishing point, the immensity of the quiet of America's grasslands lowering in upon you, and yet shore life—with all of its wild demands—still a boat or pontoon journey away.

Finally, I stopped at Double Ditch historic site to watch the sunset and meditate on American independence.

Double Ditch has unfortunately been "improved" by way of a sidewalk that thrusts a white bureaucrat's straight line right into the heart of the mounded, curved, circular world of the Mandan, and now there is a bench overlooking the river. I was just about to sit down on the bench when it struck me that, if you want to experience Double Ditch, you need to lie down in the grass.

I lay on the grass for a long time in that dreamy half-dozing way.

The sun was half an hour from setting, in a perfectly cloudless sky. It was as bright a sun as I have ever seen, overwhelming even when I tried to avert my gaze. It was a like a gargantuan Fourth of July sparkler held by an adolescent sun god, but this one would never fizzle out. The sun seemed to be saying, "I know North Dakota has long winters wherein my performances tend to be wan sun and that you endure more than a few gray, overcast days. Here is your compensation."

Sunset, I knew, would be roseate, pink, orange and charcoal, and that it would linger forever. But the sun was still pouring out BTUs as if there were no tomorrow. It was not the yellow disk of a child's painting, but an atmospheric phenomenon of overwhelming metallic white light pulsating across the western sky with the slightest tincture of bleached yellow in it.

I lay on the grass for a long time feeling the first tentative little wavelets of cool air make inroads against the lingering heat of the day. It was that perfect, almost imperceptible breeze. That's always my favorite moment of a summer day in Dakota.

Here's a life lesson. I was restored to something like soul-body integration by the mere fact of surrendering to the place, the river, the sky, the grass, and the sun. A river, any river, is one of the best metaphors for life.

My reverie was broken by the whistle of bottle rockets and the concussion of firecrackers. I stood up, stretched toward the river, and walked to my car. There in the parking area were four teenagers all leaning against a car, trunk open, a cooler on the ground before them, taking turns igniting the lesser fireworks. They looked at me a little nervously as I walked to my car. I wanted very much to think of a graceful and non-preachy way to communicate to them that Double Ditch is a very important archaeological site, a Mandan Indian village site, a sacred place in North Dakota, and it might be better if they took their gathering elsewhere. But I knew that nothing I could say, no matter what strategy I used, would do anything but offend them and brand me as a tedious old killjoy.

Freedom is a paradox. That's the meaning of the Fourth of July. *7/8/08*

Phase One is Over,
but the Real Dangers are Yet to Come

For most of the last week I have been a sandbag factotum. At Horizon Middle School, then at Fort Mandan, and finally at the big sandbag throwdown at the commerce center down by the airport, I have filled and lugged, lugged and filled, until my back ached and my soul glowed from being a part of something bigger and infinitely more important than my little life. In the past week, I have spoken only a handful of sentences (for a change) as I let myself be absorbed into the magnificent army of volunteers who have done what they can do to save Bismarck and Mandan. The harder I worked with my hands the better I felt.

At the Northern Plains Commerce Center last Sunday, I was walking down the line looking for an open work station when I saw a middle-aged couple filling white sandbags in front of a mountain of sand. Nothing remarkable in that, but then I did a literal double take. I recognized the couple as Jack and Betsy Dalrymple, the governor of North Dakota and the First Lady. There they were in jeans and T-shirts quietly filling sandbags—no handlers standing by anxiously working cell phones, no security detail, no staff photographer making sure the moment got proper public attention. They were just part of the crowd of nameless volunteers. This was no photo op in which the governor is whisked in to be seen filling a couple of sandbags and then whisked out to supervise the crisis from behind a desk. They were there by themselves, and they had made themselves indistinguishable from the other 1,460 volunteers at the commerce center, and they were there for a long time.

Two thoughts came to me in that instant. First, Jack and Betsy Dalyrmple are very remarkable people. Very few leaders (anywhere) would be capable of this sort of selflessness. Second, North Dakota is a totally amazing and very unusual place.

Now the first phase of the great flood of 2011 is over. Call it the Breastwork Phase. For all of the pain it has caused to individuals living along the river, phase one has been characterized by a certain euphoria and excitement.

As I wrote this at mid-week, most of the news was encouraging.

First, Bismarck and Mandan had done what they could to protect North Dakota's second largest population center from the high water projected by the US Army Corps of Engineers. It has been a huge, complex, and brilliantly coordinated community effort. If you add up the number of things that could have gone wrong, and the number of things that have been done with stunning efficiency on very short notice—to prepare for a flood that could not have been predicted—you brim with sheer admiration and civic pride. When the number of dump trucks, truckloads, pallets, sandbags, dikes and levees, skid steers, volunteers, man (and woman) hours, houses protected, and the value of property saved from the disaster is finally tallied up later this year, this is going to be one of the handful of greatest stories in North Dakota history. I don't know about you, but I feel nothing but gratitude and profound respect for the work of Bismarck mayor John Warford, Mandan mayor Tim Helbling, and David Sprynczynatyk, the commander of the North Dakota National Guard, among many others.

Second, the Missouri River has been scouring its bed in such a way as to deepen its channel through Bismarck and Mandan and thus absorb the increased releases more comfortably than anyone predicted.

Third, by mid last week, the amount of water being released from Garrison Dam was finally greater than the amount of water coming into Lake Sakakawea at Williston. The six mainstem dams on the Missouri River between Glasgow, Montana, and the bottom of South Dakota are all full or very nearly full. That makes the Corps of Engineers nervous no matter when it happens because it means that there is no excess storage capacity in the Pick-Sloan system. Two days of heavy rains in eastern Montana right now would create a catastrophe.

> "I recognized the couple as Jack and Betsy Dalrymple, the governor of North Dakota and the First Lady. There they were in jeans and T-shirts quietly filling sandbags—no handlers standing by anxiously working cell phones, no security detail, no staff photographer making sure the moment got proper public attention."

Full and brimming reservoirs make the corps (and all of us) extremely nervous in early June 2011 because the entire Rocky Mountain snowmelt has to flow through or over those dams in the next two months. In other words, we've now—just barely—absorbed the April-May (spring thaw) rise, but the much bigger June-July (snowmelt) rise is still to come. That's why the second phase of the flood of 2011 (the Siege) is going to last a couple of months. The corps is trying to flush as much water through the system as it can, as fast as it can—but without destroying Bismarck, Fort Yates, Pierre, Yankton, and Sioux City—primarily to free up some storage space for the massive snowmelt that is now about to descend on all of us.

If everything goes just right, the corps will be able to maintain control (barely) of the unruly Missouri River in a year when the entire Missouri-Mississippi system is in one of its periodic and history-making floods. But we must not lower our guard for a moment. We have not yet won the battle, not by a long shot. There is a significant possibility that the waters yet to come out of Montana will overwhelm the Pick-Sloan system. As you read this, we are literally in a desperate fight against time. Meanwhile, the gigantic volume of water that has to pass through Bismarck and Mandan between now and Labor Day is going to do everything it can to eat the temporary breastworks we have thrown up. It would be almost impossible to exaggerate the lifting power of the Missouri when it is on the rampage.

This is a slowly developing story. The Siege Phase is going to be characterized by exhaustion, impatience, and extreme frustration.

Stay tuned. *6/12/11*

This column, and the four that followed, brought some pretty serious criticism from people who live in the Missouri floodplain. The common ground of their criticism was that I should not be defending the US Army Corps of Engineers. One resident said that "there would be hell to pay" by the Corps once he and his neighbors had time to organize and direct their anger. Looking back, I continue to believe that the Corps behaved admirably in a crisis that could not have been predicted and that our propensity to treat the Corps as a scapegoat is an indication that we have not learned the lesson of the flood of 2011.

LESSONS FROM THE FLOOD

At some point, the Missouri River flood of 2011 will be over. The dikes and breastworks will be dismantled and hauled away. Folks will finally get back into their sodden homes. Some of those homes will be beyond repair. Others will be reclaimed, with lots of money and infinite scrubbing. Life in North Dakota will return to something like normal. For many families, however, life will never quite be the same after the summer of 2011. If we are wise, all of us will change the way we think about the Missouri River.

If there is any good news in a natural disaster that has displaced people and damaged property all the way from Dillon, Montana, to New Orleans, it is that the great flood of 2011 has reminded us that the Missouri-Mississippi is an integrated continental river system, not a fragmented set of local river units. Try as it might, the Missouri has not managed to break free of the industrial strait jacket we built to contain it over the last half century, but it has certainly taught us a new respect for its magnificent power and will, and it has forced us to realize that it doesn't work to think of what Meriwether Lewis called the "endless Missouri River" in such segmented terms as "Upper and Lower Basin," or the "Garrison to Bismarck stretch," or the "navigation channel."

The failure of the human imagination between 1944 and 2010 has been to think of the Missouri River as a plumbing problem rather than as a complex organic system of cottonwood trees, oxbows, sandbars, meanders, wildlife habitats, floods, droughts, pallid sturgeons, and human communities. The best way to manage the future of the Missouri River is agree to see it not as a problem to be solved but as an organic (almost living) multiplex that needs to be approached with equal doses of engineering and humility.

As we try to make sense of what happened and why, we should try to avoid three temptations.

First, we should resist simply blaming the Corps of Engineers and arguing that if the river just had been properly managed, the flood could have been avoided. I'm not saying the corps is blameless. When this is all over, there will be plenty of time to investigate. Undoubtedly the corps will itself wish it had done some things differently. But by any rational measure, the corps has prevented a bad flood from being an infinitely worse one over a river system that drains 40 percent of the continental United States. Undoubtedly the river can be managed better in the years to come—partly by taking advantage of what we have learned this year—but simply blaming the corps is taking the easy way out of this natural disaster. Enlightened communities do not take the easy way out; they respond to crises with creativity rather than righteousness. Just blaming the corps is like "rounding up the usual suspects" at the end of the Humphrey Bogart film *Casablanca.*

> "If there is any good news in a natural disaster that has displaced people and damaged property all the way from Dillon, Montana, to New Orleans, it is that the great flood of 2011 has reminded us that the Missouri-Mississippi is an integrated continental river system, not a fragmented set of local river units."

Second, we should avoid looking on the flood of 2011 as a "one-of-a-kind perfect storm" that is not likely to occur again. The 2011 floods on the Souris, the Red, and in the Devils Lake basin, coupled with the three thousand-mile flood on the Missouri River should teach us that we are in the heart of a significant wet cycle that has, among other things, closed scores of roads across North Dakota, prevented farmers from planting their crops, consumed thousands of acres of farmland around Devils Lake, and decimated Minot and the Souris River towns. It's not important at the moment to determine whether this is just a natural (but very pronounced) wet cycle or a barometric sign of global climate change. That debate is, in some respects, a distraction. What's important is that we realize that there is no reason to believe that the year 2011 has been randomly or uniquely wet, and that things will "return to normal" in the years to come. We may be moving into a new normal. The "software" we created in 1944 to manage water on the upper Great Plains may be no more useful to us now than Windows 95 or Windows Millennium.

Above all (third), we should avoid the urge to "fix" the problem by just getting more ruthless about "taming" the Missouri River. In the face of the flood of 2011, it would be a natural twentieth century temptation to build more dams (on the Yellowstone, for example), throw up permanent levees in south Bismarck and Mandan, rip rap more of the "free flowing" stretches of the river, add more storage capacity to the existing dams, and abandon (in a righteous huff) the conservation initiatives that have been undertaken along the Missouri River in the last ten or fifteen years. Tempting as "still more engineering" is, the flood of 2011 shows us the poverty of trying to manage the Missouri River in an exclusively industrial manner. Of course, we had to dam and channelize the Missouri River Valley to make it livable and to create an economic engine for North Dakota and other western states. It was a great human achievement. The problem is that, in our love affair with rebar and concrete, we almost lost our ability to think of the Missouri as a wild, mighty and wonderful river. We forgot that—to be healthy—rivers have to behave in some measure according to their natural dynamics, and that every human intervention represents a set of costs. Just ask the Mandan, Hidatsa, Arikara, and Lakota.

> "The failure of the human imagination between 1944 and 2010 has been to think of the Missouri River as a plumbing problem rather than as a complex organic system of cottonwood trees, oxbows, sandbars, meanders, wildlife habitats, floods, droughts, pallid sturgeons, and human communities."

The industrial model works (most of the time) and—given the 1954-2010 riverside development pattern —it would be insane to dismantle much of the existing river infrastructure. But as the twenty-first century begins we need to step back and create a more flexible, more organic, more humble, more thoughtful, and more respectful way of living beside one of the world's greatest rivers. *7/8/11*

I think this is the most important of the columns I have written about the Missouri River. I am aware, of course, that in the midst of a natural disaster, people are unlikely to want to step back to think philosophically about the nature of rivers and the technological overreach of industrial man.

THE FUTURE OF NORTH DAKOTA

Taking the First Steps

Toward a Cultural Accord

Behind the seemingly trivial issue of whether sports teams at the University of North Dakota can continue to call themselves the "Fighting Sioux," there exists a gulf that divides white and Indian cultures and keeps North Dakota stuck in a disintegrated phase of its history. It's what University of Colorado historian Patricia Limerick calls the "Legacy of Conquest."

Drive onto any reservation in North Dakota. It's a different world, a different America on the other side of that suddenly assuring windshield. The signs of cultural stress are so palpable that you wonder how such disparities can be tolerated in so decent a state, in so prosperous a nation. And yet, first impressions aside, there are plenty of good energies at work on the reservations and, as North Dakota's great novelist Louise Erdrich has shown, there is a deep aquifer of authenticity and imperturbable love medicine just below the chaotic surface.

As the twenty-first century begins, at a time of great transition on the northern Great Plains, I believe the moment has come for the two cultures to come together in a new spirit of understanding and mutual generosity of spirit. If whites and Indians can hammer out an agreed-upon narrative about the things that happened between 1864 and 1950, and find a way to assign and acknowledge responsibility without tripping into blame, defensiveness, self-pity, and defiance, it might be possible to heal some deep, festering wounds. It might even be possible for us together to create a new North Dakota that is more interesting than the sum of its parts.

The two North Dakotas need to work at reconciliation, because that is what enlightened communities do. But it can even be better than that. The presence of Indians in North Dakota (as compared, say, to Kansas) is one of our greatest cultural assets. If we can learn to live together in a more symbiotic way and find a way to blend our best energies, North Dakota could become one of the most remarkable places in North America.

It sounds pretty unlikely, I know. Plenty of people in both communities will snort: you're wasting your breath, why would we even want to reconcile, the gulf is unbridgeable, and—frankly—much worse.

There are approximately thirty-four thousand American Indians in North Dakota. That's 5.4 percent of the state. Indians are the fastest growing population in North Dakota. The high Indian birth rate is all that prevents our overall population from shrinking.

If we are going to close the gulf, white North Dakotans are going to have to acknowledge some truths, take some responsibility, and help to fix some problems. Here are just two of the many unresolved issues we ought to address.

First, there is the problem of the Indian land base. The Fort Laramie Treaty of 1851 guaranteed the Mandan, Hidatsa, and Arikara, for example, all the land bordered by the Missouri and Yellowstone Rivers on the north, the Heart and the Little Missouri on the south, and the Powder River on the west. That was 12.6 million acres, solemnly promised for as long as the grass grew and the waters flowed.

Today, thanks to a series of "adjustments" forced upon the tribes by the United States government, the Fort Berthold Indian Reservation comprises only 988,000 acres, less than 8 percent of the 1851 homeland. Actually, it is much worse. Don't be fooled by those solid patches of color that are labeled Standing Rock Indian Reservation and Spirit Lake Indian Reservation on the North Dakota highway map. Those indicate the overall size of the reservations, but they misrepresent the land ownership patterns within the reservation's boundaries. 526,883 acres on the Fort Berthold reservation are owned by non-Indians. That's 53 percent. In other words, more than half of what appears to be the reservation actually belongs to white folks who happen to live there. That's the legacy of the Dawes Act (1887).

> It would be profoundly helpful if the people of North Dakota (and the United States) in some simple, unambiguous, sincere, and humble way took responsibility and apologized for the shattering impact of their industrial conquest of the Missouri.

Nobody can realistically argue that all of the original 12.6 million acres should be returned to the three tribes. But some of it can and should be returned. Even a modest repatriation would take us a long way down the road of reconciliation.

At the very least we should all support efforts of the tribes to buy up—with their own money—available white-owned acreage within the boundaries of the existing reservations. In other words, it should be our goal to reduce the checkerboarding as much as possible and to help to make sure that the sliver that is left of Indian country is truly Indian-owned, inhabited, and administered.

Second, the damming of the Missouri River in the Dakotas in the mid-twentieth century was an unmitigated disaster for the Indians who lived in the bottomlands that Lake Sakakawea and Lake Oahe have inundated. The Three Affiliated Tribes not only lost 152,360 acres to a project that they objected to with all the resources at their disposal in 1946, but the acres they were forced to sacrifice were the most productive and most densely populated on the reservation. Three hundred twenty-five families had to be "relocated," fully 80 percent of the reservation population.

It was a Mandan, Hidatsa, Arikara holocaust.

It is virtually impossible for non-Indians to fathom the grief and anger and bewilderment that the damming of the Missouri River has wrought.

The best way to get a partial sense of it is to read Paul VanDevelder's book, *Coyote Warrior*.

The distinguished Lakota writer Elizabeth Cook-Lynn has written that the damming of the Missouri "severed the spiritual artery" of the peoples who lived along its banks. The distinguished Indian historian and philosopher Vine Deloria Jr. said that the damming of the Missouri was the greatest crime against American Indians of the twentieth century.

It's not clear what we can do about this. Breaching a dam or two would solve the problem, of course, but we must attempt to live in a world of actual possibilities. Monetary reparations already have been made and more are sure to come, but lucre only buys time and silence, without resolving the bedrock issue. It would be profoundly helpful if the people of North Dakota (and the United States) in some simple, unambiguous, sincere, and humble way took responsibility and apologized for the shattering impact of their industrial conquest of the Missouri. Possible?

Probably, all this sounds like "the wildest chimera of a moonstruck brain." Maybe it is. So let's start with an easy one. Let's retire "Fighting Sioux" and then carefully nurture the little tendril of good will it sprouts.
3/8/08

I chose the dates 1864 and 1950 because 1864 was the year that General Alfred Sully marched US troops into today's North Dakota to chastise "the Sioux" for their role in the Minnesota Uprising of 1862. Plains historians say that before that year the Lakota and Dakota of today's North Dakota had had few encounters with white people, none of them in battle. 1950 represents the period in which the great dams on the Missouri River were authorized and built, the final act of gross destruction of upper Missouri River Indian culture. Garrison Dam was completed in 1954.

North Dakota:

Let It be a Place, Not a Platform

A few days ago, I had the opportunity to address a large group of rural telephone cooperative board members and about one hundred state legislators. The topic that was set for me was "The Magic of North Dakota."

It is my favorite topic.

A friend of mine in New York, learning of my intentions, raised his eyebrow and said, "Can't wait to hear this … the 'magic' of North Dakota?"

My speech consisted of several arguments. First, I asserted that the magic of North Dakota comes from a combination of three factors: the landscape, the character of the people, and our heritage. Take any one of these away, and North Dakota is a mere platform rather than a place.

For about half an hour, I listed what I regard as the ten specific sources of North Dakota's magic. Finally, I spent a little time exploring the threat to the magic. I think the landscape, character and heritage of North Dakota are all being eroded, while we, Nero-like, play the fiddle song of prosperity.

Here, in a nutshell, is my list.

1. The endlessness of our landscape. In West Virginia long ago, I met a man who asked where I was from. When I answered, he said, "The Great Plains. That's a lot of country all spread out." In the last ten days, I have driven 3,198 miles up and down the Great Plains, to Kansas and back again twice. The endlessness of the Great Plains is amazing—even at times shocking.

2. The emptiness of our landscape. It's always been pretty empty, and now it's really empty—and rural depopulation is not nearly over yet. Thriving city-states like Bismarck and Fargo, a wide range of scattered marginal towns and endless empty country in between. There's a lot of pavement for very few vehicles. Don't break down.

3. The fauna. On any given day, if you really want to, you can see antelope, deer, elk, prairie dogs, feral horses, and buffalo. If you are lucky, you also can see bighorn sheep, coyotes, and a moose. And if you are touched by grace, you might just maybe possibly someday see a mountain lion or a wolf. The main reason you can see all of these creatures, by the way, is the twin existence of Theodore Roosevelt National Park and the Little Missouri National Grasslands. All praise to federal land supervision.

4. North Dakota's in-betweenness. We are a transition state, partly mid-western and partly western. I would not want us to be Minnesota, though Fargo and Grand Forks seem to yearn for that. I would not want us to be Montana. We get energies from both paradigms. That makes North Dakota a kind of unsettled place, a sometimes hard to define place, a place of cultural tension. Some people like to say that, at statehood in 1889, a geographic mistake was made: it should have been East Dakota and West Dakota rather than North Dakota and South Dakota. I disagree. Just as the atom is held together by the "curve of binding energy" between protons and electrons, so too North Dakota has a fascinating curve of binding energy between, say, Grassy Butte and Grafton.

5. The rawness of North Dakota. The climate here is on the whole moderate, but for about forty scattered days in a good winter, it is unbelievably cold, at times almost unbearably cold. The wind blows here more than in most other places, and we have come to terms with it. In my reckoning, there are only about ten days of drive-you-crazy wind per year in North Dakota. This is a state where you ignore the elements at your peril. I love the most violent thunderstorms, too, the ones that make you wonder if you are going to be metamorphosed into bratwurst.

6. American Indians. We are fortunate to be the home of a large and increasingly visible and assertive Native American population. The Mandan, Hidatsa, Arikara, Ojibwe, Dakota, and Assiniboine remind us that North Dakota was once a very different place, operating by a fundamentally different set of cultural liturgies. The white conquerors of other plains states, most notably Kansas and Texas, did their best to rid themselves of Indians early on. Thank goodness that did not happen here. The fact that North Dakota is a two-culture state creates serious challenges and tensions, but it contributes to the magic.

7. North Dakota is bisected by one of the world's greatest rivers, Meriwether Lewis's "mighty and heretofore deemed endless Missouri River." We've done our best to put the anarchic and capricious Missouri into a Corps of Engineers straitjacket. For a long time in Great Plains (and American) history, utility trumped magic. That era is coming to an end. With luck and good leadership, we are going to restore some of the magic.

8. Manageable scale. As someone said at my dinner table, North Dakota could be characterized as "a small town with a long street." In North Dakota, it's not six degrees of separation, but two or three. We still have only a single area code. This is a state where you can run into your United States senator in a grocery store. I always hide my Twinkies.

9. Our agrarian heritage. From 1889 until about 1989, we were Thomas Jefferson's "chosen people of God," a state of family farms, small villages, and stewardship values. As the twenty-first century begins, we are making the awkward and painful transition from our family farm past to a more diversified and cosmopolitan future. This is the single most significant dynamic at work in North Dakota today. We periodically are made aware of how agonizing this transformation really is, but we do our best to keep a poker face. That, in my opinion, is a mistake.

10. The sheer improbability of living here. On one of the appalling wind days, or when it is so cold and blustery that it virtually rips the bark right off of your exposed flesh, or when you hanker for Thai cuisine, you have to stop and ask yourself: Why do I choose to live here and not elsewhere? If you could live in Minneapolis or Santa Monica or Missoula, where a new Olive Garden restaurant is not regarded as a major cultural amenity, why would you choose to live in a cold, isolated, windswept, low-wage, emptying place, whose highest peak is a chalk butte at 3,506 feet? It's a mystery. But the improbability of North Dakota is one of its greatest charms.

So there's my list. The threat, which I will explore at a later date, is that we are industrializing our rolling hills and Badlands landscape with unprecedented greed and gumption, and siting our industrial fixtures with no regard to the heritage of the Great Plains. We are walking away briskly from our agrarian roots and values. And we are paying far too little attention to the rich heritage of our white and Indian history.

But hey, we are more prosperous than ever before, and the Legislature is going to toss money around as if there were no tomorrow and no yesterday. *12/6/08*

If We've Never Had It So Good, Why Are We So Uncertain?

The twenty-first century spirit of North Dakota?

Everyone lives somewhere. Everyone is from somewhere. People everywhere are, on the whole, loyal to the place they grew up, the place they call home, the place where their roots are deepest.

We live in a wide-open prairie and Plains landscape that strikes most Americans as flat, dull and uninspiring. We live in flyover and drive-through country. Once, when I extolled the beauties of U.S. Highway 85 between Bowman and Belle Fourche, SD, a young woman behind a hotel desk listened politely and said, "Yeah, driving that road is like sitting in a chair looking at wallpaper all day long." OK, it's not for everyone.

Our place is North Dakota. We know it's not big and powerful like Texas, not hip like Hawaii or California or even Colorado. It's not on the short list of states known for their landscape beauty. On a spectrum that runs from sublime to dreary, North Dakota is usually ranked by others pretty close to the dreary goalpost. We natives like North Dakota. Some of us even love it, but I think we all harbor a quiet anxiety that our affection has more to do with habit and loyalty than with any objective assessment.

We North Dakotans tend to pour on the loyalty a little because we feel that our state needs that, that there is something to defend, to justify, to protect against North Dakota's detractors. Whenever I hear North Dakotans say, "It's a great place to raise kids" (for export?), or "Ever been on the L.A. 405 freeway during rush hour?" or, our favorite cliche, "Keeps the riff raff out," I cringe a little even though all those things are true in their way.

I am head over heels in love with North Dakota, and I will never again live anywhere else. And yet the minute I drive over the line into Montana I find myself saying, sometimes out loud to myself, "Whoa, what I love most about the North Dakota landscape is humbled by the magnificence of Montana."

North Dakota is for most, including most of us, an acquired taste. The beauties of the landscape are subtle enough to be overlooked by most people, including some of our own. Our people are unspectacular—decent, hardworking, honest—but unspectacular. I like to say we are a little clunky (not to mention chunky). Some people object to this characterization, but I mean it as praise.

North Dakota is an isolated, windswept, and at times bitterly cold place at the center of the continent. That sounds like a liability (compared to, say, Malibu, California, or South Beach, Florida.), but somehow we've decided that it's a kind of virtue, if only for what it says about the gumption of people who have chosen to live here when they might well live somewhere else. For all of our insecurity, we feel a kind of superiority over people who live easier lives in easier places.

This place shapes us. Our hunch is that it shapes us more than most other places shape other people, because the severities of the weather and the unbelievable openness of the landscape prevent us from pretending we live in everywhere/nowhere. In some of the communities in which I have lived outside of North Dakota, it has been possible to become oblivious to place, as we go from house to office to mall to restaurant to house again. Anyone who attempts to become so abstracted in North Dakota is soon brought up short. That's the glory of living here.

This is a good time in North Dakota. The state has a gigantic and growing budget surplus. Unemployment is low. Wages are up. Fargo, Bismarck-Mandan, and Grand Forks are booming. The economy is clearly diversifying in ways that the leaders of the last generation said were essential to our economic future. On top of all that, farm commodity prices are spectacular. Thanks to ethanol, there appears to be an unlimited market for corn.

> "Nothing that we have done or can conceive of doing seems to make North Dakota any less isolated, less backwatery, or less seemingly remote from the main traffic lanes of American life."

Although most of the evidence is anecdotal, it feels like more young people are choosing to stay in the state (particularly the cities), and it seems that folks who cast their lot elsewhere are moving home in greater numbers—in the prime rather than the twilight of their lives. The energy corridor is buzzing. The coming, apparently permanent, energy crisis means that our oil is going to be extracted and our coal is going to be dug up and burned. Wind generators are going to change the face of North Dakota, as are more smokestacks and their yellowy effluents. This time, the energy boom cash flow is going to be staggering and some significant fraction of it is going to stay here. I'm sorry to report that we appear to have decided we are not going fuss much about the environmental and social cost this time around.

It would be possible to conclude, with former Prime Minister Harold Macmillan of Great Britain, that "we've never had it so good."

We are even thinking that we may be one of the few beneficiaries of global warming. We talk this way only in our jokes, but we do actually wonder if North Dakota would become a more attractive place if the winters moderated a little.

North Dakota is far and away the most egalitarian place I have ever lived. Not only is the middle class wider here than elsewhere, almost fulfilling Thomas Jefferson's dream of a middle class that occupies virtually the whole spectrum, with a tiny number of rich at one end and an even tinier number of poor at the other, but throughout North Dakota history, the richest of our citizens have tended to behave as if they were less wealthy than in fact they were. It has been regarded as gauche, shameful—un-North Dakotan—to act like a rich person, even if you were. When my father became moderately prosperous late in his career, he really wanted to drive a Cadillac, but he wouldn't purchase one because he did not want to be thought of as a man who could afford to drive a Cadillac. North Dakota is still a place where people feel a little sheepish about having more than the next guy. Something at the core of the American dream of a classless society has lingered longer in North Dakota than in any other place. It's changing now, quite rapidly. Is that good?

> "If we continue to crowd into our cities, and tilt the demographics of the state towards the Minnesota border, and the great majority of us have fewer real ties to the land, how are we going to sustain our sense of place?"

North Dakotans are, on average, more prosperous than ever before. They have more access to the fruits of life than any previous generation of North Dakotans. (When I was growing up, for example, it was difficult to get fruits and vegetables out of season.) They have more mobility than ever before. And generally speaking, they are more sophisticated, better connected, better educated, better traveled and more in tune with the wider world than ever before. My goodness, we are in danger of becoming just like everyone else, except that we hail from North Dakota. Is that really what we seek? Is that good?

In the course of my lifetime, North Dakota has changed in important ways. In the 1960s and '70s, we regarded ourselves as a progressive farm state with vibrant communities and a bright future. The world would always need food, we reckoned, and we knew how to grow it. In the 1980s and 90s, we underwent a serious identity crisis. We were pretty certain that the state was in decline—economically, demographically. There was widespread disquietude and disillusionment. People speculated half-seriously that the state might have to revert to territorial status. That was the period of the "emptied prairie."

Since the millennium, things have turned around—sort of. It's not that the rural outmigration has ended. Far from it. But psychologically, the people of North Dakota have, I think, come to terms with the exodus in a way that defies logic. A fairly large number of the rural communities that are still reasonably viable have exhibited a resourcefulness and a sheer will to survive that is little short of heroic. Hats off to them.

From 1880 (or so) until 1980 (or so), we were a farm state, where the majority of our people had real ties to agriculture. Since 1980, and particularly since the advent of the Information Age (first Web site in the world: 1991), we have been making the transition from our Jeffersonian to our post-Jeffersonian era. The future appears bright. There is ample evidence to inspire optimism. And yet there is a wide pool of uncertainty not far beneath the surface of our current prosperity. There also is a nagging feeling that we have turned away from our farm heritage, from the set of economic and social dynamics that made us who we are.

As the first decade of the twenty-first century comes to an end, we Dakotans have two brooding fears, I believe. First, we fear that no matter what we do, no matter how many amenities we provide, no matter how many jobs we create and no matter how close our pay scale approaches the national average, our young people are not going to wish to stay and spend the best years of their lives here. Nothing that we have done or can conceive of doing seems to make North Dakota any less isolated, less backwatery, or less seemingly remote from the main traffic lanes of American life. Most of the children we raise so well are going to build their lives elsewhere. There is something heartbreaking in that.

The cold and the isolation—these have been the fundamental problems of North Dakota life, and our sorrow is that Thomas Friedman's flat world does not really make any difference.

Our second fear is that the current prosperity and optimism about the future will end, perhaps abruptly. Energy booms bust. Commodity prices collapse. Deep and sustained droughts can break the heart of a prairie people. They have done so before. We know we are unwisely dependent on the federal farm program. We know that the Senate of an increasingly urban country cannot be expected to vote gigantic funds for rural stabilization forever. Our superb and powerful senators cannot be expected to serve—or live—forever. Take away the farm program and the research dollars that Sens. Byron Dorgan and Kent Conrad have steered our way, and what's left of North Dakota?

In short, what if this is nothing more than a brief period of prosperity in the midst of a long journey of decline?

Questions:

If the cities and the Red River Valley thrive, but the rural countryside becomes a landscape of decline, depopulation and disillusionment, are we still North Dakota?

If we are no longer Jefferson's agrarians—the farmers, and children and cousins of farmers whom he called "the chosen people of God"—and we are making the transition into the post-agrarian phase of our history, then who exactly are we at the beginning of the twenty-first century? If we are not an agrarian people, what kind of people are we? What kind of people do we want to be?

If our character has been shaped by family agriculture and ethnicity, and the best that is in us has to do with canning, quilting, neighborliness and self-reliance, how long and how well can we maintain those values in an increasingly urban, abstracted, mediated, and distracted era?

If we continue to crowd into our cities, and tilt the demographics of the state toward the Minnesota border, and the great majority of us have fewer real ties to the land, how are we going to sustain our sense of place? How are we going to maintain what land ethic we have and indeed develop a deeper and more enlightened understanding of how people and place intertwine to produce sustainable communities?

How much energy development is enough, and what does it matter to a people who increasingly live away from the zones where extraction occurs?

I have always felt that North Dakotans were different from other folks in the United States—not greatly different from people of the other Great Plains states, but significantly different from people in New Jersey and California and Louisiana. I have felt too that the reward we got for living in a harsh, isolated and (to most people) undesirable place was that we were, frankly, a cut above other people in integrity, core values, community, modesty of spirit, neighborliness, and respect for the golden rule and the rule of law.

A lifetime of hectic travel, here and abroad, has convinced me that this is not merely a compensatory myth. There is something special about us that has nothing to do with microbreweries, surfing, or purple mountain majesties. But it is becoming less true. And my fear is that it will slip away. Worse, I fear that we are letting it slip away.

We have been a basic and decent people who, without fanfare or self-love, grow more food than we consume. What could be more beautiful and honorable than that?

My biggest fear is that our success as a twenty-first-century state will come at too great a cost to our character. I'm not sure that there is anything we could do about this, but I believe strongly that if we are going to face this challenge, it will require leadership that I do not now see on the horizon.

The next North Dakota Legislature will have somewhere between $800 million to a billion dollars to spend. It is our money. How the Legislature chooses to invest that money will tell us a great deal about the spirit and the future of North Dakota. *2/21/08*

This essay is longer than the others. It was written for a special edition of the Bismarck Tribune. A great deal has changed between 2008 and 2012, but my questions about our troubled state identity persist.

Byron Dorgan left the US Senate in 2010. Kent Conrad retired in 2012.

ENERGY
AND THE SPIRIT
OF NORTH DAKOTA

Bakken Workers Scarce

Last week, I had the good fortune to dine in Bismarck with twenty high level employees of a large oil company, a company that does considerable business in western North Dakota. My official role was to provide a little after-dinner lecturette about "our state North Dakota." You know: 47th in population, 19th in area. Three distinct regions: Red River Valley, Prairie Pothole, western slope. Outmigration. Meadowlark, the telephone pole (state tree) and the chokecherry. Yadda go ta North Dakota, where there's cattle and there's wheat and there's folks that can't be beat.

As you can readily see, I had nothing much to contribute to our guests, who were mostly from a place called Houston, but I eagerly signed on for the dinner in the hope of learning something about the future of oil development in our region.

I started by delivering a rather extensive lecture reviewing everything I know about oil. I quote my lecture in its entirety: "It's some kind of liquid carbon, isn't it? I've heard that up from the ground comes a bubbling crude?" Having thus established my street cred, I had the good sense to shut up and listen. One of the most important rules of life, especially for those prone to hold forth, is that you never learn anything while you're talking.

I peppered our petroleum industry guests with questions for more than an hour. Here's what they taught me.

One: The Bakken oil pools at a depth of about ten thousand feet. But you don't just drill straight down those two miles and—voila. Once you reach ten thousand feet, you begin horizontal drilling another nine thousand or so feet. (Fascinating explanation, here, of how the pipe turns the corner). Now we've sunk almost four miles of pipe and still no oil. At this point water at extremely high pressure is forced down the pipe. This requires a lot of water, a great deal of power, and just imagine the pumping rigs. These jets of water shatter the shale that straddles oil, thus pooling a larger concentration of oil in one subterranean spot. Now you can pump the oil to the surface.

It's extremely expensive to get at Bakken oil, but once you reach crude, the flows can be amazing.

The Bakken field was first discovered in 1953, but there was then no profitable way to extract it. Now, thanks to the staggering world price of oil and dramatically better drilling technologies, it makes sense (and $) to develop the field.

Two: There's lots of oil out there, but not nearly as much as the hype suggests. If the Bakken formation is systematically developed, all the company reps agreed that it will be a gigantic event in the history of North Dakota, one that will change the economic and social face of the state, but it will not be a gigantic event in the history of world oil development. It will not change the world oil equation. It will not drive down the price of oil or the gasoline in your SUV. It will, however, buy a little time as the world seeks out viable alternatives to its oil-based energy habits.

How much oil is down there? Unbelievable amounts. Some estimates run to hundreds of billions of barrels. Ah, but as the company folks explained, the real question is how much of that oil can be recovered even at 2008 prices. Nobody knows for sure, but the best current estimates are between 2.5 billion and 4.3 billion barrels. American oil consumption is 20 million barrels per day.

Three: The industry folks say that even extensive development of the Bakken field will leave what they call a light environmental footprint. Compared to classical Texas or California drilling, the wells will be widely dispersed. The fact that horizontal drilling is required to access the oil means that the wells can be positioned where they cause the least domestic and aesthetic disruption. The pneumatic shattering of the shale that envelops the oil represents no environmental danger to the surface, to underground aquifers, or to the geological stability of the region.

Getting the oil out of the Williston basin to refineries and tankers is a bigger challenge, but industry experts say that the large volume of oil involved and the projected long life of the field mean that a pipeline infrastructure will be created that will bring real (and unprecedented) efficiency to the process.

Four: Assuming that oil prices do not collapse or drop below $100 per barrel, it is safe to assume that all the recoverable oil will be coming out of the ground over the next 30 years. The oil execs have three half-big concerns.

First, they are having a really hard time finding oil workers. Brace yourself for this. Given the amount of hectic oil development around the world and a shortage of oil field workers, the companies are finding that workers are less interested in staffing the Williston Basin than many other isolated places.

Second (and this is related), the North Dakota transportation infrastructure is woefully inadequate. From Houston or Dubai, it's hard to get to Williston and not particularly easy to get in and out of Bismarck and Minot. The visiting oil reps said the most important thing we could do to insure sensible economic development in the Williston Basin is create a much-improved air traffic infrastructure.

Third, there is a need for much greater training of oil field workers at all levels. The reps said the natural institution for such training would be Williston State College, but so far not much that is useful has been organized there. (In my view, Bismarck State would be a better choice, under the amazing new leadership of President Larry Skogen).

Finally, admittedly a bit wryly, the oil execs said that the sheer magnitude and cash flow of the Bakken development is going to create lots of restless millionaires in western North Dakota. "Your very new, very rich person is often a social nightmare," one executive said.

The only important thing I said to our guests was this: "You're in the oil business. Your job is to find and extract oil. Today Venezuela, tomorrow the Aral Sea. I'm not saying all places are equal to you, but from an industry point of view, in some sense an oil field is an oil field, and any given surface environment is regarded as a mere staging area for the extraction process. We have no terrorists here in North Dakota, and no political instability. In spite of our reputation, this is not an extreme environment like the North Sea or Prudhoe Bay.

"But we do have a very strong sense of place. Lewis and Clark passed right through the Williston Basin. Theodore Roosevelt found his conservation voice here, beginning in 1883. This is the home of the Assiniboine and the Hidatsa and the Mandan and the Sioux."

"If it is true that we do not regard the region west of the Missouri River as sacred ground, we certainly do regard it as a heritage landscape. It is really important to us that we don't impede your important work, but it is even more important to us that you remember always that this is our place, our homeland, and that our long-term future, unlike yours, is right here." *8/9/08*

This was one of my early columns on the Bakken. The oil now seems to be much deeper than ten thousand feet. Current projections are that there may be as many as 11.5 billion recoverable barrels given today's technologies and oil prices.

THE TRANSFORMATION

OF THE NORTH DAKOTA LANDSCAPE

The energy boom that has just begun to arrive on the northern great plains is going to be a doozey. It looks as if the United States is finally going to get serious about energy independence and, as former president George W. Bush asserted, the amazing breakthroughs in energy production and distribution are going to be driven by enterprise rather than government. Government will play a role, of course. Tax and regulatory policy on carbon are going to need to be very subtly crafted to invite and inspire the future without strangling the present. It's an incredibly exciting time. We

Americans are energy hogs. If we want to continue to live this way, we're going to have to bring some unprecedented ingenuity to the table, now that most of the easy oil in the world has been sucked out of the ground and into our machines.

Who would have thought ten or twenty years ago that North Dakota would become one of the epicenters of America's drive for energy independence? North Dakota now ranks fourth in crude oil production (after Texas, Alaska, and California), tenth in coal production (Wyoming, by a long measure, ranks first), and twenty-first in total energy production. And the great twenty-first century energy boom is just beginning. If the estimates of the number of recoverable barrels of oil in the Bakken field are accurate (4-5 billion), not to mention the Sanish, Three Forks, and other formations that are beginning to enter our energy vocabulary, North Dakota is going to prosper beyond the dreams of avarice.

> "We are becoming an urban state with an Australian-like outback."

This represents a revolution in the meaning of North Dakota. For the first one hundred years of its Euro-American history, North Dakota was an agrarian land. For the past twenty years or so, we have been edging away from the pastoralism that made us who we are. During the hard 1980s, North Dakota started to shop around for a new mission. Now that new mission is becoming more clear. It looks to me like some combination of the following dynamics.

Dramatically greater production on fewer farms operated by fewer farmers. If the twentieth century gave us mechanized agriculture, the twenty-first century is bringing us hyper-scientific agriculture: unprecedented genetic manipulations, bombastic yields, boutique pesticides and herbicides, GPS-driven combines, specialty crops marketed on the internet, farmstead processing of commodities into consumer products, calves with chips in them to enable us to track them from birth to Big Mac. All this utterly fascinating, and some of it a bit scary, but most of this innovation is going to occur below the radar of public attention.

Dramatic growth of our cities, especially Fargo and Bismarck, unsustainable growth and agonizing growing pains in the carbon corridor, severe decline in the population of the rest of North Dakota. North Dakota once had more towns of 2,500 or fewer people than any other state. That North Dakota is evaporating. We are becoming an urban state with an Australian-like outback. The cities of the east (Grand Forks and Fargo) will increasingly lean into Minnesota. The East-West split in North Dakota will widen and grow more tense. A decade ago it looked as if western North Dakota (that is, everything west of Cooperstown) would become "Godforsakia" and eastern North Dakota "Greater Minnesota." Now, thanks to the energy boom, the carbon belt is becoming North Dakota's Alberta. That "Alberta" is going to assert itself, beginning in the next legislative session. In the next decades, Bismarck is going to be the epicenter of tens of billions of dollars of economic activity and the coffer of the state's burgeoning carbon-culled surpluses. Under the remarkable leadership of Larry Skogen, Bismarck State College is likely to become the intellectual engine (the CPU) of applied Great Plains energy research and training. Fargo and Grand Forks are going to find this shift disturbing.

Wholesale industrialization of the landscape of western North Dakota. Even cautious experts are predicting a proliferation of roads, including four lane highways, pipelines, rail lines, storage facilities; new coal gasification plants and liquefaction plants; oil pads on virtually every other section of some parts of the state until you can walk from Minot to Wolf Point, Montana, or Medicine Hat, Alberta, at midnight by following the methane flares. And to get all that carbon out of the ground, we are going to have to divert immense quantities of water—in a land where water is scarce except in the Missouri River, where it is much scarcer than we like to think. As former Gov. Bill Guy likes to remind us, water is going to be the oil of the twenty-first century.

> " ... oil pads on virtually every other section of some parts of the state until you can walk from Minot to Wolf Point, Montana, or Medicine Hat, Alberta, at midnight by following the methane flares. "

Great pressures on the Badlands. The vast majority of the Badlands are managed by the Little Missouri National Grasslands, a division of the US Forest Service. That means that they are open to energy development. We can expect more roads, more rigs, more pads, more trucks, more dust, and probably more bridges. And—since the energy boom is going to make hundreds or thousands of new millionaires in North Dakota, and well-off people from elsewhere are going to discover the Badlands—more hobby ranches and ridgeline homes through the most scenic region of this sublime windswept state.

Welcome to the twenty-first century, Flickertail state. Are we ready? Don't you think we should all talk about this and not just brace for it? *10/24/10*

A Spirit of Place

Welcome Wagon Kit for Energy Workers

Western North Dakota is awash with industrial guests. The motels in Dickinson, Williston, Minot, Watford City, Belfield, Killdeer, and New Town are full to bursting. There are days when it is impossible to find a room in any of these places.

Man camps are sprouting up in the oil patch. There are widespread reports of people living in their pickups. Most of our guests are men. Their homes are somewhere else. They come here for a few days or a few weeks or a few months and then they leave, either to go home, or on a Caribbean bonus vacation provided by their employer, or to another energy hot spot. They are not from here and they do not plan to spend their lives here.

> "It's important for you to know a few things about us and about this place. It may seem like a windswept godforsaken landscape to you, but this is our home place and we love it here. We have a special relationship with the land. Stewardship matters to us as much as profit. We ask that you treat North Dakota with thoughtfulness and respect."

I have had the opportunity to spend a good deal of time talking with these men. They seem like smart, enterprising, lusty, and good-humored young men to me, quite different from the "oil field trash and proud of it" types I observed in my early manhood in Dickinson. They do seem a little addicted to the f-word as a routine flavor enhancer, no matter what the conversation. And, of course, they drink too much.

Whenever I converse with them, or hear them talking amongst themselves, the following theme emerges. Not much to do here. Lots of country all spread out, very few amenities. The locals are really nice and all that, but it seems like a pretty boring place. If the winters are as brutal as the locals say, how do you handle it?

I have a modest proposal, born of a combination of hope and real fear. My hope is that we can make the case for the greatness of North Dakota to our guests. My fear is that if they don't get to know this place, to appreciate its beauty, its history and its heritage, they will regard it as a mere outback that sits on top of black gold, and they will mistreat it, or its citizens, in small ways or large.

I want every guest—from executives down to the lowest rig hand or driver—to get a North Dakota Welcome Wagon Gift Bag when they check into our motels. We also need to work closely with all the companies who are bringing workers here to get these gift bags included in their training and orientation sessions. I wish the ND Humanities Council would create a quirky, funny, but serious, "North Dakota Naturalization" lecture series to fan out into the carbon corridor.

The Welcome Wagon Gift Bags would include the following:

—a specially printed state map with the words, "Welcome to Our Homeland" on the cover;

—a universal library card that could be used at any public library in North Dakota;

—a one-page laminated "History of North Dakota";

—a twenty-page pamphlet that lists the museums, historical sites, and places of extraordinary beauty in North Dakota (e.g., the Medicine Hole at Killdeer Mountain, the ICBM missile museum at Cooperstown, the Elkhorn Ranch);

—a universal ticket permitting one free admission to a range of North Dakota attractions: The ND Cowboy Hall of Fame, Fort Mandan, Bonanzaville, the Medora Musical, etc.;

—a 75-100 page book(let) that explains North Dakota: geography, history, literature, Native Americans, politics, music, painting, spirit of place, demographics, popular culture. The booklet would include statements about the plains, the Missouri River, the Badlands, buttes, grassland, and family agriculture from such writers as Theodore Roosevelt, Meriwether Lewis, de Trobriand, Elizabeth Custer, Louise Erdrich, etc.;

—an engraved copy of Governor Art Link's "When the Landscape is Quiet Again" speech;

—the latest issue of *North Dakota History* (the state historical society's quarterly) and the latest issue of *On Second Thought* (the ND Humanities Council's quarterly);

—and a welcome letter. (More on that in a moment.)

The gift bag would not include the usual tourism materials. Attraction brochures and glossy tourism magazines, pizza offers, and coupons are available everywhere already, in restaurants and hotel lobbies and gas stations. People get bombarded with this sort of thing, and they don't take it very seriously. The presence of such materials would dilute the seriousness of purpose of the gift bags When individuals open their gift bags, I want them to say, "Wow. These guys are serious about this place."

The welcome letter should say something like this:

Welcome to North Dakota. We are glad you are here. Thank you for helping us develop our resources. We want your time here to be productive but also pleasurable and satisfying. This gift bag includes materials prepared just for you that explain our history and culture and invite you to get to know this place and not merely regard yourself as stationed here. North Dakota has a more interesting history than you might guess.

It's important for you to know a few things about us and about this place. It may seem like a windswept godforsaken landscape to you, but this is our home place and we love it here. We have a special relationship with the land. Stewardship matters to us as much as profit. We ask that you treat North Dakota with thoughtfulness and respect.

Someday the energy boom will be over. When that moment comes, we want this place and its people to be unscarred.

Meanwhile, welcome to North Dakota. *11/14/10*

I still hope we will do this. I got some feelers about it, from state commerce and tourism and from a prominent businessman in Dickinson. But nothing came of it. I think we should do this anyway—with or without the oil boom—to teach others, and ourselves, what we value about this place. One thing is absolutely certain: the oil industry considers us just another extraction platform. I don't blame them. That is what one would expect. But we have the opportunity to teach them how we would like to be regarded.

A CITIZENS' COMMISSION ON THE ENERGY BOOM

Last week I drove through the energy corridor of North Dakota. It's a shocking and eye-opening experience. The transformation of western North Dakota from a sleepy pastoral backwater to a buzzing industrial landscape has been sudden and profound. The boom is changing where we live and who we are. Frankly, I think it is getting away from us.

If I were the governor of North Dakota, I would immediately appoint a ten-member citizens' commission on Energy and the Spirit of North Dakota. It would consist of one rancher-farmer who owned his (or her) mineral rights and one who didn't; a county commissioner from one of the impacted counties; two mayors, one from Williston or Dickinson and one from a smaller town in the oil corridor; a representative of the Three Affiliated Tribes; a water engineer; a representative from the coal industry; a representative of the oil industry; and a conservationist.

> "Knowledge is power. The people of North Dakota don't have the information we need to know what is at stake in the energy corridor. We can either stand by and watch this gargantuan thing just happen to us—like a tsunami—or we can devote ourselves to managing the boom and insisting that there are values in North Dakota life greater than mere profit."

I'd empower this commission to meet at least once a month, more in the beginning, and travel extensively, and give it a budget so that it could make site visits in North Dakota and elsewhere. I'd ask the Energy and the Spirit of North Dakota Commission to prepare a series of white papers for the people of North Dakota. The first would be called "The Boom So Far." Lavishly illustrated with photographs, video, and charts and graphs, it would provide descriptions and statistics about the number of wells, the volume of production, the types of companies working in the field, the ways in which North Dakotans are being employed in the energy sectors; housing; the man camps; the impact on roads, bridges, the hospitality sector; the strain on basic services (police, social services, fire departments, clinics and hospitals, emergency response personnel); the procurement and disposal of water resources for the industry; and the industrial accidents that have occurred so far, including injuries directly and indirectly related to the boom.

This white paper would be published physically and electronically, and the website would be constantly updated.

The second white paper would be called "Where We are Headed." It would work with cities, counties, the state government, and industry to try to project where this boom is likely to lead in one year, five years, ten years, and twenty years. It would attempt to anticipate what North Dakota needs to do (both in government and the private sector) to manage the boom in the most responsible way possible.

The third white paper would be entitled, "Costs, Risks, Impacts, and Flashpoints." A big boom like this is wonderful in many ways. It provides jobs. It makes some people rich. It fills the coffers of the state treasury, and that wealth is distributed by the state legislature by way of catch-up appropriation in education, social services, property tax relief, and worthy new projects and initiatives throughout the state. It contributes to American energy—not independence but at least less dependence. All this is good. But it comes with a cost. This white paper would look at those costs with candor and courage. The cost to wildlife—and therefore recreational hunting. The cost to Art Link's quiet landscape, particularly in and around the Badlands. The cost to the social structure. One rancher has oil and becomes a sudden millionaire. His neighbor, with whom he has been friends for forty years, has no oil and he watches his buddy suddenly prosper in an unprecedented way, through no hard work or merit. The cost to farmers and ranchers who don't own their mineral rights but find their operations and way of life disrupted and sometimes damaged by oil activity that they don't benefit from and cannot prevent. The cost to the traditional small town way of life. Spiraling housing costs. Congestion, traffic jams, potholes, dust, crime, domestic violence, violence against women, etc. This white paper will also begin to address what we might do to mitigate those costs, to make the boom as smooth as humanly possible.

The fourth white paper would be entitled, "Art Link's North Dakota." This one would assess the cultural, recreational, landscape, and natural resources of western North Dakota. It would try to discriminate between landscapes that are perfectly fine for industrialization and those to which we would like to give special protection, if possible. The commission would create a cultural resources map of North Dakota, and attempt to designate historic trails and historical landscapes, Native American sacred sites, and viewsheds that it would be wise to protect, if we can. There would be special emphasis on the North Dakota Badlands—our principal natural treasure.

I'm not suggesting government regulation. There might have to be some of that, but I'm more interested in the commission trying to determine if a series of cooperative agreements could be worked out with industry to pay respect to and if possible work around places that we North Dakotans agree deserve special consideration.

The fifth white paper would be entitled, "Making the Most of the Boom." The commission would explore ways in which to save and distribute the surplus, with a particular emphasis on finding ways to invest the surplus in the future of North Dakota. If we sought to target our windfall in such a way as to tune North Dakota for the twenty-first century and beyond, to use the bonus money like an Archimedean lever to position North Dakota for maximum prosperity and the maximum possible quality of life for our children and grandchildren, what steps should we take?

Knowledge is power. The people of North Dakota don't have the information they need to know what is at stake in the energy corridor. We can either stand by and watch this gargantuan thing just happen to us—like a tsunami—or we can devote ourselves to managing the boom and insisting that there are values in North Dakota life greater than mere profit. *4/24/11*

THE DYNAMICS *of* NORTH DAKOTA:

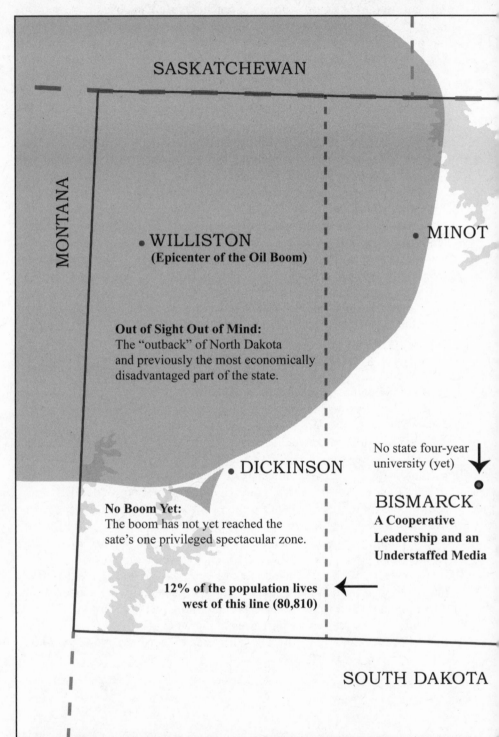

SASKATCHEWAN

MONTANA

WILLISTON
(Epicenter of the Oil Boom)

MINOT

Out of Sight Out of Mind:
The "outback" of North Dakota
and previously the most economically
disadvantaged part of the state.

No state four-year
university (yet)

DICKINSON

BISMARCK
A Cooperative
Leadership and an
Understaffed Media

No Boom Yet:
The boom has not yet reached the
sate's one privileged spectacular zone.

12% of the population lives
west of this line (80,810)

SOUTH DAKOTA

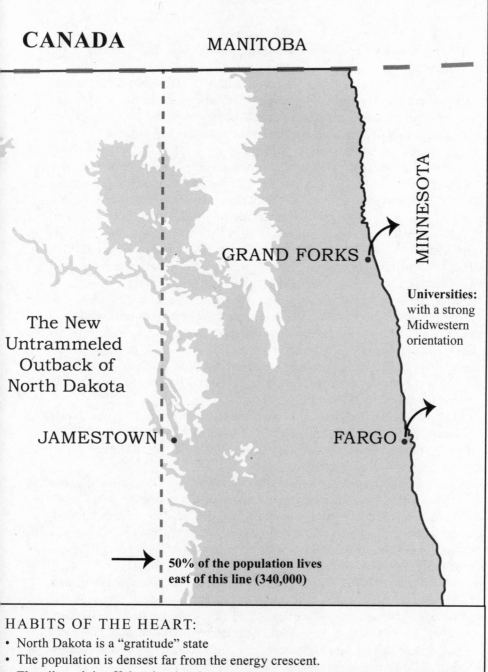

CANADA   MANITOBA

MINNESOTA

The New
Untrammeled
Outback of
North Dakota

GRAND FORKS

Universities:
with a strong
Midwestern
orientation

JAMESTOWN

FARGO

50% of the population lives
east of this line (340,000)

HABITS OF THE HEART:
• North Dakota is a "gratitude" state
• The population is densest far from the energy crescent.
• The oil patch is off the visual and even conceptual horizon of most North Dakotans
• The land in the oil patch is widely regarded as of marginal aesthetic importance

BEST FUTURE FOR THE NORTH DAKOTA BADLANDS:

WORKING RANCHES

What do we want the Badlands to look like fifty or one hundred years from now?

The Little Missouri River Valley is a broken landscape corridor that enters North Dakota modestly south of Marmarth and steadily widens and deepens and becomes more dramatic as it moves north toward Watford City and then suddenly turns east toward its confluence with the Missouri River proper.

By the time the Little Missouri Valley reaches the North Unit of Theodore Roosevelt National Park, it has learned to carve up the countryside so effectively that we can honestly speak of the "Grand Canyon of the Little Missouri."

Through the middle of this orgiastic, tumbled, god-blasted maze of bluffs and buttes and earth-buttresses runs the hapless, but vitally important Little Missouri River, which carries silt and water in equal proportions. Except for a few weeks (sometimes days) per year, the river is so water-starved that you can wade through it with nonchalance.

You can sit in it if you choose a gravelly patch. In fact, it's typically so shallow that you can lie down in it, feet-first downstream toward the Gulf of Mexico, and luxuriate in the laving of the warm sluggish current. One of my favorite activities in the world is to sit in the Little Missouri River fully clothed on a July or August afternoon hour after hour reading a book about the West.

You cannot do that in the Red. You cannot do that in the Mouse. You cannot do that in the Missouri.

The North Dakota Badlands are a magic landscape. They are North Dakota's "Montana." The appeal of the Badlands is that they are so different from the rest of North Dakota, which visitors tend to call "flat," but we prefer to call "rolling plains."

Tucked into the southwestern corner of a state that Eric Sevareid called a blank spot at the center of the North American continent is an exotic and self-contained region of "otherness," a wild, stark, magnificent landscape with a unique aura and a distinctive history that involves Theodore Roosevelt, an impulsive French nobleman and colorful, fiercely independent cattlemen. The whole package is irresistibly "dee-lightful."

It's ours. And there's a national park in the heart of it, commemorating three things: the intrinsic beauty of the Badlands; the fact that one of the greatest of all Americans lived here and acknowledged that this place, beyond all others, got under his skin; and the conservation philosophy that Roosevelt developed in part here, which led him to do more for wise-use conservation of our natural resources than any other president of the United States.

The Badlands have looked more or less the same for tens of thousands of years. They had perfected their eerie magic long before humans ever tip-toed from the safe forest and lake belts out onto the treeless and arid Great Plains, and they will look more or less the same when the human project finally withdraws. It's the short term that is problematic.

What makes the Badlands so attractive to the human spirit is that we have mostly left them alone. Mr. Jefferson's rectangular survey grid system of section line roads breaks down on the lip of the Little Missouri River Valley. That's always a sign that something wild is about to happen.

Almost none of the Badlands corridor is farmed. Where it is tilled, it really shouldn't be, at least from an aesthetic perspective. Bridges are rare: Marmarth, Medora, the Long X on U.S. 85, the once-Lost Bridge on ND 22. Good reason to be exceedingly skeptical of all new bridge (and low water crossing) proposals. The human population is sparse, dispersed and diminishing.

> "One of my favorite activities in the world is to sit in the Little Missouri River fully clothed on a July or August afternoon hour after hour reading a book about the West. "

There are only two towns on the Little Missouri River in North Dakota, and three more in the Badlands country. Medora (population ca. 100) gets most of the attention because of the musical and the pitchfork fondue, and because it is the portal of the national park, but Marmarth (population 140) is more enchanting, anarchic and improbable in its oxbow-oasis-at-the-end-of-the-world way. Killdeer (713), Grassy Butte (252) and the megalopolis Watford City (1,435) are wild and windswept Badlands towns. Think how much less interesting North Dakota would be without them.

As the twenty-first century begins, the left-aloneness of the North Dakota Badlands is seriously endangered. And when you cease to leave the Badlands mostly alone, the indefinable hypnotic appeal of the corridor begins to evaporate. We need to face the fact that the Badlands can be drilled, graded, bridged, ranchetted, paved, "improved," and even recre-ationed to death.

If you have seen the Bitterroot Valley in Montana, or the Flathead Lake region, or Telluride or Aspen in Colorado, you know what can happen when a spectacular landscape attracts too much improvement. In my view, we are already at tilt on oil development (rigs, thumping oil pumps, scoria roads, methane flares, pad and waste ponds) and there is clearly going to be much more of it in the years ahead. Hobby ranches and ridgeline homes make perfect sense to those who own them, but represent a kind of bane and scar to almost everyone else.

The best way to save the North Dakota Badlands is to "conserve" the existing for-profit family ranching system that has been in place since T.R. and the Marquis arrived in 1883. The working ranches in the Little

Missouri River Valley are widely diffused and tucked into the contours of the land. Their environmental impact is low. Their infrastructural "footprint" is lighter than that of any other economic activity.

Their mission is to produce good grass year after year—which means that ranchers essentially perpetuate how the Badlands would look if humans were not there at all. Under difficult conditions, today's ranchers continue to exemplify the rugged independence and self-reliance that has been the heart of the American frontier experience. They are a living, hardworking and colorful link to the romantic cowboy heritage of the grazing country of the American West.

I'd rather see heritage ranchers like Merle and Linda Clark of Marmarth or Robert and Ann Hanson of Amidon on the land than newcomers of any stamp. They know what we have and they know precisely how to keep it pristine. *2/28/09*

For the last couple of decades, environmentalists have been heavily critical of ranchers on the public lands. While I agree that we need to make sure that the public lands of the American West are not overgrazed, I believe that ranchers are far and away the best users and stewards of those lands, in close cooperation with sensible federal grazing policies. Emphasis: sensible.

GOOD NEWS AND BAD NEWS:

WE ARE LIVING ON MANNA

The oil well fire north of Arnegard was still burning when I wrote this, and I'm guessing it will still be burning when you read this. Once the big equipment owned by Boots & Coots Well Control International of Texas gets here, the fire will be put out and the well capped, and the first serious industrial accident of the Bakken boom will be over.

It won't be the last.

Boots & Coots will be back.

Enormous and unprecedented prosperity has come to North Dakota, the least likely of places to get rich quick. While the rest of America thrashes about in a sea of private anguish, public dispute and red ink, with 9.5 percent employment, North Dakota is at full employment (and begging for hospitality workers in the oil crescent), and our state budget surplus is spectacular-and growing.

What's happening on the streets of Madison, Wisconsin, is not happening here because we have money and they don't. The rest of the country, led by the crippled giant California, is agonizing about how to meet the fiscal demands of government services without increasing the tax burden on America's beleaguered citizenry. Out here on the plains, we have the luxury of smirking our way through debates about which insect best represents the sovereign state of North Dakota, because we are swimming in cash. The question here—as opposed to Wisconsin—is not whose lives do we have to damage with draconian budget cuts, but what kinds of increases can we sustain in the long run and who gets to sidle up to the trough first?

> "The hard-working and self-reliant people of North Dakota could not themselves dig up a single barrel of oil from the Bakken shale. There is no backhoe or auger for that. We have to import corporate giants from somewhere else to raise the oil. It need hardly be said that they don't engage in this colossal industrial activity on our behalf. They go wherever the money is. We plan to stay here forever."

I don't want to sound too—well, North Dakota—but it's important to remember that we are the accidental beneficiaries of a kind of funny money and it is temporary funny money at that. It is pure geological happenstance that western North Dakota sits on top of a gigantic oil field. The pioneers who proved up North Dakota between 1868 and 1930 came here to farm. They knew (or soon learned) that farming is just plain hard work, that it involved endless hours of arduous physical labor (plus milking), and that if you worked almost unbearably hard and never spent a nickel you might just die land rich (though still cash poor), and leave something to your children. It's difficult to think of any people in America who have earned their modest prosperity more honestly than we have—and in one of the most challenging climates on earth.

That heritage has made us a conservative people in the best sense of the term.

Now suddenly, the Saudi Arabia effect has set North Dakota on fire. An agrarian people has suddenly become a windfall people. An oil executive I had dinner with a year ago said, "There is nothing more dangerous than a sudden millionaire." The hard-working and self-reliant people of North Dakota could not themselves dig up a single barrel of oil from the Bakken shale. There is no backhoe or auger for that. We have to import corporate giants from somewhere else to raise the oil. It need hardly be said that they don't engage in this colossal industrial activity on our behalf. They go wherever the money is. We plan to stay here forever.

The sheer volume of industrial activity that is going to occur on North Dakota soil in the years and decades ahead is inevitably going to result in some oil fires, oil spills, vehicular accidents, workplace (and recreational) injuries, higher crime rates, a strain on social services, a higher cost of living, and a significant increase in violent deaths—some of them industrial fatalities and some of them homicides. The infrastructure of the seventeen oil counties is already shattered. We are going to have to spend vast amounts of money to make vastly larger amounts of money.

We are very fortunate to have this oil beneath our farms and ranches. Still, the Bakken boom is transforming much more than the landscape of North Dakota, and we need to go forward with open eyes.

Five times in the last two weeks—during a period of dangerously cold weather—I have seen individuals crouched at the end of the State Street (US 83) off ramp on I-94 holding cardboard signs explaining that they are stranded or homeless, and can you possibly help. This, in my experience, is unprecedented. In a coffee house the other day, three Hispanic men sat grumbling joyfully over their lattes about how they could not keep up with the demands on their construction company. They were moving back and forth between Spanish and excellent English. I was admiring their language skills and feeling ashamed to be so pathetically monolingual, when I looked over and saw two decidedly home grown, middle-aged women eyeing these men with deep distrust. When I made momentary eye contact with one of the Dakota matrons, she crossed her eyes fiercely and invited me nonverbally to join her in her disgust that "this sort of element" was moving into North Dakota. Meanwhile, wherever I go—restaurants, bars, gas stations, coffee shops—I see clusters of Alpha males from elsewhere talking in loud, boastful, aggressive tones about how they are going to get rich quick by doing this or selling that. When they talk about our quiet landscape from which they intend to extract "wealth beyond the dreams of avarice," they are frequently sarcastic and dismissive. I heard one fellow say, "Geez, why can't God put his oil in places you'd want to visit?"

For the first time, I have begun to lock my door.

I find that heartbreaking. *3/13/11*

I would have thought that this one—reminding us that we are a people who have a tradition of earning our modest wealth and being skeptical and conservative about "funny money" and accidental windfalls—would strike a chord with most North Dakotans.

The Goose is Laying Golden Eggs—
All that Glitters is Not Gold

Like almost everyone else, I regard the energy boom as a good thing for North Dakota. The state treasury is rolling in cash. The oil bonanza has immunized us from the most severe national recession since the 1930s. There are jobs for everyone who wishes to exert him or herself, and the boom has driven up wages for everyone. We've spent the last three decades wringing our hands about rural outmigration and rural decline. Now suddenly, people are moving to North Dakota by the thousands, and soon by the tens of thousands. Towns like Killdeer, Watford City, Stanley, Ross, Belfield, New Town, and Tioga are bursting with activity. Dickinson and Williston cannot build motels fast enough to keep up with the hectic demand. The North Dakota economy is now more diversified than ever before. And this boom, we are told, will be measured in decades rather than a few hectic years.

Three cheers!

Nobody wants to kill the goose that is laying such golden eggs for the people of North Dakota, but I feel increasing anxiety—even alarm—about how the Bakken and Three Forks-Sanish oil booms are transforming our landscape, our communities, our character, and our values.

Here are a few of my concerns:

—We must protect the most beautiful places in North Dakota from industrial blight. At minimum, we should have the discipline to protect the three units of Theodore Roosevelt National Park (and their viewsheds); the Killdeer Mountains; the still pristine sections of the greater Little Missouri River Valley; the confluence of the Missouri and the Yellowstone Rivers; places sacred to the Mandan, Hidatsa, and Arikara; and the I-94 corridor west of Dickinson to the Montana border. We cannot protect these places with sympathy alone. We have to negotiate development agreements with the oil industry to work around these state and national treasures. That's going to take creative and courageous leadership.

—I don't want the larger (the less spectacular) landscape of North Dakota to be ruined by rapid industrialization, either. The quadrant where all of this activity is taking place is far from the population and media centers of North Dakota. If every one of the 670,000 North Dakotans took a two-day drive through the energy corridor, I believe there would be widespread alarm coupled with an unmistakable people's call for an intelligent chastening of the boom. Western North Dakota is in the throes of an industrial revolution that is literally overwhelming our capacity to absorb it in a sane and orderly fashion. That oil's not going anywhere (see below, page 345).

In fact, it becomes more valuable with each passing day. We can afford to slow this pandemonium down.

—I don't want the basic character of North Dakota to be destroyed by the social distortions that gold rushes inevitably bring. We are a modest agrarian people tucked away in a backwater of North America. We have become the people we are because we have always earned our modest prosperity the hard way—by discipline, saving, and unstinting labor. Historically, North Dakota has been one of the most equalitarian and small-d democratic places in America. How do we hold on to all that is wonderful in the North Dakota character in the face of such glistering temptation? Suddenly, we have won the lottery. Beware.

—I worry about outdoor recreation, hunting, fishing, hiking, stargazing. I worry about our wildlife.

—I worry about the social impacts of the boom as much as about the impact on our landscape. You know the litany: drunk driving, meth and other drugs, vandalism, domestic violence, sexual assault, escort services, the strain on traditional county and local social infrastructure, including public education, health care, and welfare services.

—I want the oil boom to benefit all of North Dakota (not just one quadrant) and every North Dakotan, not just those who own mineral rights or have economic interests in the oil patch. We need to find creative ways to use the windfall to lay the economic and cultural foundation of the twenty-first century in North Dakota. In other words, we need to invest our surpluses wisely to prepare for the after-boom, to further diversity our economy, and to create the best-educated and most culturally remarkable state on the Great Plains. This is doable. We just need strong and creative leadership.

—I worry about the Saudi Arabia effect. Oil-rich places tend to make three colossal mistakes.

First, because the new revenues are sudden, vast, and accidental ("funny money," not really earned), governments begin to spend profligately. I share the concern of North Dakota's fiscal conservatives, including former Governor Ed Schafer, that if we keep raising the baseline of public expenditure (for education, government, infrastructure, etc.), we will soon reach an unsustainable plateau. Meanwhile, there is a tendency to give the people tax relief and to become more and more addicted to oil revenues. This is always a mistake.

Second, the real productivity of an oil-rich people tends to decline. It's a lot easier to make good money by sticking a straw into the ground than by milking cows, planting grains, selling insurance, or teaching children to read. Already we see that young people in North Dakota are abandoning college (and sometimes high school) to hurtle into the oil fields, where they can easily earn $75-140,000 per year driving a water truck. We will collectively pay a huge social price for this in the future.

> "We need to drive the energy boom, not be driven over a cliff by it. We need to manage the transformation of our landscape and our people, not just chase after the juggernaut with a broom and dustpan to clean up the messes. We need to insist upon smart development, not "drill baby drill.""

Third, an ugly class system tends to set in. Those who own oil (or oil rights) and those who control access to that oil usually set themselves up as the new masters of the community. They buy luxury cars, build McMansions, and gate themselves off from their "mere" fellow citizens. Meanwhile, the "have oil nots" find their rents jumping beyond their ability to pay, the costs of routine services skyrocket, and the quality of their lives (traffic congestion, dust, rudeness, vandalism, and serious crime) diminish dramatically.

We need to drive the energy boom, not be driven over a cliff by it. We need to manage the transformation of our landscape and our people, not just chase after the juggernaut with a broom and dustpan to clean up the messes. We need to insist upon smart development, not "drill baby drill."

We're not just another energy arena. We're North Dakota. *9/18/11*

I got some serious push-back on this column. But lots of thanks. Several regional newspapers reprinted it. One of the local developers, from Watford City, ND, actually thrust his finger at my chest at a public event and said, "This is our moment. This is the moment we have been waiting for all of our lives. We are not going to let anything get in the way of it." And turned and walked away.

In the Spirit of Janus:

Looking Back and Especially Forward

Welcome to 2012. This is the year we have to decide.

It's New Year's resolution time. Some people make them and some don't, but even those who don't make them tend to take some time at the end of the year to review their lives, their habits, their unrealized dreams, and resolve to address some issues—even if they are militant about not writing out formal resolutions.

2011 was the year the Bakken oil boom took possession of the state of North Dakota. When I moved back to North Dakota six years ago, it was still a kind of long shot, a pipe dream. By 2011, it was a massive on-the-ground phenomenon that had taken root thirteen thousand feet into our soil. The Bakken was easily the biggest story of the year 2011, the dominant narrative of North Dakota both at home and in the national consciousness. The Bakken oil boom is already, in its infancy, one of the biggest stories in North Dakota history, joining the Homestead Act, the transcontinental railroads and the Dust Bowl as events that changed this place forever. If we are not very careful, when the history of North Dakota is written in the year 2500, the story will look something like this: "From statehood in 1889 until about the millennium, North Dakota was a quiet farm state. After two little starter oil booms in the 1950s and 1980s, at the beginning of the twenty-first century new technologies permitted an oil extraction phenomenon so gargantuan that when it ended thirty years later, western North Dakota had been transformed into an industrial park. The population of the state had risen to nearly a million people. North Dakota had become the richest state per capita, but at a social, recreational and environmental cost that put unprecedented pressures on the traditional values of what had once been the nation's most agrarian place."

This is the year in which we have to decide if we are going to manage and chasten the Bakken oil boom or just shrug our shoulders and let it sweep over us no matter what it does to the land, the identity, and the character of North Dakota. Up until now we have been so grateful for the boom—for the jobs it has provided, the prosperity, the budget surplus, the sense of state renewal and optimism—that we have mostly just looked on and nodded. But things have begun to change. You can sense it more than you can actually measure it, but in the course of the last few months, the people of North Dakota, and especially western North Dakota, have begun to worry that the boom is getting away from us, that it is too much, too fast, too ruthless, too "costly," and that there is a significant chance that it is going to wreck that which we love.

I believe it is still possible to tame and target the boom, without in any way jeopardizing its mighty benefits to the people of North Dakota (and American energy independence). I believe it is still possible for us to slow it down a bit, savor it a little, and build in some protections for those who are not beneficiaries of the biggest oil rush in North America: hunters, elderly people on fixed incomes, surface owners who do not own their mineral rights, North Dakotans who have to use the same roads that have been commandeered for industrial traffic, lovers of the Badlands, and average citizens who want nothing more than safe, civil and orderly communities in which to live.

We need leadership. If it is already coming from the top down, we need to see it and hear it step up more to the bully pulpit, and assure us that all will be well. The people have legitimate concerns. Those concerns need to be addressed in candor by our elected representatives. The sense that most North Dakotans have is that our state government has essentially adopted the role of industrial cheerleader for the extraction economy, that it is working harder to strew roses before the path of the oil industry than it is to protect the long-term interests of the people of North Dakota. It may be an unfair assessment, but it is very widely held. If, on the contrary, the leadership is going to come from the people—if they are going to demand that state government chasten the boom and restrain the kinds of destructive excesses that are otherwise inevitable—2012 is the year in which we are going to have to assert ourselves. It is almost, but not quite, too late. A year from now, the cries of anguish from Watford City, Williston, Medora, Belfield, Killdeer, Stanley, Tioga, Ray, and Dickinson are going to be shrill.

The last thing I ever heard former North Dakota Gov. Art Link say, a few days before his death on June 1, 2010, was, "That oil is not going anywhere. We don't need to be in any hurry to bring it to the surface. It gets more valuable every day. We can afford to take some time in developing the field, to protect the land and the people of North Dakota."

So here's my New Year's resolution, and one I ask each of you to make. Everyone who cares about North Dakota needs to carve out the time in the first months of 2012 to drive around the oil patch for a day or two. Here's the route I recommend: Start in Minot. Drive west on US Highway 2 to Stanley and Ross.

> "I believe it is still possible for us to slow it down a bit, savor it a little, and build in some protections for those who are not beneficiaries of the biggest oil rush on the North American continent: hunters, elderly people on fixed incomes, surface owners who do not own their mineral rights, North Dakotans who have to use the same roads that have been commandeered for industrial traffic, lovers of the badlands, average citizens who want nothing more than safe, civil, and orderly communities in which to live."

Then detour up N.D. Highway 40 to Tioga and work your way west to Ray. Drop down U.S. Highway 85 to Williston, where you will try to have lunch. Then drive south through Alexander to Watford City, and over to Mandaree by way of N.D. Highway 23. When you reach "Lost Bridge" on N.D. Highway 22, take a good look around, for late in 2011 the government of North Dakota cheerfully authorized a large oil field right smack in that fabulous stretch of the Little Missouri Badlands. Drive through Killdeer, once the best little cowboy town in North Dakota, and then finish your trek in front of the new Theodore Roosevelt statue on the grounds of the Stark County Courthouse.

Ask yourself how Roosevelt would manage the boom.

2012 is the year we North Dakotans are going to decide whom we intend to be in the twenty-first century. *1/1/12*

A Reluctant Endorsement
for the Keystone Pipeline

For four or five months I have been trying to make sense of the Keystone Pipeline controversy. The proposed $7 billion, 1,700-mile pipeline would transport oil from Hardesty, Alberta, to Houston and Port Arthur, Texas. The pipeline would not cross the state of North Dakota, but it would benefit North Dakota by providing an efficient and safe method of transporting oil from the Bakken oil field to distant refineries.

North Dakota currently ranks fourth in US oil production (after Texas, Alaska, and California), and is likely to rank third or even second before long. We are producing more than five hundred thousand barrels of oil per day. Virtually all of that oil has to go somewhere else to be refined. Getting it out of North Dakota is a serious logistical problem. The Keystone Pipeline would approach the border of North Dakota at Baker, Montana, just over from Marmarth. An access facility at Baker would serve as an on ramp for Bakken oil.

The vast quantities of oil being extracted from beneath the prairie of western North Dakota can find their way to refineries by one of three transportation systems: railroads, highway trucks, or pipelines. No system is entirely immune to industrial accidents (oil spills), but a well-built underground pipeline is without question the safest and most reliable method of transporting oil, and the one that puts the least pressure on the social structure of North Dakota, as well as its existing infrastructure.

The national (and indeed international) controversy about the Keystone Pipeline has little to do with North Dakota. A list of environmental and landowner organizations too impressive to be ignored opposes the Keystone project, as well as somewhere between fifty and one hundred members of Congress. The Obama administration has serious doubts about the wisdom of the pipeline and is attempting to slow down the process. The president's decision (last Wednesday) to reject the current pipeline proposal is not the end of the story. Obama made it clear that TransCanada is welcome to return with a revised proposal that, among other things, will be re-routed to protect the sandhills of western Nebraska. If the president is re-elected in 2012, I believe he will reluctantly approve the pipeline—while expressing his serious misgivings at the same time.

> "In an increasingly dangerous world, where the remaining large deposits of conventional oil seem to lie under unstable or unfriendly regimes (Iran, Iraq, Saudi Arabia, Russia, Venezuela, Nigeria), knowing that Canada has the second or third largest oil reserves in the world should be a source of deep comfort to the people of the United States, even if tar sands oil is not ideal from an environmental point of view. Canada is our best friend in the world. It may be that the Monroe Doctrine is going to become even more important in the twenty-first century than it was in the nineteenth."

The arguments of pipeline opponents move from the specific to the general. The pipeline may threaten wetlands and wildlife habitats along its path. It will transect seventy rivers and streams, including the Yellowstone, the Missouri, the Platte, and the Arkansas. It will cross (or now perhaps skirt) the fabulous and fragile sand hills of Nebraska, and it will cross the Ogallala Aquifer, the vast underground lake underlying eight Great Plains States. The Ogallala supplies 30 percent of the nation's irrigation water and provides domestic water to more than two million people. A serious oil spill could be catastrophic.

Those are just the siting and spill issues.

Landowners in Nebraska have also complained about the high-handedness of TransCanada, which has allegedly threatened to use eminent domain to secure the pipeline's path if farmers and ranchers do not cooperate in leasing the right of way.

The larger issue has to do with our future relationship to carbon. Pipeline opponents, led by environmental essayist and activist William McKibben, argue that building the Keystone Pipeline endorses and indeed deepens our addiction to the carbon economy at a time when the United States should be doing everything in our power to develop a new energy paradigm that is not so harmful to the health of the Earth. If we are serious about addressing the problem of global climate change, serious about reducing the carbon "footprint" of the industrial nations of the world, we should be concentrating our ingenuity into developing alternative energy sources rather than "rewarding" a particularly dirty carbon source—the Alberta tar sands.

The rap against the tar sands is that they are extremely expensive to exploit and that the oil they release is "dirty fuel," producing two or three times more carbon emissions than conventional oil, plus additional toxins. If we are serious about moving toward a lighter industrial footprint and a greener civilization, opponents say, the Keystone Pipeline is precisely the sort of "energy solution" we should reject. Pipeline opponents argue that even those who are skeptical about global climate change should reject the Keystone project simply because the tar sands are such an expensive, cost-ineffective, and toxic source of oil.

I see the merits of the arguments on both sides of the Keystone issue. I have been reading everything I can get my hands on, talking with everyone I know (ad nauseam), and wrestling with the dilemma we all find ourselves in. There is no clear path to an enlightened future.

Still, on balance, I think we should hold our noses and build the thing. Here's why.

Two things are absolutely certain. First, Canada is going to continue to develop the Alberta Tar Sands whether we approve the pipeline or not, and nothing the United States can do would prevent that development. Second, Alberta's oil is going somewhere. If it doesn't pass through the Keystone Pipeline to refineries in the United States, it is going to flow toward the west coast of Canada, where it will be transported to China. In other words, we cannot "save the planet" by refusing to authorize the pipeline. We just give China a strategic advantage at the beginning of a century in which that rising nation of 1.3 billion consumers is going to be our principal international rival and antagonist. From a geopolitical perspective, that makes no sense. It may turn out to be a colossal mistake.

Furthermore, whether we like to admit it or not, we continue to be hopelessly addicted to oil (and carbon generally), and no viable green alternative is yet in sight. The United States already gets 20 percent of its oil from Canada. That number is likely to rise. In an increasingly dangerous world, where the remaining large deposits of conventional oil seem to lie under unstable or unfriendly regimes (Iran, Iraq, Saudi Arabia, Russia, Venezuela, Nigeria), knowing that Canada has the second or third largest oil reserves in the world should be a source of deep comfort to the people of the United States, even if tar sands oil is not ideal from an environmental point of view. Canada is our best friend in the world. It may be that the Monroe Doctrine is going to become even more important in the twenty-first century than it was in the nineteenth. The international consternation over Iran's threat to close the Straits of Hormuz reminds us of just how fragile the West's oil supply continues to be.

Besides, from a purely selfish point of view, the Keystone Pipeline is a godsend to North Dakota at a time when our infrastructure is being overwhelmed by oil production. *1/22/12*

I knew I would be criticized for writing this, but I had no idea how vicious some of it would be. The Keystone Pipeline has become a barometric measure of where you stand on global warming and a post-carbon future in the world's energy supply. Many of my friends expressed deep disappointment in me, and plenty of others denounced me in highly personal terms. Some called me a fraud, a stooge for industry, a sell-out, an idiot. I wrote what I think sensible and sane, but tried to make the case for the other side, too. If I had written to say that we should not build the pipeline, I would have expressed the same reluctance. I regard this as a no-win situation. Things to remember: Canada has an energy policy. Canada is complying with the Kyoto accord, which the United States refused to sign. Not a single American soldier is needed to keep the oil flowing from Alberta, but we have fought at least two, maybe three, resource wars in the Middle East to keep that oil flowing towards us.

At the same time, I am not at all sure that I am right about the Keystone. In the best of all possible worlds, we would not need to develop the tar sands. It is not the most desirable oil in the world, and I am a firm believer that humans are causing global climate distortions that threaten the stability of the planet. It seems to me that wisdom is having the capacity to doubt your "certitudes," and to realize that you may be full of beans about things you think you know.

My best sense, as I try to look at the Keystone through a geopolitical (rather than an environmental) lens, is that sometime around 2075, when China China China is the core of our national anxiety, we are going to thank God that we had the foresight to build the Keystone Pipeline.

But I may be full of beans.

WHEN THE LANDSCAPE
IS QUIET AGAIN

We do not want to halt progress

We do not plan to be selfish and say "North Dakota will not share its
energy resources."

No, we simply want to insure the most efficient and environmentally
sound method of utilizing our precious coal and water resources for the
benefit of the broadest number of people possible.

And when we are through with that
and the landscape is quiet again,

When the draglines, the blasting rigs, the power shovels and the huge
gondolas cease to rip and roar!

And when the last bulldozer has pushed the last spoil pile into place,

And the last patch of barren earth has been seeded to grass or grain,

Let those who follow and repopulate the land be able to say,

Our grandparents did their job well.

The land is as good and, in some cases, better than before.

Only if they can say this will we be worthy of the rich heritage of our
land and its resources.

—Governor Arthur A Link, Mandan, ND *October 11, 1973*

We do not want to halt progress.
We do not plan to be selfish and say
"North Dakota will not share its energy resources."
No . . . we simply want to insure
the most efficient and environmentally sound method of
utilizing our precious coal and water resources for the
benefit of the broadest number of people possible.

And when we are through with that
and the landscape is quiet again ---
when the draglines, the blasting rigs,
the power shovels and the huge gondolas,
cease to rip and roar:

And when the last bulldozer has pushed
the last spoil pile into place,
and the last patch of barren earth has been seeded to grass or grain.

Let those who follow and repopulate the land be able to say
Our predecessors did their job well.
This land is as good and
in some ways,
better than before.
Only if they can say this will we be worthy of the rich heritage of
our land and its resources.

Arthur A. Link
Governor - 1973-81

ACKNOWLEDGEMENTS

This book would not exist if it were not for the great Sheila Schafer. For several years she has suggested that I publish a collection of my newspaper columns. Sheila (shy-la) is one of my favorite people on earth. She has been one of my most faithful readers, and she is never afraid to tell me when I am full of beans. When I printed out all of my columns (351 as of today), I asked her to divide them into three piles: Yes, No, and Maybe. She chose. Sheila and I share a deep love of North Dakota, though we often express it in different ways. It would have been worth moving home to North Dakota if only to have Sheila in my life. Although she is now eighty-seven years old, and not in perfect health, she is always the youngest person in every room she enters. A few days ago, I called to check up on her. She said, "I cannot talk right now. I've got fifteen more minutes on the treadmill." We still disagree about whether Theodore Roosevelt had a soft spot in his heart for murderers, so long as they were men of the West rather than urban thugs. I know I have a soft spot for Sheila. Death has come for her three times since I met her, and each time she has told him to go jump in the lake. My father, whom I adored, had his bags packed.

I would not be in North Dakota at this point in my life had it not been for Jim Fuglie, one of my oldest and dearest friends. At the last Thanksgiving of my mentor Everett C. Albers's life, at my mother's house in Dickinson, Jim said to me the wisest thing I ever heard. I was living in Nevada at the time. He said, "When you know where you want to be, the rest will follow." Jim never says an uninteresting thing. His Thanksgiving koan broke a logjam of indecision. That's Jim. He's my favorite North Dakota problem solver. I am immensely grateful for his friendship. If I could be on Bullion Butte with anyone on earth, it would always be with Jim.

When I was formulating my plans to move back to North Dakota after a quarter century elsewhere, I wrote to Ken Rogers to ask if the *Bismarck Tribune* might be willing to let me write a weekly newspaper column. I'd never done anything like this in my life. Ken checked with his publisher and senior editors and said the *Tribune* would publish me on Sundays in the Dakota section. That was more than six years ago. Throughout that time Ken has been my editor and my protector, and he has talked me down from 1,350 words per column to an ironclad 900, the way you talk someone down from the window ledge on the 57th floor of the Chrysler Building. I am immensely grateful. I have told him many times that writing for the *Bismarck Tribune* has been one of the greatest satisfactions of my life. It has enabled me to get to know North Dakota and North Dakotans in a way that would have been impossible without this weekly forum for observing this place and trying to make sense of the future.

It may seem ironic that I wish to thank Leonard Baenan of Mandan, since he nearly caused me to quit before I even got started. A few days after my first column appeared, in October 2005, Mr. Baenan, whom I had never met, wrote a nasty letter to the editor of the *Tribune*, wondering why they were wasting their space printing my thoughts. The gist of the letter was that Leonard wanted me to know that nobody was particularly eager to hear from me, and who did I think I was to presume that I had something interesting to say? I was so upset by his letter that I seriously considered packing it in. That's only happened twice in almost six years, but the first time was truly devastating. Perhaps I had been away too long. Mr. Baenan and I later made our peace and became pen pals, but not before I had a long night of the soul. I am, in fact, deeply indebted to him. He taught me two invaluable lessons. First, that no matter how hard I tried to please, there always would be critics and detractors. It comes with the territory. Second, that it was extremely important that I try to envision the readers of my columns while I wrote them; in other words, to try to read what I write through their eyes, and to make sure that I make my point clearly, if possible, in a way that cannot be misunderstood as something else. Leonard taught me that I was not writing my newspaper column for myself but for readers of the *Bismarck Tribune*. In other words, Leonard taught me that it is a mistake to write whatever I happen to think in whatever style seems most useful without trying to assess how it will be received by someone who doesn't know me, who brings a different background or a different sensibility to the Sunday paper. Had I not figured that out, I would have gone silent—voluntarily or at the request of the *Tribune*—long, long ago.

I want also to thank the two women who wrote me my favorite "fan letters." They were hand-written, and they came in the mail. One said: "Dear Mr. Jenkinson, Thank you for the columns you write in the Bismarck Tribune. I look forward every Sunday to reading what you write. I always take a deep breath when I begin because they are so damn long. But I am never sorry."

The other letter came from an elderly woman who lives in a care facility across town. She said, "Mr. Jenkinson, I am writing to invite you to marry me so that I can go along on the wonderful adventures you write about in the Bismarck Tribune. But I want you to hurry, because I am 93 years old." There is such a thing as pure delight.

There is no way I can ever thank my friend Melanie Carvell enough. Melanie is the director of the Women's Health Center in Bismarck. She is also a physical therapist. And she is an outstanding triathlete who has competed all over the world. She makes the finest bean hot dish on earth. I call it "Bean Thing," which she does not much appreciate. Melanie is the best person I have ever known. Because she's a gifted athlete and I am Mr. Schlump, I had never heard of her before I moved back to North Dakota.

Like everyone else, I had heard of the legendary Carvells of Mott. I met Peggy Carvell when I was in college, and I knew Kevin Carvell, for many years the eastern North Dakota director for US Senator Byron Dorgan, and before that a journalist. In early 2006, I wrote a column about a trip I took to Disney World with my mother and daughter. It was entitled, "Mamas, Don't Let Your Children Grow Up to Be Cheerleaders," and it made a good deal of fun of the fifty thousand obnoxious high school cheerleaders we ran into at Disney World that week. Melanie wrote gently to rebuke me for satirizing cheerleading, which, she said, is excellent for character building and the development of teamwork skills. That's Melanie. She always makes Pollyanna look like Imelda Marcos with facial piercings and Goth tattoos. Thus began a friendship that has made all the difference in my life. Melanie and her husband Charles have made my life in North Dakota happier and more satisfying in so many ways. If there were only one North Dakotan, I would nominate Melanie. She represents the very best of us.

Dr. Larry Skogen invited me to lunch shortly after he returned to North Dakota to take up his post as the president of Bismarck State College. We moved back home to Dakota at about the same time. He said he was impressed with a column in which I said there are conversations we North Dakotans need to have with each other, whether we want to or not, and that we should not just blunder into the future, but make enlightened choices about who we want to be and what we choose to value in the twenty first century. We had lunch at the Peacock Alley. We instantly became good friends. We have traveled the West together. If we were transplanted back to 1804, he would have lasted no more than three hours on the Lewis and Clark Expedition, and I probably would have lasted less than a week. But at least I would not have whined. Larry is what is technically known as a "weenie" when it comes to mosquitoes and solar radiation, snow, rain, sleet, and dark of night, or clutter of any sort, but he is a natural leader and a man of great innovation, not to mention a serious historian of the American West. We lecture together at Bismarck State College, where I am happy to be his straight man. He's a gifted college president and one of the best things that have happened in Bismarck-Mandan in recent years. His optimism and his conviction that the future is a story we can write in any way we choose has given me the confidence to keep raising questions about North Dakota as we pass from the agrarian past to an uncertain, but extremely promising future.

I want to thank my mother Mil Jenkinson for being such a good sport. I write about her from time to time, partly because she is such a wonderful companion in my life, one of my closest friends, and a fellow adventurer; and partly because she is good column fodder. In the words of our mutual hero Huck Finn, I have told the truth about her—mostly. She speaks in colorful phrases, and she is game for just about any improbable adventure. I am so fortunate to have her in my life. In fact, I cannot imagine my life without her.

We travel together. We talk about everything. We laugh a lot whenever we are together. I am so glad I inherited her genes and outlook. If I could order up any mother in the world, from 1-800-MAMA, it would always be her.

Thanks, too, to my administrative assistant Nancy Franke. She lives in the state of Washington, but without her I would not be able to function. We are almost never in the same zip code, which is good, for she would undoubtedly whup me if she could get her hands on me. She handles the calendar, which is like trying to push one hundred snakes to Marmarth in a grocery cart. Given my incessant travels, some of them outside the territorial limits of the United States, Nancy has been called on many times to find an electronic path between my laptop and Ken Rogers's desk at the *Bismarck Tribune*. She has never failed. Without her I'd be lost. With her, I'm still pretty lost, but the fault is not hers.

In the course of my time as a *Tribune* contributor, I have only once written my column by hand. When I was making a 173-mile solo hike from Marmarth (my favorite North Dakota place) to Juniper Campground in the North Unit of Theodore Roosevelt National Park, I stopped at Sully Creek State Park south of Medora at about the halfway point of my journey. It was the hottest summer in North Dakota history. Charles and Melanie Carvell met me there. They brought fresh fruit salad and cold sodas, which I devoured like a character out of a Jack London story. I handed my hand-written copy to Charles. He typed it and took a memory card of some sort to Ken Rogers at the *Tribune*. Other than that, I have literally filed all of my other columns by way of email. I have been inside the offices of the *Bismarck Tribune* only twice, once on unrelated business. I guess I owe Al Gore some heartfelt thanks.

There are a handful of people I would like to throttle, frankly, but they shall remain nameless. I've had a little trouble with a few little people with cramped souls and free-floating aggressions. In the course of the last five years I have learned a good deal about how to avoid getting entangled in the lives of bitter, unsleeping people who are sporting for a fight. They are legion. I have been lucky to avoid most of them.

I feel open contempt for the cowards of the *Tribune*'s anonymous blog site, who prefer name-calling to rational argumentation. I expose myself fifty-two times a year, at considerable length, accompanied by a photograph of my face, and I always put my name to whatever I write. There is some danger in this. I try always to show respect for opinions different from my own. My email address is printed on the bottom of every column. My phone number is published in the phone book. Instead of addressing me like mature adults, these folks dash off a vicious sentence or two, often ungrammatical, usually ignorant of the basic facts of the case, and then hide behind a curtain of electronic anonymity. If they had to sign their names to the verbal assaults they make on me and anyone else who sees the world differently, they wouldn't dare post them. If they had to walk through the door of the *Bismarck Tribune* to deliver their venomous blather, they wouldn't dare write what they write. I don't usually read what they spew forth, and I never respond to anonymous anything. If they write to me personally, I always respond with what Jefferson called "artificial good humor." I take criticism pretty well. I don't take anonymous hate mail well at all.

My friend Deb Dragseth of Dickinson State University has read each of my columns in advance and served as a kind of weekly reality check for me. A handful of far flung friends, including Annie and Wes Hall, Joni Kinsey, Stacy Cordery, Sherry Manning, and Robbie and Joanne Bock, read my columns as they come off my computer and provide excellent advice and feedback. I wish to give special thanks to Valerie Naylor, who has taken me on some of these adventures and who always reads what I write with thoughtfulness and helpful suggestions.

Most of all, I want to thank all of you for taking the time to read what I write. You have no idea how much pure joy that gives me. My goal is to be as great an advocate of North Dakota as this place has ever seen. I aspire to be a cultural leader as well as a commentator. I want the people of North Dakota to take our homeland more seriously, to develop a greater spirit of place, and to preserve this low-contoured windswept place as if it were paradise. Because it is paradise. I don't actually know how many people read what I write, and I certainly don't exaggerate my influence, which I'm pretty certain is close to negligible. Still, I love writing my newspaper column, and I believe it is the best body of work I have ever undertaken. The cumulative result is a sustained love song to North Dakota. I don't know anyone who has written about our seasons and our counterintuitive beauties more. Without readers like you, I would not have written all these words, and the words I would have written instead would have been about something much less important than North Dakota. So thank you. If you stopped reading my words, Ken would have to cut me loose.

Thanks to Lillian Crook, Christine Hogan, Joe Satrom, Stephenie Ambrose Tubbs, Suzanne Russ, Richard McCallum, Richard Brauhn, David Borlaug, and Beverly Everett. I owe David Borlaug special thanks. He has done more than I deserve to put scaffolding under some of my dreams. Thanks to Wendy and Arik Spencer (though he continues to evade his waterfall promise), Kevin Kirkey, Rhonda Smith, Nancy Krebsbach, and Ethel Mart.

I want to single out my friend Sarah Trandahl for special thanks. This book has been much more challenging than it seemed when we began, and Sarah has seen it through the process with great skill and even greater patience and perseverance. In a project like this, there is always someone who makes the difference. Sarah has cheerfully played that role.

Thanks to the artist Leon Basler, whose drawings grace the pages of this book. I first met Leon at a Lewis & Clark event, where his simple illustrations of buttes won my admiration. When I moved into my house in north Bismarck,

Leon created a painting of the Little Missouri River as it winds around Bullion Butte. It has pride of place above my fireplace. He agreed to make a series of very simple line drawings for this book. I love them.

Finally, very special thanks to my wonderful friend Kimberly Jondahl. Although she is as busy as anyone I know, she has stepped in to help see a number of my projects through to completion. Frankly, some of them would never have seen daylight without her patient and thorough labors. Kim is my fellow author. I hope to join her some day as the writer of a banned book! She has cleaned out the Augean stables of my files on a number of occasions. She has to endure my organized chaos and I have to endure her very weak puns.

I love North Dakota with all of my heart, and never wrote a sentence about Nevada or Colorado or even Minnesota during my lives there.

I'm so glad to be home.

—Clay Jenkinson

BOOKS CITED BY CLAY IN HIS COLUMNS

An occasionally annotated bibliography

The Analects of Confucius.

Bhagavad Gita. This book has a special place in my life. When I was at the University of Minnesota, I considered taking courses in Sanskrit. My Greek professor advised against. If you work hard at it, he said, you might just read the bulk of ancient Greek literature in a lifetime. But you can never read more than a fraction of the unbelievable mass of Sanskrit literature. Read what little you wish in translation.

The Bible. I continue to prefer the cadences of the King James Version (1611) even though it is not as accurate as the New Revised Standard Version. When I lived on a farm in Kansas, I read the book of John in koine Greek with a Lutheran preacher friend named Dave. I'm fond of the Jerusalem Bible, too. When I quote the Bible in my column, I tend to use the King James Version unless I have some specific reason for preferring a different phraseology or translation.

The Book of Mormon. 1830. If you want to read an amazing book, try *The Mormon Murders: A True Story of Greed, Forgery, Deceit, & Death* by Steven Naifeh and Gregory White Smith. 1992. A lapsed Mormon named Mark Hofmann had a short but amazing run as maybe the greatest forgery artist in human history.

Koran.

Edward Abbey. *Desert Solitaire: A Season in the Wilderness.* 1868. Abbey is a kind of countercultural guru of the environmental movement. This is the only one of his books that I love, though his essay, "Down the River with Henry Thoreau" is amazing.

Aeschylus. *The Oresteia.*

Louisa May Alcott. *Little Women.* 1868-1869.

Sherman Alexie. *Reservation Blues.* 1995.

Alexie. *The Toughest Indian in the World.* 2000.

Stephen Ambrose. *Undaunted Courage: Meriwether Lewis, Thomas Jefferson, and the Opening of the American West.* 1996.

Rick Atkinson. *Crusade: The Untold Story of the Persian Gulf War.* 1993. You cannot read this book without realizing something about our capacity to bring another nation to its knees, to knock out, more or less at will, not just the military infrastructure of another sovereign nation, but its capacity to function in purely civilian terms. It's breathtaking. It would seem to me that what we did in 1991 and again in 2003 is in direct violation with the Geneva Conventions. Certainly it violates any notion of a Jeffersonian republic.

St. Augustine. *City of God.*

St. Augustine. *Confessions.*

Jane Austen. *Emma.* 1815.

Austen. *Mansfield Park.* 1814.

Austen. *Northanger Abbey.* 1818.

Austen. *Persuasion.* 1818.

Austen. *Pride and Prejudice.* 1813. One of my daughter's favorite books. Mine, too.

Austen. *Sense and Sensibility.* 1811. This is my favorite of Austen's novels.

Mary Austin. *Land of Little Rain.* 1903.

Nicholson Baker. *The Size of Thoughts: Essays & Other Lumber.* 1997. I first read Baker's *Vox* back during the Monica Lewinski years. That's not much of a novel, but I fell in love with Baker's work. Nothing he writes is uninteresting. He's a miniaturist. One of my favorite Baker essays is about books as furniture.

Jeremy Bernstein. *Oppenheimer: Portrait of an Enigma.* 2004. This is not my favorite book about Oppenheimer, but it is the one that introduced me to the photography of Philippe Halsman.

Kai Bird and Martin Sherwin. *American Prometheus: The Triumph and Tragedy of J. Robert Oppenheimer.* 2005. This book won the Pulitzer Prize. It's an amazing biography of a great and troubled man. Oppenheimer made many mistakes in the course of his remarkable life, but he did not deserve the way he was treated by the Cold Warriors in the mid-1950s.

James Boswell. *The Life of Dr. Samuel Johnson.* 1791. I still have the first copy of the *Life of Johnson* I ever owned and read. It's a paperback abridgement. One of my favorite professors, Robert Moore, of the University of Minnesota, insisted that I should read it over the summer of my sophomore year. I did. I have read it four or five times since, each time with unlimited joy. It's regarded as the finest biography of the English language.

Rachel Calof. *Rachel Calof's Story: Jewish Homesteader on the Northern Plains.* 1995. This is the Little House stories on steroids, or Laura Ingalls Wilder noir. One of the most fascinating homestead accounts ever written.

Willa Cather. *My Antonia.* 1918. When Mr. Shimerda says, "Teach, teach my Antonia," I invariably burst into tears. Although this may be the greatest Great Plains work of fiction, I hate the ending. I'm not even slightly interested in the life of Jim Burden. I don't want to see Antonia wrinkled and toothless. There is, I think, something patronizing about Cather's ending.

Elizabeth Cook-Lynn. *Aurelia: A Crow Creek Trilogy.* 1999. Ms. Cook-Lynn came to Bismarck to speak at our Missouri River humanities symposium at the beginning of the Lewis & Clark bicentennial. She was angry and amazing.

Jared Diamond. *Guns, Germs, and Steel: The Fates of Human Societies.* 1998.

Vine Deloria, Jr. *God is Red.* 1973.

Deloria, Jr. *Custer Died for Your Sins: An Indian Manifesto.* 1969.

Raymond Demallie. *The Sixth Grandfather: Black Elk's Teachings Given to John G. Neihardt.* 1986. If it is possible to be even more interesting than *Black Elk Speaks*, this is that book.

Charles Dickens. *Bleak House.* 1852-1853. It's hard to say which is Dickens' greatest novel. One of my professors at Oxford, asked about this very question, said, "It depends on which one you have read last." I have not read all of Dickens, but my hierarchy runs *Great Expectations, Pickwick Papers, Bleak House, David Copperfield* . . . I do not like *A Christmas Carol* much at all. Unfortunately, it is most people's Dickens, unless they were forced to read *A Tale of Two Cities* in high school.

Dickens. *Great Expectations.* 1860-1861. My daughter has read this classic. Long ago I taught it. The book, more than any other in Dickens, lends itself to a Freudian analysis.

John Donne. *Biathanatos.* 1608. This is not a book for the faint of heart. But it is immensely important in the history of western civilization's response to suicide. The Romans honored heroic suicide. Christian society honored martyrdom but not suicide. Donne regarded martyrdom as a *kind of suicide.* He even argued, perhaps blasphemously, that Jesus was a holy suicide who *gave up the ghost* on the cross.

Louise Erdrich. *The Beet Queen.* 1986.

Erdrich. *Love Medicine.* 1984.

Erdrich. *The Master Butchers Singing Club.* 2003.

Erdrich. *The Painted Drum.* 2005. North Dakota should give Erdrich the Rough Rider Award—now! She is our greatest living writer.

Erdrich. *Tracks.* 1988.

Edward Fitzgerald. *The Rubaiyat of Omar Khayyam.* 1947.

F. Scott Fitzgerald. *The Great Gatsby.* 1925.

James W. Foley. *The Voices of Song.* 1916.

Karen Joy Fowler. *The Jane Austen Book Club.* 2004.

Hamlin Garland. *A Son of the Middle Border*. 1917. This is one of the two greatest plains autobiographies. Garland had South Dakota roots. He was a friend of Theodore Roosevelt. He is best known for his collection of short stories, *Main Traveled Roads*. The other great autobiography is Eric Sevareid's *Not So Wild a Dream*. Sevareid spent his first years in Velva, North Dakota.

Edward Gibbon. *The History of the Decline and Fall of the Roman Empire*. 1776. Nobody reads "the greatest book of the eighteenth century" anymore. The first volume was published in the same year as the Declaration of Independence.

Philippe Halsman. *Philippe Halsman's Jump Book*. 1959. It's worth it just to see Richard Nixon jump.

David Freeman Hawke. *Those Tremendous Mountains: The Story of the Lewis and Clark Expedition*. 1980. This is the book that started me down a long path in trying to make sense of Lewis and Clark. Until I read it, I was unaware that Lewis had died just three years after the expedition's return, and almost certainly by suicide. I have been trying to make sense of his suicide ever since.

Adolf Hitler. *Mein Kampf*. 1925. I have never read it. I have read in it and on a handful of occasions I have tried to make a run at it. It's a pretty awful book in a range of ways. But one of my heroes, William L. Shirer, said that the big mistake we made was not reading it, because in it Hitler spelled out his plans, including the final solution. Hitler's original title was *Four and a Half Years of Struggle against Lies, Stupidity and Cowardice*. His publisher forced the change of title. I remember reading (somewhere) that there were several hundred thousand grammatical issues in the original manuscript.

Homer. *The Odyssey*. In the handful of the world's greatest books, this one ranks extremely high. My favorite translation is by Richmond Lattimore, though most scholars and serious readers prefer Robert Fitzgerald.

L. Ron Hubbard. *Dianetics: the Modern Science of Mental Health*. 1950. In my book on Meriwether Lewis, I cited one of Hubbard's ideas about communication and human relationships. This raised some eyebrows. I'm an idea opportunist: if it is an insight, who cares where it comes from? Besides, I have a dozen or so friends who are Scientologists, and they are without question the most self-actualized and productive people I have ever met.

Zora Neale Hurston. *Their Eyes Were Watching God*. 1937. I had to teach this at the University of Nevada at Reno. When we were told that this would be one of the central texts of the semester, I rolled my eyes. But then I read it. The fact that I first reacted with skepticism, and then discovered that my close-mindedness had kept me away from a book of great beauty and insight, is a kind of parable.

Kay Redfield Jamison. *Night Falls Fast: Understanding Suicide*. 1999.

Clay Jenkinson. *The Character of Meriwether Lewis: Explorer in the Wilderness*. 2011. This is the most important book I have written, and the best piece of intellectual work in my life.

Clay Jenkinson, ed. *A Vast and Open Plain: The Writings of the Lewis and Clark Expedition in North Dakota*. 2004. This anthology of the journals of Lewis and

Clark, plus other documents, was published by the State Historical Society of North Dakota. Using the University of Nebraska text of the journals, we broke new ground by printing the journal entries of each member of the expedition, captains, sergeants, and privates, on the day they were written, rather than printing Lewis and Clark first, and the "lesser diarists" in subsequent volumes. Plus we printed the weather data (carefully kept at Jefferson's insistence) at the beginning of each day's entry.

Jack Kerouac. *On the Road.* 1957. Every three or four years I reread this book. Of all the road books in American literature, it is unquestionably the best. It holds up.

W.P. Kinsella. *Dance Me Outside.* 1977. This is my favorite book of Native American fiction.

Kinsella. *Scars: Stories.* 1978.

Aldo Leopold. *A Sand County Almanac.* 1949. My high school English teacher Agnes Oxton gave me a paperback copy of this book for my graduation gift. She wrote in it, "Maybe some day you will write a book." I credit her with so much in my life. It's the little things like that moment that make all the difference. Who knows if I would ever have become a writer had she not said those words to me?

Sinclair Lewis. *Main Street.* 1920. Lewis has unfortunately been largely forgotten. This is a mistake. I love *Main Street* and *Babbitt* and *Elmer Gantry.* North Dakota is not Gopher Prairie, Minnesota, but Lewis's savage indictment of small town values continues to have the capacity to skewer North Dakota's habits and mindset.

Patricia Limerick. *The Legacy of Conquest: The Unbroken Past of the American West.* 1987.

David Lodge. *Changing Places: A Tale of Two Campuses.* 1975. All of Lodge's books are wonderful. But this one is the best.

John Avery Lomax. *Cowboy Songs and Other Frontier Ballads.* 1910.

Jack London. "To Build a Fire." 1908. I am not particularly fond of London's novels, but I love his short stories. I remember buying a Penguin Edition of the stories in England when I was homesick for the American West, and reading them through one weekend.

Richard Manning. *Grassland: The History, Biology, Politics, and Promise of the American Prairie.* 1995.

George E. Mowry. *The Era of Theodore Roosevelt: 1900-1912.* 1958.

John Milton. *Paradise Lost.* 1674. This is the epitome of Twain's definition of a classic: a book that everyone praises and nobody reads. I have been trying to make a run at it again for the past few years, but something else always intervenes. And yet it is a book that rocked my world when I first read it at the University of Minnesota.

John Neihardt. *Black Elk Speaks.* 1932. This is one of the most important books about the Great Plains.

George Orwell. *1984*. I haven't read it since, well, 1984, when it seemed a little dated.

John Wesley Powell. *Arid Lands Report*. 1878. Had we listened to Powell, the 100th Meridian, which passes through Bismarck, Pierre, North Platte, etc., would have been the line of demarcation between the Jeffersonian cadastral grid system (square miles, townships), and a more flexible system designed to accommodate the aridity of the American West. Powell argued that the traditional grid would create conditions of failure (through no fault of the homesteader) west of the 100th Meridian. I call my house in north Bismarck Meridian House in honor of Powell, who was absolutely right about the West.

Theodore Roosevelt. *Autobiography*. 1913. Of all the presidential autobiographies, this is one of the handful of the best. *Grant's Personal Memoirs of U.S.* Grant is almost universally regarded as the finest.

Roosevelt. *Hunting Trips of a Ranchman*. 1885.

Roosevelt. *Ranch Life and the Hunting-Trail*. 1896.

Roosevelt. *The Rough Riders*. 1899.

Roosevelt. *The Wilderness Hunter*. 1893.

O.E. Rolvaag. *Giants in the Earth*. 1927. If you haven't read this book, do! Among the essential books for every citizen of the Great Plains to read, *Giants in the Earth*, Willa Cather's *My Antonia*, Hamlin Garland's *Son of the Middle Border*, Kent Haruf's *Plainsong*, and Larry Woiwode's *Beyond the Bedroom Wall*.

Joseph Sax. *Mountains without Handrails: Reflections on the National Parks*. 1980. This book has had a huge influence on my thinking. It's short, and full of insights about the relationship between humans and technology.

William Stafford. *The Way It Is and Other Poems*. 1998

John Steinbeck. *Acts of King Arthur and His Noble Knights*. 1976.

Steinbeck. *America and Americans*. 1966.

Steinbeck. *Cannery Row*. 1945.

Steinbeck. *East of Eden*. 1952.

Steinbeck. *The Grapes of Wrath*. 1939. This is one of the top five American novels. The rest of Steinbeck is great, but if all but one book had to be shredded forever, I'd keep *Grapes of Wrath*. I first read it in high school, where teachers were scandalized that Rose of Sharon saved a dying man by offering him her breast. The novel just gets better every time you read it.

Steinbeck. *Journal of a Novel: The East of Eden Letters*. 1968.

Steinbeck. *Of Mice and Men*. 1937.

Steinbeck. *The Red Pony*. 1937.

Steinbeck. *Tortilla Flat*. 1935.

Steinbeck. *Travels with Charley*. 1962.

Jonathan Swift. *Gulliver's Travels*. 1726. This is one of those books people forget to reread. It is usually billed as a children's novel, but it is anything but that. It is one of the greatest works of English literature. I read it again every couple of years.

Henry David Thoreau. *Walden* or *Life in the Woods*. 1854. My desert island book. My *Fahrenheit 451* book. If I could only keep one American book, this would be it. Like all great classics, it is a new great book every time. Lots of people find Thoreau annoying, and the first chapter, "Economy" trips up lots of readers, but if you give yourself to the book, it gives back wonderfully. I read it while preparing this book for the press. This time, without wishing to, I found myself reading it as a lens on the North Dakota oil boom. It's pretty sobering reading from that perspective.

Leo Tolstoy. *Anna Karenina*. 1873-1877. This is actually one of my favorite novels. My friend and mentor Ray Frazer used to say it had "the best first 100 pages in all of literature." On his recommendation, I read it without putting it down back in 1982 or so. In my view, it has the best final 100 pages in all of literature. TR didn't like the book much—he disliked Tolstoy's apparent acceptance of the adultery at the center of the novel.

Tolstoy. *War and Peace*. 1869. Roosevelt borrowed this immense novel from Medora von Hoffman, the wife of the Marquis de Mores. He seems to have borrowed a French translation. He wrote the title as *La Guerre et la Paix*.

Mark Twain. *The Adventures of Huckleberry Finn*. 1885. If *Walden* were not my favorite American book, this would be it. I've read it a dozen times, and always with pure admiration.

James Welch. *Fools Crow*. 1986.

E.B. White. *Charlotte's Web*. 1952.

Laura Ingalls Wilder. *Little House on the Prairie*. 1935. The Little House books got under my skin when I was a boy, ten or eleven years old, and they left a serious mark. Every Christmas I read the Christmas chapter in *Little House on the Prairie* to my daughter, and every year I cry when Pa gets choked up that Mr. Edwards swam across the swollen creek to deliver Santa's gifts to Laura and Mary.

Wilder. *The Long Winter*. 1940.

Owen Wister. *The Virginian*. 1902. Wister and TR were friends. With Remington, they helped to create the cowboy myth. Not all North Dakota ranchers and cowboys admire TR, but they should, if only for the ways in which he celebrated the cowboy life and helped to make it a central part of American mythology. One chapter of *The Virginian* is set in Medora. The novel was dedicated to Roosevelt.

INDEX

A

Abbey, Edward 103, 139, 201
ABM protest march 59-60, 120-122
Acts of King Arthur 92
Adams, Abigail 146
Adams, John 99, 114, 130-132, 254
The Aeneid 128
Aeolus 195
Afghanistan 87, 151-153
Agriculture, future of 270-271, 319
Ahmadinejad, Mahmoud 210
Albers, Albert 147
Albers, Everett C. 142, 144-147, 344
Albers, Gretchen 147
Alberta tar sands 338-341
Aldrin, Edwin (Buzz) 142
Allen, Jay 264
Allen, Steve 85
Allen, Woody 234-235
Amazon River 282
Ambrose, Stephen 125, 139
"America the Beautiful" 29
American Indians 2, 29, 78-80, 117-118,
    126-128, 147-150, 152, 175, 178, 231,
    264-266, 284, 290, 292, 298, 302-
    304, 306, 318, 324, 325, 333
American Prometheus 84
Analects of Confucius 104
The Andy Griffith Show 106, 141
Antaeus 34
Antelope 3, 28, 82, 177, 183, 215,
    235-237, 247, 290
Appropriation (see cultural appropriation)
Aquinas, Thomas 32
Arches National Park 29, 103, 139, 231-232
Arid Lands Report 137
Armstrong, Lance 16
Armstrong, Neil 142
Augustine, Aurelius (Saint) 92, 132, 142
Austen, Jane 92, 97
Austin, Mary 137
Autobiography (Theodore Roosevelt) 89, 91
Autumn 35-37, 38-39, 41-43, 44, 46, 51,
    173, 182-184, 237

B

Bacon, Francis vi, 104, 124, 170
Badlands *passim*, vi, vii, 11, 14, 26, 27, 39,
    41-43, 46, 89, 93, 94, 113, 115, 132-135,
    135-138, 148-149, 164-166, 167-169,
183-184, 198-208, 209-212, 212-213,
230-232, 256, 267-268, 274-275,
276-279, 320, 322, 325, 328-330, 337
Baenan, Leonard 3, 345
Baier, Lowell 149
Bakken Oil Field 62, 316-318, 330, 332,
    336, 338
Ball, Lucille 85
Bankhead-Jones Act 273
Barcalounger 17, 157, 172
Barge traffic 282-284
Basler, Leon 193-195, 348
Bates, Katherine Lee 29
Beach Boys 249
Beans 18, 21
Bear Butte 236, 264-266
Bear, Keith 118
Beatles 16, 59, 118, 288
The Beet Queen 147
Belle Fourche River 217
Berle, Milton 85
Bernstein, Jeremy 84
Bhagavad Gita 83, 104, 123, 124
Biathanatos 142
Bible 18, 33, 60, 98-99, 104, 122-124,
    128, 171, 182, 187, 234, 240
Bicycle 14, 16, 200, 226, 248
Billings County 148, 166, 188, 190,
    267-269, 274-276, 277
Bin Laden, Osama 105, 107, 216, 237
Bird, Kai 84
Black Butte 194, 211, 215
Black Elk Speaks 123, 124
Black Robe 104
Blair, Tony 119
Blizzards 3, 22, 39, 47, 52, 144, 186
Bobcat (skid-steer) 15, 20, 45, 64, 82, 186
Bodmer, Karl 179-181, 231
Bodmer's Overlook 180-181
Bogart, Humphrey 297
Bohl, Kristi 5-6
Bock, Joanne & Robbie 348
Bonanzaville 322
Book of Mormon 123
Boone, Daniel 89, 269, 278
Boone & Crockett Club 140-141, 149
Boots & Coots Well Control International 330
Borlaug, David i, 105-108, 348
Borscht 68
Boswell (Mother's dog) 28
Boswell, James 10, 105
Bowden, Charles 190-192
Brauhn, Richard 348
Bridge (Billings County) 267-269

Brinkley, Douglas 138
Bronte, Charlotte 247
Bryan, William Jennings 271
Buchanan, James 101
Buffalo 88, 106, 126, 139, 140, 181, 183-184, 213, 290, 305
Bullion Butte 33, 194, 207, 209-212, 215, 225, 269, 277, 344, 349
Bureau of Land Management 148
Burns, Ken 125
Burroughs, John 137
Bush Foundation 150
Bush, George W. 210, 318
Buttes 3, 21, 67, 81, 168, 178, 193-195, 211, 215-217, 218, 322, 328, 348

C

Cameahwait 127
Cannery Row 92, 94
Cannes Film Festival 146
Cannonball River 216
Carhenge 24
Carrey, Jim 114
Carvell, Charles 204-206, 346
Carvell, Kevin 346
Carvell, Melanie 16, 17, 18, 33, 35, 58, 167, 168, 200, 207, 345-346, 347
Carvell, Peggy 346
Casablanca 297
Cassiopeia 31, 35
Castle, Carl 13
Castle Rock Butte 216
Cather, Willa 67, 92, 99
Cave Hills 217, 231
Cawley, Rebecca 105
Cedar River 217
Celsius, Anders 169
"Center of the Nation" 217
Chandler, Raymond 22
Changing Places 92
Channing, Carol 85
Charbonneau, Jean Baptiste 127
Charbonneau, Toussaint 106, 126-128
Charlie's Angels 141
Charlottes's Web 104
Chase Lake NWR 138, 277
Chaucer, Geoffrey 92
Chautauqua 119, 145-146
Checkerboarding 303
Cheney, Richard 116
Cheerleading 57-58
Chimney Butte 210
Christmas 11, 13, 24, 47, 48, 52, 66, 72, 222, 230, 235, 238-240, 258-260

Churchill, Winston 56
Cincinnatus 154
Citizens' Commission on the Oil Boom 323-325
The City of God 92, 142
Clark, Dick 85
Clark, George Rogers 89
Clark, Julia Hancock 289
Clark, Merle & Linda 330
Clinton, William Jefferson 115
Coffee Houses 96 104, 172, 332
Coleridge 181, 199
Collins, John 126
Colter, John 126, 127
Columbine shootings 101
Confessions 92
Conrad, Kent 311, 313
Conservation 42, 88-92, 135-138, 138-141, 166, 201, 267-269, 273-276, 324, 328-330
Constitution of the United States 29, 100-102, 117, 122-124,131, 160
Cook-Lynn, Elizabeth 304
Copernicus 32
Cordery, Gareth 213-214
Cordery, Simon 213-214
Cordery, Stacy 213-214, 348
Cottonwoods vi, 11, 14, 17, 21, 25-26, 39, 42, 64, 65, 66, 117, 169, 180, 182, 185, 202, 208, 209, 290, 297, 298
Cowboy Songs and Other Ballads 90
Cowboy poetry and song 88-90
Coyotes 3, 6, 14, 28, 48, 66, 95, 96, 97, 126, 205, 226, 227, 305
Coyote Warrior 284, 285, 304
Crazy Horse 29, 87, 246, 265
Crazy Horse Memorial 254
Crazy Horse Monument 87, 246
Crockett, Davy 89
Crocus (see pasque flower)
Crook, Lillian 195-196, 348
Cross Ranch 24
Crow Buttes 217
Crown Butte 194
Cruise, Tom 216
Cruzatte, Pierre 126
Cultural appropriation 78-80, 119, 264-266, 302-305
Custer Died for Your Sins 78
Custer, Elizabeth 322
Custer, George Armstrong 231, 290

D

Dakota: A Spiritual Geography 201
Dali, Salvador 85
Dalrymple, Betsy 294
Dalrymple, Jack 294
Dante 6
Darwin, Charles 21, 32
Dawes Severalty Act 303
Declaration of Independence 29-30, 31,
    88, 107, 129, 135
Decline and Fall of the Roman Empire 125
Deers Ears Butte 216
Deloria, jr., Vine 78, 304
Department of Motor Vehicles 6
Desert Solitaire 103, 201
Devils Tower 42, 198, 211, 231, 232, 266
Diamond, Jared 73
Dianetics 123
Dickens, Charles 92, 99, 104
Dickinson State University 144, 149-150, 348
Disney World 56-58
Donne, John 49-50, 51-52, 92, 142
Dorgan, Byron 149, 311, 313, 346
Dostoevsky, Fyodor 92
Double Ditch Indian Village 31, 292-293
Dragseth, Deb 348
Dunne, Finley Peter 103
Durango, CO 23, 24
Dust Bowl 93, 148, 274, 336
Dylan, Bob 59, 118

E

East of Eden 92
Easter 14, 15, 189, 193-195
Eaton, Howard 139
Eberts, Ken and Norma 138-141, 148, 165
Eberts Ranch 138-141, 148-149, 164-166,
    268, 273-276
Einstein, Albert 63
Ekalaka, MT 29, 81-82
Electoral College 100
Eliot, T.S. 98, 203
Elisabeth II 119
Elk 20, 232, 305
Elkhorn Ranch 41, 42, 133, 135, 138-141,
    148-149, 164-166, 198, 207, 208, 267-
    268, 273-276, 322
Ellison, Keith 122-124
Elvis 61, 63
Emma 97
"The Emptied Prairie" 187-189, 190-192, 267
Enlightenment 124-125, 129-131, 180
Era of Theodore Roosevelt 114

Erasmus, Desiderius 118-119
Erdrich, Louise 69, 147, 322
Everett, Beverly 41-43, 348

F

Fahrenheit, Daniel Gabriel 169
Feldner, Tom 182
Fergus Falls, MN 19, 64, 73, 96, 222-224,
    234, 239, 246, 248, 288
Ferrell, John R. 284
Field, Joseph 62
Field, Reuben 62, 126
Fighting Sioux 79-80, 147, 302-304
Fillmore, Millard 101
Finnegan, Red Headed Mike 116
Fitzgerald, F. Scott 97
Five Point Butte 210
Fleishkuechle 5, 145
Flood Control Act of 1944 282, 286
Flood of 2011 294-296
Foley, James 90-91
Fort Laramie Treaty 1851 303
Fort Lincoln 125
Fort Mandan 7, 12, 63, 64-65, 125-128,
    173, 294-296, 322
Fort Union 179-181
Foster, Patty 254-255
Fourth of July 27-30, 39, 86-88, 105-109,
    196, 222, 293
Fracturing (fracking) 316
Franke, Nancy 201, 347
Franklin, Benjamin 131
Frazier, Ian 201
Frein, George 256
Frenzel, Joe & Sandi 197
Freud, Sigmund 32, 47
Friedman, Thomas vi, 134, 311
Friendship 112-114
Frost, Robert 237
Fuglie, Jim 113, 168, 170, 174, 195-197, 344

G

Galileo 32
Garden 15, 17, 18, 19-21, 25, 33, 34, 95, 169-
    171, 172-174, 185, 206, 243-245, 248
Garland, Hamlin 73
Garrison Dam 284, 290, 295, 304
Garrison Diversion 284
Gettysburg 139
Gibbon, Edward 125
Gleason, Jackie 85
Glenn, John 142
God Is Red 78

Goode, Virgil 123
Gore, Al 347
GPS technology 13, 199, 201, 207, 319
Grand Canyon 29, 91, 198, 268, 328
Grand Forks 8, 9, 70, 95, 121, 146, 160,
    190, 216, 235, 270, 272, 284, 306,
    309, 319, 320
Grand River 117, 217
Grand Union Hotel 288
The Grapes of Wrath 92-94
Grassland 21, 34, 42, 174, 180-181, 214,
    274, 292, 322
Grassy Butte vi, 306, 329
Great Compromise 102
Great Conversations 100
Great Expectations 99
The Great Gatsby 97
Great Plains 201
Great Plains Chautauqua 119
Greenwood, Lee 87
Grinnell, George Bird 137, 140
Griswold Clark 28, 72, 168, 259
Grizzly bear 28, 63, 245
Gulliver's Travels 99
Guthrie, Woody 66
Guy, William L. 61, 120-122, 320

H
Halsman, Philippe 83-85
Hall, Annie 348
Hall, Wesley 348
Hamilton, Alexander 100, 131
Hamlet 92
Hammarskjold, Dag 85
Hannity, Sean 123
Hanson, Jon 146
Hanson, Ann 330
Hanson, Robert 205, 330
Harding, Warren 101
Harry Potter 105, 176, 213
Hatzenbuhler, Milo 69
Hawke, David Freeman 142
Haystack Butte 216
Hazleton, ND 68-70
Heart Butte 194
Heart River 195, 217, 303
Heaven 12, 14, 33, 93, 175
Hemings, Sally 132
Hepburn, Audrey 85
Heet 8, 95
Heibling, Tim 295
Heitkamp, Heidi 119
Hemingway, Ernest 62
Hercules 141, 144

Hilton, Paris 216, 239
Hiroshima 83
Hoeven, John 119, 151, 192, 210
Hogan, Christine 348
Holmgren, Douglas 113, 244
Homer 99, 104, 242
Homestead Act 336
Hoses 11, 15, 37, 45, 47, 177, 179
Hubbard, L. Ron 123
Huckleberry Finn 26, 99, 211, 245, 253,
    291-293, 346
Hughes, Howard 5
Hume, David 124
Humphrey, Annie 118
Hunting 75-77, 268, 278, 324, 334
Hunting Trips of a Ranchman 14, 91, 141, 274

I
Iacocca, Lee 104
The Iliad 104
Impeachment 100
Indian Summer 15, 39, 41, 46, 182
Indians (see American Indians)
International Courts of Justice 102
Inyan Kara 11, 12
Iraq 87, 116, 151-153, 229

J
Jacobs, Mike 31, 60-61, 159, 160, 191, 241, 260
James, Jesse 90
Jamison, Kay Redfield 142
Jefferson, Thomas 2, 7, 20-21, 29-30, 63,
    73, 86-88, 92, 99, 100, 101, 114, 115,
    122-125, 126, 129-132, 137, 141-143,
    169-170, 172, 179, 180, 188, 222, 224,
    233-235, 254, 270-271, 289, 291, 307,
    309, 311, 329, 348
Jenkinson, Catherine 3, 13-14, 27-28, 56-
    58, 97-99, 105, 166, 170, 202, 208,
    216-217, 225-227, 229-230, 230-232,
    234-235, 235-237, 238-240, 240-242,
    245-247, 249-250, 251-253, 253-255,
    256-257, 258-260
Jenkinson, Charles 23-24, 25, 46-48, 67, 212-
    214, 217, 222-224, 241-242, 256-257, 288
Jenkinson, Mil 3, 27-28, 56-58, 66, 200,
    222-224, 229-230, 234-235, 243, 247,
    255, 256, 258-260, 346-347
Jesus 18
Jobs, Steve 41
Johnson, Lyndon 115
Johnson, Samuel 63, 124
Jondahl, Kimberly 349

Joplin, Janis 59
Journal of a Novel 92
Judicial term limits 101
Judith Landing 289
Jump Book 84
Jupiter 13, 35, 179
Jusseaume, Rene 127

K

Kabala 47, 71
Kaye, Bruce 164
Keillor, Garrison 13, 65, 68, 86, 157
Kent State University 59, 120-122
Kerouac, Jack 82, 118-119, 245
Kerry, John 115
Keystone Pipeline 338-341
Killdeer Mountains 211, 322, 333
King, Martin Luther 59
Kinsey, Joni 348
Kittredge, George Lyman 89
Koran (also Quran) 104, 122-125
Kupchella, Charles 147
Kyi, Aung San Suu 229

L

Lake Agassiz 272
Lambrecht, Bill 285
Land of Little Rain 137
Lawn mowers 19, 47, 71, 248
Lawson, Michael 285
Leopold, Aldo 137, 141
Letters 99, 240-242
Lewis, C.S. 112-113
Lewis, Jerry 85
Lewis, Sinclair 68
Lewis & Clark 7, 11, 12, 23, 61-63, 65,
    82, 106, 118, 125-128, 141, 141-143,
    173-174, 179-181, 231, 266, 278, 285,
    288-291, 292, 318, 346
Library of Congress 122-124
Life Magazine 84
Life of Dr. Samuel Johnson 105
Limerick, Patricia 285, 302
Lincoln, Abraham 115, 228, 271
Lincoln Memorial 265
Link, Arthur A. 154-156, 158-160, 271,
    322-325, 337, 342-343
Link, Grace 154-155
Link, Harvey 156
Link, John 154-155
Little Big Horn 139
Little Heart Butte 211
Little House on the Prairie 2, 38, 260

Little Missouri National Grasslands 166,
    211, 274, 276, 305, 320
Little Missouri River *passim* vi, 3, 11, 33,
    35, 39, 42, 90, 138, 139, 140, 148-149,
    164, 167-168, 176, 182-183, 183-184,
    194, 195, 195-196, 198-209, 211, 212,
    215, 225, 231, 236, 253, 267-269, 275,
    277, 284, 303, 328-330, 333, 349
Little Missouri River Trek 198-209
Little Women 241
Locke, Kevin 117-119
Lodge, David 92
The Log from the Sea of Cortez 92
Logging Camp Ranch 194, 205
Lomax, John Avery 89-90
London, Jack 8, 38, 347
Lone Butte 211
Lonetree Wildlife Management Area 60
Long, John D. 116
Lopez, Barry 2
Loren, Sophia 85
Lostwood National Wildlife Refuge 277
Lothspeich, Roger 205, 273
Love Medicine 147
Luther, Martin 103

M

Macmillan, Harold 309
MacMurray, Fred 251
McCallum, Richard 348
McClusky Canal 60
McGrath, Thomas 145
McKibben, William 339
McKinley, William 116
McKuen, Rod 141
McQuade, Sam 255
Madison, James 124, 129-131
Main Street 68
Makoche Recording Studios 117-118
Maltese Cross Ranch 138, 208, 210
Manning, Sherry 348
Maple River 94
Marmarth vi, 3, 167, 182, 188, 190, 193, 196,
    198, 200, 201, 205, 206, 207, 213, 216, 232,
    236, 267, 269, 328, 329, 330, 338, 347
Marshall, John 102
Martin, Dean 85
The Master Butchers Singing Club 147
Maximilian, Prince 180
Meadowlark 3, 6, 12-13, 14, 66, 156, 172,
    210, 215, 244, 248, 316
Medora 21, 38, 41, 90, 115, 132, 134, 135,
    138, 139, 198, 205, 206, 208, 210,
    213, 367, 275, 329, 337, 347

Medora Grazing Association 274, 276
Medora Musical 11, 12, 27, 33, 36, 246, 322, 329
Mein Kampf 104, 123
Melville, Herman 145
Memorial Bridge 286-289
Meteorites 32, 34
Of Mice and Men 92
Milton, John 92, 104
Minnesota Uprising 304
Mississippi River 29, 103, 282-284, 289-290, 291, 295, 296-298
Missouri River vi, 26, 27, 35, 64, 70, 77, 94, 106, 126, 128, 142, 173, 175, 179, 180, 182, 189, 194, 272, 282-298, 303, 304, 306, 320, 322, 328, 333, 339
Missouri River bibliography 285
Mitchell, John 121
Moab, UT 29, 103
Moffat, Jaccinda 23, 24
Mohammed 125
Mondavi, Margrit 234
Mondavi, Robert 233-235
Monroe Doctrine 339-340
Monticello 20, 88, 139, 141, 234
Moon 25, 30, 32, 34-35, 37, 119, 142, 156, 172, 205, 228
Moreau River 217
Mores, Marquis de 132-135, 206, 328, 329
Mosquitoes 11, 212, 346
Mossett, Amy 128
Mount Rushmore 87, 106, 115, 141, 246
Mount Vernon 139
Mountain lion vi, 201, 210, 225, 305
Mountains without Handrails 290
Mountbatten, Lord 85
Mowry, George E. 114
Muir, John 136, 141
Murrow, Edward R. 85
Mustang Ranch 6
My Antonia 99

N
NCAA 147-150
Nagasaki 83
Napa Valley 233-235
National Endowment for the Humanities 90, 146
National Forests 88, 137, 139, 148-149, 148, 166
National Guard 120-123, 151-153, 295
National Monuments 88, 137, 166
National Park Service 143, 148-149, 165
National Parks 30, 88-91, 137, 139-140, 246

National Reserves 151-153
National Wildlife Refuge System 88, 137-138, 139, 277
Naylor, Valerie 12, 38-39, 168, 183-184, 209-212, 230-232, 348
Nekoma, ND 59-61, 120, 122
Nero 305
Nevada 4, 6, 77, 176, 270, 344, 349
Newlands Reclamation Act 137
New Yorker 86
Nicandri, David vi
Night Falls Fast: Understanding Suicide 142
Nile River 282
Nilsson, Rob 146
Niobrara River 217
Nixon, Richard 84-85, 101, 121
Nonpartisan League 72, 146, 159
North Dakota Cowboy Hall of Fame 322
North Dakota Heritage Center 145
North Dakota History 322
North Dakota Humanities Council 142, 144-147, 245, 322
North Dakota Horizons 38
North Dakota National Guard 120, 153, 295
North Dakota Welcome Wagon Kit 321-323
Northern lights 3, 30-32, 39
Northern Lights 146
Notre Dame 265, 278

O
Obama, Barack 116, 339
The Odyssey 99, 242, 245
Ogallala Aquifer 339
Oil boom vii, 43, 159, 244, 270-273, 276, 278, 309, 318-320, 323-325, 330, 333-335, 336-338, 338-341
Old Faithful 28
Olson, Michael 229, 284
On the Road 82, 245
On Second Thought 322
Oppenheimer, J. Robert 83-85
Ordway, John 12
Orwell, George 60
Ostroushko, Peter 157
Outmigration vii, 2, 310, 316
Owl Butte 216
"Ozymandias" 230, 233

P
Paine, Thomas 131, 230
The Painted Drum 147
Pal (my Holstein) 96, 222
Paradise Lost 92

Parthenon 278
Pasque flower (crocus) 11, 14, 38, 94, 172, 193, 212
Peale, Charles Willson 20, 169
Pearl Butte 194
Penates 178
Perry, Patti 167-168, 188, 190-192, 198-199
Petrified Forest 212-214, 230-232
Pick-Sloan Plan 285, 286, 290, 295
Pieper, David 149, 273-276
Piepkorn, Merrill 64-65
Pinchot, Gifford 136-137
Platte River 215, 217, 230, 339
Pompey's Pillar 266
Potter, Tracy 125
Powell, John Wesley 137
Prager, Dennis 123
Prairie dog 212, 215, 305
Pretty Butte 194, 211, 216
Prometheus 83
Pryor, Nathaniel 126

R

Rainy Buttes 194, 211, 215
Ranch Life and the Hunting Trail 91
Rattlesnakes 205, 212
Reading habits
    At bars 9
    In the river 33, 202, 328
    My father's chair 46
    At the kitchen table 71
    Slow reader 92
    In the zone 93
    Under the covers with flashlight 97
    We read alone 98
    Reading books at the same time 99
    Desultory reading 103
    While walking 175
    On the deck 248
    While shopping 250
Reading, Lord vi
Red Cloud 29
The Red Pony 92, 94
Red River 70, 216, 270, 272, 283-284, 297, 311, 316, 328
Redwoods 91
Reisner, Marc 285
Remele, Larry 146
Remington, Frederic 91
Reno, NV 2, 4, 5, 77, 176, 266, 288
Republic 62
Retton, Mary Lou 57
Reunion Bay 126
Rhodes, John 120-121

Rhubarb 64-65, 248
Rhubarb Festival 64-65
Richards, Eugene 190-191
Ring, Ben 32
Robin Hood 90
Robinson Crusoe 99
Rocky Mountain National Park 247
Rogers, Ken viii, 13, 344, 347
Rolvaag, O.E. 38, 67
Roosevelt, Alice 139, 164, 274
Roosevelt, Edith 116
Roosevelt, Mittie 139, 164
Roosevelt, Theodore *passim*, 7, 8, 14, 24, 30, 37, 41-43, 52, 76, 88-91, 103, 106, 114-116. 133-135, 135-138, 138-141, 148-149, 164-166, 182, 193, 199, 206, 208, 210, 212-213, 257, 258, 267-269, 273, 274, 278, 317, 322, 328, 338, 344
Rorschach Test 84
Rosa, Salvator 180
Rototiller 15, 18, 33, 95, 172, 185, 248
Rough Riders 115
The Rough Riders 103
Rumsfeld, Donald 116
Running 15
Russ, Suzanne 348
Russell, Bertrand 85
Ryburg, Donna 186
Ryburg, Virgil 186

S

Sacagawea 29, 106, 127, 128
Sagamore Hill 140, 274
Sahlstrom, Ed 146, 226
St. Peters of Rome 232, 265, 278
A Sand County Almanac 137
Sandhills 81, 339
Sandoz, Mari 217
Sanish Formation 319, 333
Saskatchewan 11
Satrom, Joe 119, 149, 348
Saudi Arabia effect 331, 334
Sax, Joseph 290
Schafer, Ed 119, 334
Schafer, Sheila ii-iv, 3, 11, 12, 185-186, 229, 344
Schlump, Mr. 16, 200, 345
Schollaert Hills 194
Schneiders, Robert Kelley 285
Seasonal Affective Disorder 24-25, 52
Second Amendment 101
Sentinel Butte 210-211
Seuss, Dr. 145, 239
Sevareid, Eric 68, 328
Shackleton expedition 70

Shakespeare 92, 104, 169, 229
Shane 231, 250
Sheheke-shote 126-128
Shelley, Percy Bysshe 230, 233
Sheyenne National Grasslands 276
Sheyenne River 189, 216, 284
Shiloh 139
Shore, Dinah 85
Silvers, Phil 85
Simon and Garfunkel 246
Sisyphus 213
Sitting Bull 29, 117, 119, 139, 290
Skelton, Red 85
Skogen, Larry 286, 317, 320, 346
Slavery 102, 129, 291
Slide Mountain (butte) 215
Slim Buttes 216
Sloan, Mara 240
Solon 100
Solstice 24-27, 38, 50-52,
Son of the Middle Border 73
Snow Shoveling 10
Snowbirds 9, 173, 195
Snowblower 10, 13, 15, 47, 48, 71-72, 185-186
Souris River 297, 328
South Korea 87
Speer, Albert 31
Spring 5, 10-12, 12-14, 15-16, 17-19, 19-
    22, 38, 40, 51, 66, 81, 94-97, 172-174,
    193-195, 248-250
Sprynczynatyk, David 151, 295
Square Butte 21, 211
Stafford, William 227
Starbucks 5, 191, 195
Stars 7, 31-32, 34, 179, 202-203, 289
Star Wars 65
State Bank of North Dakota 72-74
Steele, Danielle 104
Stegner, Wallace 30, 291
Stein, Gertrude 187
Steinbeck, John 92-95, 286-287
Stevenson, Adlai 85
Straus, Dick 73-74, 94, 95, 222, 228, 240,
    244, 246-247, 259, 288
Straus, Rhoda 19, 20, 28, 36, 64, 73-74,
    96, 170, 177-178, 222-224, 228, 234,
    243-245, 246-247, 248, 258, 288
Straus, Susan 222-224
Stump Lake NWR 138
Sturgis Bike Rally 264-266
Suchy, Andra 156-158
Suchy, Ben 156-158
Suchy, Chuck 37, 156-158
Suchy, Linda 156-158

Suicide 63, 106, 142-143, 192
Sully, Alfred 304
Sullys Hill National Game Preserve 60, 137
Summer 17, 24-27, 33-35, 38-39, 40, 41,
    46, 51, 64-65, 72-74, 113, 166, 167,
    168, 170, 176, 182-184, 194, 196,
    208, 246, 247
Swenson, David 117-119

T

Tancredo, Tom 116
Teepee Buttes 194, 215
Thanksgiving 222-224, 228-230, 235-237,
    238, 344
Their Eyes Were Watching God 99
Theodore Roosevelt National Park 14, 38,
    41, 133, 139, 164, 167, 168, 198, 206,
    207, 212-214, 230-233, 268, 277, 305,
    328, 333, 347
Theodore Roosevelt statue, Dickinson
    338
Thomas, Dylan 144, 177
Thoreau, Henry David 20, 28, 30, 93, 136,
    141, 167, 170, 201, 202-204, 209, 214
Thorson, John E. 285
Three's Company 62
Three Fifth's Clause 102
Three Forks Formation 319, 333
Three Stooges 145
Thunderstorms 3, 17, 25-26, 36, 39, 93,
    158, 168, 172, 175-176, 182, 202, 206,
    244, 251, 306
Tocqueville, Alexis de 83
Tolstoy, Leo 92
Tomatoes 15, 17, 18, 19, 20, 21, 25, 33-
    35, 36, 52, 74, 95, 169-170, 177-178,
    206, 245, 248
Tortilla Flats 92
Tracks 147
Trains 14, 46, 66-67, 135, 268
Trandahl, Sarah 180-181, 348
Trans-basin diversion 282
TransCanada Corporation 338-341
Travels with Charley 92, 93, 286-288
Tristani, Michael & Jeanette 68-70
Trobriand, Regis de 322
Truman, Margaret 85
Tubbs, Stephenie Ambrose 106, 348
Turner, Frederick Jackson 88, 160
Twain, Mark 92, 104
Twin Buttes (near Bowman) 21, 215
Twin Buttes (town) 42, 211

U

Uecker, Korliss 286-288
US Army Corps of Engineers 283, 286, 290, 292, 294-296, 297, 306
Unabomber 27, 107-108
Undaunted Courage 125
United Nations 85, 102, 210
University of North Dakota 8, 68, 79-80, 121, 147, 302-304

V

VanDevelder, Paul 285, 304
Van Gogh, Vincent 247
A Vast and Open Plain: The Writings of the Lewis and Clark Expedition in North Dakota 173
Velveeta 68, 69
Venus 95
Verendrye, Pierre Gaultier de Varennes 290
Vergil 128
Vickers, Deanna 149-150
Vickers, Lee 149-150
Vietnam 39, 59, 120-122, 152
Virginia Tech shooting 101
The Virginian 91
The Voices of Song 90
Voltaire 124

W

Walden Pond 136, 139, 164, 209
Walden 27, 30, 136, 167, 201, 203, 205, 209
Waldera, Jean 146
Walker, Etta 202, 227, 239, 254, 257, 270
Walking 10, 26, 46, 66, 95, 97, 173, 175, 178, 184, 189, 200, 202, 207, 208
Wallman, Kris 60-61
Walter Reed Army Hospital 153
War and Peace 61
War Powers 101
Warford, John 295
Washington, Booker T. 145
Washington, George 115, 131
Wayne, John 231
Weed whackers 19
Weinstein, Jack 68
Wemyss, Nina 234
Wendell, Barrett 89
Wheat 3, 13, 20, 29, 72-74, 76, 122, 156, 222, 237, 246-247
"When the Landscape is Quiet Again" 155, 160, 322, 342-343

Where Seldom Was Heard a Discouraging Word: Bill Guy Remembers 121
White, Richard 283
White Butte 168, 194, 211
White Cliffs (Missouri River) 288, 290
White River 217
Whitman, Walt 194
Wilder, Laura Ingalls 12, 194, 260
Wilson, Mary Louise Defender 118
The Wilderness Hunter 91
Wilderness proposal 276-279
Wilderness Warrior: Theodore Roosevelt and the Crusade for America 138
Wind *passim*, 3, 7, 8, 10, 14, 16, 22-24, 26, 31, 38, 44-45, 46, 48, 52, 68-70, 70, 73, 173, 174, 180, 182, 183, 186, 188, 193, 195-197, 231-232, 236, 239, 264, 271, 276-278, 306
Windsor, Duke and Duchess 85
Wine 14, 19, 42, 71, 75, 164, 173, 197, 207, 212, 214, 233-234, 288
The Winning of the West 91
Winter 7-9, 10-11, 12-14, 16, 38-39, 40-41, 44-45, 50-53, 70-72, 182, 185-186, 193, 293, 306, 321
Wister, Owen 91
Woiwode, Larry 69
Woodstock 122
Wordsworth, William 210
Worster, Donald 285

Y

Yeats, William Butler 145
Yellow Corn 127
Yellowstone National Park 27-28, 58, 91, 105, 106, 137, 231, 247
Yellowstone River 27, 106, 126, 180, 215, 245, 285, 289, 298, 303, 333, 339
York 106
Yosemite National Park 29, 91, 136
Yugoslavia 113